THE LEGACY OF SOLOMON ASCH:

Essays in Cognition and Social Psychology

Solomon E. Asch

THE LEGACY OF SOLOMON ASCH:

Essays in Cognition and Social Psychology

Edited by
IRVIN ROCK
University of California, Berkeley

LEA LAWRENCE ERLBAUM ASSOCIATES, PUBLISHERS
1990   Hillsdale, New Jersey   Hove and London

Lawrence Erlbaum Associates, Inc., Publishers
365 Broadway
Hillsdale, New Jersey 07642

Library of Congress Cataloging-in-Publication Data

The Legacy of Solomon Asch: Essays in cognition and social psychology
edited by Irvin Rock.
    p.   cm.
Includes bibliographical references.
ISBN 0-8058-0440-4
1. Cognition.   2. Social psychology.   3. Perception.   4. Gestalt
psychology.   5. Asch, Solomon E. (Solomon Elliott), 1907–   .
I. Asch, Solomon E. (Solomon Elliott), 1907–   .   II. Rock, Irvin.
BF311.C5487   1990
153—dc20   90-30570
                                                            CIP

Printed in the United States of America
10   9   8   7   6   5   4   3   2   1

Contents

Preface

This volume, a tribute to Solomon Asch, reflects the many areas of psychology to which he has made fundamental contributions: to cognition, perception, social psychology, and personality theory. His contributions also reflect a deep interest in theoretical psychology, notable for his extension of Gestalt psychology to topics beyond those dealt with by the founding fathers. Thus he stands as one of the few generalists of this century. This volume is divided into sections that correspond to these diverse interests. A unifying thread running through all of Asch's writings is his abiding humanistic concerns. These come together in a reiterated theme: the belief in the ultimate rationality of human conduct.

In varying ways, the list of contributors reflects Asch's interests and his influence, as well as his institutional connections. Some were his graduate students and research assistants at the New School for Social Research and at Rutgers University. Others were his faculty colleagues at the New School, Swarthmore College, Rutgers, and Pennsylvania Universities. However, quite a few of those whose essays appear in this volume were not directly his students or departmental colleagues, but are themselves important psychologists who have been deeply influenced by his ideas, research, and style of thinking.

The first chapter in this volume is a biography of Asch, tracing his career as an investigator. Therefore not much need be said here by way of preface. However, I do want to mention two points about Asch that distinguish him from most of his contemporaries, including many outstanding psychologists. There is, first, the point already made, the breadth of his interests. Then, there is the interesting fact that Asch's list of publications is unusually short (see pages 293–295). But what a list it is! Virtually every paper, to say nothing of his book, *Social Psychology*, is now a classic, a landmark contribution, constituting a paradigm that has given birth to many replications and variations that have since been published. If others have emulated Asch, it is not because his work has been facile or fashionable—far from it—but because it has been penetrating and provocative.

Recently, Asch's *Social Psychology* has been reissued, unrevised, with a foreword expressing his thoughts about the book and about developments in psychology since its publication almost four decades ago. It is hoped that the reappearance of this classic, long out of print, will invite newer generations to study it, and that, supplemented by this volume of essays, it will serve to inspire us all and to perpetuate the lines of thought initiated by this exemplary man.

We thus present this volume to our friend, colleague, and mentor, with affection and admiration.

Irvin Rock
Berkeley, California

BIOGRAPHY

1 On Solomon Asch

John Ceraso
Rutgers University

Irvin Rock
University of California, Berkeley

Howard Gruber
Teachers College, Columbia University

Solomon Eliot Asch, whom his friends call Shlaym, was born in Warsaw, Poland in 1907, but grew up in Lowicz, a little town not far from Warsaw:

> A small religious environment where the relation of people to the forces around them was very near and strong. In that setting man is very important, not just to himself, he's important in the scheme of things, and this feeds an interest in human nature.
>
> I was brought up at a time of great anxieties, big fears, great dangers. But I remember a little incident of another kind when I was a child. I must have been about seven. The war [WWI] had just started; it was Passover evening and there was the first Seder. Everything was prepared; it was a glowing ceremony, and we children were up late for the first time. Then I saw my grandmother fill a cup of wine for each of us including the children; and in addition, another cup. Then I saw a chair in which nobody sat. I was sitting next to an uncle of mine and I asked what this meant. He said that the prophet Elijah comes into every Jewish home on Passover. That is why there is a chair prepared for him, and at the proper moment in the ceremony the door is opened to admit him and that he takes a sip of the cup of wine meant for him.
>
> I was completely fascinated and astounded that the prophet Elijah would in one night stop at all the Jewish homes in the world. I said to my uncle, "will he really take a sip?" and he said, "oh yes, you just watch when the time comes, watch the cup."—it was filled to the brim—"and you'll see that it goes down." And when the moment came, my eyes were glued to the Prophet's cup; I looked and looked and then it seemed to me as if perhaps it did go down a little! Well, except for a few details, that is just about the story of an experiment I was to do years later as part of the group pressure studies.
>
> In that variation, as in others, there was a standard line and three comparison

3

lines. The task was to choose one of three lines equal to the standard. Is this clear? One of the three lines was markedly longer—or shorter—than the standard; no one chose it. The other two lines were equal to the standard and to one another; thus there were two correct alternatives. The majority that preceded the critical subject was always correct, always choosing an equal line. In addition, the majority was always unanimous: it always chose the same equal line, but shied away from the other. In short, the majority was correct, unanimous *and* one-sided.

Under these conditions ninety per cent of the minority subjects went with the majority, shunning the other correct alternative. This was by far the strongest pro-majority effect I obtained. However, the significance of this effect was not the same as in the main body of the study: the effect was not mainly about independence. Here the relevant question shifts: why did these minority subjects stay so close to their majorities? The answer is hardly in doubt. The minority noticed the features of the situation, and in particular wondered about the unchosen and equal line. They reported that the rejected, equal line was 'almost' but 'not quite' equal to the standard. The procedure created a doubt that was decisive. In this case there *was* safety in numbers. No such doubt attached to the chosen line.

Don't ask whether what happened to me at the age of seven was responsible for an experiment that came forty years later—I don't know. When I thought or talked about it, the Passover incident would come back to me. As far as I can remember, the thought wasn't there when I planned it. Still I came to think of it as my 'Passover' experiment' (Gruber, 1971).

Along with a great many others, Asch's family migrated to the United States in 1920. They lived on the Lower East Side of New York, then a haven for many immigrants—Jews, Italians, Irish.

His wife, Florence, tells what it was like for him to come to a new country:

A naturally reserved, very shy boy of thirteen (he once said, "it was easier for me not to breathe than not to be shy") and *without* language! Shlaym learned English by reading Dickens. He was put into the 6th grade of P.S. 147, the neighborhood public school. His most vivid memory of that early period was a complete inability to comprehend what was said. Slowly he began to catch on, and 1½, or 2 years later he found himself in Townsend Harris High School (Asch, F., 1989).

That school was attached to the City College of New York and admission was selective. It is remarkable that when Asch was at Rutgers-Newark, Gruber, Lehrman, and Rock, three other members of the Psychology Department, had also attended this small elite high school.

After Townsend Harris, Shlaym went to City College where he majored in both literature and science, earning a Bachelor of Science in 1928, age 21.

Toward the end of my undergraduate days, I heard that there was a science called psychology, and I assumed—wrongly—that its concerns coincided with mine. So you might almost say that I came into psychology by mistake. I had formed my impression of what psychology might be from reading William James and a philosopher here and there—Santayana, Royce (Gruber, 1971).

In spite of the gap between his own concerns about human nature and the kind of psychology he was exposed to in his first courses, Asch went on to graduate studies at Columbia University. While he did not work much in social psychology at Columbia, he was attracted to anthropology, and attended seminars with Ruth Benedict and Franz Boas. Later, this led to a summer fellowship arranged by Gardner and Lois Murphy, with the help of Boas and Benedict. It permitted the Aschs to spend a summer in observations of Hopi children. The aim was to explore how the children became members of their culture; how they became "Hopified." Based on this experience he wrote a paper, "Personality development of Hopi children" (Asch, 1932a). It was unpublished, but was cited briefly by Klineberg (1940), and at some length by Murphy, Murphy, and Newcomb (1937). Among the anecdotes cited is one he used later in his teaching, although his students were hardly aware that Asch had been the observer:

> The teacher, a Mid-Westerner who was trying to inculcate American ways in the Hopi, sent some children to the blackboard to do an arithmetic problem, asking them to face the class as soon as they were done. Instead:
>   The quickest children, when they were through, waited and looked about inconspicuously to their right and left, and when all were ready, they all turned around together. Needless to say, the teacher had to abandon this practice. (Asch, 1932a, cited in Murphy et al., 1937).

His master's thesis was done under the supervision of Woodworth. The research (Asch, 1929) was a dry statistical analysis of data provided by Woodworth of the test scores of 200 children (although Asch still believes there was an interesting idea in it). Except for a certain careful way of presenting things, one does not, strain as one may, hear Asch speaking in his own voice. There are a few sentence order inversions and other oddities that remind us of his European origins. This and the dryness of style are in sharp contrast to his later masterful and eloquent prose.

Asch was married to Florence Miller in 1930, and their son, Peter (now a Professor of Economics at Rutgers University), was born in 1937. The unity and steadfastness of his intellectual life are matched by the steady quality of his long marriage to Florence. Anyone who has seen them together knows what an easy, good-humored rapport there is in that household.

Florence Asch (1989) tells of their first meeting:

> Where did we meet? In a library of course—where else? On East Broadway on the famous Lower East Side (where we lived a few blocks away from each other—but wrote each other constantly) the home of the Jewish intelligentsia, and working class. What a wonderful library that was. I haven't seen such a beloved library

before or since—including the Bodleian. I can still remember the way the sun shone thru the windows—and its special smell. The books were old and well-thumbed. When new books arrived, not often, they became old in two weeks—everybody scrambled for them. On Friday nights after the library closed (at 9 P.M.) everybody went walking on East Broadway. There was loud talk and much argument. Two favorite topics: "What is the meaning of life?", "Is there a God." The first time we met in the library (1926), Shlaym asked to walk me home. He told me years later that he never knew how he got the courage.

Asch's doctoral dissertation (Asch, 1932b) was on a problem that was given to him, as was commoner then than now, by his supervisor, H. E. Garrett, who: "wanted me to find out whether all learning curves had the same form. You can see the Middle Ages from which I date, so I don't like to think about that study at all." A little quaintly, the title page of the published version identifies him as "Tutor, Department of Philosophy, Brooklyn College."

Something important happened to Asch at Columbia. He tells about this in describing an episode that will probably sound familiar to every experimental psychologist.

When I was a graduate student at Columbia, maybe in my second or third year, something happened to me suddenly as I was sitting in the psychology reading room reading a paper by Thorndike on the law of effect. That law was a big thing in those days. Much revolved around it in that peculiar world. And then, for the first time, I had what seemed like an idea. I was quite shocked, because I thought of myself as one who studies what other people say and think. I had no clear notion I would ever do anything of the sort that these important people were doing and though I was a shy youth, I immediately rushed down to the Department Chairman and talked to him about the problem. I didn't even give myself a chance to think about it, and told him I would like to work on it.

Now the problem was a curious one. I was reading an experiment in which Thorndike had people look at lines of different lengths—having them judge the lengths, but he didn't give them information about their accuracy. Thorndike was trying to show that without such information, they won't improve their judgments. And, of course, information to Thorndike meant reward. If the subject said "two," and you said "That's right," you were rewarding him. And I said to myself: But if the law of effect is right it should be possible for me to produce wrong judgments by following the law of effect. I'm going to show a person a set of lines in random order, and just ask him or her to say this is 1, the shortest line, that is line number 2, etc. Every time he gives a judgment I'll tell him what the correct judgment is. But I'll introduce one twist: in the middle of the set, say at lines 4 and 5, whenever he says 4, I'll say 5, and whenever he says 5, correctly, I'll say 4. Years later, I found a notebook with ideas, ideas about experiments and some questions, that I had kept while at Columbia. This was after I started the group pressure studies. I wasn't particularly close to social psychology at Columbia, but there I found the plan for the group pressure study. I had completely forgotten it. When I read the notebook it was entirely new to me. (Gruber, 1971).

For Asch, the group pressure study was indeed a test of the law of effect, since the group is administering rewards and punishments which, according to the law of effect, should change the subjects' judgments. There is a quasi-religious feeling in Asch's objection to the arbitrariness of the law of effect. As he put it at one point, the laws of psychology must not be "just concocted by God."

Unquestionably, Asch's encounter with Gestalt psychology was the intellectual event of his life. He had some knowledge of it during his graduate student days. Gardner Murphy (1930), then a young faculty member at Columbia, gave *Gestalttheorie* a fairly full and very sympathetic treatment in his *Historical Introduction to Modern Psychology*. But it was not until Wertheimer came to the United States that Asch's encounter with Gestalt thinking really took hold. He recalled: "When I read in the New York Times one day that Wertheimer was coming to the New School for Social Research (later also known as the University in Exile) as a refugee, I said to myself that I must see him." (Gruber, 1971).

Note that Gestalt psychology did not just happen to Asch, he sought it out. By the time he met Wertheimer he had completed his formal training, so he never actually studied with him, but did get to know him well. It was not only the technical side of Gestalt psychology that drew him, but:

> Wertheimer's inner qualities, the way he looked at psychological questions. They were for him more than simply technical questions that we had to study. He had a truly aesthetic approach. When he of spoke of certain ways of thinking as "ugly," he meant it. He represented to me a kind of ideal of what a psychologist should be. For the first time I was meeting a man whose range of interest and whose concern with human questions was what psychology needed. It was exactly the dimension I had not encountered in anyone before, or, I might add, since. (Gruber, 1971)

It is true, as we have seen, that Asch had certain developed interests antedating this encounter: his youthful and abiding interest in human nature, his immersion, willy nilly, in research on learning, and his concern for problems of meaning and truth. But all these interests were assimilated into the context of Gestalt theory, and thereby transformed.

During the early 1940s, while at Brooklyn College (where he began his teaching career), he was editing the manuscript of Wertheimer's *Productive Thinking* (published in 1937). Asch used the unpublished work as the basis for his course on the psychology of thinking. His personal relationship with Max Wertheimer lasted until the latter's death in 1943. He then replaced his mentor as chairman of the psychology department at the New School.

At Brooklyn College Asch had a powerful impact on the lives of a number of students, among them Howard Gruber and Dorothy Dinnerstein; both later joined him to form the Institute for Cognitive Studies at Rutgers. He collaborated with colleagues Max Hertzman and Helen Block Lewis on studies of stereotyping and halo effects in social judgments. Dinnerstein and Gruber worked with Asch and

Witkin on the studies of the perception of the upright and discovered that performance on that task was related to gender and personality. Dinnerstein also worked with Asch on his *Social Psychology,* and, at Swarthmore, on the group pressure studies.

One of us (Gruber) reports his early recollections of Asch:

> My very first class in psychology was a lecture, at Brooklyn College, by Shlaym, replacing the regular teacher, Witkin, who was absent that day. It must have been in September, 1939. Shlaym talked about the Lewin, Lippit, and White experiments on experimental social climates. I was enthralled. So from the very first day, the pertinence of scientific psychology to social issues was a given.
>
> Later, I took a course on the psychology of thinking with Shlaym. We went over Wertheimer's *Productive Thinking,* working from the manuscript that Shlaym was editing. I was often the one who went to the blackboard and explained how I had solved a geometry problem. Wertheimer's book became for me the standard to strive for, and he and Asch have always been looking over my shoulder during my work on thinking.
>
> Shlaym was in Ithaca for a time when I was a graduate student at Cornell. I remember a conversation we had about materialism while taking a walk. I used the old argument, if I kick a stone I feel it. By the consequences of our actions we know the world, and that is its reality; something like that. Shlaym replied in his super-dignified way—that the question was too important for such an easy answer. I was impressed, and since then have always thought of Shlaym as the person who directed me toward the importance of deepening an inquiry.
>
> Asch was beginning his group pressure work just as I left for the army in January or February of 1943. The word reached me from friends: "people stick to their guns!" It was electrifying. Then he moved from Brooklyn College and started finding that the number of "yielders"—even in this perceptually highly structured situation—was disappointingly large. We have all had to learn to swallow that result, along with the lessons of the Nazi successes, and with the findings of Zimbardo and Milgram telling us that conformity is international.
>
> I regard my shadow box research (see Chapter 9 in this volume) as a part of that story, an attempt to study the conditions under which people can synthesize different perspectives and thereby transcend the limitations of a single point of view. It is not about conformity or nonconformity, but about some aspects of the search for truth, and that is a preoccupation that goes back to my early contacts with Asch.

Another of us (Rock) met Asch a few years later at the New School for Social Research and has this to say:

> I first met Shlaym in 1948. My teacher, Martin Scheerer, introduced us. He was sitting at the front desk of an empty classroom at the New School doing some writing. In those days the Psychology Department had two rooms which served as secretarial office, faculty office, seminar room, and laboratory, and these rooms were shared by faculty, secretary, and students. No one could possibly think or write there, and that was why Shlaym was in the empty classroom. But he did not at

all mind, nor did he expect more in the way of *facilities*. The image I have retained of him working in that classroom fits perfectly with the point Lee Ross makes in this volume where he contrasts the style of Shlaym's *Social Psychology* with the merchandising aspects of many contemporary textbooks on the subject (see Chapter 5, pp. 93–94). Nothing I learned about Shlaym thereafter necessitated any change in this image of his Spartan devotion to the world of ideas.

To explain what Shlaym has meant to me I have to tell that, until graduate school, I had a poor academic and intellectual record. I was a poor speller, poor memorizer, poor reader, and a slow thinker. But in graduate school I found out that thinking, particularly independent thinking, was important, and, much to my surprise, my teachers seemed to find that I had some ability in this direction. As to Shlaym, when I had an idea, his eyes lit up and he let me know he valued it. When I told him in 1955–1956 about my experiments showing no benefit of repetition in forming associations, his support—along with that of only very few other people— sustained me during the period when this work began to draw the fire of all the "big guns" in psychology. In 1963 he invited me to teach a class in learning and memory at Swarthmore and did me the great honor of attending it regularly. It is hard to overestimate just how important it was to a young investigator to merit the praise of a man of Shlaym's stature.

There is another aspect of my relationship with Shlaym that has meant much to me. Despite his well known devotion to and respect for Gestalt psychology and his leadership role in its extension to social psychology and its dissemination in America, he never expressed the slightest annoyance or fault-finding when my research led me to question one of another of the Gestalt tenets. Not the slightest trace of dogmatism was ever in evidence. The message was implicit but it was clear: What mattered was "truth."

In 1947 Asch joined the faculty of Swarthmore College, but retained his connection with the New School. At that time, Swarthmore had become the major home of Gestalt psychology in America, with the New School as a kind of annex. Mary Henle who had been at Bryn Mawr replaced Asch at the New School. The faculty at Swarthmore included Köhler, Prentice, and Wallach. Asch, Wallach, and occasionally even Köhler gave classes one night a week at the New School. Swarthmore emphasized undergraduate education and the students were quite gifted. Many distinguished psychologists received their undergraduate education there.

Another of us (Ceraso) tells of working with Asch at Swarthmore in the mid 50s.

Of all my recollections of Shlaym there is one which somehow comes to mind when I think of him. I had been a graduate student at the New School and Mary Henle recommended me to Asch who was looking for someone to assist him in his research. As his research assistant at Swarthmore I was often present when he would give a talk about the work we were doing. I noticed that very often, when someone asked a good question, he would ask them to repeat it, "So that I am sure I understand your question." Now, what at first seemed odd to me was that the question was invariably one which we had already spent many hours discussing. As any one who has worked with Asch knows, an important part of the job is to think along with him as he attempts to penetrate the complexities of a problem. What a wonderful experience that was for me! So, usually, we would know where the question cam from and where it went. Why then did Shlaym treat it as new, as one he had never thought of before? Well, for one thing, by treating it as new he gave respect to both the questioner and the question. But, more important, I believe that Asch, in his Socratic way, doesn't think of a good question as new or old, answered or unanswered. He regards it as providing yet another opportunity to take a fresh look at a difficult problem, and a chance to see it in a new and deeper way.

At Swarthmore, Asch formed a strong relationship with Köhler. Köhler died in 1967 and Asch wrote the obituary which appeared in The American Journal of Psychology. What Asch wrote tells us as much about him and his values as it does about Köhler.

Those who met Köhler knew that they were in the presence of a remarkable human being. A tremendous part of what he communicated he did through the qualities of his person. His bearing conveyed a measured balance of vitality, intelligence, and feeling. There was an unsullied integrity about him; no gesture was incompatible with his overall values. His scientific individuality, the art of thinking and investigation that he exemplified, were rooted in the larger pattern of his character. With him science did not shrink the man. Scientific activity was for him part of the life of civilization, not its replacement. He could not tolerate injustice; the necessity to act in accordance with the requirements of the situation was strong in him, strong enough to prevail over a shyness and aversion to public activity. Köhler was one of the few academic persons in Germany who did not remain silent in public about Nazi excesses. One thinks of these as lofty qualities, and indeed the life of Köhler was one of high seriousness, but one must not omit his deep enjoyment of nature and persons and his constant play of keen humor. In some ways he exemplified a style of life and character that is rapidly receding into the past. A bold and incisive mind that helped bring psychology into the twentieth century, he retained a serene confidence in the validity of human striving and values. There are few in any generation of his stature. (Asch, 1968b)

Asch spent 19 years at Swarthmore, and left in 1966 to found (with John Ceraso, Dorothy Dinnerstein, Howard Gruber, and Irvin Rock) The Institute for Cognitive Studies at Rutgers University. In 1972, Asch went to the University of Pennsylvania as Professor of Psychology where he remained until he retired in 1979. He now lives in Princeton, New Jersey.

Asch's many honors include two Guggenheim fellowships, residences at the Institute for Advanced Study at Princeton, the Nicholas Murray Butler Award from Columbia University, the Distinguished Scientific Contribution Award of the American Psychological Association, and membership in the American Academy of Arts and Sciences.

In addition to his work in social psychology, Asch has made significant contributions to the study of perception, metaphor, learning and memory, and person perception. These works are unified by two related themes; a holistic approach to cognition, and an emphasis on the rationality of mind.

In the 1940s Asch and Witkin began their collaboration on the effect of the visual frame of reference on the perception of the upright, culminating in their four classic articles published in the Journal of Experimental Psychology in 1948. The series won an award, then given annually by the APA, for the best experiments of the year, quite an honor for Asch who had never published in the field of perception before, or since for that matter. While this research later came to be known as the rod-and frame effect (see the Chapters by Rock and by Ebenholtz in this volume) it actually encompassed more than just the effect of a tilted frame on a rod contained within it. Some of the experiments made use of a mirror to tilt the actual scene (a procedure originally used by Wertheimer [1912] who referred to the ''righting'' of the scene after a short period of inspection) and other experiments made use of tilted rooms. The immediate impetus for these experiments was a paper published by Gibson and Mowrer (1938) in which they maintained that gravity receptors were the major factors in determining what directions appear to us as vertical and horizontal in the world, Wertheimer's mirror experiment to the contrary notwithstanding. But the Gestaltists had argued that objects are perceived with respect to how they relate to the visual frame of reference and Wertheimer's demonstration with a mirror was certainly compelling phenomenological evidence for this belief. Duncker's work on motion induced by a surrounding reference frame also supported this view.

Asch and Witkin (Asch & Witkin, 1948a, 1948b; Witkin & Asch, 1948a, 1948b) introduced an important variation; they included a rod within the scene with which to *measure* the direction that appeared upright. One might say that here was an interesting fusion of the experimental approach of American psychologists of Asch's generation with his way of thinking about Gestalt psychology. Of course, H. A. Witkin was a major determinant of the course of this research, and perhaps with a similar mixture of influences. These studies revealed a powerful impact of the visual frame of reference on the phenomenal upright, a result that seriously challenged Gibson's earlier claim. The 1948 papers are rich in facts and observations about how subjects deal with the conflicting information and make fascinating reading even 40 years later. Witkin and his collaborators continued the investigation with an emphasis on individual differences in field dependence that also became well known (see Witkin, Lewis, Hertzman, Machover, Meissner, & Wapner, 1954).

Asch's influence has been most significant in the field of Social Psychology and that work is characterized, as is all of his work, by careful and elegant thinking, ingenuity in experimental design, and a concern with basic issues and assumptions. The focus of a number of his studies is the demonstration of the Gestalt principle that one cannot describe the result of a stimulus array as the summation of the fixed properties of the elements which make up the array. For example, in the studies of the forming of impressions of persons (Asch, 1946), he showed that the order in which a list of traits was given could affect the resultant personality impression. Also, some traits seemed to be more central than others, so that substituting "warm" for "cold" would affect the overall impression and change the meaning of each of the individual traits. We have already seen how contextual determination was treated in his studies on the perception of the upright.

His concern with cognition and the rationality of cognitive processes is continuous with the Gestalt position on the veridicality of perception. The Gestaltists believed that the perceptual system is designed to yield an objective picture of the real world, and it does this by following certain principles of organization. It can happen that one may at times misperceive, but the misperception is accounted for by the same rules which apply to veridical perception; for example, Wertheimer's laws of grouping account for the articulation of the visual field into objects, but camouflage, which works by the same grouping principles, can also work to conceal objects.

The theme that the person actively constructs his world is also seen in the work on prestige suggestion (Asch, 1948). Does a person blindly give high value to a statement attributed to Jefferson, and low value to the same statement when attributed to Lenin? Asch showed that the situation is more complex than that. People will give different value to a statement when it is attributed to Jefferson than when it is attributed to Lenin because the *meaning* of the statement is different in the two situations. The meaning of an utterance is constructed in the context of what the person knows, or believes, to be the convictions of the person who produced it. In these days of schema and frame theories of comprehension this analysis would be readily accepted, but Asch's views were very provocative at the time they were presented, and had great influence.

Asch is perhaps most widely known for his pioneering work on independence and conformity (Asch, 1956). The issue is, "how does one understand the tendency of individuals to conform to the group?" The experimental paradigm he developed to study the question is, as Roger Brown put it, "an epistemological nightmare." The subject is confronted with a standard line and three variable lines, one equal to the standard and the other two obviously different in length. The subject hears the unanimous judgment of other subjects (three or more is all it takes) that one of the unequal lines is, in fact, equal to the standard. The group judgment contradicts what the subject sees clearly with his or her own eyes. Whether one yields or resists, the experience is powerfully distressing. Indeed, there is some evidence that those who resist are more affected than those who yield. Asch argues that the situation is disturbing because it brings into conflict two powerful forces by which we construct reality; our own subjective experience, and intersubjective agreement. The assumption that the world as we see it is the same world seen by others is brought into question. The study does not tell why people conform or why they are independent, but, rather, puts the question in a much broader perspective; social behavior is seen as involving a coordination of ones own perspective with the perspective of others, and people act in what they consider to be a "mutually shared" field. It is the blatant disconfirmation of the assumption that we all share the same world which is so distressing. The procedure developed by Asch and the variations on it are endlessly fascinating and have influenced the work of many other psychologists.

The concern with objectivity took another turn with his work on metaphor (Asch, 1955, 1958). In this work Asch examined the proposition that metaphors are simply social conventions. That is, one learns to associate the word "cold" with a certain type of personality. He examined such sensory terms and their reference to personality in a number of languages (Old Testament Hebrew, Homeric Greek, Chinese, Thai, Malayalam, and Hausa). He found wide agreement between these languages in the assignment of sensory terms (hot or cold person, deep or shallow thinker) to psychological traits. Language and thought are not the result of rote associative connections, but reflect the attempt of the person to deal with the real properties of people and objects.

In the 1950s Asch returned to the topic of learning where, as we have seen, he had done his earliest research, and published a series of experimental and theoretical papers on that topic. The dominant position at that time was that learning could be described as the association of temporally contiguous events, and the events that were associated were stimuli and responses. Asch took issue with these assumptions. In contrast to the stimulus-response characterization of human learning Gestalt psychologists believed that perceptual and conceptual processes left behind a memory trace; an internal representation of the percept or the idea. Asch joined this issue thru the study of associative symmetry (Asch, 1968a; Asch & Ebenholtz, 1962a; Asch & Lindner, 1963).

If one describes a paired associate as a stimulus-response pair, then it does not make conceptual sense to say that a response can give rise to a stimulus. Nevertheless, backward associations do occur in human paired associate learning. S-R theorists dealt with this awkward fact by arguing that in learning an A-B pair, *two* S-R associations were formed; a forward association, where A was the stimulus and the production of B was the response, and a backward association, where B was the stimulus and the production of A the response. The evidence for this theory was that forward associations are stronger than backward associations. Asch and Ebenholtz presented evidence which suggested that there was only one, symmetrical association and that forward- backward differences could be accounted for by differences in item availability, a non-associative property of the traces themselves. It is interesting to note that their general position is now widely accepted. The work of Collins and Quillian (1972), and of Anderson and Bower (1973) has made current the idea of memory as an internal representation of the presented information and this concept is now dominant in the field. The idea of "activation" as a property of memory traces is also indispensable in present thinking, and is quite similar to Asch and Ebenholtz's concept of trace availability.

A second theme in Asch's work on learning is the distinction between unitary and nonunitary associations (Asch, 1962, 1969; Asch, Ceraso, & Heimer (1960); Asch & Prentice, 1958). It is astonishing that this important distinction had been neglected for so long, particularly when one realizes that the founders of associationism, Locke, and especially Hartley, had specifically discussed the analogous distinction between simultaneous and successive associations (Herrnstein & Boring, 1966; pp. 348–355). Asch created a simple paradigm through which he demonstrated that simple properties, such as shape and color, would enter into association much more readily when they were parts of the same unit than when they were parts of different units. Ceraso's chapter in this volume reports work directly related to Asch's research. One senses that the web of issues surrounding the concept of the unit has finally become a "hot" topic in psychology. This is largely due to the recent work of Treisman (1986) that has provoked excitement about an issue which should have been dealt with long ago.

The third aspect of Asch's work on learning and memory deals with the concept of association itself. In a series of papers (Asch, 1964, 1968a; Asch & Ebenholtz, 1962b; Asch, Hay, & Mendoza, 1960) Asch has attempted to show that even when dealing with more traditional associative paradigms the concept of association encounters difficulties and complications.

The free recall of items from a serially presented list, for example, had been treated by postulating sequential associations between the list items which mediated their recall. Asch and Ebenholtz (1962b) presented evidence suggesting that, in fact, recall of material from a serially presented list occurs readily even when the conditions which foster interitem association are not present. In order to deal with the kinds of difficulties Asch's studies revealed, association theorists have employed concepts such as "association with position." But Asch has pointed out that these concepts themselves entail further problems, For example, the concept of "position" is itself relational, it does not refer to a particular position in space. One learns that an item is at the beginning, the middle, or the end of a series. Neither can one identify position temporally. For example, Asch, Hay, and Mendoza (1960) showed how the same temporal series would be learned differently when presented in different spatial patterns.

When one thinks of Asch, and a few others, attempting to develop a cognitive theory of learning at that time, in the face of massive opposition, the analogy to the group pressure studies becomes irresistible.

As we have seen, then, Asch is one of the few experimental psychologists who has contributed to the many fields into which psychology is now divided and who has also elaborated a comprehensive view of man; each study can be seen in its own right and also in relation to this more comprehensive view. The broadest statement of his position was given in his 1952 book, *Social Psychology*. The book reflects his belief that people, given a chance, will behave reasonably and decently. His friends know how deeply Shlaym cares about social issues and the human condition and how his work flows from these concerns. Happily, a reprint of the book was made available by Oxford Press in 1987. Some sense of the aims and contents of the book can be gotten from the preface Asch wrote for the Oxford edition.

He describes the state of psychology at the time the book was written:

> The dominant American direction was behaviorism; it rested largely on the findings and conclusions of Pavlovian conditioning and British Associationism, as filtered through the American milieu. The overarching concept was habit—it was concerned with how habits are formed and changed. Psychoanalysis served as a secondary but important adjunct. As applied to social psychology, it was about how persons deceive themselves (and others); in particular how persons and groups are misled by instinctual forces. Historical circumstances make for odd alignments, and this is what happened with the peculiar affiliation during the 1930's in America between the alien and mostly incompatible currents of behaviorism and psychoanalysis. Mainly they shared one affinity; both worked (although in distinctive ways) from the premise of human irrationality; both strove for a general psychology on that foundation. This notion was not altogether clear, but neither was it easy in the climate of the time to counter the premise of irrationality. People do go mad, and even when apparently sane they are capable of killing one another by the millions. Thus, despite many obscurities, these unlikely partners were made to mesh—conditioning and association on the one hand and psychoanalytic processes on the other—and the combination appeared acceptable to many.

Asch also pointed out that the legacy of World War I, the great depression, and the growing threat of World War II, all fed into a cynicism concerning human beings. He then described his intentions in writing the book:

> It was about that time (in the 1930s and 40s) that I became somewhat acquainted with gestalt ideas and began to think of a work in social psychology. My own convictions were not notably more prescient than those of my contemporaries, yet I did persist in a few points. First, the work was to be about fundamental issues of human psychology: it was to clarify problems more than to provide solutions. My intention was to produce, in contrast to the prevalent non-cognitive versions, a phenomenological psychology in which social facts and processes held central place. The account of human experience would of necessity be cognitive, but the emotional dimensions of human existence were not to be slighted. Not to sound too grandiloquent, I aimed for a treatise on human nature, informed by recent gestalt strivings—a psychology with a human face. The foregoing aims of course presupposed the necessity to portray human beings as a whole, not as a collection of mechanisms or facts. The opening chapter of the book examined in a critical light what I called ''doctrines of man,'' or entrenched assumptions that were taken for granted and that few stopped to question. Among these themes was a systematic underestimation of human intellectual capacities and potentialities. It was not diffi-

cult to understand or even to sympathize somewhat with this position, but it was less easy to justify the glib ways in which it was adopted. Surely it is not the mission of psychologists to mouth the preconceptions of their day. The consequences of this theme, usually lamentable, spurred me to explore several related questions that lent themselves to concrete investigation. Ironically, many investigators were friendly to these efforts and tried to carry them forward, without however departing in the slightest from their irrationalistic starting point. As I was to discover, my medicine was evidently not sufficiently powerful. It did earn me though the suspicion in the eyes of some of my colleagues of being a "rationalist." My own position was far more modest, if not trite; I did hold that under certain conditions people are capable of acting reasonably.

Another problem that engaged my attention concerned the powerful assumption that human motives and actions are self-centered, that the ego is for each the center of the world. So unquestionable did this proposition seem that it virtually amounted to an axiom: social psychology was not only about individuals, but individualistic at the core. This belief found no place for the person as citizen, as the bearer of rights and duties, capable at times of public spirit.

In preparation for this volume some contributors sent along reminiscences of Asch and what he and his work meant to them. We have already incorporated some of this material, and though there is not enough space to include it all, we don't want to omit what Roger Brown, and Henry Gleitman gave us.

Roger Brown:
"When we examine the characteristics of instinct and habit we discover a curious thing about them: they are not *human*." That wonderful sentence telling social psychologists we had nothing to lose but our chains is from Solomon Asch's textbook. The book was published in 1952 and that was the year I first taught social psychology; by departmental decree, with little background, in a cold winter, at Harvard University. The only thing in my head was instincts and habits, then called learning theory, based on animal experiments, and so, the first time through, the social psychology I offered was a kind of Dollard and Miller (1950) liberalization of Clark Hull (1943). There were external stimuli, big "S's," and overt responses, Big "R's," and a lot of little "s's" and little "r's" desperately mediating between them and everybody was working to satisfy the hunger drive. That first time through students would scratch their heads and say: "There must be more to social psychology than this." "No, no," I assured them, "that's it, that's the lot."

"All societies of which we have knowledge possess some form of medicine and rules of hygiene. In all societies we find personal names, modes of greeting, hospitality, feasting, games, and athletic sports. . . . Facts of this order offer a threat to the belief that the invariant properties of men are to be found solely at the earliest stages of development. . . . (Asch, 1952, p,78)". Professor Asch was visiting at Harvard in the early 1950's when I was an instructor and I heard him give many talks and seminars. In true elementaristic fashion I brought the great experiments into my course one at a time over some years: group forces on the modification of judgments (conformity); structural factors in the understanding of assertions (critique of the doctrine of suggestion); universal aspects of metaphor; person perception. At first each was unconnected with the serious business of instincts and habits, a "box" in a textbook, something too good to leave out but impossible to integrate with the drossy stuff around it.

How I loved teaching Solomon Asch's experiments! How *have* I loved teaching them and writing about them for all these years. But it has to be done right. A flat statement of the outcomes gives neither understanding nor pleasure. You must always read again the original presentations so that you can preserve the tensions of the argument and the student can appreciate the beauty of the thinking.

His experiments did not stay in the boxes I put them in. They exerted *forces*. They transformed my course in social psychology and my thinking about social psychology, creating in me an appetite for what is universally and peculiarly human.

Henry Gleitman:

It was late at night, sometime in the 50s, as I was about to leave after a visit to the Asch's. Florence had gone to bed an hour or so before, having previously plied Shlaym and me (mostly me) with a generous number of her magnificent Old Fashioneds. I had been arguing with Shlaym. I was always arguing with Shlaym, sometimes about Greek Tragedy, and sometimes about American Learning Theory. That particular night I had tried to convince him that one could make a case for Neal Miller's attempts to interpret certain complex human phenomena in S-R terms. Just why Shlaym kept on listening, I'm not quite sure, even now. Perhaps he really wanted to find out what was going on in Yale just then (though I doubt it). Or perhaps he was just being kind to a brash young man (which is more likely). Or perhaps he regarded me as a traveller returning from a far-off land who brought back amusing tales of Anthropophagi and men whose heads do grow beneath their shoulders (which is even more likely). In any case, he listened to me gravely, and nodded, and then, just as I put on my coat and was about to leave, he smiled and asked: "Yes, Henry, but can a rat play Iago?"

What a puckish, devastating comment! At the most obvious level, it was a supreme—and oh so gentle—putdown. For of course Shlaym knew of my deep interest in acting and directing. And of course he knew that the one part I truly ached to play was Iago. (What actor doesn't?)

I eventually realized that Shlaym's sly question had a much deeper and less personal meaning as well. For what is it that a rat can't possibly do, no matter how many rg's we may choose to grant it? The answer is that it cannot lie or pretend. Like Iago. And if it can't do that, it assuredly cannot take the further step of pretending to pretend. Like the actor who plays Iago. Or any actor on a stage.

I regard Shlaym as one of the deepest—perhaps *the* deepest psychologist I have ever met. As a young man I didn't realize just how deep he was. I hope he'll regard my comments about the theater [Chapter 8] as an indication that I finally understood his little joke.

We began this biography with Shlaym speaking about his childhood. It seems appropriate to end with his recent thoughts about psychology. This comes from the preface to the 1987 Oxford edition of his Social Psychology:

Today social psychology appears almost unrecognizably different from what existed in the 1950s when this book was written. The field has expanded enormously: it now resembles more an international combine than the corner grocery of the past. New topics have sprung up, old ones have vanished. More to the point, behaviorism as it existed has apparently lost its old force, and the emergence of gestalt views is almost universally acknowledged.

Why then am I not ready to beat the drums of victory, to proclaim that my hopes have been vindicated, and that a new day has dawned in the study of mankind? Why the sense of unfulfilled perspectives? Why do I sense, together with the current expansion, a shrinking of vision, an expansion of surface rather than depth, a failure of imagination? Have the changes that transpired in recent decades been more than skin-deep? Why the outcroppings of piecemeal ways of thinking during a supposedly gestalt revolution? Why are the stirring contributions so eerily rare as one leafs through volume after thick volume? Has there in fact been anything like a gestalt revolution in American social psychology? The evidence is, I think, not convincing. And is not the current cognitive psychology, despite the striking change of language it has introduced, perhaps too often a guise for a newly attired behaviorism, a species of the increasingly mentioned cognitive behaviorism? More important, why is not social psychology more exciting, more human? The reexamination of basic assumptions that was needed in the 1950s is, I believe equally necessary today. Busyness is no substitute for serious analysis.

It is not my intention to end on a negative note. Indeed I have never sided with those who held that social psychology is a marginal, inbetween discipline; to me it was and remains as ultimate as physics. Therefore I am hopeful of its future, even though that may require insights not yet on the horizon but struggling to come to the surface.

REFERENCES

Anderson, J. R., & Bower, G. H. (1973). *Human associative memory.* New York: Wiley.
Asch, F. (1989). *Letter to Irvin Rock.*
Asch, S. E. (1929). *A study of scatter on the Stanford revision of the Binet scale.* Unpublished MA thesis.
Asch, S. E. (1932a). *Personality development of Hopi children.* Unpublished paper.
Asch, S. E. (1932b). An experimental study of variability in learning. *Archives of Psychology, 143,* 1–55
Asch, S. E. (1946). Forming impressions of personality. *Journal of Abnormal and Social Psychology, 41,* 258–290.
Asch, S. E. (1948). The doctrine of suggestion, prestige, and imitation in social psychology. *Psychological Review, 55,* 250–276.
Asch, S. E. (1952). *Social psychology.* Englewood Cliffs, NJ: Prentice-Hall.
Asch, S. E. (1955). On the use of metaphor in the description of persons. In H. Werner (Ed.), *On expressive language* (29–38). Worcester, MA: Clark University Press.
Asch, S. E. (1956). Studies of independence and conformity: I. A minority of one against a unanimous majority. *Psychological Monographs, 70,* 1–70.
Asch, S. E. (1958). The metaphor: a psychological inquiry. In R. Tagiuri & L. Petrullo (Eds.), *Person perception and interpersonal behavior* (pp. 86–94), California: Stanford University Press.
Asch, S. E. (1962). A problem in the theory of associations. *Psychologische Beitrage, 6,* 553–563.

Asch, S. E. (1964). The process of free recall. In C. Scheerer (Ed.), *Cognition: Theory, research, promise* (pp. 79–88). New York: Harper and Row.

Asch, S. E. (1968a). The doctrinal tyranny of associationism. In T. R. Dixon & D. L. Horton (Eds.), *Verbal behavior and general behavior theory* (pp. 214–228). Englewood Cliffs, NJ: Prentice-Hall.

Asch, S. E. (1968b). Wolfgang Köhler. *American Journal of Psychology, 81,* 110–119.

Asch, S. E. (1969). A reformulation of the problem of associations. *American Psychologist, 24,* 92–102.

Asch, S. E., Ceraso, J., & Heimer, W. (1960). Perceptual conditions of association. *Psychological Monographs, 74*(3), 1–48.

Asch, S. E., & Ebenholtz, S. M. (1962a). The principle of associative symmetry. *Proceedings of the American Philosophical Society, 106,* 135–163.

Asch, S. E., & Ebenholtz, S. M. (1962b). The process of free recall: evidence for non-associative factors in acquisition and retention. *Journal of Psychology, 54,* 3–31.

Asch, S. E., Hay, J., & Mendoza, R. (1960). Perceptual organization in serial rote-learning. *American Journal of Psychology, 73,* 177–198.

Asch, S. E., & Lindner, M. (1963). A note on "strength of association." *Journal of Psychology, 55,* 199–209.

Asch, S. E., & Prentice, W. C. H. (1958). Paired association with related and unrelated pairs of nonsense figures. *American Journal of Psychology, 71,* 247–254.

Asch, S. E., & Witkin, H. A. (1948a). Studies in space orientation: I. Perception of the upright with displaced visual fields. *Journal of Experimental Psychology, 38,* 325–337.

Asch, S. E., & Witkin, H. A. (1948b). Studies in space orientation: II. Perception of the upright with displaced visual fields and with body tilted. *Journal of Experimental Psychology, 38,* 455–477.

Collins, A. M., & Quillian, M. R. (1972). How to make a language user. In E. Tulving & W. Donaldson (Eds.), *Organization and memory.* New York: Academic Press.

Dollard, J., & Miller, N. E. (1950). *Personality and psychotherapy.* New York: McGraw-Hill.

Gibson, J. J., & Mowrer, O. H. (1938). Determinants of the perceived vertical and horizontal. *Psychological Review, 45,* 300–323.

Gruber, H. (1971). *Unpublished interview of S. E. Asch.*

Herrnstein, R. J., & Boring, E. G. (1966). *A Source book in the history of psychology.* Cambridge MA: Harvard University Press.

Hull, C. L. (1943). *Principles of behavior.* New York: Appleton-Century-Crofts.

Klineberg, O. (1940). *Social psychology.* New York: Holt.

Murphy, G. (1930). *Historical introduction to modern psychology.* New York: Harcourt, Brace, World.

Murphy, G., Murphy, L. B., & Newcomb, T. M. (1937). *Experimental social psychology.* New York: Harper & Row.

Treisman, A. (1986). Properties, parts, and objects. In K. R. Boff, L. Kaufman, & J. P. Thompson (Eds.), *Handbook of perception and human performance* (Vol. II, Chap. 35, pp. 1–70). New York: Wiley.

Wertheimer, M. (1912). Experimentelle studien über das sehen von bewegung. *Zeitschrift für Psychologie, 61,* 161–265.

Wertheimer, M. (1937). *Productive thinking.* New York: Harper & Row.

Witkin, H. A., & Asch, S. E. (1948a). Studies in space orientation: III. Perception of the upright in the absence of a visual field. *Journal of Experimental Psychology, 38,* 603–614.

Witkin, H. A., & Asch, S. E. (1948b). Further experiments on perception of the upright with displaced visual fields. *Journal of Experimental Psychology, 38,* 762–782.

Witkin, H. A., Lewis, H. B., Hertzman, M., Machover, K., Meissner, P. B., & Wapner, S. (1954). *Personality through perception: an experimental and clinical study.* New York: Harper & Row.

II SOCIAL PSYCHOLOGY

2 Politeness Theory: Exemplar and Exemplary

Roger Brown
Harvard University

ABSTRACT

The Theory of Politeness of Penelope Brown and Stephen C. Levinson (1987) is offered as an example of the kind of human invariant arising out of interaction discussed by Solomon Asch in his *Social Psychology* (1952). Politeness means acting so as to take account of the feelings of others. The feelings taken account of are those concerned with positive face (the wish to be approved of) and negative face (the wish to be unimpeded, free from imposition). It is the central claim of Politeness Theory that there are many verbal strategies of politeness and that the selection of a strategy is governed by the degree of estimated risk of face loss. Risk of face loss increases with the power of the hearer over the speaker, with the horizontal social distance between speaker and hearer, and with the ranked extremity of the imposition in a given culture. Politeness is represented as a system, not a bundle of habits; the system in broad outline is thought to be a human invariant, but at specified points cultural values must be supplied; politeness is central to human nature but not biological; politeness theory is explicitly rooted in a general intellectual position. In these and other ways politeness theory meets Solomon Asch's high standards for social psychology.

In his 1952 textbook Asch said that he expected to find universal systems arising out of interaction that have produced motives and capacities as central to the nature of man as biological needs. Today we have a theory of politeness which is an exemplar of the kind of invariant system Asch described. Politeness theory is also, I think, exemplary or worthy of imitation. For whom is it exemplary? For experimental social psychology today.

INTRODUCTION TO THE IDEAS
IN POLITENESS THEORY

In 1978 Cambridge University Press published a 300-page paper on politeness by Penelope Brown, a Cambridge anthropologist, and Stephen Levinson, a Cambridge linguist. This book-length paper was awkwardly packaged with a very short essay on questions and the book itself given the title *Questions and Politeness* (Goody, 1978). It very quickly went out of print. I read the paper about 5 years ago and it seemed to me to be some kind of masterpiece which had never found the right readership. In the spring of 1987, however, Cambridge Press reissued the paper as a book called *Politeness; Some Universals in Language Usage* and I learned from a new 50-page review of research on the theory that it had many admirers.

Politeness means acting so as to take account of the feelings of the other person. That means on the whole being less straightforward and uncomplicated than if you disregarded the other's feelings. Polite speech is to be contrasted with maximally efficient speech, which is sometimes called "Gricean," after Paul Grice (1975) who set down the four maxims governing such speech. These are: the Maxim of Quality—"Tell the truth"; the Maxim of Manner—"Be unambiguous"; the Maxim of Quantity—"Say all that is necessary but no more"; and the Maxim of Relation—"Be relevant." Politeness takes more time and effort, but politeness systems are universal in languages and for most of us on most days the work of politeness constitutes a substantial part of the total talking we do.

The Brown–Levinson theory deals only with politeness in linguistic forms, but the authors believe the entire theory could be constructed in terms of nonverbal behavior, in terms of bows, smiles, and personal distance instead of forms of address and request, apologies, and thanks. Verbal and nonverbal politeness considerations came together to powerful effect in the trial of Bernhard H. Goetz. Troy Canby, one of the men Goetz shot, testified that he (Canby) had walked up to within 4 or 5 feet of Goetz (stranger distance) and said, "Mister" (deferential address), "can I have $5.00"? (indirect request). According to Goetz's taped statement, the youth who approached him drew close (intimate distance) and smiling menacingly (nonverbal threat), said: "Give me $5.00" (imperative request). The difference between homicide and self-defense hinged on six points of contrast in politeness theory. As you see, we are not always in an Emily Post world with the topic of politeness.

Positive Face and Positive Politeness; Negative Face and Negative Politeness

The feelings that politeness takes account of are of just two kinds: those concerned with positive face and those concerned with negative face. The authors acknowledge a large debt to Erving Goffman (1967, 1971, 1976) and dedicate their book to him. Positive face is every person's *want* (the authors' carefully chosen word) to have his public self-image appreciated, approved, and ratified by others, not all others for all aspects of face, but the significant ones for each aspect. Very exactly expressed, what each person wants is that others want for him what he wants for himself: health, honor, happiness. Negative face is also a matter of wants: Every person's want to be free from imposition and distraction and to have their personal prerogatives and territory respected.

Positive politeness is simply defined as any effort to meet positive face needs. The phrase "Have a good day," renewed daily, is a quintessential act of positive politeness: The speaker wishes for the hearer what the hearer wishes for himself. Brown and Levinson identify and illustrate 15 varieties of positive politeness. These include attending to and showing concern for the other's health, appearance, possessions, etc., emphasizing in-group identity by using familiar forms of address, a common dialect, slang, ellipsis that works because of shared past experience, seeking areas of agreement (the weather at least), avoiding disagreement on politics, people, but also books, movies, whatever, and giving gifts that may be either material or psychological.

Learning to recognize substrategies of positive politeness takes practice. On one occasion when Mr. Gorbachev was in Washington in the fall of 1987 he and the President were sitting together awaiting the arrival of their wives. Mr. Reagan suggested that the two men simultaneously look at their watches just as the women arrived. They did so and the newspapers reported smiles and a flow of good feeling. What kind of positive politeness was this? In-group identity. The meaning was: "We husbands—kept waiting by our wives. It's the same all over the world."

Positive politeness—familiar address, in-group references, compliments, and sympathy—is the everyday exchange of friends and intimates. In a recent long distance phone call with a fellow-psychologist and friend, we two praised one another's most recent papers, expressed a shared dislike of APA conventions, recalled with pleasure the happy days of the Harvard Center for Cognitive Studies, inquired about the health of family members, deftly avoided reference to a known point of disagreement, and ended with requests to "Take care. Have a good semester, etc." In a sense, nothing was said, but you have to have words to carry the melody.

In the Brown–Levinson theory, however, all forms of politeness are linked to what the authors call "intrinsic face threatening acts" (or FTA's). The politeness strategy called "positive politeness," which consists of 15 substrategies, is specifically addressed to FTA's that threaten the positive face. Positive politeness is an effort to redress or make up for a threat, specifically, to the positive face or desired self-image.

Negative politeness is defined as any effort to meet negative face wants, and there are 10 subvarieties. Negative face is threatened by an imposition on freedom of action or any challenge to prerogatives or territory, and negative politeness is designed to redress just the specific FTA that creates the occasion for politeness. The most common speech act requiring negative politeness is a request that is an imposition, and one general principle of negative politeness is to minimize the size of the imposition, guarantee its nonrecurrence, call attention to any pleasant aspects. Another general principle of negative politeness is to make it very clear that the request cannot be coerced. One does not use the Gricean imperative: "Write me a letter of recommendation today," but one of the many indirect request forms that all languages make available; e.g. "I wonder if you feel that you know me well enough to write a letter of recommendation." Always leave the hearer an "out" as in the preceding. Give deference to the hearer and abase yourself so as to convey the absurdity of any notion that you might be able to coerce compliance. On the same principle, do not seem to be confident of compliance with your request, take nothing for granted, be pessimistic. And, finally, explicitly acknowledge your indebtedness and apologize.

All of the substrategies of negative politeness can be found in the letters of former students making requests which they think of as impositions because a long time has passed since they were last heard from or because they never worked closely with you or for whatever reason. Here are a few from my files:

1. "May I ask one last favor of you (hopefully) for a while?" (The request will not recur.)
2. "I wouldn't blame you if you tossed this letter right out, without ever reading it." (Pessimism)
3. "Can you spare me just five minutes of your time?" (Minimizing the imposition)

The next example is from a Korean student and the negative politeness has an extravagance that is a pan-cultural, pan-linguistic regional characteristic of the Far East (with China a partial exception):

These papers come from my notes of what I read. So I'm afraid that it would be an absolutely meaningless and unnecessary job for you to read these bulky papers. You might think it a waste of time. I ask you not to bother yourself with these and just regard them as traces of my work.

It is a little hard to find the request there, but the papers were, after all, on the desk. Of course even negative politeness can be manipulated with wit:

I'm sending you something to read (please don't groan! It is not another tedious article). It's a *story*. I think you won't mind reading it and besides it's a present. You don't, for a change, need to play editor at all with it. It's a present. It's a Trojan Horse. I'm applying for a Writing Fellowship here and would like to list you, etc.

After these excesses of negative politeness, it is refreshing to read a more usual request from a current student in good standing who does not think a letter of recommendation is an imposition:

Sorry to bother you at Thanksgiving, but here are 15 jobs I have applied for.

There is some evidence that the negative politeness strategy of minimizing a request is the first that children learn. Elizabeth Bates (1976), working with Italian preschool children in Rome, introduced each one to la Signora Rossi, a grey-haired hand puppet with a large supply of sweets, who would give the child one if asked, and did so. The Signora then confided that she liked children who were *molto gentile* and so she would, if asked very, very nicely, give a second sweet and for still greater politeness even a third. Under this politeness pressure almost all children from 2 years on knew enough to say *per favore,* but some, in addition, reduced *biscotto* to *biscottino* or *caramello* to *carmellino.* And some, charmingly, reduced their requests by whispering them.

An adult nonverbal example of the substrategy of minimization may be seen at large formal lectures when a member of the audience must leave before the end. The person leaving will typically go into a "little-me" crouch and tiptoe out on tiny cat feet. Thereby minimizing the imposition on the speaker and other audience members.

As an example of the subtlety of politeness theory I offer its treatment of conventionalized indirect questions, a form of negative politeness. A request such as "Pass the salt" threatens to impose on the hearer's freedom, if only in a small way, and when expressed in the straightforward Gricean imperative, the threat is evident. English is rich in circumlocutious alternatives: "Can you reach the salt?"; "Is there any salt down there?"; "We need the salt"; "Would you mind passing the salt?" Functionally these are all requests, but grammatically they are questions or statements. Indirect requests like these turn out to be constructed in a principled way. The simple imperative "Pass the salt" will not accomplish its purpose unless certain contextual prerequisites are satisfied: (1) There should be salt within reach of the hearer; (2) The speaker should genuinely want salt; (3) The hearer should have no fixed objection to passing the salt—and so on. If these circumstances are satisfied, then the world is ready for "Pass the salt" to have its intended effect. The circumstances that comprise a happy environment for imperatives are called "felicity conditions" (Searle, 1975) in speech act theory. Indirect requests more polite than the imperative such as "Can you pass the salt?" all either question a felicity condition or call attention to a felicity condition and in that way satisfy the hearer's negative face by leaving him an "out." It is as if the speaker thought the hearer might not be remiss at all; perhaps there is no salt or perhaps he cannot reach it or has religious scruples about passing it (Gordon & Lakoff, 1971; Labov & Fanshel, 1977).

If Brown and Levinson left the matter there, the sensitivity of their linguistic intuitions could be faulted because it is obvious that indirect requests like "Can you pass the salt?" are not processed in terms of grammatical form but are understood to be requests even by very young children (Bates, 1976). To answer "Can you pass the salt?" by saying "Yes, I can" is either a joke or a snub. Of course, Brown and Levinson know this and so they call such indirect requests "fully conventionalized,'' which is to say that frequent use has turned them into functional requests whatever their grammar. However, they add, the original derivation still has enough semantic life in it to give indirect polite requests like ''Would you mind passing the salt?'' the feel of a compromise between a selfish wish to have the salt and a face-considerate reluctance to impose. In speech processing terms this means that both the functional meaning and the literal meaning are computed, and Herb Clark and his associates (Clark, 1979; Clark & Lucy, 1975; Clark & Schunk, 1980) have found ways to demonstrate experimentally that this is so.

What finally makes the analysis of polite requests impressive is the fact that they are derived in the same way, from felicity conditions, in some languages not related to English—possibly in all (Blum-Kulka, 1982; Fraser, 1978). Brown and Levinson (1978, 1987) have shown that in Tamil and Tzeltal indirect requests are based on felicity conditions as they are in English. R. Brown and Gilman (1989) have recently shown that the same is true of polite requests in Early Modern English (1500–1700) as used by Shakespeare. The phrases are now archaic: *I entreat you, I do beseech you, Prithee, If you will give me leave, If it please you.* However, they all either express the sincerity of the speaker's wish or else inquire about the willingness of the hearer to comply and these are both felicity conditions.

OUTLINE OF THE THEORY

The core of the Brown-Levinson theory of politeness is graphically represented in Fig. 2.1. The point of view is that of the speaker. The mental processes modeled are his and they are assumed to be swift and unconscious, though I will generally have to use words that suggest deliberation. The problem the speaker is considering is whether or not to perform some single face-threatening act (or FTA) and if the decision is to perform it, then how to perform it, in what way. An FTA is a communication and it seems to be true that many, even most communications are in some way face threatening. The FTA is addressed to the hearer, and taking account of the feelings of the hearer poses the problem of politeness. The relevant feelings concern positive face and negative face and have already been described. An ''on record'' speech act has a single unambiguous interpretation and the speaker may be held accountable for it whereas an ''off record'' speech act has more than one reasonable interpretation and speaker accountability for any single interpretation is in doubt.

There are five numbered politeness strategies in Fig. 2.1:

1. Do the FTA without redressive action, baldly.
2. Do the FTA on record with redressive positive politeness.

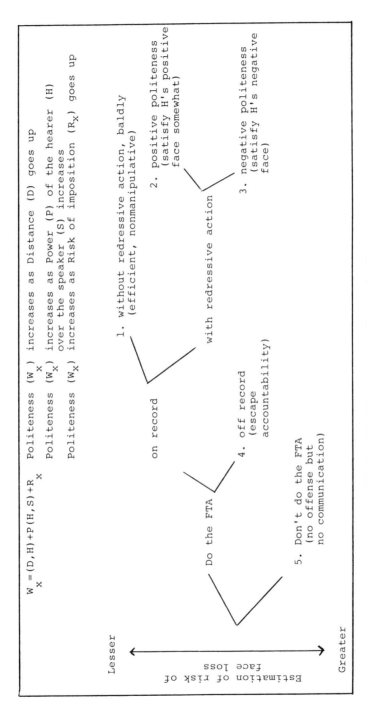

FIG. 2.1. The Brown-Levinson theory of politeness.

29

3. Do the FTA on record with redressive negative politeness.
4. Do the FTA off record.
4. Don't do the FTA.

These five strategies are actually superstrategies because the theory identifies numerous more specific varieties of each. The principal empirical claim of the theory is that the five superstrategies are ordered as in Fig. 2.1 against a scale of lesser to greater estimated risk to face. The authors make another claim of which they seem less confident but which in my own preliminary work (R. Brown & Gilman, 1989) looks very promising. "The more *effort* a speaker expends in face-saving work, the more he will be seen as trying to satisfy the hearer's face wants . . . the greater the number of compatible outputs—the more the speaker may be judged as at least trying to be polite (Brown & Levinson, 1987, p. 143)." If someone says, "I have no right to ask this and I would not do it if I were not desperate and unable to handle it myself," we do not expect the FTA to be "Can you tell me the time?" The politeness windup has been disproportionate to the FTA.

Figure 2.1 says that when risk is minimal the FTA may be done in a Gricean way which is on record without redressive action, baldly, and when risk is maximal, the theory advises "Don't do the FTA." The three remaining strategies are associated with intermediate risk levels. An on-record strategy is a way of doing the FTA that leaves the speaker's intention unambiguous and so makes the speaker fully accountable. An off-record FTA does not permit an unambiguous assignment of intention to the speaker and so any interpretation made is deniable and the speaker is not accountable.

Politeness theory holds that the selection of strategies is universally determined by just three variables. Two concern the relationship between speaker and hearer: vertical social distance or "power" (P) and horizontal social distance or "solidarity" (D). These are the same dimensions that R. Brown and Gilman used in 1960 to describe the semantics of European pronouns of address as typified by the French *tu/vous* (T/V) distinction and which have been reported since 1960 to be the dimensions underlying pronominal (and other) address in at least 28 different languages, many of them unrelated (Alrabaa, 1985; Fang & Heng, 1983; Friedrich, 1966; Kempff, 1985; Kroger, Wood, & Kim, 1984; Lambert & Tucker, 1976; Levinson, 1977, 1982; Mehrotra, 1981; Paulston, 1987; Yassin, 1975; and others).

While power and distance are postulated to be universal determinants of politeness, the personal characteristics that enter into the calculation of power and distance vary both culturally and historically. Race, sex, age, generation, kinship, occupation, religion, and language have all figured prominently, and the "samba clubs" of Rio de Janeiro and the "benevolent societies" of New York's Chinatown teach us that almost any personal characteristic can serve in this way. If we looked only at cultural features, externally viewed, we should see a high degree of cultural relativism, but if we look at intracultural meanings in terms of

P and D, we see universality or invariance. This is the general position that Asch took on cultural relativism in his *Social Psychology* (1952).

Pronouns of address have relational rather than referential meanings and in this way they are like kin terms. Just as it is not a property of a person to be always addressed as *dad* or *son,* so it is not a property of a person to be always addressed as T or as V; in both cases the form used varies with a relation, the relation between speaker and addressee. The very important difference between kin terms and pronouns is that the former (unless "extended" or "fictive") serve to relate only some members of a social group with some others whereas the latter serve to relate each one to each other one and so constitute a fully connected language of relationship. If the dimensions governing such relational forms are universal across languages, then such dimensions would seem to have a privileged fundamental status for the analysis of social life. On present evidence they are universal and, in politeness theory, they are called "power" and "distance," symbolized as, respectively, "P" and "D."

There is a third variable that affects the choice of a politeness strategy and this is the intrinsic extremity of the face-threatening act. In the culture and situation in question, how much does the FTA interfere with self-determination (negative face) and approval (positive face)? The assumption made is that there will be a fairly constant ranking of impositions in terms of expenditures in time, expertise, and goods and also a ranking of threats to positive face in terms of desired attributes like honesty, honor, and generosity. The necessary operations are not all at hand but the idea is clear: Asking for a loan of $5 is less of an imposition than asking for a loan of $50; criticizing someone's life work is a greater imposition than criticizing a necktie.

Brown and Levinson combine additively the three variables affecting the selection of a strategy into the formula $W_x = D(S,H) + P(H,S) + R_x$ which in words says that the weightiness or riskiness of FTA_x is a function of the social distance between speaker and hearer plus the power of the hearer over the speaker plus the culturally ranked intrinsic threat posed by the FTA. In crude operational terms W should be greater if H is a superordinate than if H is a subordinate; W should be greater if S and H are new acquaintances than if S and H are old friends; and W should be greater if R is a request to borrow a car than if R is a request to borrow a book. Experiments so far have mostly used written scenarios that use two values of one variable while holding the other constant.

We know how riskiness or weightiness is compounded. But what exactly is the relation between weightiness levels and numbered strategies? It might appear to be a kind of stimulus-response prediction (with both stimuli and strategies rank ordered), but that is not what the authors intend. Brown and Levinson (1987) make it very clear that politeness strategies are to be thought of as goal-oriented plans, not simple responses, and they add:

> The wonders explored in cognitive psychology, linguistics or artificial intelligence have no counterparts in social theory. . . . Here we merely scratch in a groping

way, the surface of one area of interaction, and we wish to draw the attention of social scientists to the richness and complexity of the assumptions and inferences upon the basis of which humans understand and cooperate with one another. (p. 56)

With respect to Fig. 2.1, the theory claims universality for the strategies and their ordering and, in he formula, for P, D, and R. What clearly varies by language and culture are the factors figuring in the calculation of the weightiness variables. On the molecular level of substrategies there are occasional structural and functional correspondences that are as pan-linguistic as indirect requests. The more usual case is to find some function like hedging an imposition expressed by a variety of forms—for example, particles, adverbs, prosodics, and kinesics—with the formal mix varying by languages.

Examples of positive politeness and negative politeness have already been given but little has been said about the outlying strategies. The first, "on the record without redress, baldly," is the maximally efficient Gricean speech introduced as a general contrast to all forms of politeness. Speech becomes Gricean whatever the relation between speaker and hearer in certain circumstances that override all considerations of politeness such as extreme urgency ("Fire!" "Stop, thief!" "Help me!") or noisy channels ("I'll call back!" "Fasten seat belts."). The surgeon in the operating theater is an ultimate Gricean with his "scalpel," "sponge," "retractor," and so is the 18-month child with his "cookie," "milk," "doggie." In Fig. 2.1, however, Gricean speech is associated with minimal values and that seems to be right. Taking off several layers of politeness is one of the comforts of coming home where D is low and so is P.

Brown and Levinson are students of total systems, linguistic and cultural, and they almost never speculate about individual differences, but a psychologist cannot forbear. I know a few people who have personal styles that are Gricean. They do not do the work of politeness in much the spirit that some housekeepers do not do windows. All the Griceans I call to mind are males and all have very high standing in some profession. Brown and Levinson suggest that individuals will cooperate in mutual face maintenance unless one can manipulate the other into maintaining his face without reciprocation, and probably high-ranking males are the ones for that job. In opting out of a cultural system, stylistic Griceans acquire a "character" in the eye of conventional people. They do not, I think, come across as "abrasive." So far as I have been able to tell by unsystematic observation, abrasive people use the code of manners but they get it wrong. Gricean man seems aloof rather than abrasive. One of my Gricean acquaintances has the nickname "All Signal, No Noise." That says it.

Off-record speech (Strategy No. 4) is called for when there is high risk but not so much as absolutely to prohibit the FTA. The idea is to communicate your intention with enough ambiguity so that you cannot be held strictly accountable. The Brown-Levinson treatment is elegant. Since the hearer must *interpret* what he hears, must go from what is said to something hinted at, there must be a "trigger" to alert him to do more than the usual amount of interpretive work. What should the trigger be? Some violation, the theory proposes, of the Gricean Maxims of Cooperative Conversation. The speaker must say too little—or too much—must say something not clearly relevant, must be vague or self-contradictory. A trigger is a signal to look for what speech act theory calls an "implicature" or "inference," something implied by what has been said, together with the situation and the personalities involved.

In Act III of *Othello*, Iago, Othello's ensign, intends to make Othello believe that Desdemona and the honorable Cassio are secret lovers. This is not something he can say given the difference of power and the extremity of the accusation, but it is something he can insinuate, off record.

Act III, Scene *iii*,
Iago. "Ha! I like not that." (Ellipsis violating the Maxim of Quantity)
Othello. "What dost thou say?" (Registering the violation)
Iago. "Nothing, my lord; or if—I know not what." (Vague, contradictory, and
   elliptical, violating the Maxims of Quality, Quantity, and Manner)
Othello. "Was not that Cassio parted from my wife?"
Iago. "Cassio, my lord? No sure I cannot think it. That he would steal away so
   guilty like, hearing you coming." (Hint, violating the Maxim of Relevance)

Finally, there is Strategy No.—4 Don't do the FTA, which is the strategy to adopt when the risk of speaking is prohibitively great. One might think it impossible to provide an example since it is necessary to know not only that something was not said but that it was thought and suppressed. Dramatists, however, have ways of representing inner life. Shakespeare, in *Hamlet, King Lear, Macbeth,* and *Othello* used the psychological soliloquy. Hamlet in Act I, Scene *ii,* is asked by his uncle and now stepfather: "How is it that the clouds still hang on you?" and he answers: "Not so, my lord, I am too much in the sun." For an attentive and well-prepared audience Hamlet's response is off record. We can infer the meaning: "too much in royal favor," with a pun on "son." The king makes no response to the speech and it is fair to suppose that it simply seems oddly irrelevant. When Hamlet's mother, the queen, urges "cast thy nighted color off" Hamlet speaks only of the intensity of his grief. From what he says to them, Claudius and Gertrude could not infer his thought:

O, most wicked speed, to post
   With such dexterity to incestuous sheets! (I, *ii,* 156–157)

which is expressed in the soliloquy that immediately follows upon their exit, and which ends:

But break my heart, for I must hold my tongue (I, *ii,* 158).

That is Strategy No. 4 Don't do the FTA.

Even in its basic claims politeness theory is bold, but it is still bolder than I have indicated. In addition to all else, the theory aims to provide a conceptual apparatus for characterizing the distinctive affective tone of interaction in different cultures, what Brown and Levinson call the ethos of a culture. And fascinating work has been done on this level. Shoshana Blum-Kulka (1982) of Hebrew University has obtained strong evidence that Israelis speaking Hebrew do less facework, go in for less politeness, than most nationalities. Where an American asking directions would say: "Excuse me, can you tell me how to get to the railway station?" an Israeli would say: "Excuse me, where's the railway station? This transfer of politeness system from one language to another makes Israelis sound rude in a second language to native speakers of that language.

Information on the use of the American Sign Language (Schive, personal communication) suggests that the deaf in North America communicate in an extremely direct Gricean way among themselves with little more than a "please" sign to soften impositions. This is an important lead to follow because informants say that solidarity is very high among the deaf and power differences slight. Ursula Bellugi, an authority on the American Sign Language, tells me that everyone, regardless of stature, is addressed in the same way: name sign without title. What is more, if someone in the deaf community does you a favor, you are expected to reciprocate but not necessarily to the one who benefited you. Anyone in the community will do. In effect, they pool their tips. These are the circumstances in which Gricean speech is supposed to flourish.

Politeness theory has also made work on women's speech and men's speech (the two are sometimes called "genderlects") more systematic. Robin Lakoff's book *Language and Women's Place* (1975) stimulated work that resulted only in a hodge-podge collection of constructions and words seemingly more common in the speech of one sex than in the speech of the other, but these collections are not easily conceptualized or related to any general theory. Using the formula for assessing the weightiness or riskiness of an FTA, we start with the hypothesis that women in general have less power than men and so ought to rate any given FTA as riskier in cross-sex conversation than a man will and be less disposed to produce it. Interruptions in a conversation are threats to positive face in that they show no concern for the wishes of the other and they are also threats to negative face since they impede the other. Zimmerman and West (1975) and West (1979) found that in casual cross-sex conversations more than 90% of the interruptions came from men. The differential power (or status) interpretation is strengthened by findings that high status men interrupted low status men and high status women interrupted low status women. Penelope Brown in her field work in Mayan Tenejapa (1979, 1980) found women highly vulnerable to men, with wives, sisters, and daughters liable to be beaten and marriageable women subject to abduction. Brown found that women among themselves used a lot of positive politeness, being mutually supportive as it were. Women speaking to men used a lot of negative politeness—minimizing impositions, giving deference, being diffident. From men they received relatively direct Gricean speech, unredressed by politeness.

A social psychologist studying politeness theory is continually reminded of exchange theory (a theory that every sort of personal benefit and cost can be usefully treated in terms of ideas borrowed from economics) and led to wonder whether the two theories are not somehow connected. The parallels are slightly obscured by the fact that politeness theory proceeds one FTA at a time and nothing is actually exchanged in a single speech act. However, if we imaginatively project the speaker and hearer forward and backward in time, it will usually be the case that the individual speech act is a link in a two-way exchange process that need not be entirely verbal but may include nonverbal actions of all kinds as well as material benefits and costs. Honest Iago, rousing the green-eyed monster in Othello, was retaliating for Othello's preferment of Cassio. In this case the linguistic acts are remote in space and time from the costs to which they are responsive, but there are two kinds of politeness (Coulmas, 1981) that are immediately responsive—thanks and apologies—and from these we may learn something about how politeness relates to exchange.

A speaker says thanks immediately following his receipt of some benefaction—a compliment, a favor or gift. A speaker apologizes (''excuse me,'' ''forgive me,'' etc.) immediately after delivering some malefaction (a criticism, insult, or injury). In both cases the act of verbal politeness is offered in exchange for something that may be verbal (a compliment or criticism) but need not be. In both cases, thanks and apologies, the full social routine includes a third step in which the hearer, having been thanked or apologized to, says ''not at all'' or ''don't mention it'' or, in French, ''de rien'' and in German ''bitte.'' The fact that this third step is often exactly the same phrase in both thanks and apology routines shows how closely similar the two are. In saying ''not at all,'' the hearer makes light of the benefaction he has delivered or of the malefaction he has suffered.

A thank you is a form of positive politeness intended to recompense a positive politeness, and an apology is a form of negative politeness intended to make reparations for a threat to either positive or negative face. It seems clear that the extravagance of the form ought to be proportionate to the weightiness of the prior deed. If someone dives into the icy Potomac to save your life, a perfunctory ''Thanks a lot'' will not suffice, and if you carelessly smash into someone's new car, a simple ''Excuse me'' is inadequate. On the other hand, if you forget to bring home a magazine from the drugstore, saying ''Oh my God, can you ever forgive me?'' does not sound quite serious. If thanks and apologies are meant to pay off an indebtedness, then politeness theory is that part of exchange theory that makes explicit what will count as subjective equivalents of various benefactions and malefactions. If it does that at all well, it is an important addition to exchange theory.

I myself do not think that thanks and apologies are adequate to produce a trade balance. However warmly you thank a host and hostess, however convincingly you moan over the incomparable cuisine, it is not, in the end, enough. To even accounts you must reciprocate more materially, perhaps in kind—dinner for dinner—but if not in kind, then the subjective equivalent in some currency more costly to you than thanks. "Words," it has been truly said, "are cheap." For smashing up someone's car, not even the deepest apology is sufficient recompense. One wants the name of the insurance company.

If thanks and apologies are not enough to balance accounts, what function do they serve? I think they acknowledge the debt. There is a Japanese word often used to close indebtedness routines that says it: *sumimasen* which means, literally, "this is not the end," or "it is not over." The exchange is not over until the benefit has been repaid or the damage recompensed. Verbal politeness is perhaps comparable to a check or an I.O.U., something that can be issued on the spot as an assurance of intention to pay. The extravagance of the thanks or apology seems to be proportionate to the magnitude of the good or harm. I suspect that the level of politeness functions like the size of a check to acknowledge a greater or lesser debt and an intention eventually to repay more or less.

EXEMPLAR AND EXEMPLARY

Politeness theory is an example of the kind of invariance in social behavior to which Asch directed our attention. Politeness arises out of interaction as a kind of implicit agreement to respect one another's face. Viewed externally, acts of politeness would suggest a complete cultural relativism, but when they are considered in terms of their meaning there seems to be one universal system. The motives or wants that develop in connection with politeness are peculiarly human and, if less peremptory than the biological needs we share with animals, are, nevertheless, very strong. Politeness is not a stimulus-response network but a system of planned strategies governed by means-end rationality and a scale of estimated risk. There are no biological drives anywhere in it and no habits, but it is *human*.

For whom is politeness theory exemplary or worthy of imitation. For some experimental social psychologists it is because of these features.

1. Its propositions are intended to be true at the level of the human species with certain variables explicitly identified as requiring culture-specific values.

2. It is pan-cultural and pan-linguistic from the start rather than finally, if ever.

3. It is about evaluation but is not itself evaluative. Implicit values are not concealed in its concepts as they often are in theories associated with experimental social psychology.

"All very well," the experimentalist might reply, "but is politeness theory true?" Brown and Levinson set themselves a constructivist task, not a hypothesis-testing task. Their construction is rooted in speech act theory and in the perceptions of Erving Goffman. It draws on many kinds of evidence from several different disciplines and was put together with Tamil and Tzeltal in mind as well as English. It is not a ramshackle creation that collapses with the first serious criticism; a lot of hard thinking and fine sociolinguistic intuition went into it. These constructed virtues make politeness theory worthy of all the attention it is getting but they do not establish its truth. Experiments are needed and are now appearing (e.g., Baxter, 1984; Holtgraves, 1986; Holtgraves, Srull, & Socall, in press). But the experiments are coming late rather than early. This may be, for a change, a good thing.

REFERENCES

Alrabaa, S. (1985). The use of address pronouns by Egyptian adults. *Journal of Pragmatics, 9,* 645–657.

Asch, S. E. (1952). *Social psychology.* Englewood Cliffs, NJ: Prentice-Hall.

Bates, E. (1976). *Language and context: The acquisition of pragmatics.* New York: Academic Press.

Baxter, L. A. (1984). An investigation of compliance-gaining as politeness. *Human Communication Research, 10,* 427–456.

Blum-Kulka, S. (1982). Learning to say what you mean in a second language: A study of the speech act performance of learners of Hebrew as a second language. *Applied Linguistics, 3*(1), 29–59.

Brown, P. (1979). *Language, interaction and sex roles in a Mayan community: A study of politeness and the position of women.* Unpublished doctoral dissertation, University of California, Berkeley.

Brown, P. (1980). How and why women are more polite: Some evidence from a Mayan community. In S. Connell-Ginet, R. Borker & N. Furman (Eds.), *Women and language in literature and society* (pp. 111–136). New York: Prager.

Brown, P., & Levinson, S. C. (1987). *Politeness; Some universals in language usage.* Cambridge, England: Cambridge University Press.

Brown, R., & Gilman, A. (1960). The pronouns of power and solidarity. In T. A. Sebeok (Ed.), *Style in language* (pp. 253–276). Cambridge, England: M.I.T. Press and John Wiley.

Brown, R., & Gilman, A. (1989). Politeness theory and Shakespeare's four major tragedies. *Language in society. 18,* 159–212.

Clark, H. H. (1979). Responding to indirect speech acts. *Cognitive Psychology, 11,* 430–477.

Clark, H. H., & Lucy, P. (1975). Understanding what is meant from what is said: A study in conversationally conveyed requests. *Journal of Verbal Learning and Verbal Behavior, 14,* 56–72.

Clark, H. H., & Schunk, D. H. (1980). Polite responses to polite requests. *Cognition, 8,* 111–143.

Coulmas, F. (1981). Poison to your soul: Thanks and apologies contrastively viewed. In F. Coulmas (Ed.), *Conversational routine: Explorations in standardized communication situations and prepatterned speech.* The Hague: Mouton.

Fang, H., & Heng, J. H. (1983). Social changes and changing address norms in China. *Language in Society, 12,* 495–507.

Fraser, B. (1978). Acquiring social competence in a second language. *RELC Journal, 9*(2), 1–26.

Friedrich, P. (1966). Structural implications of Russian pronominal usage. In W. Bright (Ed.), *Sociolinguistics* (pp. 214–259). The Hague: Mouton.

Goffman, E. (1967). *Interaction ritual; essays on face to face behavior.* New York: Pantheon.

Goffman, E. (1971). *Relations in public.* New York: Basic.

Goffman, E. (1976). Replies and responses. *Language in Society, 5,* 257–313.

Goody, E. N. (Ed.). (1978). *Questions and politeness.* Cambridge, England: Cambridge University Press.

Gordon, D., & Lakoff, G. (1971). Conversational postulates. In *Papers from the Seventh Regional Meeting of the Chicago Linguistic Society,* Chicago, pp. 63–84.

Grice, H. P. (1975). Logic and conversation. In P. Cole & J. L. Morgan (Eds.), *Syntax and semantics: Speech acts* (Vol. 3, pp. 41–58). New York: Academic Press.

Holtgraves, T. (1986). Language structure in social interaction: Perceptions of direct and indirect speech acts and interactants who use them. *Journal of Personality and Social Psychology, 51,* 305–314.

Holtgraves, T., Srull, T. K., & Socall, D. (in press). Conversation memory: The effects of speaker status on memory for the assertiveness of conversation remarks. *Journal of Personality and Social Psychology.*

Kempff, R. (1985). Pronouns and terms of address in *Neues Deutschland. Language in Society, 14,* 223–237.

Kroger, R. O., Wood, L. A., & Kim, V. (1984). Are the rules of address universal? III. Comparison of Chinese, Greek, and Korean usage. *Journal of Cross-Cultural Psychology, 15,* 273–284.

Labov, W., & Fanshel, D. (1977). *Therapeutic discourse.* New York: Academic Press.

Lakoff, R. T. (1975). *Language and women's place.* New York: Harper and Row.

Lambert, W. E., & Tucker, G. R. (1976). *Tu, vous, usted.* Rowley, MA: Newbury House.

Levinson, S. C. (1977). *Social deixis in a Tamil village.* Unpublished doctoral dissertation. Department of Anthropology, University of California, Berkeley.

Levinson, S. C. (1982). Caste rank and verbal interaction in Tamilnadu. In D. B. McGilvray (Ed.), *Caste ideology and interaction* (pp. 108–124, 198–203). Cambridge, England: Cambridge University Press.

Mehrotra, R. R. (1981). Non-kin forms of address in Hindi. *International Journal of the Sociology of Language, 32,* 121–137.

Paulston, C. B. (1976). Pronouns of address in Swedish: Social class semantics and a changing system. *Language in Society, 5,* 359–386.

Searle, J. (1975). Indirect speech acts. In P. Cole & J. L. Morgan (Eds.), *Syntax and semantics: Speech acts* (Vol. 3, pp. 59–82). New York: Academic Press.

West, C. (1979). Against our will: Male interruptions of females in cross-sex conversation. In J. Orsanu, M. Slater, & L. Adler (Eds.), *Language, sex, and gender. Annals of the New York Academy of Science, 37,* 81–97.

Yassin, M. A. F. (1975). *A linguistic study of forms of address in Kuwaiti Colloquial Arabic.* Unpublished doctoral dissertation, Leeds University.

Zimmerman, D. H., & West, C. (1975). Sex roles, interruptions, and silences in conversation. In B. Thorne & N. Henley (Eds.), *Language and sex; Difference and dominance.* Rowley, MA: Newbury House.

3 Asch's Moral Epistemology for Socially Shared Knowledge[1]

Donald T. Campbell
Lehigh University

ABSTRACT

From 1938 on, Asch has pointed out our ubiquitous dependence upon the reports of others for our knowledge of the world. Most conformity studies should be reinterpreted as illustrating this process (rather than showing the character defect of suggestibility). The Aschian moral norms for socially achieved knowledge are:

Trust: It is our duty to respect the reports of others and be willing to base our beliefs and actions on them.

Honesty: It is our duty to report what we perceive honestly, so that others may use our observations in coming to valid beliefs.

Self respect: It is our duty to respect our own perceptions and beliefs, seeking to integrate them with the reports of others without deprecating them or ourselves.

Social consensuses based on this morality have a much better chance of being valid than do consensuses where agreement per se has been the goal. The paper concludes by positioning Asch's epistemology within the typologies of current philosophical discussions.

---

[1]We are certain to see a growth of "Asch Studies," as scholars restudy his contributions, reconstruing their relevance for contemporary and future intellectual concerns. Just as philosophers are paying close attention to the psychologies of Piaget, Gibson, and others, so too they should be attending to Asch, and on several issues beyond the one addressed here.

Most important of these is his contribution to a unified phenomenology encompassing both philosophical and experimental perspectives. Note that while Merleau-Ponty (1962, 1963) cites Gestalt psychology extensively in borrowing criticisms of behaviorists and atomistic associationists, he scolds the Gestaltists for retaining the natural-scientific world view. But he himself falls into it, in

For most of the last 200 years, the epistemology of science has been merged with an individualistic epistemology of ordinary knowing. Recently, however, self-critical philosophers of science have come to recognize not only that science is a social product, but that any theory as to how scientific beliefs might increase in validity must include social-process components. Independently arising from disparate traditions, a new social epistemology has been emerging from within mainstream philosophy. *Synthese* (Volume 73, Number 1, October, 1987) devotes a whole issue to the topic. There is also a new journal, *Social Epistemology* (Taylor & Francis, publishers). I have been able to list some 30 philosophers now participating in the social epistemology of science (Campbell, 1986b). Fuller (1988) and Hull (1988) have devoted whole books to the topic.

Asch has been contributing to such a social epistemology since 1940 and earlier. His contributions have been specific and seminal, in contrast with the abstractly programmatic statements of most of the currently participating philosophers. However, like a number of these philosophers, Asch recognizes that a social epistemology must include moral or ethical norms. His great *Social Psychology* (1952/1987) is profoundly different from the social psychologies that have preceeded and followed it. It is deeply committed to the importance of the experienced world of a highly rational[2] knower. But it is also more thoroughly social, portraying that knower as heavily dependent on others, and as especially gifted in perceiving how those social others perceive the world.

---

doing the phenomenology of a brain-damaged patient who had lost sexual affect (Merleau-Ponty, 1962, Chapter 5), shifting to a hypothetical "phenomenology of the other one" (Campbell, 1969). Husserl's own search for prescientific certainty is increasingly regarded as failed (e.g., Adorno, 1983). The important agenda of phenomenology needs restating without its "my-own-experience-only" foundationalism. Asch's *Social Psychology* (1952, 1987) is a great beginning.

Philosophers today are actively reconsidering cultural relativism (e.g., Krausz, 1989; Hollis & Lukes, 1982; Jarvie, 1984). While a frame-of-reference relativist for visual perception, Asch has gone against the overwhelming majority of his fellow social psychologists by rejecting cultural relativism (Asch, 1952/1987, chapter 13). While I have identified myself as a cultural relativist (Campbell, 1972; Segall, Campbell, & Herskovits, 1966), there may be little difference between Asch's and my own point of view, since I emphasize that were our perceptual processes radically different we could not confirm that we were communicating, and hence could not learn the nature of the differences (Campbell, 1964).

[2]Asch would prefer that I refer to his view of human beings (both experimenters and experimental subjects) as intelligent, or reasonable, basing their actions on reasoned judgment after weighing the evidence. "Rational" sounds too formalistic and forbidding, and he himself has avoided using it. I have, however, persisted in using it as the most convenient term for contrasting with the reflex automation model of humans, or the passive-suggestible model, etc. Whenever the word *rational* appears in what follows, read it as my shorthand summary of what *I perceive* to be Asch's perspective, not directly his perspective.

The reader is hereby warned. I am deliberately dramatizing the contrast between Asch's views and those of most social psychologists, in an effort to achieve in readers the required Gestalt-shift into his perspective. But with my different background and agenda of interests, I never get it quite right. There is no substitute for a thorough and leisurely reading of Asch himself. I hope this essay inspires many readers to undertake this.

Asch from the first (Asch, 1940, 1948; Asch, Block, & Hertzman, 1938), has rejected the model of passive, mindless, "suggestion," "imitation," or "conformity" which is characteristic of the vast literature that goes under these names. Instead, in these experiments, rational persons are intelligently using the information about the beliefs of others that is provided in order to improve their own knowledge of the world. It is the human predicament that the overwhelming bulk of our knowledge of the world is dependent upon the reports of others, most of it achieved without cross-validation through our own individual experience. It is reasonable and required that we believe and use the reports of others. "Trust" is a better term for what is observed in these experiments than is "conformity." Even if we end up disagreeing with others in achieving our own rational, coherent view of the world, we should do this respecting the corationality of our social fellows, striving for a point of view that integrates the information they have provided with our own beliefs and perceptions, disparaging neither their views nor our own. This rational respect for one's own perceptions and beliefs also stands in contrast with the doctrines of prestige-suggestion and conformity, which imply slavish imitation or irrational dependence.

Conformity experiments deliberately break the normally existing rational grounds for trust and self-respect by drastic experimental artificiality. Through deception they create a setting in which trust is *locally* unjustified. Typically, they have also employed settings in which one's own independent sources of knowledge are minimal or nonexistent, thus overlooking the respect for one's own discrepant information that is normally shown in the process of integrating the new information provided by others. Adopting an Aschian perspective we can see that in the Sherif (1936) autokinetic situation it is highly rational to respect the reports of others. Most of what Sherif demonstrated is a necessary part of any cooperative strategy for knowing the world, an essential to socially-vicarious knowing, rather than being a bias or character weakness such as the terms "suggestibility" or "conformity" seem to imply.

To dramatize the gestalt shift or reversal of perspectives involved here, I am tempted to make some psychology-of-science speculations: Most of the hundreds of existing conformity studies have been done by researchers who are themselves very conformant to current fads in their discipline. Along with this, they have implicitly created a deprecating social distance between themselves and those fellow human beings whom they have duped into "conforming." It is as though the term "subjects" had unconsciously evoked its political meaning, becoming a synonym for "slaves" or "serfs." How provocatively paradoxical it is that Asch, who reinterprets most of the "conformity" found in the laboratory studies as what I would call "rational trust," has been himself most stubbornly independent of the consensuses among his fellow social psychologists, most willing to be isolated and out of tune with the Zeitgeist.

When there is reference to "the Asch experiment" without further specification, it might be the ordering of trait terms in forming impressions of personality that is being referred to (Asch, 1946), but is usually the group pressure studies in which 6 to 8 confederates lie about what they see (Asch, 1952, 1956). But I believe that the study to a considerable extent surprised and disappointed Asch, in finding more irrational conformers (albeit a minority) than he had expected. Instead, in my judgment, the best prototypical experiment to use in teaching Asch's point of view is his great experiment on "the meaning of politics" (Asch, 1940), which I first learned of through Krech and Crutchfield's *Theory and Problems of Social Psychology* (1948, pp. 338–340). (It is cited, but not discussed, in Asch's [1952/1987] own text.) In this study, students were asked to rank ten professions on "intelligence" (and on some other favorable traits). When doing this independently, the profession of "Politics" was ranked quite low (8.1). Subjects who had first been told that 500 other college students had ranked "Politics" number 1, gave an average rating of 4.1, a result which, had he stopped there, would be indistinguishable from the usual conformity experiment. But Asch went further, and asked his participants to give examples of what they had in mind by "Politics" when they rated it. The second group had in mind statesmen, admired public leaders, presidents, and governors. The first group (and a third group told that fellow students had ranked "Politics" tenth) had in mind ward heelers, minor functionaries in corrupt political machines. What the "information" provided had done was to change the object being ranked, to disambiguate in one direction or another the ambiguous term "Politics."

In an early paper (Campbell, 1961) that attempted to review all of the conformity literature from an Aschian point of view, I identified the purest Asch model as the "Resolved Composite." One's respect for the reports of other's beliefs and for one's own knowledge is maximized when one can find an interpretation that is fully compatible with both. Binocular resolution was my model: Where the views presented to the two eyes are discrepant, if they can be resolved, the discrepancy adds information about the distance of the various objects. If those respected social fellows who ranked "Politics" as requiring the most intelligence were thinking of "outstanding statesmen," then my view of the world and theirs can be reconciled without discarding or disparaging either. Respect for the corationality of self and other has been maximized.

Even though in Sherif's autokinetic-effect conformity experiment (calling for judgments of the length of movement of a pin-point of light in an otherwise dark room) there is almost no grounding for an own-opinion, Asch (1952, pp. 487–492) shows how participants are puzzled and disturbed by the discrepancies between their own perceptions and those reported by their fellows, and strive to achieve an understanding that respects both. He does this by reporting in some detail on the unpublished masters study of his student H. G. Sperling, who used Sherif's experimental setting, augmented by collecting phenomenological reports. In extending this effort, I report on an unpublished honors thesis done by Bruce Holzman under my direction at Northwestern University in the early

1960s, employing the same laboratory set-up used by Jacobs (Jacobs & Campbell, 1961). In that setting, subjects reporting alone gave average movement estimates of 3.8 inches during the 5 seconds the light was on. This value we used for an estimate of the "own opinion" that has to be resolved with the report of the confederate (who always gave the first oral response).

One of the sources of ambiguity available for resolution in this setting is the distance of the light from the observer. Were the light to be much farther away than one had assumed, this would explain how the other (the confederate) could be competently and sincerely reporting in the range of 15 or 16 inches, instead of the 3 or 4 inches one perceived oneself. To test whether this mode of search-for-resolution was being employed, Holzman asked at the end of each session for estimates of how far away the light had been, and used three experimental treatments in which the confederates estimates were always zero, or averaged around 11 inches, or averaged around 17 inches. Here are his results (as I find them recorded in old lecture notes):

	Confederate Says Zero	Control (No Confederate)	Confederate Averages 11"	Confederate Averages 17"
Average estimate of movement by naive respondent (inches)	1.35	3.86	8.24	10.19
Average post-session estimate of distance of light (feet)	8.31	8.38	10.43	10.61

The rank order of the distance-away estimates, and the significant overall trend, I take as convincing evidence of some degree of effort to resolve the discrepancy by using this perceptual equivocality. (The light was actually about 12 feet away. There were some auditory grounds for estimating its distance, and although participants were brought in blindfolded, spatial knowledge of the hall and waiting room set limits on the possible distance.)

The Aschian rationality agenda can be extended to more than just "resolved composites." In many settings, the average judgment of several observers or raters is more reliable as well as more valid than that of a single judge. Such totaled or averaged ratings conform well to the statistical models underlying reliability estimates for multiple item tests. The increase in reliability produced also increases validity, if there is any validity to begin with. Thus it is also rational to pool the reported perceptions of one or more others with one's own perceptions, even if one has to do this as an averaging process. In my review (1961), I called these "compromised composites." For those many conformity studies that make this inference possible, there is clear evidence that one's own perceptions are given considerable weight. In the autokinetic situation, our participants weighted the reports of a single self-confident confederate 2.6 times as heavily as what we presumed to be their own perceptions (Campbell, 1961, p. 112; Jacobs & Campbell, 1961). In Asch's much less ambiguous "Politics" study, the participants weighted the reported views of their supposedly 500 fellow students only 1.1 and 1.3 times their own (Campbell, 1961, p. 112). Most of the 100-odd studies I reviewed can be summarized as showing that the stronger the rational grounds for trusting one's own view, and the weaker the rational grounds for trusting the reported views of others, the less the "conformity."

The 1961 review also had a category of "Dominated Composites" in which only one source, self or other, saw expression, epitomized by those stereoscope experiments presenting unresolvably discrepant pictures to the two eyes. Were I to rewrite this section today, I would augment it with the concept, borrowed from William James, of "ambivalence as optimal compromise" (Campbell, 1965, pp. 304–306). In that form, apparently total depreciations of one's own view could still be interpreted as holding available in reserve an unexpressed own view (a "recessive" still there though covered up by a "dominant"), rather than a cognitive erasure of it.

Asch (1952) recommends this combination of respect for the reports of our social fellows, respect for our own perceptions, and rational search for interpretations which deny the validity of neither, not only as describing much of the behavior disparaged as suggestibility or conformity, but also as the requisite strategy for human knowing, given that we are so totally social and given our unavoidable epistemological predicament. Thus his theory of human knowing involves moral imperatives.[3] An extended quote illustrates his social-epistemological moralizing style, and introduce a further complication:

> Let us now consider the import of the observations for the role of individuals in the social process. Social existence presupposes, we have seen, the achievement of consensus; but consensus, if it is not to be an empty or treacherous gesture, must have validity. The meaning of consensus collapses when individuals act like mirrors that reflect each other. Precisely because we live in an environment that is in a powerful way mediated by the psychological processes of others does the integrity of the individual's contribution play an indispensable role. If reliance upon mutual understanding and purpose is to have meaning, each must rely in an ultimate way upon his own understanding and purpose. The need for consensus demands that individuals should be able to refuse agreement when they see no way of reaching it. When individuals abrogate their capacity to think and judge in their own way, when they cease to relate themselves independently to things and persons, when they surrender initiative and delegate it to others, they are altering the social process and

---

[3]Technically, these are *mediational* moral norms (Campbell, 1979b) for those who have made a more ultimate value choice in favor of improving the validity of beliefs and extending the domain covered by competent believing (a.k.a. "knowledge").

introducing into it a radical arbitrariness. The act of independence is productive from the social point of view, since it is the only way to correct errors and to steer the social process in accordance with felt requirements. On the other hand, the act of yielding is anti-social because it spreads error and confusion. Sharing itself is not enough; it can produce the spectacle of millions marching under the banner of a frightful Weltanschauung. Shared action that rests on the voluntary or involuntary suppression of individual experience is a malignant sociological process. By the same token, group action must have a wholly different dynamics and power when its purpose and ideas rest on the insight of its human members.

We have implied above that independence and its failures in social life are in some respects significantly similar to what was observed under the experimental conditions described here. This inference needs to be justified, since the experimental situation was quite special and in many ways not representative of ordinary or even unusual social circumstances. For example, many social influences are possible because the facts are remote and complex, because they are not directly given and crystal clear. This is but one of the special conditions the experimental situation contains. In the absence of further evidence we cannot rigorously justify the relevance of the present observations to the conditions that persons generally face, but it seems fruitful to assume that there is a relation. There can be no doubt that personal independence and the lack of it are facts crucial for social life. There are times when one must choose between stark alternatives that have very much to do with the question of independence. Germans who lived near concentration camps could not escape the choice of breaking with their social order or of forcibly suppressing a range of facts and refusing to bring them into relation with their daily experience. But one also observes the relevance of these processes under less stringent conditions. Those who strive to think independently and not merely to repeat current slogans are playing a role in the social process quite different from those who veer away from ideas because they are threatening or who deny all reason to a side when it is out of favor. It is probably incorrect to suppose that states and tyrants achieve insidious aims entirely by giving a plausible account of themselves. What happens often is that people partly meet those who manipulate them. The threat of unpleasant consequences makes them more amenable to the tyrant's kind of "reason," which they allow to soften the edge of their scrupulousness by adopting a "dignified" alternative to autonomy. Social and political life would be far healthier if the yielder in most of us were less active and adroit. (pp. 495–496)

May I summarize Asch's epistemological moral imperatives in my own words as follows:

1. (Trust) It is our duty to respect the reports of others, and to be willing to base our beliefs and actions upon them.

2. (Honesty) It is our duty to report honestly, so that others may use our observations in coming to valid beliefs.

3. (Self-respect) It is our duty to respect our own perceptions and beliefs, and

to seek to integrate them with the reports of others without deprecating them or ourselves.

Were collective cognitive competence the only, or the socially dominating, goal, then it seems to me that the rational and moral naive participant in the group-pressure experiments should have said: "You fellows are probably right. After all, your 7 pairs of eyes are, collectively, better than my one pair. If I were to wager on which line is longer, I would wager with you that line A is longer. But it is my duty to you, for the validity of your final decision on the fact of the matter, to report that I see line B as longer." Translated into the two conditions of report that Asch employed, the epistemologically moral participant should have conformed when asked to report in private to "which line do you *believe* is longer?" (i.e., do you "believe," not "perceive"). However, when asked to report in public, one should show nonconformity, reporting what one saw with one's own eyes, so that one's report could be depended upon by the others in making their decisions. Exactly opposite from this epistemological norm, Asch's (1952, 1956) naive participants showed much more conformity in *public* reports than in *private* reports. (This is a very dependable finding, corroborated by eight other studies cited in my 1961 review.)

This outcome does not prove that Asch's model of optimal strategies for cooperative knowing is wrong (even though I surmise he would have been happier with the opposite outcome). But it does show that the human animal (even in its group-pressure exemplars) has more dominant imperatives than collective competence. Most of Asch's participants did honestly report their dissenting view, and showed their respect for their fellow students in their discomfort in having to disagree, and in their relief when debriefed. The public conformers also showed sensitivity to the three moral norms, both in their discomfort during the experiment, and in their chagrin upon debriefing. But I take the direction of the discrepancy as showing that consensus per se (independent of its validity) generally takes priority over validity. Consensus clears the way for collective action. Human nature, for these purposes, may have been shaped in an ecological niche in which collective action was more adaptive than either uncoordinated individual action, or collective *in*action, as a response to inconsistent, incomplete, or incompetent information. In that ecology, there may have been a meta-rationality in preferring consensus to truth, if the two were in conflict. Of course, there would no doubt also have evolved a rational preference and adaptive advantage for valid consensuses over invalid ones for most situations, if these did not unduly prolong the collective decision process. And the privately retained knowledge of the individual's own discrepant perceptions would have persisted (rather than have been erased) as a resource for building alternative consensuses if collective action failed.

Science, however, supposes itself to operate in a different ecology than did our neohuman tribes, valuing truth more than consensus per se. In science's ideology, public reports should maximize individual honesty (and perhaps private wagers on the truth should maximize respect for trusted colleagues). Scientific beliefs depend overwhelmingly on trust in the reports of others, and that trust will be most rational and valid if these colleagues have followed what I perceive to be Asch's cognitive morality.

There are two major social-psychological sources for fraud in science. On the one hand, there are the institutional social traps that require publishable papers (whether valid or not) for institutional survival as a scientist (e.g., to get tenure, or to get future grants). These are often overwhelming motives, and lead scientists to suppress and disguise the weaknesses of their own studies, and even falsify their data where embarrassing replication efforts are unlikely, or in arenas in which failures at replication are so common that they are not humiliating. Journal editors who attempt to raise standards by rejecting articles which confess to imperfections, universities that attempt to improve themselves by requiring more publications in those editor's refereed journals, and granting agencies that give grants to successful publishers without regard to the replication history of the grantees previous "findings," all conspire, however unconsciously, to make the trust of published scientific articles less rational. (Asch's very short list of publications, by far the shortest of anyone receiving Psychology's "Distinguished Scientific Contributions Award" [*American Psychologist,* December, 1967, Volume 22, pp. 1128–1130], indicates his stubborn refusal to be trapped by the publish-or-perish incentive system.)

But equally important for the occurrence of fraud in science is the fact that research teams and scientific networks are strikingly like the ordinary human groups exemplified by those of Asch's experimental subjects who valued consensus more than truth. The fear of breaking consensus which keeps those scientists who know of (or suspect) fraud by others from speaking out; the guilt feelings of those who do blow the whistle; and the ostracism and retaliation received by whistle blowers; all demonstrate the hazards to scientific truth coming from our human social preference for consensus, adaptive perhaps in some tribal past, but dysfunctional (and immoral) as a part of a scientific search for truth.

Asch's moral imperatives for cooperative knowing, *trust, honesty,* and *self-respect,* may not be as descriptive of humans as rational knowers as he had hoped, but they retain validity at two other levels: as ethics or moral norms for the collective enterprise of seeking truth, and as a hypothetical sociology of scientific validity (e.g., Campbell, 1979a, 1986a).

While most sociologists of science militantly avoid the issue of truth for the beliefs and belief changes they study (as reviewed in Campbell, 1986a), we need to entice them into a speculative comparison of different social belief-transmission and belief-change systems, speculating as to which would be more likely to improve the fit between beliefs and a real world those beliefs refer to (speculatively assuming that there exists such a referent, an assumption unacceptable to many of the best of the current crop of sociologists of science). The product would constitute a hypothetical sociology of scientific validity. We could interpret the ideology of the scientific revolution of the 16th and 17th century as such a conjectural sociology of scientific validity (Campbell, 1986a). Habermas' (1970a, 1970b) "ideal speech community," so similar to Asch's perspective, is clearly both a set of moral norms for optimizing validity (as well as emancipatory norms) and a conjectural sociology of scientific validity (except for being too idealistic to be implementable).

INTRODUCING ASCH TO PHILOSOPHERS

In this final section, I relate what I perceive to be Asch's overall epistemological position to issues current in philosophy's epistemological discussions. Although I encourage psychologists to eavesdrop, I am addressing philosophers in this section.

I judge Asch to be an *antifoundationalist*. While the perceptions of the individual knower are to be respected, they are not infallible, but instead are context-dependent, relative to a frame of reference. In a preliminary section on individual knowing, he asserts, "The perceived localization of particular objects is 'relationally determined', being a function of the organization of the entire visual field" (Asch, 1952, p. 56); thus a person presented with a distorted visual field will tend instead to see it as normal. He illustrates this by reference to Duncker's (1929) research on induced movement, "If one observes in a darkened room a point of light surrounded by a rectangular contour or frame, which is slowly moved to the right or left, one sees the point moving in a direction opposite to that of the frame, which he sees as stationary. The movement is compelling and entirely indistinguishable from objective movement [of the point, with the frame stationary]. Nor is the movement impaired if the observer fixates the point. . . . On the other hand, moving the point induces no movement in the frame" (Asch, 1952, p. 58).

For the epistemologist this illustrates that even such *"primary qualities"* as the motion or fixed location of objects *are not directly known*, but are, rather, "constructed in the brain" at a preconscious level. In his own research with Witkin (Asch & Witkin, 1948; Witkin & Asch, 1948) it was demonstrated that a tilted frame distorted the perception of an upright, and in later research, that if one built a whole experimental room that could be turned and tilted around a seated person, the physical movements of the room would instead be perceived as one's own movements in the opposite direction. In its epistemological implications this is the opposite of (and thoroughly refutes) James Gibson's (1979) "direct realism," which has influenced many philosophers.[4]

---

[4]However, if Gibson be read only as emphasizing that no *conscious* inference processes are involved, Asch would agree. "The processes that correspond to phenomenal facts are only part of a wider field of cortical process with which they are in constant interaction. Many internal processes . . . are not at all represented in awareness" (Asch, 1952, pp. 68–69).

I would like to relate Asch's epistemology to the issue of *coherence theories*. Two such are under discussion in philosophy today. In the continental tradition, there is the contrast between a Hegelian coherence theory of "truth" and a correspondence theory of *the meaning* of "truth" (Rescher, 1973). I believe that Asch would reject the Hegelian tradition in which coherence is to be sought as an ultimate goal, as an end in itself, and constitutes the definition of *truth*. I place him, rather, in the tradition of Quine (1951) and Lehrer (1974), in which a *coherentist strategy of belief revision* is contrasted with a rejected atomistic perceptual foundationalism. This is compatible with a fallibilist ontological realism, and even with a correspondence meaning of the term *truth*. (After all, conspicuous "correspondence theorists" such as Quine or Popper (1959) have never believed that one could employ it as a truth test, directly comparing beliefs with reality itself.)

Asch's frame-of-reference relational determination of basic perceptions, which is rooted in Gestalt psychology, is not accompanied by a skeptical rejection of ontological, physical realism. Our usually valid perceptions, and indeed our discovery of occasional illusory perceptions, are achieved in spite of this epistemological predicament, which I, at least, take to be fundamentally relativistic and unconsciously presumptive. I believe that Asch must join Quine (1951), and me, in seeing the considerable "objectivity" which we do achieve as the product of a search for coherence in as broad a frame of reference as possible. It is this expanded framework that enables us to recognize some perceptions as illusory.

Asch seems to me to be clearly in the *"naturalistic epistemology"* camp (Kornblith, 1985; Quine, 1969) which, while still a minority position within philosophy, is a growing one. But among naturalistic epistemologists, his emphases on conscious experience and rationality are atypical, and make him potentially more reconcilable with those mainstream epistemologists who espouse a perceptual foundationalism. This is facilitated by the fact that most of these foundationalists agree that perception is fallible (albeit preponderantly reliable) (see Campbell & Paller, 1989, for citations). Asch provides the detailed analysis of our epistemological predicament that should be substituted for their nonspecific acknowledgements of perceptual fallibility.

The naturalistic epistemology movement as a whole has been individualistic and biological in emphasis (e.g., justifying trust in vision by reference to biological evolution, in an approach fully as appropriate to a solitary as to a social species). For the most part, it is only when extending this naturalism to an epistemology of scientific knowledge that philosophers have felt the need for social process specification (e.g., Giere, 1985). In contrast, Asch's epistemology for an individual's ordinary knowledge is overwhelmingly social. He is undoubtedly correct in this, and when the naturalistic epistemologists get beyond programmatic statements and into details, they should incorporate Asch's insights. One feature of his social epistemology is particularly unique, a naturalistic contribution to the philosophers' old "problem of other minds." Asch insists that the perception of other persons is profoundly different from the perception of inanimate objects, and that phenomenally we experience their pains and joys "directly." This is not to deny unconscious quasi-inferential neurological processes, presumptively utilizing fallible cues of facial expression, tone of voice, etc., but rather to emphasize that the conscious experience resulting has phenomenal immediacy, and that conscious, rational, inference processes are typically lacking.

Sociology of knowledge and sociology of science traditions are nowadays merging with naturalistic epistemology, and a major point of view is the "social constructionist" (to the references in Campbell, 1986a, add Latour, 1987; Collins, 1985; Barnes, 1982; Knorr-Cetina & Mulkay, 1983). I see Asch, as well as myself, as also social constructionists, since the beliefs one has about the world are collective social products. The social constructionists call attention to the relativity of belief thus resulting. At the level of *epistemological* relativism, I see Asch as joining them: One cannot know for sure that one's beliefs are true, as they are all dependent on the assumed completeness of the available frames of references, most of them socially provided.

The bulk of the social constructionists go on from there to ontological relativism, agnosticism, or nihilism. The goal of *truth* or *objectivity,* they assert, must be given up as naive and incoherent since consensus is all we can be sure science achieves. I see Asch as departing from them at this point. If we are to be rationally authentic to our experienced purposes, we must retain the *goal* of knowing how the world is in a way that is independent of our particular vantage point and limited frame of reference. In this regard, all consensus processes are not equivalent. Some of them, as found in science when working at its best, can be seen to be rationally more likely to improve the validity of the resulting beliefs. These are the ones that follow the Aschian epistemological morality. Consensuses achieved where consensus itself has been the ultimate goal must be sharply distinguished from consensuses discovered in the collaborative search for truth.

ACKNOWLEDGMENT

I would like to acknowledge advice and encouragement from my colleague and friend Robert E. Rosenwein in the preparation of this essay.

REFERENCES

Adorno, T. W. (1983). *Against epistemology: A metacritique.* Cambridge, MA: The MIT Press.
Asch, S. E. (1940). Studies in the principles of judgments and attitudes: II. Determination of judgments by group and by ego standards. *Journal of Social Psychology, 12,* 433–465.

Asch, S. E. (1946). Forming impressions of personality. *Journal of Abnormal and Social Psychology, 41,* 258–290.

Asch, S. E. (1948). The doctrine of suggestion, prestige and imitation in social psychology, *Psychological Review, 55,* 5.

Asch, S. E. (1952). *Social psychology.* Englewood Cliffs, NJ: Prentice-Hall. Reprinted, Cambridge University Press, 1987.

Asch, S. E. (1956). Studies of independence and conformity: I. A minority of one against a unanimous majority. *Psychological Monographs, 70*(9) (whole number 416).

Asch, S. E., Block, H., & Hertzman, M. (1938). Studies in the principles of judgments and attitudes: I. Two basic principles of judgment. *Journal of Psychology, 5,* 219–251.

Asch, S. E., & Witkin, H. A. (1948). Studies in space orientation: I. Perception of the upright with displaced visual fields; II. Perception of the upright with displaced visual fields and with body tilted. *Journal of Experimental Psychology, 38,* 325–337, 455–477.

Barnes, B. (1982). *T. S. Kuhn and social science.* New York: Columbia University Press.

Campbell, D. T. (1961). Conformity in psychology's theories of acquired behavioral dispositions. In I. A. Berg & B. M. Bass (Eds.), *Conformity and deviation* (pp. 101–142). New York: Harper & Row.

Campbell, D. T. (1964). Distinguishing differences of perception from failures of communication in cross-cultural studies. In F. S. C. Northrop & H. H. Livingston (Eds.), *Cross-cultural understanding: Epistemology in anthropology* (pp. 308–336). New York: Harper & Row.

Campbell, D. T. (1965). Ethnocentric and other altruistic motives. In D. Levine (Ed.), *The Nebraska symposium on motivation, 1965* (pp. 283–311). Lincoln: University of Nebraska Press.

Campbell, D. T. (1969). A phenomenology of the other one: Corrigible, hypothetical and critical. In T. Mischel (Ed.), *Human action: Conceptual and empirical issues* (pp. 41–69). New York: Academic Press. Reprinted in D. T. Campbell (E. S. Overman, Editor), *Methodology and epistemology for social science: Selected papers.* Chicago, IL: University of Chicago Press, 337–359.

Campbell, D. T. (1972). Herskovits, cultural relativism, and metascience. In M. J. Herskovits, *Cultural relativism* (pp. v-xxiii). New York: Random House.

Campbell, D. T. (1979a). A tribal model of the social system vehicle carrying scientific knowledge. *Knowledge, 2,* 181–201. Reprinted in D. T. Campbell (E. S. Overman, Editor), *Methodology and epistemology for social science: Selected papers.* Chicago, IL: University of Chicago Press, 489–503.

Campbell, D. T. (1979b). Comments on the sociobiology of ethics and moralizing. *Behavioral Science, 24,* 37–45.

Campbell, D. T. (1986a). Science's social system of validity-enhancing collective belief change and the problems of the social sciences. In D. W. Fiske & R. A. Shweder (Eds.), *Metatheory in social science: Pluralisms and subjectivities* (pp. 108–135). Chicago, IL: University of Chicago Press. Reprinted in D. T. Campbell (E. S. Overman, Editor), *Methodology and epistemology for social science: Selected papers.* Chicago, IL: University of Chicago Press, 1988, 504–523.

Campbell, D. T. (1986b). Science policy from a naturalistic sociological epistemology. In P. D. Asquith & P. Kitcher (Eds.), *PSA 1984,* Volume 2. East Lansing, MI: Philosophy of Science Association, 14–29.

Campbell, D. T., & Paller, B. T. (1989). Extending evolutionary epistemology to 'justifying' scientific beliefs. (A sociological rapprochement with a fallibilist perceptual foundationalism?) In K. Hahlweg & C. A. Hooker (Eds.), *Issues in evolutionary epistemology* (pp. 231–257). Albany, NY: State University of New York Press.

Collins, H. (1985). *Changing order: Replication and induction in scientific practice.* Beverly Hills, CA: Sage Publications.

Duncker, K. (1929). Ueber induzierte Bewegung. *Psychologische Forschung, 12,* 180–259.

Fuller, S. (1988). *Social epistemology.* Bloomington: Indiana University Press.

Gibson, J. J. (1979). *The senses considered as perceptual systems.* Boston, MA: Houghton Mifflin.

Giere, R. N. (1985). Philosophy of science naturalized. *Philosophy of Science, 52,* 331–356.

Habermas, J. (1970a). On systematically distorted communication. *Inquiry, 13,* 205–218.

Habermas, J. (1970b). Toward a theory of communicative competence. *Inquiry, 13,* 360–375.

Hollis, M. & Lukes, S. (Eds.). (1982). *Rationality and relativism.* Cambridge, MA: The MIT Press.

Hull, D. L. (1988). *Science as process.* Chicago, IL: University of Chicago Press.

Jacobs, R. C., & Campbell, D. T. (1961). The perpetuation of an arbitrary tradition through several generations of a laboratory microculture. *Journal of Abnormal and Social Psychology, 62,* 649–658.

Jarvie, I. C. (1984). *Rationality and relativism.* London, England: Routledge & Kegan Paul.

Knorr-Cetina, K. D., & Mulkay, M. (Eds.). (1983). *Science observed.* Beverly Hills, CA: Sage Publications.

Kornblith, H. (Ed.). (1985). *Naturalizing epistemology.* Cambridge, MA: The MIT Press.

Krausz, M. (Ed.). (1989). *Relativism: Interpretation and confrontation.* Indiana: University of Notre Dame Press.

Krech, D., & Crutchfield, R. S. (1948). *Theory and problems of social psychology.* New York: McGraw-Hill.

Latour, B. (1987). *Science in action.* Cambridge, MA: Harvard University Press.

Lehrer, K. (1974). *Knowledge.* Oxford, England: Clarendon Press.

Merleau-Ponty, M. (1962). *Phenomenology of perception.* London, England: Routledge & Kegan Paul.

Merleau-Ponty, M. (1963). *The structure of behavior.* Boston, MA: Beacon Press.

Popper, K. R. (1959). *The logic of scientific discovery.* New York: Basic Books.

Quine, W. V. (1951). Two dogmas of empiricism. *Philosophical Review, 60,* 20–43.

Quine, W. V. (1969). *Ontological relativity.* New York: Columbia University Press.

Rescher, N. (1973). *The coherence theory of truth.* Oxford, England: Clarendon Press.

Segall, M. H., Campbell, D. T., & Herskovits, M. J. (1966). *The influence of culture on visual perception.* Indianapolis, IN: Bobbs-Merrill.

Sherif, M. (1936). *The psychology of social norms.* New York: Harper & Row.

Witkin, H. A., & Asch, S. E. (1948). Studies in space orientation: III. Perception of the upright in the absence of a visual field; IV. Further experiments on perception of the upright with displaced visual fields. *Journal of Experimental Psychology, 38,* 603–614, 762–782.

Comments on D. T. Campbell's Chapter

Solomon E. Asch

Alone among American psychologists Professor Donald Campbell has grasped and scrutinizes here a theme central to my thought: that there is an inescapable moral dimension to human existence. It follows that investigation must take account of that proposition. Yet psychologists have been among the most determined opponents of this claim, predictably in the name of what they deem to be science. They hoped, at least in their technical activities, to be above the fray. No wonder I am grateful to my friend Don Campbell for his insights, as well as for his generous comments.

Campbell applies here an evolutionary perspective to questions of consensus; it forms the core of his exposition. In this connection he speaks of human nature being "shaped in an ecological niche" and he proposes to explain certain specific findings in terms of a "meta-rationality in preferring consensus to truth, if the two are in conflict" (p. 46)

The general reason for this procedure is evident: If one stresses, as Campbell does, the place of rationality in human judgment, one must account for it in evolutionary terms. This is an important, bold step; to expand an area of discourse beyond conventional limits can mark an indispensable advance in thinking.

Here a question arises: Is Campbell's reference to evolutionary rationality more than assertion? Does it mark an actual advance in thinking or does it only transfer the observed rationality of social judgment back to unobserved evolutionary events? The answer is not certain. I am confident though that it was valuable to state the problem, and that it will press for resolution. Also, I am intrigued by the thought that an evolutionary process may have, contrary to all I

53

was once taught, an aspect of rationality, even if the detailed steps remain as yet unspecified.

Let me mention two ways to advance Campbell's inquiry. The first is about consensus. Since the problems are in part psychological, a phenomenological mode of analysis appears necessary. Phenomenology is essentially unprejudiced description, as free as possible from theoretical preconception. Despite its unpretentiousness this approach has not fared well in the American climate. To illustrate, terms such as *independence, conformity, consensus, norm,* are not self-explanatory, despite their apparent simplicity and obviousness. They all refer to rich and complex ideas; they all need to be explicated, to have their inner structure revealed. Failure to do so can obscure problems Fortunately there are examples of superb phenomenological description. True, phenomenological and evolutionary concepts are far apart, yet I am confident that clarification of either can dispel confusion.

Second is the need for a dynamic theory of psychological forces. Here, in contrast to the first point, much of the groundwork remains to be done. For example, I am thinking of the sense of necessity when facing a syllogism in logic, or the compelling sense of fitness when engaged in an esthetic or ethical choice. It is evident to me that such vectors are intensely active with issues of independence, and that conforming to a majority against one's conviction generally goes with the stinging experience that one has violated a requirement. The only thinkers to address these questions have to my knowledge been the Gestalt pioneers. Köhler's brief but illuminating essay on psychology and evolution reprinted in *Documents of Gestalt Psychology* (edited by Mary Henle), comes nearest to Campbell's concern. Those steps are important but incipient. Also, I see little encouragement in current theories of motivation, including those of a psychoanalytic character.

There are wide areas of agreement about matters of consensus between Campbell and myself. However, we do not see entirely eye to eye on the empirical level. For the sake of simplicity I will refer mainly to my work.

Campbell cites the well-established finding that young adults ''showed much more conforming in public reports than in *private* reports'' (p. 46). From this finding he draws the conclusion ''that consensus per se (independent of its validity) generally takes priority over validity'' (p. 46). Clearly ''consensus per se'' stands here for false consensus.

(1) It does not strike me at all as strange that it is painful to disagree with others in public, particularly when one is assailed by self-doubt and disturbed about the source of one's difficulty. Rather I am encouraged by this finding: it assures me that the people studied were sensitive to the forces around them; that they responded with feeling; and—if this expression be permitted—that they were human in the good sense of this term. The finding also demonstrates that these people were vulnerable, that they suffered temptation and pain. I do not at

all take these to be signs of moral blemish. Rather, I would be concerned if they could not respond in these ways.

(2) I do not want to pass over without comment the fact that the people studied were independent in private, when public surveillance was withdrawn and when they were confronting only themselves. This outcome is intuitively understandable but it would be wrong to treat it as self-evident. Indeed, I find it significant, intriguing, and highly worthy of reflection.

(3) I question Campbell's conclusion that false consensus *generally* prevails over validity. It certainly did not in studies I have done which, I believe, bear most directly on the issue under discussion. Under those conditions independence of majorities was by far the strongest force at work. It is fair to ask: Why didn't the young people in my study generally prefer the tranquilizing semblance of truth to what they perceived to be true?

For some reason Campbell appears to minimize the forces of independence as he proceeds, in striking contrast to his emphasis at the outset (p. 39). Scholars will rightly agree on the necessity to be wary when addressing this problem, where an easy optimism is worse than useless. However I miss at the end a clear reference by Campbell to the love of truth as a psychological reality, and of the power it can command. This in no way detracts from the importance of his contribution overall.

4 The Role of Evaluation in Impressions of Persons

Dean Peabody
Swarthmore College

ABSTRACT

Forty years ago, Asch (1946) did pioneering studies on impressions of persons. Subjects were given certain "Stimulus" traits, and later made inferences to other "Response" traits. One interpretation of the effects obtained is the "evaluative theory": the most important determinant is evaluative consistency between the different traits. This chapter states an "alternative theory": the decisive determinants are the descriptive aspects of traits, not the evaluative ones.

Four general principles summarize the alternative theory. One needs to distinguish between evaluative and descriptive aspects, and also between *determinants* of particular trait judgments and *factors* that summarize the relations among them. Evaluative aspects are more general, and so affect the factors; as determinants, they are pervasive but less important than descriptive aspects. The two theories are then compared for three major results of the Asch studies: the *Warm–Cold* variation, the primacy effect, and changes of meaning. These comparisons support the alternative theory, not the evaluative theory.

It was once common to go on a blind date—a social engagement with a person previously unknown. This was arranged by someone else—often one's roommate. One might become overanxious and ask the roommate beforehand: "What kind of a person is this anyway?" The roommate replies without hesitation: "This person is intelligent, skillful, industrious, determined, practical, and cautious." "That's very interesting," one might comment, "but is this person warm or cold?" Depending on the answer, one might form very different impressions of this person.

Such an incident would be a "real life" counterpart of the pioneering studies on impressions of persons conducted by Asch (1946) 40 years ago. In his main study, two groups of subjects were asked to assume that a hypothetical person was characterized by seven traits, one of which varied between the groups: *Intelligent—Skillful—Industrious—Warm* or *Cold—Determined—Practical—Cautious*. The subjects were first asked to write a summary of their impression of the person. They were then asked to select, from each of 18 pairs of opposite traits, the one that agreed more with their impression. It is convenient to use a stimulus-response terminology: The subjects were given certain "S-traits," and later made inferences to other, "R-traits." Such trait inferences thus provide a general technique that can be applied to impressions of persons.

Asch's (1946) results showed large differences between the "Warm" and "Cold" variations. How should these differences be interpreted? One persistent type of interpretation emphasizes evaluation—how much the impression is favorable or unfavorable. *Warm* is good, and *Cold* is bad. *Warm* will therefore result in a more favorable impression. In general, the evaluative theory holds that the determinant that is primary (most important or decisive) is evaluation—e.g., good S-traits lead to good R-traits and bad S-traits lead to bad R-traits. Recently, Roger Brown (1986) restated the evaluative theory. Because Brown's restatement is closely argued and brilliantly written, it is fitting to use his version to represent the evaluative theory. It is also fitting to follow Brown, and concentrate on the issues raised by Asch's (1946) original studies.

As Asch (1952) emphasized, psychological theories has implications about human nature. If the evaluative theory is correct, then people are simplistic and irrational. Therefore, it is important to see whether the evaluative theory is true. I opposed the evaluative theory 20 years ago (Peabody, 1967). Much has been learned in the meantime. It seems appropriate to restate clearly why the evaluative theory is wrong.

Two separate issues are involved in Asch's (1946) studies. Asch's own main interest was in how the effects of several S-traits combine—whether according to additive or to configural rules—and he used seven S-traits from the beginning. In contrast, the second issue concerns the evaluative interpretation of the effects of even a single S-trait. This issue is our primary interest here.

This chapter has two main sections. The first section presents four general principles. These principles define the "alternative theory" that will be compared with the evaluative theory. The second section compares these two theories with regard to three major results of Asch's (1946) study.

FOUR PRINCIPLES

1. Trait judgments combine evaluative and descriptive aspects. "Trait" judgments are those that can be expressed using trait adjectives. They involve a combination of evaluative and descriptive aspects. The judgment that "X is

TABLE 4.1
A Scheme for Separating Evaluative and Descriptive
Aspects of Traits: Examples from Two Sets

Descriptive Contrast			
X		Un-X	
a. Generous (+)	vs.	Stingy (-)	
b. Extravagant (-)	vs.	Thrifty (+)	
X		Un-X	
a. Light-hearted (+)	vs.	Grim (-)	
b. Frivolous (-)	vs.	Serious (+)	

stingy'' involves the evaluative aspect "X is bad,'' and the descriptive aspect "X tends not to spend money.'' Hence, trait judgments involve a logical "confounding'' between evaluative and descriptive aspects. This point seems fairly clear when it is stated explicitly, so the explicit presentation can be brief. Consider only the limiting cases. Some adjectives, such as *good* vs. *bad* or *likable* vs. *unlikable,* are entirely or primarily evaluative. On the other hand, there are a few "neutral'' trait adjectives that have no clear evaluative direction, and are almost entirely descriptive. In a classification of 571 common trait adjectives (Peabody, 1985), there were less than 3% such cases. The remaining 97% had a definite evaluative direction, as well as descriptive aspects.

What is the implication of this point for the evaluative theory? Because of the confounding between aspects, one cannot simply apply the evaluative theory when any effects may be due to descriptive aspects. In an attempt to meet this problem, Peabody (1967) classified trait adjectives into sets designed to "unconfound'' descriptive aspects from evaluation. Table 4.1 gives two examples of such sets. In the scheme used in Table 4.1, each set includes two pairs of opposite traits. Each pair (row "a'' or "b'') involves both an evaluative contrast (+ vs. -) and a descriptive contrast (X vs. Un-X). Thus, each pair involves a confounding of evaluative and descriptive contrasts. But, comparison *between* the two pairs in each set permits an unconfounding of the two contrasts.

Traits that can be classified so as to complete the scheme in Table 4.1 will be called evaluatively "reversible'' traits. There are also many traits that cannot be so classified, and so are "nonreversible.''[1] For purposes of Peabody's (1967) initial attempt to unconfound evaluative and descriptive aspects, nonreversible traits were omitted. They were added much later, in the study of Peabody (1984), which moved toward a representative selection of all trait-adjectives.

Thus, almost all traits have evaluative as well as descriptive aspects, but

[1]Peabody (1967) also included sets of traits that were "partially reversible.'' These involved three of the four combinations from Table 4.1, as compared with two pairs for "reversible'' and one pair for "nonreversible'' traits. However, such partially reversible traits were not used in the later selection by Peabody (1987).

reversible traits have the special advantage of providing a straightforward logic for separating these aspects, and for showing whether evaluation is of primary or secondary importance.

   2.   *One needs to distinguish between (a) the **determinants** of any particular trait judgment, and (b) the relations between these judgments, including any **factors** that summarize these relations.*   Consider the following model. Suppose that trait judgments resemble Spearman's theory of intelligence: Any particular trait judgment includes a general (evaluative) component and a specific (descriptive) component. Assume further that the specific (descriptive) components are decisive in determining the direction of any judgment. Then the evaluative theory—which holds that evaluation is the decisive determinant—would be clearly wrong.

   In contrast, suppose one considers the correlations between judgments, and the factors summarizing these correlations. There would be only a single factor involving the general (evaluative) components. On these assumptions, evaluation would be the only factor, but never the primary determinant. Hence, evidence about *factors* is not conclusive for the evaluative theory which is about *determinants*.

   How well does this model apply to trait judgments? Evidence suggests that the evaluative aspects tend to be general as in the model. Accordingly, any specific aspects are descriptive. The main departure from the model is that there are also descriptive aspects that are not very specific but of intermediate generality, and that relate to many (although not to all) trait judgments—analogous to Thurstone's "group" factors for intelligence. For example, for both the sets in Table 4.1 the descriptive contrasts (X vs. Un-X) are included in a quite general one between "Loose" impulse-expression versus "Tight" impulse-control.

   The implications for the evaluative theory are clear. The evaluative theory holds that evaluation is the decisive *determinant* of particular trait judgments. This theory could be false, even if evaluation is important in the *factors* for the correlations between judgments.

   3.   *Determinants: (a) The evaluative aspects have pervasive effects; (b) The descriptive aspects have larger effects.*   The evaluative aspects are general, and so have pervasive effects for inferences between any two traits. This point has been well documented by Norman Anderson (e.g., 1981), whose analysis of traits uses only the evaluative aspects (ratings of likability). (Like Asch, Anderson was primarily interested in the combining of several S-traits, but he favored the "additive" types of combination that Asch opposed.) Anderson uses several S-traits, and their likability ratings are combined according to some mathematical formula. This calculation is compared with an actual rating of the combination of traits. There are no R-traits; the only dependent variable is this rating

of likability for the combination. This approach allows for the testing of point (3a), for which Anderson provides impressive evidence.

However, Anderson's approach cannot be used to test the effects of descriptive aspects. For this purpose one must include dependent variables other than evaluation or likability. Peabody (1967) made use of the traits selected to fit the scheme shown in Table 4.1. Subjects were asked to make inferences between these traits. The critical items were those where there was a choice between evaluative consistency and descriptive consistency. Sets of complete evaluative reversals, like those in Table 4.1, each provide four critical items: Select as an S-trait any one of the four traits. The two traits from the other row are the alternative R-traits. The subject is then offered a choice between evaluative consistency and descriptive consistency—e.g., Is an *Extravagant* person likely to be *stingy* or *generous?* Altogether there were 70 critical items; for all of them the mean inference was in the direction of descriptive consistency. The example suggests that this result is obvious, and almost ludicrously so. Apparently, the evaluative theory is obviously wrong, once it is clearly tested.

This point has the most direct implications for the evaluative theory. The evaluative aspects have moderate but pervasive effects on trait inferences. Nevertheless, one can propose that descriptive aspects are decisive in determining all trait judgments. One can prove this only where the descriptive aspects can be opposed to the evaluative aspects. For such cases—the critical items—100% of the results go against the evaluative theory.

4. Factors: The usual factors combine evaluative and descriptive aspects. Factors summarize what is common to several traits. The scheme in Table 4.1 can be used to illustrate the possible factors. Table 4.1 shows each trait as a combination that confounds an evaluative aspect ($+$ vs. $-$) and a descriptive aspect (X vs. Un-X). Theoretically, there could be separate unconfounded factors for the evaluative components—general evaluation—and for the descriptive components—in this case, "Loose" impulse expression versus "Tight" impulse control. Indeed, such unconfounded factors *can* be produced by deliberate rotation (e.g., Peabody, 1984; Peabody & Goldberg, 1989). However, the factors usually considered—e.g., those produced by Varimax rotation—are *not* unconfounded in this way, but are combinations of evaluative and descriptive components (like the individual trait terms in Table 4.1). These usual factors are designed to approach "simple structure," and to be aligned close to the relevant variables—e.g., the trait terms. But these traits combine evaluative and descriptive aspects. It follows that the usual factors will represent a similar combination—a combination of general evaluation and some relatively general descriptive aspect.

Present evidence (Peabody, 1984; Peabody & Goldberg, 1989) suggests that there are five or six such factors relevant to impressions of persons. However, for the R-traits used by Asch, only two factors play a major role, and one other a minor role. The two major factors include traits from the two rows—marked "a" and "b"—of Table 4.1. If one interprets "a" and "b" broadly, the traits relevant to the two factors can be called type-a and type-b traits; this emphasizes that the two factors have opposing descriptive directions. These factors also include other (nonreversible) traits; the traditional factor labels emphasize these latter traits.

In Table 4.1, two pairs of traits are marked "a": *Generous* vs. *Stingy* and *Light-hearted* vs. *Grim*. These traits are included in a factor with interpersonal traits involving affiliation (e.g., *Warm* vs. *Cold*). This factor is often called "Agreeableness." The other two pairs of traits in Table 4.1 are marked "b": *Thrifty* vs. *Extravagant* and *Serious* vs. *Frivolous*. These traits are included in a factor with traits concerning conscientious performance (e.g., *Reliable* vs. *Unreliable*). This factor is often called "Conscientiousness." In addition to the two major factors, a minor role among Asch's traits is played by those related to judged intelligence. These traits may appear on an "Intellect" factor, but they may also appear on one of the major factors.

The implications of this point for the evaluative theory are clear. The two major factors "a" (Agreeableness) and "b" (Conscientiousness) both involve evaluation. According to the evaluative theory both types of traits should give similar results determined by evaluation. However, the descriptive contrast is reversed between these two types of traits. If the evaluative theory is false, the two types could give very different results.

INTERPRETING ASCH'S RESULTS

This section considers three major results of Asch's (1946) studies—the main study with the Warm-Cold variation, the primacy effect, and changes of meaning. In each case, consideration is given to the "evaluative theory" supported by Brown (1986)—that the results can be explained by evaluative consistency between Asch's traits. This theory—that evaluation is the primary determinant—will be compared to the position summarized in the previous section. This latter might be called the "descriptive-evaluative" theory. It holds that evaluation is a secondary determinant as compared with the descriptive aspects, and will simply be called the "alternative" theory. It will be shown that the evaluative theory does not account for any of the major results, whereas the alternative theory does so. Brown's support of the evaluative theory is not to be found in any general statement, but in the consistent use of interpretations that correspond to the theory.

In each study, Asch's subjects were given certain S-traits, and wrote summaries of their impressions. From these summaries, one might already find qualitative evidence about effects of the S-traits. To get more quantitative results, Asch's subjects also made inferences to 18 R-trait pairs. Asch (1946) presented these results using the percentage of subjects who, for each R-trait pair, selected the more favorable trait rather than the more unfavorable one. Thus, percentages greater than 50% indicate a choice of the favorable term; percentages less than 50% a choice of the unfavorable term. The evaluative theory implies that these percentages should be similar for different R-traits; the alternative theory implies that they may be systematically different.

The Main Study: The Warm-Cold Variation

Asch's main study—the Warm-Cold variation—was introduced earlier. Subjects were given seven S-traits: *Intelligent—Skillful—Industrious—Warm* or *Cold—Determined—Practical—Cautious*. They made inferences to the 18 pairs of R-traits. The results are presented in Table 4.2. The R-traits are arranged according to the size of the difference between the *Warm* and the *Cold* versions.

The predictions from the evaluative theory are straightforward. Among the S-traits, *Warm* is good and *Cold* is bad. In Table 4.2, the R-trait pairs are

TABLE 4.2
Asch (1946): The Warm-Cold Variation
Percentages Choosing the Left-Hand Term

Pairs of R-Traits	Warm N=90	Cold N=76	Difference
Type-a traits (Agreeablness)			
1. generous--ungenerous	91	8	83
2. good-natured--irritable	94	17	77
3. humorous--humorless	77	13	64
4. happy--unhappy	90	34	56
5. popular--unpopular*	84	28	56
6. humane--ruthless	86	31	55
7. sociable--unsociable	91	38	53
8. altruistic--self-centered	69	18	51
Intelligence traits			
9. wise--shrewd	65	25	40
10. imaginative--hard-headed	51	19	32
Type-b traits (Conscientiousness)			
11. restrained-talkative	77	89	-12
12. important--insignificant*	88	99	-11
13. reliable--unreliable	94	99	- 5
14. serious--frivolous	100	99	1
15. persistent--unstable	100	97	3
16. strong--weak*	98	95	3
17. honest--dishonest	98	94	4
18. good-looking--unattractive*	77	69	8
Means: Type-a traits	85	23	62
Type-b traits	92	93	-1

* = Debatable traits

arranged so that the left-hand term is always more favorable. Hence, the evaluative theory should predict consistently higher percentages (in choosing the left-hand term) for *Warm* than for *Cold,* so that the *Warm-Cold* difference should be consistently positive.

The results in Table 4.2 clearly do not fit this prediction of consistent effects. Instead, the R-trait pairs divide into different groups. The first eight pairs (numbered 1–8) do show very large effects, with differences greater than 50%. The last eight pairs (numbered 11–18) show very small effects. Two pairs (numbered 9 and 10) show intermediate effects. The two large groups are related to the traits of type-a and type-b that were defined earlier. The first group includes pairs related to type "a" in Table 4.1 (*generous* vs. *stingy*) and to the factor called "Agreeableness." The last group includes pairs related to type "b" in Table 4.1 (*serious* vs. *frivolous*) and to the factor called "Conscientiousness." The two intermediate traits are related to intelligence or the intellect.

Several of Asch's R-traits are questionable selections as representative trait adjectives, and would be excluded from a more painstaking selection like that of Norman (1967)—as representing "social stimulus values" (*popular—unpopular*); evaluative terms (*important—insignificant*); ambiguous terms (*strong—weak*); or doubtful personality traits (*good-looking—unattractive*). These terms are marked in the tables as "debatable traits." It is debatable whether they belong with the other traits of the relevant type, although they give similar results.[2]

The evaluative theory predicts comparable results for all types of traits, and so cannot explain the actual results. How *can* these results be explained? Rosenberg, Nelson, and Vivekananthan (1968) explicitly stated the basic explanation—that there are two major types of traits. *Warm* and *Cold* are the only S-traits that are closely related to some of the R-traits—those called here Type a (Agreeableness)—and so produce large effects. But *Warm* and *Cold* are not related to other R-traits—those called here Type b (Conscientiousness)—and so do not produce large effects. However, these latter R-traits are related to some of the other S-traits: *Intelligent, Skillful, Industrious, Determined, Practical,* and *Cautious.* Accordingly, *all* the results on these R-traits tend to be well above a chance 50%.

Rosenberg et al. (1968) present several figures illustrating these relations as

---

[2]One could also ask about changes between 1946 and 1989. A major change—a least for American college students—is that "Loose" impulse expression became more favorable relative to "Tight" impulse control. *Extravagant* becomes barely unfavorable, and *Thrifty* barely favorable. In the pair *restrained* vs. *talkative, restrained* was the more favorable and the pair therefore of type-b (Conscientiousness). Nowadays, *talkative* may be rated favorably, and the pair could become of type-a (Agreeableness). A related change occurred for *honest,* which once was closer to type-b (Conscientiousness)—e.g., Abraham Lincoln walking for miles to return a few pennies. Nowadays, *honest* could be closer to *frank* and so to type-a (Agreeableness)—e.g., Abraham Lincoln is "up front" in telling his wife that he stole the pennies, and still loves Ann Rutledge.

two dimensions, and Brown (1986) reproduces some of these figures. These presentations are generally helpful, but sometimes misleading. One dimension includes *Warm* vs. *Cold* plus the R-traits called here Type a (Agreeableness). Rosenberg et al. (1968) label this dimension "Social Good-Bad." A second dimension includes the other S-traits, the R-traits of Type b (Conscientiousness), plus some traits related to intelligence. Their label for this dimension—"Intellectual Good-Bad"—is misleading; it overemphasizes the intelligence traits and neglects the Conscientiousness traits. This dimension is meant to account for the type-b traits, but none of these refer to the intellect.

Linguistic intuitions: Ands or Buts.   As a psycholinguist, Brown (1986, pp. 390–392) tries to buttress the evaluative theory with linguistic intuitions about the use of *and* or *but.* The clearer cases involve the use of *but,* with its implication of inconsistency ("but") or consistency ("but not"). For example, Brown cites the combination "a generous but unhappy person" as supporting the evaluative theory. This interpretation assumes that these two traits are inconsistent, and that the relevant inconsistency is an evaluative one.

Is this interpretation correct? Brown's examples use Asch's R-traits, but the traits from Table 4.1 permit a more precise analysis. One possibility is that evaluative inconsistency is combined with descriptive inconsistency (e.g., if the two traits were opposites of type a, or opposites of type b). In such cases, the use of *but* represents both kinds of inconsistency and so is theoretically indecisive— "generous but grim" or "serious but extravagant." Most of Brown's examples (including "generous but unhappy") are of this inconclusive sort. Another, more decisive, possibility is that evaluative inconsistency is combined with descriptive consistency. The alternative theory predicts cases with *but not* (implying consistency): "generous but not extravagant"; "serious but not grim"; etc. Such cases should not exist according to the evaluative theory; there is no evaluative consistency and *but not* should be unnecessary. Thus, these examples of linguistic intuitions do not support the evaluative theory.

The Primacy Effect

Asch (1946) compared two series of S-traits: *Intelligent—Industrious—Impulsive—Critical—Stubborn—Envious* and *Envious—Stubborn—Critical—Impulsive—Industrious—Intelligent.* The two series are in reverse order. Suppose that the traits given first have a greater influence. This is the "primacy effect."

The primacy effect may be widespread, and by no means confined to impressions of persons. For example, Brown's (1986) own order of presentation may benefit from this order effect: He begins detailed discussion of Asch's results with the Primacy effect (where the inadequacy of the evaluative theory is perhaps less obvious), and postpones until the end detailed discussion of the Warm-Cold variation (where the need is belatedly conceded for something more than a single evaluative dimension). The same effect has been used in the present chapter to the opposite end, by discussing the Warm-Cold variation first.

The primacy effect tends to occur whenever (a) all the information is to be unified, and (b) there is no prior information—e.g., an impression of one person who was previously unknown. Both Asch (1946) and Brown (1986) have theoretical explanations of primacy. Asch's would use the Gestalt principle of "relational determination": Psychological effects are not determined by a particular stimulus, but by a relation between stimuli—e.g., between a particular stimulus and its context. In the primacy effect, the initial items have no previous context, but provide a context for the interpretation of the later ones. In Brown's explanation the earlier items provide more information. This explanation seems plausible, except for the assumption that the information is entirely about evaluation. Why are there some 4000 trait adjectives in English, if the information is to be reduced to a single choice between *good* and *bad?*

In discussing the Warm-Cold variation, Asch (1946, p. 264) noted that the results were not evaluatively consistent, and explicitly opposed the evaluative theory—"a halo tending toward a consistently plus or minus evaluation." Thus, he should be a natural ally in opposing the evaluative theory. However, in the case of the primacy effect, he did discuss the S-traits using evaluative terminology. By analogy with another famous study by Asch, it seems that in this case the evaluative theory has become a unanimous majority facing a minority of one. As in the analogy, the minority position still has one thing on its side—the evidence.

Effects among the S-traits?   The most important results are for inferences from the two orders of S-traits to the 18 pairs of R-traits. But Brown (1986, pp. 401–405) also proposes that certain effects occur already among the six S-traits, and these proposals will be considered first. One may begin with some points that were noted by Asch: At the two ends of the series are traits that are clearly favorable (*Intelligent, Industrious*) or clearly unfavorable (*Envious*). The other three traits from the middle of the series are neutral or somewhat unfavorable (*Impulsive, Critical, Stubborn*). These "intermediate" traits are therefore somewhat inconsistent with the traits that have clear evaluations. What could the theories say about this situation?

Consider first the alternative theory. The descriptive relations among traits are decisive, but there are also pervasive evaluative relations. For a unified impression, there is therefore a problem to integrate the three intermediate traits with, for example, the two favorable traits. Subjects may give comments relevant to this problem.

Brown's proposals go further. He tries to apply Peabody's (1967) scheme (see Table 4.1) to support the very evaluative theory that Peabody opposed. This could be the "unkindest cut of all." Brown proposes first that the intermediate traits (*Impulsive, Critical, Stubborn*) are like the traits in Table 4.1 (i.e., they are "evaluatively reversible," in contrast to the other three traits which are "evaluatively nonreversible"). These proposals agree with Peabody's (1987) classification of 571 traits. Thus, for the three intermediate S-traits, there are related traits that are descriptively similar but clearly favorable in evaluation—Brown proposes *Spontaneous, Discriminating, Resolute.*

Brown's (1986) main proposals are more radical and more debatable: The intermediate traits actually change to the meanings of these related traits—in order to be evaluatively consistent with the initial traits in each series. Consider the actual series *Intelligent—Industrious—Impulsive—Critical—Stubborn—Envious.* This series would become the following "list of meanings": *Intelligent—Industrious—Spontaneous—Discriminating—Resolute—Envious* (Brown, 1986, p. 404). These proposals should have some empirical implications. Apparently, the (transformed) intermediate traits should not be treated by the subjects as problems whose integration requires further explanation. Such problems should occur only abruptly at the end, when the opposing nonreversible traits are encountered. The subjects' summaries should be paraphrased as: "A generally good person, but there is a problem about *Envious,*" or (with the opposite order) "A generally bad person, but there is a problem about *Intelligent* and *Industrious.*" The intermediate traits should not need special mention.

The alternative theory has different implications: Changes in meaning may occur to produce descriptive consistency, but they need not occur just to produce evaluative consistency. The (largely unchanged) intermediate traits pose problems for the subject to integrate into a unified impression, and this may produce explanatory comments. This alternative interpretation fits the examples of subjects' summaries presented by Asch (1946). The summaries do comment on the intermediate traits. Brown (1986, p. 397) quotes one of these summaries from Asch (1946):

> The person is intelligent and fortunately he puts his intelligence to work. That he is stubborn and impulsive may be due to the fact that he knows what he is saying and what he means and will not therefore give in easily to someone else's idea which he disagrees with. (p. 270)

Asch's subject should not need to comment on "stubborn" and "impulsive" if their meanings had already become evaluatively favorable as "resolute" and "spontaneous." Thus, this example does not seem to support Brown's interpretation. But Brown cheerfully cites it as if it did. One can conclude that there is no clear support for these proposals.

Effects on the R-traits. The more obvious results of the primacy study are the inferences to the 18 pairs of R-traits. Asch's (1946) results for the R-traits were examined with care. Although many of the results made sense, the trait pairs that showed the very largest order effects seemed implausible. A natural hypothesis was that these results might be due to chance, and so would not be repeatable in a replication. Accordingly, I carried out, using 60 Swarthmore College students in 1988, a replication of the experiment in Asch (1946), following his procedure as closely as possible. Both sets of results are presented in Table 4.3. The arrangement of the R-traits is similar to that used in the preceding table.

Consider first what is *similar* between the results using either order—i.e., the general effect of this set of S-traits. These results *are* systematic relative to the two types of traits, and consistent between the original results and the replication. The situation is summarized by the means at the bottom of Table 4.3. The percentages are below 50% for the first four means for the type-a traits (Agree-

TABLE 4.3
The Primacy Effect
Percentages Choosing the Left-Hand Term

Pairs of R-Traits	Order Intelligent to Envious N=34 N=35	Envious to Intelligent N=24 N=25	Difference
Type-a traits (Agreeableness)			
humorous--humorless	52 (35)	21 (32)	31 (3)
sociable--unsociable	56 (37)	27 (48)	29 (-11)
happy--unhappy	32 (24)	5 (16)	27 (8)
popular--unpopular*	35 (41)	14 (25)	21 (16)
good-natured--irritable	18 (20)	0 (4)	18 (16)
humane--ruthless	36 (25)	21 (29)	15 (-4)
generous--ungenerous	24 (26)	10 (12)	14 (14)
altruistic--self-centered	6 (0)	5 (8)	1 (-8)
Intelligence traits			
imaginative--hard-headed	26 (14)	14 (21)	12 (-7)
wise--shrewd	18 (9)	17 (12)	1 (-3)
Type-b traits (Conscientiousness)			
reliable--unreliable	84 (86)	91 (68)	-7 (18)
persistent--unstable	82 (88)	87 (76)	-5 (12)
important--unimportant*	85 (94)	90 (80)	-5 (14)
serious--frivolous	97 (94)	100 (76)	-3 (18)
honest--dishonest	80 (59)	79 (64)	1 (-5)
strong--weak*	94 (84)	73 (88)	21 (-4)
good-looking--unattractive*	74 (62)	35 (52)	39 (10)
restrained--talkative	64 (29)	9 (33)	55 (-4)
Means: Type-a traits	32 (26)	13 (22)	19 (4)
Type-b traits	83 (74)	71 (67)	12 (7)

Note. Numbers represent the percentage of subjects who chose, for each trait pair, the more favorable alternative which is shown on the left. Results without parentheses are from Asch (1946). Results with parentheses are from the replication.

* = Debatable traits.

ableness). The comparable means are above 50% for the type-b traits (Conscientiousness). This pattern is basically similar to the *Cold* version of the *Warm* vs. *Cold* study. *Envious* substitutes for *Cold* in determining unfavorable judgments for lack of Agreeableness on the type-a traits. Some of the other S-traits determine favorable judgments on the type-b traits. These results are not of course consistent with the evaluative theory, which predicts a comparable degree of favorableness for all R-traits.

The "primacy" effect itself would refer to *differences* between the two orders, as shown in the right-hand columns of Table 4.3. Here Asch's original results suggest some limited primacy effect (which would not support the evaluative theory). But the replication shows no notable or systematic effects. For most of the type-a traits Asch's results showed a modest effect, but this is not replicated. Asch's results showed no effect for the majority of the type-b traits, but then relatively large effects for three pairs—especially *restrained* vs. *talkative*. It was the implausibility of this last result that suggested the need for replication. The replication does indeed not confirm this result. But it also suggests that there is no notable or systematic primacy effect altogether. The primacy effect thus ends here not with a bang but a whimper. Such an effect is plausible theoretically, and presumably may show up under some circumstances. But using Asch's arrangement, no replicable effect was found, no effect for which one would need to compare theoretical explanations.

The preceding section questioned Brown's (1986) proposal that changes in meaning result from evaluative inconsistency. The next section demonstrates the alternative theory—that changes in meaning result from descriptive inconsistency.

Changes of Meaning

Asch (1946) reported several experiments relevant to changes of meaning. Some of the clearest cases come from his experiment IV, where he reported changes for *Warm* and *Cold* in the following contexts:

    A. *Obedient—Weak—Shallow—Warm—Unambitious—Vain*
    B. *Vain—Shrewd—Unscrupulous—Warm—Shallow—Envious*
    C. *Intelligent—Skillful—Sincere—Cold—Conscientious—Helpful—Modest*

In this study, Asch reported qualitative results based on the subjects' summaries. He reported that in series A, *Warm* became "dependent" instead of "central"—e.g., a "dog-like affection." In series B, a "more extreme transformation" was observed. In series C, there was a similar change for *Cold*. Asch compared series C directly with the *Cold* version of the main study, where *Cold* did not change meaning. The four results may be summarized with regard to change of meaning for *Warm* or *Cold:* series A—a change for *Warm;* series B—

a big change for *Warm;* series C—a big change for *Cold;* the main study—no change for *Cold* or *Warm.*

How could the evaluative theory account for these results? The account would depend on the evaluative inconsistency of *Warm* and *Cold* with the other S-traits. In series A and B, the other S-traits are generally bad and therefore inconsistent with *Warm.* In series C, the other S-traits are generally good, and so inconsistent with *Cold.*

How could the alternative theory account for these results? For the alternative theory, changes of meaning are not determined by evaluative inconsistency, but by descriptive inconsistency. *Warm* and *Cold* are type-a traits. Many of the S-traits are related to type-a traits and have implications for *warm* vs. *cold.* Thus, in series A and B, the change for *Warm* is not because the other S-traits imply *bad,* but because they imply *cold*—and this implication is stronger for B than for A. *Warm* changes meaning because it is inconsistent with this implication. In series C, the change for *Cold* is not because the other S-traits imply *good,* but because they imply *warm.* In the main study, the other S-traits (type-b traits) imply *good* but not *warm,* and there is no change of meaning for *Cold.*

To provide a direct check on this interpretation, new data were obtained from 28 subjects in 1987. The subjects made inferences to a *warm* vs. *cold* response scale from each of the relevant S-traits. For the individual S-traits, the percentages are given in the right-hand column of Table 4.4. The relevant averages of these percentages for groups of traits are summarized in the left-hand column. Note that some traits are common to series A and to series B. Hence, for series A one would combine the traits that are only in series A (these traits themselves average 58%) with the traits that are common to series A and series B (these traits average 15%). One would thus obtain an overall average for all five of the other S-traits in series A (41%, shown as "All A" at the bottom of Table 4.4). In a similar way, some traits are common to series C and to the main study. In the end, one needs to account for the four averages at the bottom of Table 4.4.

The predictions of the alternative theory should be compared with these averages. In series A, with a change in meaning for *Warm,* the other S-traits should imply *cold.* (The result is 41% *warm,* 59% *cold*). In series B, with a big change for *Warm,* the other S-traits should strongly imply *cold.* (The result is 13% *warm,* 87% *cold*). In series C, with a big change for *Cold,* the other S-traits should strongly imply *warm.* (The result is 82% *warm,* 18% *cold.*) In the main study, with no change, the other S-traits should have no clear implication between *warm* and *cold.* (The result is 48% *warm,* 52% *cold*). Thus, the results can all be predicted, but by the alternative theory, not by the evaluative theory.

This section has considered three major results of Asch's studies—the main study with the Warm-Cold variation, the primacy effect, and changes of meaning. The evaluative theory was examined in relation to these results, and to additional proposals made by Brown (1986) that might have supported this theory. None of the results or proposals supports the evaluative theory. They generally support an alternative theory emphasizing descriptive judgment.

TABLE 4.4
Changes of Meaning for Four Series

Series A: Change for Warm
Series B: Big change for Warm
Series C: Big change for Cold
Main Study: No change for Cold or Warm

Inferences from other S-traits to warm (vs. cold)[a]

S-Traits	Means for Trait Groups	Individual Traits
A only	58%	
Obedient		64%
Weak		63
Unambitious		48
A and B	15	
Shallow		27
Vain		4
B only	11	
Unscrupulous		18
Shrewd		7
Envious		7
C only	92	
Helpful		100
Sincere		96
Modest		88
Conscientious		86
C and Main study	61	
Intelligent		63
Skillful		59
Main study only	42	
Cautious		55
Industrious		41
Determined		36
Practical		34
All A	41	
All B	13	
All C	82	
All Main study	48	

[a]Subjects used a seven-step response scale, labeled warm vs. cold. The percentage of subjects responding in the warm direction is estimated here by including one-half of the midscale responses.

DISCUSSION

Giving Evaluation its Due

Those who are attracted to the evaluative theory ignore the points concerning the role of the descriptive aspects. My own problem is the opposite one; I am generally alert to the descriptive aspects but I am tempted to ignore the points concerning the role of evaluation. In my first trait-inference study (Peabody, 1967), this led to a mistake in interpreting the factors. It is appropriate to acknowledge this once again, and to consider whether it affects the presentation here.

In this first study, the primary concern was with determinants and not factors—to demonstrate point (3b) that the descriptive aspects were the decisive determinants. Traits were selected to provide a variety of critical items to test this point, and they did so decisively. At this time, I was largely innocent of knowledge about personality factors. Nevertheless, it seemed worthwhile to have a look at any factors that might summarize the correlations among the items. The data matrix included the means for inferences from 90 S-traits to 40 R-trait scales. It seemed equally promising to analyze this matrix either way—the correlations among the S-traits across the scales or the correlations among the scales across the S-traits. I was looking for dimensions that were "unconfounded"—i.e., entirely evaluative or entirely descriptive. The factors from the analysis of scales therefore seemed difficult to interpret. (In retrospect, it is clear that this is because these—now-familiar—factors combined evaluation and description.) In contrast, in the analyses of the S-traits, the factors were very easy to interpret as unconfounded descriptive dimensions. In doing so, one could ignore evaluation altogether. It was only later that it became clear what had happened to evaluation in this analysis: The means of the S-traits represented differences in general evaluation (averaged across all the R-trait scales). When correlations were taken between the S-traits, they were taken around these means, and general evaluation was removed from this analysis in advance. This had the positive heuristic effect of providing clear-cut definitions of the descriptive dimensions. But, it seemed (wrongly) to ignore the existence of general evaluation.

I acknowledged this point early (Peabody, 1970), and consistently since then have stressed the importance of recognizing the role of evaluation—an evaluative component among the factors, and evaluation as a determinant that is pervasive although not decisive. One should give evaluation its due.

Beyond Impressions of Persons

The roles of evaluation and liking are not limited to impressions of persons and trait inferences. For example, among the cognitive consistency theories, the theories of balance and congruity are stated primarily in terms of liking and evaluation (e.g., Heider, 1957; Osgood & Tannenbaum, 1955; Rosenberg & Abelson, 1960). These theories are based on the pervasive role of evaluation, and tend to ignore the role of descriptive aspects.[3]

---

[3]Asch (e.g., 1952, Ch. 15) questioned such an emphasis on evaluative consistency in relations between a "source" (e.g., Jefferson or Lenin) and an "assertion" (e.g., advocating "a little rebellion"). The meaning of the assertion changed in relation to the source (e.g., Jefferson advocates agitation, Lenin revolution). This relation is essentially a descriptive one.

Still closer comparisons for impressions of persons are with two other cases: judgments about actual individuals or about groups of people—traditionally called "personality ratings" and "stereotypes." All three cases involve "trait judgments"—judgments that can be expressed using trait adjectives. They therefore all raise the same issues about the roles of evaluative and descriptive aspects. (Examples: Impressions involving inferences from *Warm;* judgments about an extraverted individual; judgments about "Italians." In all cases, any *single* trait judgment—e.g., as *generous* or *light-hearted*—would confound evaluation and description. But other judgments—as *extravagant* vs. *thrifty,* or as *frivolous* vs. *serious*—could show that the descriptive aspects are more important.)

Data are now available comparing trait inferences directly with personality ratings (Peabody & Goldberg, 1989), and with judgments about nationality groups (Peabody, 1985). These comparisons show striking similarity among the three cases. As regards determinants, the evaluative aspects are not decisive over the descriptive aspects (as the evaluative theory implies). As regards factors, these are comparable in the different cases. In short, the other two types of trait judgments generally agree with the present analysis. It would be equally possible to apply the evaluative theory in all three cases, but it would be equally mistaken.

A Deep Question

In his introduction to his book *Social Psychology,* Brown (1986, p. xi) says that the interesting arguments in social psychology change rapidly, but there are some "deep questions" that change hardly at all. One such deep question is "To what extent are human beings irrational or rational?" Theories that people are irrational have been popular in most of the history of psychology.

How does this issue relate to the evaluative theory? If people follow the evaluative theory, they are being irrational. It is against logic and experience that other persons are consistently good or consistently bad. Brown (1986, pp. 395–396) clearly agrees with this appraisal. Brown also believes that in impressions of persons, people generally do follow the evaluative theory, and so are irrational. But this latter belief is mistaken.

The preceding section compared impressions of persons with two other cases of trait judgments: personality ratings and stereotypes. All three cases raised similar questions regarding the roles of evaluation and description, and in all three cases the evidence supported answers that are similar. However, the usual *interpretations* of the three cases are dramatically different. These differences can be illustrated, both in general and for the distinctive case of Roger Brown. Impressions of persons are included in "person perception" and in "cognitive social psychology"; these are treated as the source of many potential "biases" (of which evaluative consistency is only one). Such biases may also be extended to judgments about actual persons. (Here the counterpart of the evaluative theory was traditionally called the "halo effect".) But there is a strong countertrend among personality psychologists that these judgments can be valid, both in principle and in fact. Brown (1986, p. 424) supports this latter view; personality ratings are an "Actual Reflection" of real personality. They are therefore not irrational but rational.

Judgments about groups ("stereotypes") were traditionally considered irrational, but this question has been reopened since the 1970s. Roger Brown is one of a very few who had already argued earlier that stereotypes might not be as irrational as was then assumed. His position included a rejection of the evaluative theory as applied to stereotype judgments, which involve descriptive as well as evaluative aspects (e.g., Brown, 1986, p. 596). Thus, both stereotypes and personality ratings do not follow the evaluative theory. On the other hand, Brown treats impressions of persons as following the evaluative theory and so as irrational. In this sense, his interpretations are inconsistent. In contrast, Asch (1952) argued consistently, for every problem he considered, that people were more rational than was assumed by other doctrines of human nature.

Why the evaluative theory?   The evidence shows that the evaluative theory is wrong. Why then has it been so popular? Brown (1986, p. 389) says that the evaluative theory is the "simplest," and this is surely its major attraction. It is simpler to deal only with the evaluative aspects which are pervasive and general, than to consider the variety of descriptive aspects. Simplicity is traditionally considered an asset for a theory. But it is not when the subject matter is less simple. So it is with impressions of persons. People are not so simple as the evaluative theory.

AUTHOR NOTE

I would hope that it would be obvious from the text that I admire as psychologists Roger Brown as well as Asch, both of whom have been my teachers. Hence, my opposition to Brown's interpretation is in the spirit of evaluative inconsistency: How could such a good psychologist have supported such a bad theory?

I am endebted for suggestions to Sarah E. Hampson and to Lewis R. Goldberg.

Correspondence should be addressed to: Dean Peabody, Swarthmore College, Swarthmore, PA 19081

REFERENCES

Anderson, N. H. (1981). *Foundations of information integration theory: Foundations, Vol. 1*. New York: Academic Press.
Asch, S. E. (1946). Forming impressions of personality. *Journal of Abnormal and Social Psychology, 41*, 258–290.

Asch, S. E. (1952). *Social psychology*. Englewood Cliffs, NJ: Prentice-Hall.

Brown, R. (1986). *Social psychology, the second edition*. New York: The Free Press.

Heider, F. (1957). *The psychology of interpersonal relations*. New York: Wiley.

Norman, W. T. (1967). *2800 personality trait descriptors: Normative operating characteristics for a university population*. Ann Arbor: Department of Psychology, University of Michigan.

Osgood, C. E., & Tannenbaum, P. H. (1955). The principle of congruity in the prediction of attitude change. *Psychological Review, 62*, 42–55.

Peabody, D. (1967). Trait inferences: Evaluative and descriptive aspects. *Journal of Personality and Social Psychology Monograph, 7* (Whole No. 644).

Peabody, D. (1970). Evaluative and descriptive aspects in personality perception: A reappraisal. *Journal of Personality and Social Psychology, 16*, 639–646.

Peabody, D. (1984). Personality dimensions through trait inferences. *Journal of Personality and Social Psychology, 46*, 384–403.

Peabody, D. (1985). *National characteristics*. New York: Cambridge University Press.

Peabody, D. (1987). Selecting representative trait-adjectives. *Journal of Personality and Social Psychology, 52*, 59–71.

Peabody, D., & Goldberg, L. R. (1989). Some determinants of factor structures from personality-trait descriptors. *Journal of Personality & Social Psychology, 57*, 552–567.

Rosenberg, M. J., & Abelson, R. P. (1960). An analysis of cognitive balancing. In M. J. Rosenberg et al. (Eds.), *Attitude organization and change* (pp. 112–163). New Haven, CT: Yale University Press.

Rosenberg, S., Nelson, C., & Vivekananthan, P. S. (1968). A multidimensional approach to the structure of personality impressions. *Journal of Personality and Social Psychology, 9*, 283–294.

5 Recognizing the Role of Construal Processes

Lee Ross
Stanford University

ABSTRACT

This chapter reviews the role that subjective interpretation or "construal" processes play in a number of classic and contemporary social psychological phenomena. I begin by noting Asch's own seminal discussions of social and contextual influences on subjective construal, and the importance of such influences on impression formation, persuasive communication, and conformity. I then proceed to review some of my own more recent work on inferential biases and shortcomings—noting in each case the relevance of uncertainty and variability in the process of social and situational construal. In particular, I argue that each bias or shortcoming reviewed, and each resulting phenomenon, can be traced in part to a failure on the part of actors and/or observer to make *adequate inferential allowance* for influences *of* construal, and influences *on* construal—influences long ago discussed and documented by Solomon Asch.

My personal contact, and friendship, with Solomon Asch began in the fall of 1976 when he was beginning a 1-year stay as a fellow at the Center for Study in the Behavioral Sciences. I had just coauthored a paper (Ross, Bierbrauer, & Hoffman, 1976) that offered an "attributional analysis" of the classic Asch conformity paradigm, and he graciously invited me to the Center, which was located on a hilltop overlooking the Stanford campus, in order to discuss it. The focus of that initial meeting, as I recall, soon shifted from the narrow concerns of my paper to the current state of social psychology; and, before the afternoon was over, we agreed that we would meet regularly at the Center over the months ahead so that I could bring him up to date on any recent advances in our field—

"advances," he assured me with a twinkle in his eye, that he had "probably missed" during the years he had spent devoting himself anew to problems in perception.

Needless to say, I learned a great deal more than I taught during our year-long tutorial. My senior colleague remained unconvinced that the "advances" I heralded—in particular, the fruits of a decade of solid research in attribution theory, and some very recent attempts to pursue more general inferential and judgmental shortcomings—either were particularly new or particularly promising. Meanwhile, I gained a new respect for Asch and for intellectual traditions that my own work, and that of other young social psychologists of my cohort, had drawn upon so heavily without our acknowledgment. This respect was further enhanced when I finally sat down and read Asch's seminal 1952 text—a work that I had occasionally cited but one which, except for it's chapter dealing with group influences on judgments, I had never explored in any depth.

My contemporaries and I, it became evident, had become preoccupied with a task and a challenge very relevant to ideas that were eloquently presented in Asch's text and that were implicit in many of his most important experiments. To understand, predict, or control human behavior, Asch cautioned us continually, we must take into account the subjective interpretations or *construals* of the relevant social actors. Attempts to formulate behavioral laws that would associate objectively defined stimulus events and objectively defined responses, he argued, are likely to achieve very limited success at best; and as he pointed out in discussing the famous Hartshorne and May (1928) studies, attempts to find large and robust correlations in the behavior individuals display across different objectively defined situations are unlikely to fare any better. The problem of *meaning,* especially socially defined meaning, cannot be ignored; and research strategies that seek to finesse the problem must inevitably yield shallow research and theory.

The link between Asch's insight and the endeavors of contemporary psychology has become increasingly clear. Social psychologists have been preoccupied with one particular aspect of social meaning, that is, the problem of response attribution or assigning of personal versus situational causes to behavior, and the discernment of the actors' personal attributes on the basis of such behavior. (See Jones & Davis, 1965; Kelley, 1967, 1973; also, Ross, 1988; Nisbett & Ross, 1980; Fiske & Taylor, 1984). Over the same period mainstream cognitive psychologists increasingly began to elaborate the role of dynamic knowledge "schemas" (Bartlett, 1932; Piaget, 1936; Rumelhart, 1976) or "scripts" (Abelson, 1976, 1981; Schank & Abelson, 1977) both in facilitating the comprehension of written and spoken language and in guiding the interpretation of everyday events. While the problem of meaning or construal that Asch pointed to so forcefully has come to occupy increasingly greater prominence in our discipline, it is worth noting that not all of Asch's ideas and insights have been taken to heart. The *social* aspect of social cognition, that is to say the processes by which

meaning and implication are arrived at through social interaction and negotiation, has all but been forgotten by most contemporary researchers. And Asch's
advocacy (and exemplary use) of postexperimental interviews to probe the *subjects'* "definition of the situation" in order to better appreciate the significance
of their behavior has similarly fallen on deaf ears. In short, Asch's contributions
as an intellectual pioneer are beyond challenge, and they continue to offer insights about the way to do more interesting and important work that remain fresh
and useful three and a half decades after the initial publication of his text.

In this chapter I discuss the aspect of my own research that I believe is most
continuous with Asch's concerns and insights. In particular I describe my attempts to link the classic problem of situational construal to a variety of phenomena in the "judgment under uncertainty" and "intuitive psychology" or
"human inference" traditions (see Kahneman, Slovic, & Tversky, 1981; Nisbett
& Ross, 1980). I seek to go beyond the now familiar contentions that people are
often forced to engage in complex tasks of situational construal, that construals
often are highly uncertain and variable across actors, and that subjective construals play a large role in governing behavior. My real thesis is that, in interpreting each others behavior and making assessments about the future, lay perceivers
and actors alike consistently fail to appreciate, and consistently fail to make
adequate inferential allowance for the very uncertainty, variability, and impact
of construal that Asch alerted us to so long ago.

CONSTRUAL INTERPRETATIONS OF SOME
EMPIRICAL PHENOMENA AND RESULTS

Asch on Impression Formation, Persuasive
Communication, and Group Influence

Before discussing my own research it is appropriate to remind the reader, very
briefly, about Asch's "construal" interpretation of three specific sets of phenomena: biases in impression formation, communicator credibility effects in
persuasion, and group influences on conformity. In all three cases Asch's insight
concerned the mediating role of subjective interpretation. That is, he recognized
that the impact of the relevant independent variables and manipulations depended, in large measure, on their capacity to alter the meanings or construals
that subjects attached to whatever information was presented and whatever
events they witnessed.

Asch's (1946) impression formation paradigm, and his findings regarding
both "primacy effects" and the seemingly disproportionate impact of "central"
dimensions or evaluation categories such as warmth versus coldness, are probably familiar to the readers of this volume. In both cases, it will be recalled, he
staunchly resisted contemporary (and subsequent) critics who tried to account for

the relevant phenomena in terms of differential attention, retention, or weighting of individual items of informations. The actual underlying sources, he argued provocatively, were more dynamic, and more configural. The meaning of specific trait discriptors (like that of any isolated bits of information), he maintained, depends heavily upon the global impressions adopted by the subject. Thus a seemingly straightforward descriptor like *intelligent* would have a very different connotation—indeed have a very different meaning to the subject—when construed in the light of a positive global impression than a negative one. The presentation of an initial item of positive information, or the introduction of an item that offers a potent organizing dimension like overall warmth or coldness, becomes so important, accordingly, not because of the attention or weight the individual item receives but because of the impactful global impressions they create which, in turn, determine the meaning that will be attached to the other items in the list.

Asch's controversial "change of meaning" hypothesis similarly invigorated debate about the communicator credibility effect demonstrated by attitude researchers in the Hovland tradition at Yale. Again, it was not difficult for investigators (e.g., Lorge, 1936) to offer straightforward, "nondynamic," explanations for the obvious finding that written arguments produced more attitude change in the undergraduates who read them when they were attributed to positively regarded (i.e., attractive, trustworthy, expert) communication sources than to negatively regarded ones. A given message associated with an attractive, high credibility source, it was proposed by those in the then dominant learning theory tradition, would be attended to more closely, recalled more successfully, regarded as more accurate and reliable, and deemed more worthy of emulation by the recipient, than would the same message when associated with an unattractive, low credibility source. Again, however, Asch (1948) offered the provocative hypothesis that the very *meaning* of a message (i.e., the "object of judgment," as opposed to the "judgment of the object") changes as a function of the source to which it is attributed. Thus, to cite Asch's classic example, an assertion to the effect that "a little rebellion . . . is a good thing" has a different (and more acceptable) meaning to the recipient when it comes from Thomas Jefferson (with "rebellion" connoting something akin to "throwing the corrupt rascals out") than it does when its reputed source is V. I. Lenin (in which case "rebellion" connotes "a bloody purge of the innocent and guilty alike").

The final phenomenon prompting a construal interpretation is the one with which Asch's name is most closely associated by contemporary social psychologists—that is, the modification of individual judgement in the face of group pressure. There is an irony worth noting here. Contemporary text books cite the "Asch experiments" (Asch, 1951, 1955) as perhaps the ultimate demonstration of the individual's dangerous and mindless conformity to the whims and views of the majority. Asch's own view, of course, was quite different. Conformity to group standards, he insisted, *generally* would reflect a rational and adaptive response, one that depended heavily upon the capacity of group consensus to influence the *object* of the individual's judgment as much as the *judgment* of that object. Thus, Asch (1940) explained in reporting an earlier and somewhat less celebrated conformity study, when one subject learns that his peers have derogated the profession of "politician," and another learns that the same profession has been rated more highly than virtually any other, the two subjects' own evaluations actually pertain to two very different types of politicians. In the first case, the assessment deals with corrupt ward bosses and political hacks (an interpretation of the object of judgment that is both consistent with the peers' derogation and likely to prompt and justify similar derogation by the subject); in the second case the assessment deals with statesmen and effective national leaders like Jefferson or Roosevelt (this time, an interpretation consistent with, and demanding of, high regard by subject and peers alike). Conformity in the classic Asch situation thus constituted an exceptional, even unique, "special case" in which reinterpretation or altered construal of the stimulus, and of the group's response to that stimulus, is all but impossible (see Moscovici, 1985; Ross, Bierbrauer, & Hoffman, 1976).[1]

The False Consensus Effect

In an early paper on attributional shortcomings (Ross, Greene, & House, 1977) my students and I pursued very simple and, it now appears, a very robust phenomenon involving biased estimates of response consensus. Our first study had subjects read descriptions of a series of hypothetical situations, each of which prompted a choice between two specified response alternatives. For each situation, subjects were asked to indicate what their own response would be, to estimate the commonness of their own and the opposite response alternative, and to assess the degree to which each alternative permitted strong and confident inferences about the actor's distinguishing personal dispositions. Our principal finding, which we termed the false consensus effect, was that the subjects who personally selected a given response alternative saw that alternative as more common, and less revealing of personal dispositions, than did the actors who chose the other alternative.

References to "egocentric attribution" or "attributive projection," and reports of findings suggestive of the false consensus effect in particular domains, had appeared sporadically in the social perception and attribution literatures (e.g., Holmes, 1968; Katz & Allport 1931; and Kelley & Stahelski, 1970). Generally, the interpretations offered for such phenomena had been motivational, centering on the actor's need to feel that his or her behavioral choices

---

[1]A followup study by Allen and Wilder (1980) has since offered direct support for Asch's construal interpretation. On the other hand, a later study by Griffin (1980) suggests that the process of "congruent" construal may play a larger role in helping the subject to justify conformity after the fact, than in mediating the conforming judgment itself in the first place.

are rational and normative. Our own initial interpretation of this bias in consensus estimates was more "informational." We argued that social actors are selectively exposed to (and likely to expose themselves to) other people who share their background, values, priorities and other determinants of response—i.e., to other people who in fact really do respond to the majority of situations in the same manner as the actors themselves. We also argued that in trying to imagine how "typical" actors might respond, the actors' own responses, the responses of others similar to themselves, and also the goals and values prompting such responses, are all likely to be more cognitively salient or "available" than the relevant alternatives. In reflecting on our results, however, we were troubled by a possible alternative explanation that we felt, at least initially, would trivialize our findings.

This alternative interpretation involved the resolution of uncertainties and ambiguities presented in the descriptions of the hypothetical situations that had been presented to our subjects. Our brief verbal descriptions had necessarily left a lot of details about situation and context to the subjects' imagination—details that inevitably would be "filled in" differently by different subjects. Consider, for example, the following situational description presented to our subjects:

As you are leaving your neighborhood supermarket a man in a business suit asks whether you like shopping in that store. You reply quite honestly that you do like shopping there and indicate that in addition to being close to your home the supermarket seems to have very good meats and produce at reasonably low prices. The man then reveals that a videotape crew has filmed your comments and asks you to sign a release allowing them to use the unedited film for a TV commercial the supermarket chain is preparing.

Now consider what is *not* specified in such a description. What exactly does this "man in a business suit" look like, and how exactly does he ask? (Is he a fast-talking huckster wearing a pinky-ring who prompts instant distaste, or a pleasant clean-cut chap whom one would hate to disappoint?) How are *you*, the potential actor, dressed at the time (in sweaty jogging togs, or in a snappy new outfit?). And what exactly did you say in the "interview," and exactly how did you say it? Beyond these details of content and context, there are questions of prior experience that would become highly relevant if the hypothetical dilemma were real (Had you seen any such commercials in the past and, if so, what had you thought of them?). There would also be additional issues about feelings and ideation. What kind of mood would you be in at the time, and what else would be going on in your life? What specific ideas, schemas, or associations would happen to be invoked by the request and by the immediate, real, context in which it occurred (fears about "being exploited," norms about "helping out someone just doing their job," joy or dread at the notoriety of "being seen on television," or perhaps something quite different)? Obviously, readers would differ in the concreteness and completeness of their construals. But the way in which you, or any other reader of the story resolves these and other ambiguities too numerous to mention would influence not only your own "hypothetical" response but also your estimates of response consensus and your assessment of the meaning of the two response alternatives. Similar uncertainties of construal, moreover, existed with respect to each of the hypothetical situations and other questionnaire items used in our false consensus studies.

Our initial reaction to this "alternative interpretation" was to regard the construal problem as an artifact to be eliminated in the most direct way possible, i.e., by having our subjects face a real dilemma, make a real choice, and make consensus estimates and personal attributions about purportedly real peers who had done likewise. Accordingly, a sample of 80 Stanford undergraduates were recruited for a study on "communication techniques." After a few preliminary remarks about the general topic, the experimenter abruptly asked them if they would be willing to walk around campus for 30 minutes wearing a large sandwich-board sign bearing a simple message (e.g., EAT AT JOE'S), and record the responses of their peers to this unusual communication technique. The experimenter made it clear to subjects that they could easily opt out of the sandwich-board study, and be rescheduled for some future study, but that he would prefer that they participate and thereby "learn something interesting while helping the research project." Subjects were subsequently asked to decide about their own participation, to estimate the probable decisions of others, and to make trait inferences about particular peers who agreed or refused to participate.

The results using this "real" conflict situation confirmed the findings of our earlier questionnaire studies. Overall, subjects who agreed to wear the sandwich-board sign estimated that 62% of their peers would do likewise, while subjects who refused to wear the sign estimated that only 33% of their peers would be willing to wear it. Furthermore, as predicted, "compliant" subjects made more confident and more extreme inferences about the personal characteristics of a purportedly noncompliant peer, while noncompliant subjects made stronger inferences about a purportedly compliant peer.

At first consideration, the success of this demonstration seemed to rule out the construal "artifact," since all participants had faced the same concrete dilemma. Upon reflection, however, we soon realized that it did nothing of the kind. Possibilities for divergent construal can remain even when the situation confronted is concrete and objectively identical for all concerned. Thus subjects who imagine that their sandwich-board adventure will prompt ridicule from the peers they encounter, or imagine that refusal to participate will be accepted with equanimity, or construe the overall situation as a test of their assertiveness, likely will refuse to wear the sign. They will also make appropriate predictions and inferences about the meaning of acquiescence versus refusal by others in that same situation. By contrast, subjects who imagine that the peers they encounter will applaud their good sportsmanship and recognize that they are contributing to science rather than making fools of themselves, or who imagine that their refusal to participate will meet with incredulity and scorn from the experimenter, or who construe the overall situation as a test of their uptightness, will agree to wear the sign; and they too will make appropriate predictions and inferences about others who elect to do likewise or otherwise in the same situation.

Our construal interpretation, it should be emphasized, depends on more than the simple assumption that subjects engage in variable construals of situation and context. It depends on the additional assumption (which, it will be recalled, provides the thesis for this chapter) that in doing so they fail to recognize, and/or fail to make adequate inferential allowance for the fact that many if not most of their peers may construe the "same" situation quite differently. In a sense, our contention is that subjects fail to recognize the degree to which their interpretation of the situation is just that—a set of constructions and inferences rather than a direct perception of some objective and invariant reality.

Overconfident Prediction and Overly Dispositional Interpretation of Behavior

Shortcomings in the performance of two important tasks of intuitive psychology—behavioral prediction and causal attribution—have provided a major focus for my research for the past decade; and, it eventually became apparent, problems of situational construal play a potentially critical role in both cases.

In an initial set of studies (Dunning, Griffin, Milojkovic, & Ross, 1990) my students and I focused on behavioral prediction. Our primary finding was that subjects, across several different social prediction tasks and paradigms, proved to be highly overconfident. That is, regardless of the type of prediction item (e.g., responses to hypothetical dilemmas, responses to contrived laboratory situations, habit inventories) and regardless of the amount and source of information available about the target of their prediction (e.g., predictions about roommates, predictions about strangers interviewed by the subject, predictions about anonymous targets shown in photos) achieved levels of accuracy remained far below the levels required to justify the subjects' expressed confidence levels. Additional analysis further revealed that although relatively higher confidence levels were associated with relatively higher rates of accuracy, the *gap* between anticipated and achieved accuracy was greatest precisely when subjects were most confident in their success. Relatively high levels of confidence also proved unrealistic to the extent that subjects knowingly or unknowingly went *against* the relevant response base rates—i.e., predicted that particular targets would idiosyncratically differ from the consensus of their peers.

In a pair of followup studies, Vallone, Griffin, Lin, and Ross (1988) extended the domain of enquiry from social prediction to personal prediction. Newly arrived Stanford undergraduates wee asked to predict their own future actions and outcomes (as well as those of their roommates) over the weeks and months of their freshman year. For every type of prediction item we studied, from academic choices and outcomes (e.g., where will I study; what major will I choose; what courses will I drop?) to social and leisure activities (e.g., will I end up close friends with my roommate, will I take part in the dorm play, will I go to San Francisco once a week?) we again found marked overconfidence, and again the gap between confidence levels expressed and rates of accuracy achieved was widest precisely when confidence itself was greatest and/or when subjects' predictions went against the relevant behavioral base rates. Moreover, while subjects were, overall, more accurate in predicting their own actions and outcomes than those of their roommates, the discrepancy between subjective certainty and objective accuracy was virtually identical in both cases. In other words, even in predicting the behavior of the person whose personal attributes and past experience they knew best—that is, *themselves*—subjects were overconfident. Furthermore, the degree of their overconfidence was greatest precisely when they assumed that their self-knowledge justified the prediction that their behavior would differ from that of their peers (and, presumably, from the dictates of the situational pressures and constraints that govern the behavior of people in general).

The overconfidence effect in personal and social prediction obviously cannot be traced to a single cause or underlying mechanism. Like most interesting and robust phenomena (including all of the ones discussed in this chapter) it almost certainly is *multiply* determined, and probably also *over*determined—in the sense that it reflects the joint impact of many different processes that may be *sufficient* to produce the phenomena in at least some contexts, without being *necessary* to do so in other contexts.

Initially, our interpretation of the overconfidence effect focused on the inveterate dispositionism of our subjects—i.e., their tendency to infer personality traits too readily, and to give those traits too much weight (and whatever situational forces and constraints are reflected in the relevant behavioral baserates too little weight) in making behavioral predictions. But the essentially parallel nature of the findings we obtained for self-predictions and social predictions forced us to recognize that premature and erroneous trait inferences could be only a part of the overconfidence story. Trait inferences about self are less pervasive than similar inferences about peers (Jones & Nisbett, 1972) and, one would assume, also more data-based and accurate; yet, confident self-predictions like confident social predictions prove to be inaccurate far more often than the predictors' confidence levels would seem to demand. Once again, further reflection prompted us to consider the role of situational construal or, more particularly, inadequate allowance for the uncertainties of such construal, in producing the relevant phenomenon.

There are, in fact, two different aspects to the construal problem as it relates to behavioral prediction. First, to predict an actor's response to a given situation—even the response of an actor whom one knows very well and whose behavior one has observed in a wide variety of previous situations—one generally must know or correctly infer the *details* of that situation, i.e., the features of content and context that determine the relative attractiveness of the available response alternatives. Second, beyond knowing the "objective" features of the situation, one must discern or anticipate the meaning of the situation from the private perspective of the actor. Uncertainty about objective features of the situation and/or their subjective construal by the actor increases the difficulty of prediction and the likelihood or error. And failure to recognize and/or make adequate *allowance* for such uncertainty promotes overconfident social prediction, both in the context of our present laboratory research and, more importantly, in everyday social experience as well.

It is worth reemphasizing that construal problems by no means disappear when it is one's own behavior being predicted. To the extent that one must guess details about the specific situations one will face, and/or the way one personally will experience these situations, construal errors are inevitable. And again, it is the failure to make adequate allowance for such uncertainty that makes one susceptible to overconfidence and the potential costs one pays for overconfidence, costs that range from mild social embarrassment to poor use of ones resources and ill-advised neglect of measures that would insure one-self against error.

Recognition of the link between construal problems and systematic dipositionist biases in the attribution process has been an equally recent theoretical development—at least in *my* theoretical development. A decade ago (Ross, 1977, 1978) I coined the term "fundamental attribution error" to label an inferential bias noted long ago by Lewin (1936) and Heider (1944, 1958). I also argued that this bias, whereby social perceivers overlook situational explanations for observed actions and outcomes, and prematurely both infer distinguishing personality traits and exaggerate their role in determining behavior, accounts in part for the didactic power of our field's classic situationist demonstrations (see Nisbett & Ross, 1980). That is, Asch's compelling conformity studies, and Milgram's (1963, 1965, 1974) later obedience studies, and many less dramatic and celebrated experimental demonstrations, all offer one common message: situational manipulations in general, and relatively subtle situational features or variations in particular, can produce behavior that one never could have anticipated from knowledge about the actors or their past behavior (see also Miller, 1986; Ross, 1988).

Notwithstanding the importance of such demonstrations, I now believe that inappropriate trait inferences, especially in everyday experience outside the laboratory, owe as much to construal failures as they do to the simple underweighting of situational forces and constraints. Specifically, inappropriate trait inferences may occur because we fail to recognize the degree to which seemingly exceptional actions and outcomes inform us not that the relevant actors are exceptional in their personal dispositions but rather that *we* have *misconstrued* the relevant stimulus situations—i.e., failed to recognize or correctly infer the true (and perhaps exceptional) nature of the situation in question, and/or failed to appreciate how that situation is perceived by the relevant actor.

Two sets of studies that my students and I have undertaken seem to provide some evidence for this "construal interpretation" of the fundamental attribution error. The first was a rather crude set of pilot studies (Ross & Penning, 1985) that looked at social perceivers' responses to one particular failed prediction. Subjects in each study were asked to predict whether each of two peers (one of whom they had judged, on the basis of a photograph, to be a "highly typical" Stanfordite; and one of whom they had judged to be an atypical Stanfordite) would prove willing to donate a small sum of money to help sponsor a "Gay Rights are Human Rights" advertisement in a campus newspaper. The amount of information provided about the specific situation confronting the actors at the point when they encountered the opportunity to make their donation varied across studies (for example in one study they were told virtually nothing about any appeal for funds, in another study they were told that the actors encountered a booth at a campus thoroughfare) but in each of these pilot studies two criteria were satisfied. First, all of the descriptions of the stipulated situations left plenty of room for construal (e.g., Were the relevant actors alone or accompanied? Was any explicit appeal directed at the person; and if so what was the content and manner of the appeal?) and second, the initial consensus of our subjects in each study was that *neither* of the actors would contribute to the gay rights ad.

At that point in the procedure, the experimenter first required all subjects to describe their own particular, detailed construal of the situation facing the two actors. Then he informed the subjects that their behavioral predictions about *both* of the actors were *wrong*—for example (in the modal case where the prediction was two refusals) that both actors had, in fact, made the small contribution sought for the advertisement. Our subjects were then asked, in a series first of open-ended questions followed by forced-choice items, to comment on their failed predictions. In particular, they were asked to tell us what could be inferred from the actors' responses. Overwhelmingly, the subjects in our three pilot studies favored dispositional explanations and inferences to situational ones. Far more subjects spontaneously offered exclusively dispositional interpretations (they're both "gay," or "liberals," or "easy marks," etc.) than exclusively situational ones ("someone they knew must have confronted them directly and asked them to contribute" or "somehow the setting must have made it very difficult to refuse"). Furthermore, when both types of factors were cited, dispositional factors were more likely to be cited first and, when forced-choice measures were employed, they were more likely to be rated as highly probable and important.

Our second set of studies (Griffin, Dunning, & Ross, 1988) took a more direct approach in attempting to link construal problems first to overconfident predictions and then to inappropriate trait inferences. We reasoned that one obvious way to determine whether subjects do or do not make adequate inferential allowance for the uncertainties associated with situational construal is to compare their behavioral predictions and trait inferences under conditions where the certainty of their construals is *manipulated*. If subjects show the same lack of conservatism under conditions where they know their situational construals to be correct as they do under conditions where they have no particular reason to believe them correct, such a finding would suggest that their assessments in the latter conditions have failed to make adequate allowance for the possibility of misconstrual.

The first Griffin et al. study conducted to test this line of reasoning dealt with self predictions. Subjects in four conditions were called upon to make predictions about the amount of time or the amount of money they would spend in a specified set of circumstances (e.g., the amount of time they personally would talk during a 60-minute roundtable discussion with four peers on the issue of abortion, or the amount of money they would spend during an end-of-the-quarter celebration in San Francisco). In all conditions, furthermore, details about context or situation were described in rather modest detail—i.e., leaving lots of room for variable interpretation or construal—and in all condition subjects were asked not only to make specific "best guess" estimates but also to furnish appropriate confidence intervals. After completing their best guesses and confidence intervals for the various situations, all subjects were asked to *reconsider* and, if they wished, to adjust their responses in light of such reconsideration.

What varied in the four conditions were the intervening instructions subjects received about situational construal. Thus the control condition subjects were given no relevant instructions during the interval between their original and their reconsidered estimates. A second set of subjects, those in the *uncertain construal condition,* were asked simply to specify their particular construal of contextual or situational details and then, with no guidance about the potential accuracy or inaccuracy of their construals, they were invited to reconsider each estimate and confidence interval. A third set of subjects, those in *certain construal condition,* were similarly asked to specify each situational construal; however, in contrast to the procedure followed in the two former conditions, in this group subjects then were told that in furnishing their second set of estimates they were to assume that their situational construals were "exactly correct." In other words, they were invited to make their reconsidered predictions and confidence intervals *conditional* on the accuracy of their prior situational construals.

The results for these three self-prediction conditions can be summarized very succinctly. In all three conditions the size of the "reconsidered" confidence intervals were, on average, virtually identical to the size of the intervals that the subjects had offered before receiving the relevant construal instructions. Thus, simply making it explicit to subjects that their predictions were predicated upon personal construals of the situation (which might or might not be accurate) did not increase the size of the confidence intervals they offered. More importantly, stipulating to subjects that they should assume their construals to be *completely accurate* (i.e., that no allowance had to be made for the uncertainty inherent in the process by which they filled in gaps in information, resolved ambiguity, or otherwise went "beyond the information given") did not *decrease* their confidence intervals. Our interpretation for this result, of course, is that subjects in both the "uncertain" and the "certain" construal conditions (as well as those in the control condition) similarly furnished predictions and offered confidence estimates that failed to make the logically warranted allowance for the possibility of inaccurate construal.

The fourth experimental condition in Griffin et al.'s initial experiment becomes important in the light of these findings and the interpretation we have offered for them. It showed that subjects can and will make allowance for the possibility of incorrect construal, provided this possibility is demonstrated with sufficient force and clarity. In this fourth condition, subjects were again invited to specify their situational construals; but, before offering any new predictions and confidence intervals, they were told explicitly to suggest respects in which their initial construals might be *incorrect* (i.e., to furnish *alternative* construals). In this condition, at last, the subjects seemed to recognize the implications of the uncertain status of the situational construals at which they had arrived. In contrast to the subjects in the other conditions their mean confidence intervals showed a significant and consistent increase (averaging over 30%, in contrast to the net changes of no more than 3% in the other three conditions.

A second study by Griffin et al. (1988) employed essentially the same reasoning and experimental paradigm to explore interpersonal inference, and it yielded essentially the same result. Subjects in the four conditions of this study all were called upon to make dispositional inferences about a peer who purportedly had behaved in an extreme fashion (i.e., the individual had monopolized a group discussion by talking for 45 minutes out of the 75 minutes allotted). Consistent with the results of Study 1, we found that subjects exhibited as little conservatism (i.e, made just as extreme and confident trait assessments) when they did so under conditions where their situational construals (and/or their guesses about the relevant *actors'* construals) were of indeterminate accuracy as they did under conditions where the complete accuracy of such construals had been stipulated and where their trait assessments were, in fact, *contingent* on that accuracy. Once again, only the explicit invitation to furnish alternative, highly divergent, construals induced subjects to make adequate inferential allowance for the general uncertainty of their construals, and for the specific possibility that they had somehow misconstrued the situation by failing to imagine situational features irrelevant to the actor's personality that might have accounted for his monopolization of the group discussion.

Perceptions of Bias and Hostility

The final research area reviewed in this paper concerns intergroup conflict and distrust. The evolution of our work (Mark Lepper has been my collaborator throughout) is worth tracing because the problem of subjective construal, and the failure to make adequate allowance for uncertainties and biases in such construal, once again provides a common thread. Several years ago, Lord, Ross, and Lepper, (1979) had shown that opposing partisans could derive support for their views from the same set of mixed and ambiguous evidence—i.e., that *polarization* of opposing beliefs occurs in response to evidence that, viewed dispassionately, should have made the two partisan groups less certain and less dogmatic about their respective positions. This work, in turn, led us to ponder the tendency for partisan groups to complain about their treatment by the media. With hindsight wisdom it became clear that the same *"assimilation biases"* that allow partisans to maintain their beliefs in the face of arguments and evidence that provide weak support for such beliefs also predispose them to perceive the media as hostile and biased. That is, to the extent that partisans accept supportive facts and arguments at face value but subject nonsupportive facts and arguments to critical scrutiny and alternative interpretation, and to the extent that they resolve ambiguities in the meaning of ambiguous evidence in a way that favors their preconceptions, the partisans would be bound to perceive objective or evenhanded evaluations of the same arguments and evidence—and those who offer them—as unobjective and unfair.

The most dramatic evidence we have been able to muster for this "hostile media" phenomenon came from a study (Vallone, Ross, & Lepper, 1985) in which we provided Pro-Arab and Pro-Israeli reviewers with videotaped news coverage immediately following the infamous 1982 massacre of civilians in Lebanese refugee camps. On measure after measure there was virtually no overlap in the evaluations offered by the two partisan groups. Pro-Arab and Pro-Israeli viewers showed agreement only in their conviction that the other side had been favored by the media, that their own side had been treated unfairly, and that the relevant bias in coverage had resulted from and was reflective of the personal interests and ideologies of those responsible for the programs.

Our data, however, also suggested the operation of mechanisms that we had *not* anticipated, but perhaps could have anticipated had we paid closer attention to arguments and interpretations offered long ago by the man whom we honor in this volume. Rather than simply disagreeing about whether the facts and arguments presented were valid, or whether the overall tone and emphasis of the programs was fair, the two partisan groups seemed to disagree about what they actually had seen. Thus both pro-Arab and pro-Israeli viewers of the same 36-minute videotapes reported that the other side had enjoyed a greater proportion of favorable facts and references, and a smaller proportion of negative ones, than their own side. Both groups also believed that the overall tone, emphasis, and message of the videotapes was such that it would lead neutral viewers to change their attitudes in a direction favorable to the other group and hostile to their own. In other words, or rather in Asch's (1952) words, the opposing partisans disagreed about the very nature of the "object of judgment."[2]

The next step in the progression of our ideas about perceptions of bias and hostility was to address a problem that our conceptual analysis suggested might thwart face-to-face negotiation between groups in conflict. If opposing groups are inclined to interpret media reports about the conflict in a highly uncharitable fashion, we reasoned, they should be even *more* inclined to look uncharitably upon, and respond negatively to, each other's proposals for conflict resolution. Our working hypothesis was very simple: We assumed that the same proposal that seems equitable and forthcoming to the partisan offering it will seem inequitable and unforthcoming to the partisan receiving it. In part, of course, this hypothesis arises from the expectation that the two sides will differ both in what they believe would be fair (in the light of their divergent views about past history and present context) and in the way they construe the terms and balance of the proposal itself. We anticipated, however, that an additional construal bias would come into play and constitute a further barrier to conflict resolution. The very act of offering a proposal, we predicted, would *change* its attractiveness (and very possibly its meaning) in the eyes of the recipient. As a consequence of having been offered, especially by an adversary, specific concessions or compromises would come to be perceived as smaller than they had been perceived (or would have been perceived) prior to the offer. Any concessions especially sought by an adversary, conversely, would come to be perceived as more significant and less appropriate to cede to that adversary.

Evidence for this pessimistic hypothesis, and for our more specific ideas about underlying construal biases, has been provided in a series of recent studies (Stillinger, Epelbaum, Keltner, & Ross, 1990). In our first study we seized the opportunity provided by a Soviet diplomatic initiative to show that the authorship of a proposal can indeed change its attractiveness and apparent balance. Early in 1986, the Soviet leader Mikhail Gorbachev made a dramatic arms reduction proposal, one that might have seemed, at least at first blush, to offer a promising basis for future negotiation. Essentially, the proposal called for a three stage reduction of nuclear weapons: In stage one, to be accomplished within the next 3

---

[2]These results may bring to mind Hastorf and Cantrils's (1954) classic paper reporting partisan perceptions of a particularly rough football game between Princeton and Dartmouth. Despite viewing the same objective stimulus (a film of the game) the Princeton fans apparently saw a continuing pattern of Dartmouth atrocities and occasional Princeton retaliation, while the Dartmouth fans apparently saw brutal Princeton provocations and measured Dartmouth responses. Vallone et al.'s results suggest that the opposing partisans, far from seeing a stimulus in which their side appeared to be the hero and the other side the villain, saw a stimulus in which their side seemed to be the villain and the other side be the hero.

to 5 years, both the U.S. and the U.S.S.R. would reduce the numbers of weapons capable of reaching the other sides territory by 50%. In stage two, to follow in the next decade, shorter range tactical weapons would be reduced and eliminated. In stage three, to begin in 1995 and end by the turn of the century, the elimination of all nuclear weapons would be completed. Accompanying this proposal was an announcement that the U.S.S.R. would extend, by 3 months, its unilateral moratorium on nuclear testing (begun 6 months earlier) and a renewed insistence that the U.S. abandon (or at least severely limit) its attempt to develop the so-called Star Wars system of space-based weapons.

Despite the simple, relatively unambiguous, and nontechnical terms of this proposal, its attractiveness, as we predicted (and as Solomon Asch would have been utterly unsurprised to discover) seemed to depend largely upon its purported authorship. When we attributed it (correctly) to Mr. Gorbachev, the majority of our survey subjects (adult citizens of Palo Alto, California) said that its provisions disproportionately favored the interests of the U.S.S.R., while only a very small minority thought it disproportionately favored the U.S. By contrast, when the proposal was purported to be Mr. Reagan's, only a small minority thought it favored the U.S.S.R. and the clear majority believed it favored the U.S. In both cases, fewer than a third of the respondents in these two conditions thought the proposal was "equally favorable to both sides." When the same proposal, however, was presented as the product of an unknown group of policy analysts, the most common evaluation (i.e., by almost half the respondents) was that the proposal was equally favorable to both sides, and only a minority thought the proposal disproportionately favored either the Soviets or the U.S.

In a second opportunistic venture, we asked Stanford students to evaluate various proposals that the University was purportedly considering in response to widespread demands that it immediately and totally divest itself of all holdings in American companies doing business in South Africa. Of particular interest were the students' ratings of two compromise proposals—one of which was a *partial divestment* plan that would have seen the University immediately divest itself of stock holdings in various companies that had been specifically linked to the South African military or police and/or been guilty of apartheid practices in the work place, and one of which would have seen the University specify a 2-year *deadline* for major reform of the apartheid system (after which total divestment would follow if such reform had not occurred). When we simply told students that the University was considering both proposals, along with many others, they were rated about equally satisfactory and equally significant. When we told students that the University was about to offer the partial divestment plan, a clear majority rated this concession to be less satisfactory and significant than the nonoffered alternative of a deadline for total divestment. Conversely, when we told students that the University would propose a deadline, the clear majority rated such a deadline as less satisfactory and significant than the plan for immediate, albeit only partial, divestment.

The same basic result was obtained when we asked students favoring immediate and total divestment to negotiate with a peer (actually an experimental confederate) who willingly championed the University's far more conservative position. Again, when concession content was held constant, whichever concession the confederate offered was devalued relative to whichever concession he withheld. More importantly, in a final study we were able to demonstrate the predicted reactive devaluation phenomenon when, at long last, the University concluded its deliberations and announced the specific measures it would undertake to show its condemnation of apartheid. Having learned in advance of the content of the plan that the University would adopt (which turned out to be a partial divestment plan similar to but more extensive than the one we had presented to subjects in our earlier studies) we took the opportunity to survey student evaluations both before and after the plan was finally announced. As predicted, the perceived attractiveness and significance of the University's plan declined significantly from the first measurement to the second—both in absolute terms, and relative to other plans and proposals that had not been enacted.

In followup research we are trying to show that such reactive devaluation really does depend, at least in part, upon differences in construal (rather than a reflexive, thoughtless, attempt to restore cognitive balance or reduce "dissonance"). We are also trying to show that concession offerers and concession recipients do, in fact, underestimate the magnitude of the differences in their respective construals and also fail to recognize that such differences are genuine reflections of the other side's interpretations, and not merely cynical negotiation ploys. Finally, we are beginning to explore various strategies for overcoming this and other cognitive barriers to successful negotiation. In so doing, we are taking to heart some of the pointed objections that Solomon Asch raised over a decade ago in our private tutorial, when I tried to champion the advances in theory and research offered by my generation of young social psychologists. That is, we are trying to do social psychology that is at once more social, more humane, and more closely directed to significant problems facing our society.

A POSTSCRIPT: REFLECTIONS ON ASCH'S 1952 TEXT

In this *festschrift* chapter I've tried to show the continuity between my empirical research, or at least my interpretation of the results of that research, and one of Solomon Asch's most important contributions to social psychology—that is, his success in focusing our discipline's attention on the problem of subjective meaning and on the active cognitive, perceptual, and social processes that govern the assignment of such meaning. In rereading his 1952 text I am struck anew by the force, and clarity, and passion, with which he combatted the objectivist and reductionist tenor of his times. Both as methodologist and careful analyst of phenomena inside and outside the laboratory, Asch set an example that few of us can hope to approach, but all of us can learn from if our goal is better and more serious work.

The term *serious* is an advised one. One cannot leaf through Asch text, which was intended for students encountering the field of social psychology for the first time, and then do likewise to a contemporary introductory text designed for the same purpose, without experiencing a twinge (or, in the case of some of us, a paroxysm) of guilt and embarrassment. One is struck by how flattering Asch's *Social Psychology*—the approach as well as the text—was to the students of the time. Unlevened with clever cartoons or multicolored art reproductions, without photographs of lovers or soldiers or protestors, without engaging interviews of contemporary contributors, it assumed that students and colleagues could be addressed in a single voice and that they all shared the author's eagerness to tackle basic intellectual and philosophical issues. With no chapter summaries, no glossary of technical terms, no bar graphs or other study aids, and no questions for review, it did little to help students prepare for exams. What it offered the student instead was an earnest invitation to participate in serious thinking about human nature, experience, and society. Somehow, without citing a thousand or more studies by hundreds of investigators on dozens of topics, as now seems standard practice, it offered students an entree to the intellectual core of our field that no contemporary text can match. Let us hope that the recent reissuing of Asch's text in paperback will give many of us the means and motive to offer our own students the same flattering and inspiring introduction to social psychology, and to the ideas of one of its giants.

ACKNOWLEDGMENTS

In preparing this chapter I have made liberal use of unpublished papers on the subject of construal written by two of my former graduate students, David Dunning (now a faculty member at Cornell) and Dale Griffin (now at the University of Waterloo). Their help is acknowledged with gratitude. I should also note that I borrowed heavily, especially in my overviews of research, from an earlier *festschrift* chapter (Ross, 1987) written in honor of my advisor Stanley Schachter, whose work and whose "Lewinian" roots I have drawn upon so heavily throughout my career.

REFERENCES

Abelson, R. P. (1976) Script processing in attitude formation and decision-making. In J. S. Carroll, & J. W. Payne (Eds.), *Cognition and social behavior* (pp. 33–46). Hillsdale, NJ: Lawrence Erlbaum Associates.

Abelson, R. P. (1981). Psychological status of the script concept. *American Psychologist, 36,* 715–729.

Allen, V. L., & Wilder, D. A. (1980). Impact of group consensus and social support on stimulus meaning: Mediation of conformity by cognitive restructuring. *Journal of Personality and Social Psychology, 39,* 1116–1124.

Asch, S. E. (1940). Studies in the principles of judgments and attitudes: II. Determination of judgments by group and by ego standards. *Journal of Social Psychology, 12,* 433–465.

Asch, S. E. (1946). Forming impressions of personality. *Journal of Abnormal and Social Psychology, 41,* 258–290.

Asch, S. E. (1948). The doctrine of suggestion, prestige, and imitation in social psychology. *Psychological Review, 155,.*

Asch, S. E. (1952). *Social psychology.* Englewood Cliffs, NJ: Prentice-Hall.

Asch, S. E. (1955, November). Opinions and social pressure. *Scientific American,* 31–35.

Bartlett, F. C. (1932). *Remembering: A study in experimental and social psychology.* Cambridge, England: Cambridge University Press.

Dunning, D., Griffin, D. W., Milojkovic, J., & Ross, L. (1990). The overconfidence effect in social prediction. *Journal of Personality and Social Psychology.* (in press).

Fiske, S. T., & Taylor, S. E. (1984). *Social cognition.* New York: Random House.

Griffin, D. W. (1988). *The role of construal processes in conformity and dissent.* Unpublished doctoral dissertation. Stanford University.

Griffin, D. W., Dunning, D., & Ross, L. (1990). *The role of construal processes in overconfident predictions about the self and others.* Manuscript submitted for publication, Stanford University.

Hartshorne, H., & May, M. A. (1928). *Studies in the nature of character: I. Studies in deceit.* New York: Macmillan.

Hastorf, A., & Cantril, H. (1954). They saw a game: A case study. *Journal of Abnormal and Social Psychology, 49,* 129–134.

Heider, F. (1944). Social perception and phenomenal causality. *Psychological Review, 51,* 358–373.

Heider, F. (1958). *The psychology of interpersonal relations.* New York: Wiley.

Jones, E. E., & Davis, K. E. (1965). From acts to dispositions: the attribution process in person perception. In L. Berkowitz (Ed.), *Advances in experimental social psychology* (Vol. 2). New York: Academic Press.

Holmes, D, S. (1968). Dimensions of projection. *Psychological Bulletin, 69,* 248–268.

Jones, E. E., & Nisbett, R. E. (1972). The actor and the observer: Divergent perceptions of the causes of behavior. In E. E. Jones and others (Ed.), *Attribution: perceiving the causes of behavior.* Morristown, NJ: General Learning Press.

Kahneman, D., Slovic, P., & Tversky, A. (Eds.). (1982). *Judgment under uncertainty: Heuristics and Biases.* New York: Cambridge University Press.

Katz, D., & Allport, F. (1931). *Students' Attitudes.* Syracuse, NY: Craftsman Press.

Kelley, H. H. (1967). Attribution theory in social psychology. In D. Levine (Ed.), *Nebraska symposium on motivation* (Vol. 15, pp. 192–240). Lincoln: University of Nebraska Press.

Kelley, H. H. (1973). The process of causal attribution. *American psychologist, 28,* 107–128.

Kelley, H. H., & Stahelski, A. J. (1970). Social interaction basis of cooperators' and competitors' beliefs about others. *Journal of Personality and Social Psychology, 16,* 66–91.

Lewin, K. (1936). *Principles of topological psychology.* New York: McGraw-Hill.

Lord, C. G., Ross, L., & Lepper, M. R. (1979). Biased assimilation and attitude polarization: The effects of prior theories on subsequently considered evidence. *Journal of Personality and Social Psychology, 37,* 2098–2109.

Lorge, I. (1936). Prestige, suggestion, and attitudes. *Journal of Social Psychology, 7,* 386–402.

Milgram, S. (1963). Behavioral study of obedience. *Journal of Abnormal and Social Psychology, 67,* 371–378.

Milgram, S. (1965). Some conditions of obedience and disobedience to authority. *Human Relations, 18,* 57–76.

Milgram, S. (1974). *Obedience to authority.* New York: Harper and Row.

Miller, A. G. (1986). *The obedience experiments: A case study of controversy in social science.* New York: Praeger.

Moscovici, S. (1985). Social influence and conformity. In G. Lindzey & E. Aronson (Eds.), *The Handbook of Social Psychology* (3rd ed). Hillsdale, NJ: Lawrence Erlbaum Associates.

Nisbett, R. E., & Ross, L. (1980). *Human inference: Strategies and shortcomings of social judgment.* Englewood cliffs, NJ: Prentice-Hall.

Piaget, J. (1936). *La naissance de l'intelligence chez l'enfant.* Neuchatel et Paris: Delachau et Niestle.

Ross, L. (1977). The intuitive psychologist and his shortcomings: Distortions in the attribution process. In L. Berkowitz (Ed.), *Advances in experimental social psychology* (Vol. 10). New York: Academic Press.

Ross, L. (1978). Afterthoughts on the intuitive psychologist. In L. Berkowitz (Ed.), *Cognitive theories in social psychology* (pp. 385–400). New York: Academic Press.

Ross, L. (1987). The problem of construal in social inference and social psychology. In N. Grunberg, R. E. Nisbett, & J. Singer (Eds.), *A distinctive approach to psychological research: The influence of Stanley Schachter.* Hillsdale, NJ: Lawrence Erlbaum Associates.

Ross, L. (1988). Situationist perspectives on the obedience experiments. *Contemporary Psychology, 33,* 101–104.

Ross, L., Bierbrauer, G., & Hoffman, S. (1976). The role of attribution processes in conformity and dissent: Revisiting the Asch situation. *American Psychologist, 31,* 148–157.

Ross, L., Greene, D., & House, P. (1977). The false consensus effect: An egocentric bias in social perception and attribution processes. *Journal of Experimental Social Psychology, 13,* 279–301.

Ross, L., & Penning, P. (1985). *The dispositionalist bias in accounting for behavioral disconfirmation.* Unpublished manuscript, Stanford University.

Rumelhart, D. E. (1976). Basic processes in reading: Perception and comprehension. In D. LaBerge & S. J. Samuels (Eds.), *Understanding and summarizing brief stories.* Hillsdale, NJ: Lawrence Erlbaum Associates.

Schank, R. C., & Abelson, R. P. (1977). *Scripts, plans, goals, and understanding.* Hillsdale, NJ: Lawrence Erlbaum Associates.

Stillinger, C., Epelbaum, M., Keltner, D., & Ross, L. (1990). *The reactive devaluation barrier to conflict resolution.* Manuscript submitted for publication, Stanford University.

Vallone, R. P., Griffin, D. W., Lin, S., & Ross, L. (1990). The overconfidence prediction of future action and outcomes by self and others. *Journal of Personality and Social Psychology.* (in press).

Vallone, R. P., Ross, L., & Lepper, M. R. (1985). The hostile media phenomenon: Biased perceptions and perceptions of bias in media coverage of the ''Beirut Massacre.'' *Journal of Personality and Social Psychology, 49,* 577–585.

6 Social and Moral Aspects of Food and Eating

Paul Rozin
University of Pennsylvania

ABSTRACT

For most people in the world, food and eating are embedded in a social context, and have strong moral and social status. The separation of food from its origins, that is to say, its decontextualization, in Western industrialized countries masks these functions of food, although they are still present. Two widespread beliefs, "you are what you eat" and contagion (once in contact, always in contact), help to account for the social and moral roles of food. These beliefs are described, and evidence is presented, some based on Asch's impressions technique, that they are operative in educated American adults. Both beliefs, and the social and moral functions of food, are manifested in the emotion of disgust.

THE PSYCHOLOGY OF FOOD AND EATING

From the point of view of any individual, the world can be divided into the self and the outside. Almost all of the material transaction in the direction of outside to self comes through one aperture, the mouth, and takes the form of ingestion (Rozin & Fallon, 1980, 1987). The mouth is the principal incorporative organ. Nothing could be more threatening or intimate than taking something into the self (body), and this occurs in every act of ingestion. On the biological level, ingestion is an absolutely fundamental and frequent necessity. However, it carries with it the significant risk of incorporating toxic or imbalanced substances. Hence, at the biological level, oral incorporation has powerful benefits and risks. It is not surprising that ingestion is an act about which people feel strongly and that liking and disliking are terms that naturally apply to foods.

When coupled to the widespread traditional belief that "you are what you eat," the scope of oral incorporation is extended to the acquisition of positive or negative behavioral or physical properties, conveyed by animal or plant foods. Since humans rarely eat one another, the social implications of the "you are what you eat" principle are limited. However, "you are what you eat" seems to be a special case of the "sympathetic magical" law of contagion (once in contact, always in contact). In the large framework of contagion, the implications for social structure, social interaction, and expanded meanings for food are rich. Now, animal and plant foods become vehicles for transmission of human properties and intentions, and every item of food bears the mark of those who participated in its preparation. This chapter is an expansion of this point.

In the following section I describe the role of food in three very different cultures, to demonstrate the variability of the social functions of food. Then, I consider some of the basic beliefs and contrasts that motivate traditional beliefs about food, and that imbue food with social significance and meaning. I will show that these same beliefs exist in modern Westerners. Finally, I consider the emotion of disgust, which perhaps best illustrates the role of food as a biological, social, and moral substance.

THREE MODELS OF FOOD IN HUMAN LIFE

The United States

For Americans, food has two principal functions. First, it is the substantive vehicle that provides nutrition. Second, it is a major source of pleasure. The social function of food for Americans is muted. Of course it provides the occasion for daily or festive family gatherings and a base for social interactions with friends and companions at work. But food is basically what is on the plate. We are rather indifferent to the particular history of the food we eat: where it came from, who prepared it, its symbolic and social significance. Indeed it would be hard for us to be otherwise, in a world where we buy our food in plastic packages, prepared by anonymous others, and grown on some enormous automated farm far away. We have culturally decontextualized food in many ways.

The Hua of Papua New Guinea

In Papua New Guinea, "The Hua understand food and eating as part of a central process that connects organic and inorganic forms" (Meigs, 1988, p. 341). Exchanges of food are linked to bonds of social alliance and solidarity, and eating and food help to define the self (Meigs, 1978, 1984, 1988). The Hua world view centers on the concept of "nu," a "vital essence" conveyed principally by food, and responsible for growth and health. An individual's vital essence is contained in all of his or her body including body residues, and in all things contacted by the body. In particular, any food gathered or hunted, or cooked by a person, contains his or her vital essence. For the Hua, a piece of food contains the residue of all those who have contactually interacted with it. This belief has serious consequences because vital essence is personalized; it includes specific properties of its source person, and conveys the source's intent as well. One can acquire particular properties of a person by ingesting foods he or she has gathered or prepared. Ingestion of food containing the nu of those with hostile intent toward the eater (either because of their relationship within the social structure or because they are specific enemies) will cause harm. On the other hand, ingestion of "friendly" nu will benefit one's health and well being. Body substances are particularly potent sources of nu. It is considered auspicious that a relative with whom one has a positive relation spits on one's foods. Within the memories of living Hua, the Hua practiced cannibalism. They consumed their parents, after the parent's natural death, in order to incorporate both their specific virtues and the benefits of their good intent.

As in many other New Guinea cultures, there is great concern about the vulnerability of males at the time of puberty. For the Hua, contact with the vital essence of potentially fertile females (those between menarche and menopause) will seriously compromise the development of boys in the period around puberty. As a result, prepubescent boys are raised separately, and permitted no contact with any food gathered or prepared by fertile females, for a period of some years.

Among the Hua, food is a social vehicle that passes personal properties and intent from one person to another, as food transactions occur. There are two underlying beliefs of some general interest to social psychologists behind the Hua view. One is that people take on the properties of what they eat (i.e., the properties of the specific food, such as a particular animal). This is the oft cited "You are what you eat" principle. The second is the more general idea that, via contact, properties are permanently passed from one entity to another. This is the sympathetic magical law of contagion.

Hindu India

I turn now to one of the great civilizations of humankind, and one that encompasses hundreds of millions of people. In Hindu India, seen most clearly in the belief of Brahmins, food is A if not THE major vehicle for maintaining social distinctions and for enacting basic moral beliefs (Appadurai, 1981; Marriott, 1968, 1976). As Appadurai describes it, "beliefs about food encode a complex set of social and moral propositions." He also describes food as a "condensed social fact" and a "biomoral substance." The sharing of food (which includes both A and B eating food prepared by C), has a homogenizing function; it equalizes the sharers, and enhances their intimacy and solidarity (Appadurai, 1981). On the other hand, avoidance of or refusal to share food, as with members of lower castes, has a heterogenizing function; it establishes rank, distance, and segmentation. Marriott (1968, 1976) has argued that the basic caste structure of Hindu India can be recovered just by looking at permitted and forbidden food transactions. The basic rule is that one cannot accept food prepared by members of a lower caste. Reciprocally, in most cases, members of higher castes can give food to members of lower castes (Marriott, 1976).

Behind these basic Hindu beliefs is a concept of the person that is very different from the Western view. The Hindu person is a "complex, unstable and weakly bounded aggregate of biomoral substance" (Appadurai, 1981). The person is not unitary, but rather divisible, and in constant transaction with the environment (Marriott, 1976). The permeable Hindu person, like all persons, has a biological and frequent need for food, at the same time that this same food constitutes a social and moral threat to the self. The principle of you are what you eat is of obvious relevance in these beliefs, as is the principle of contagion.

The social significance of food plays out richly in both daily and festive eating occasions (Appadurai, 1981; Khare, 1976). Both the quality of food served and the conditions of serving (order of serving, who eats whose leftovers) are significant aspects of each meal, which serve to define the status of the meal participants. Appadurai describes the operation of these rules, and particularly the concerns that arise in cases of ambiguity, as gastropolitics. Ambiguities arise in family meals, festivals, and in the distribution of food in the temple. For example, in the home situation and at weddings, better quality foods and earlier serving precedence go to males and to those who are older, as well as to relatives of the husband as opposed to the wife. Conflict is produced when different rules contradict each other, as when a male wife's relative and a female husband's relative eat at the same meal.

The acceptance of a new daughter-in-law into the husband's home is a complex negotiation. As an outsider and a competitor in the kitchen, the daughter-in-law is in conflict with the mother of her husband. The daughter-in-law is served last and has minimal importance in the kitchen, initially. Over time, she assumes a more important role in the family; this progress is accomplished and measured by her increasing responsibility in the kitchen and improved status at meal times.

The moral status of food derives from notions of purity and pollution that help to define the caste structure. In Hindu thought, food is a fundamental link between humans and the gods; the gods provide the environmental conditions under which humans grow food; the cycle is completed when food offerings are made to the Gods in the temple. And the leftovers (prasadam) of the offered foods (after priests, acting for the gods, have removed some) are enhanced in value by this contact with the gods (Appadurai, 1981; Breckenridge, 1986). This is a clear example of contagion.

The central moral position of food and food transactions is illustrated in a recent comparative study of moral beliefs in Hindu Brahmin and American children (Shweder, Mahapatra, & Miller, 1987). Eight- to 10-year-old children rated seriousness of breach for each of 39 cases, concerning many practices, some involving food. The most serious four breaches for the Brahmin children all concerned food. They were: (1) The day after his father's death, the eldest son had a haircut and ate chicken; (2) One of your family members eats beef regularly; (3) One of your family members eats a dog regularly for dinner; (4) A widow in your community eats fish two or three times a week. In obvious contrast to results from American children, the following offenses received a low ranking in seriousness of breach: (29) There was a rule in a hotel; invalids and disfigured persons are not allowed in the dining hall; (32) In school a girl drew a picture. One of her classmates came, took it, and tore it up (Shweder et al., 1987). Little more need be said about major differences in the meaning of food across cultures.

YOU ARE WHAT YOU EAT

I now discuss a few principles or beliefs that I believe to be the foundation for social and moral aspects of food. The belief that "you are what you eat" is almost ubiquitous in traditional cultures. This belief includes transmission of both physical and behavioral properties, and of intent. Animals, perhaps because of their more distinctive behavioral characteristics, and their closeness to humans, are more often involved than plants. At the turn of the century, James Frazer (1890/1959) in "The Golden Bough," and Crawley (1902) in "The Mystic Rose" offered abundant examples; the ancient Greek belief that eating the flesh of the wakeful nightingale would prevent a man from sleeping; avoidance of slow animals by hunters in a number of cultures; avoidance of hedgehog by adult males in Madagascar, so that they will not become shy and retiring; avoidance of deer by Dyak males so as not to become timid; avoidance of hyenas in Morocco, so as not to become stupid; consumption of lion flesh by Hottentots to induce courage and strength. Among the Hua of Papua New Guinea, Meigs (1984) has exhaustively catalogued an amazing array of food taboos, many of which illustrate "you are what you eat." One group of these are taboos of soft or reddish plant products for pubescent males, on the grounds that such entities resemble the vagina and will feminize the males.

The "you are what you eat" principle has great intuitive appeal. Generally, when things are mixed, the result is some combination of the properties of the two components. In this framework, food should impart its properties to those who ingest it. It is only our modern conception that all foods are made up of the same small set of molecules, to which they are reduced by the process of digestion, that renders "you are what you eat," in its concrete form, untenable. Indeed, "you are what you eat" is the kind of idea that one might expect to be invented independently in many cultures.

The notion that people who eat animals become more animal-like occurs frequently in both Western and non-Western cultures. The Old Testament prohibitions on ingestion of many animals have been interpreted, by Hebrew scholars, as a means of preventing the transmission of animal instincts into man (Grunfeld, 1972/1982). "This is the general principle: the nearer the animal is to the vegetable world in its habits and composition, the less likely it is to arouse the animal nature in man, and its meat becomes the more suitable for human consumption" (Grunfeld, 1972/1982). Ancient Greek writings in support of vegetarianism cite transfer of animal properties as one argument against eating animals (Dombrowski, 1984). The concern surfaces again many times in European history, from the middle ages onward (Thomas, 1983). The evidence from traditional cultures is abundant. Frazer (1890/1959) summarizes the situation: "The savage commonly believes that by eating the flesh of an animal or man he acquires not only the physical but even the moral and intellectual qualities which were characteristic of that animal or man" (p. 573).

When wedded to the contagion principle, as mentioned earlier, "you are what you eat" becomes a means for passage of characteristics between humans. One special version of this has to do with nursing. For example, among the Tairora of Papua, New Guinea (Watson, 1983), it is believed that while the father's contribution to the characteristics of his children is mediated by his semen, the mother's contribution comes principally by her contribution of a different white liquid, breast milk. Furthermore, by Islamic Law (Altorki, 1980) nursing is a sufficient condition to establish kinship, in the sense that marriage is prohibited between children who nurse from the same woman. Similarly, in urban Mali, children who nurse from the same woman are said to share blood, and cannot marry (Dettwyler, 1988).

Experiments Using Asch's "Impressions" Technique

Given both the intuitive appeal and generality of "you are what you eat," it is of interest to determine whether this belief is operative, at some level, among Americans. We knew that American adults would not openly admit a belief in "you are what you eat," in a concrete as opposed to metaphorical sense. However, we thought we might detect an unacknowledged or unconscious belief. We (Nemeroff & Rozin, 1989) have explored this possibility using the Asch impressions technique (Asch, 1946). This technique is ideally suited to detect unacknowledged beliefs, because subjects have no indication about what the aim of the study is. Since they see only one of a number of versions of a description, they have no idea what the critical variable is. College student subjects read a short, half page vignette that described a traditional culture, providing information about location, social organization, food habits, etc. Two versions of the vignette were created, which were identical except for one aspect of the food habits. In the boar-eater case the people were described as eating wild boar while hunting marine turtle for its shell, but not eating the turtle. The turtle-eater case was the exact opposite: the people were described as eating marine turtle, and hunting boar for the tusk, but not eating the boar. Each subject read only one vignette.

After reading the vignette, subjects were asked to rate adult males in the culture on a set of 21 bipolar dimensions. Prior to the main study, different subjects rated a large number of dimensions for their boarness and for their turtleness. We selected 13 dimensions that showed substantial boar-turtle differences to use in the main study, such as excitable—phlegmatic, fast-moving—slow moving, good runner—good swimmer, and aggressive—peaceful, and eight dimensions for which there was no boar-turtle difference. Boar eaters were rated more boarlike than turtle-eaters on 11.5 of the 13 marked dimensions. A more inclusive measure was created by comparing the difference in mean scores for turtle-eater vs. boar eater subjects, on each dimension, with the difference in mean scores for pretest subjects who directly rated boar and turtle properties (these ratings included all 21 attributes, including many for which there was no difference in rated boarness versus turtleness). The correlation (rho) between culture rating differences and direct boar-turtle rating differences across the 21 dimensions was .64. Note that since members of both cultures hunted both boars and turtles, the results cannot be accounted for by proximity, familiarity or the necessities of hunting; eating seems to be the critical relation.

A second study (Nemeroff & Rozin, 1989) used the same Asch impressions paradigm to compare two variants of another hypothetical culture that differed only in that one ate an almost entirely meat diet, with elephant the primary source of meat, while the other culture ate an almost exclusively vegetarian diet. The elephant-eaters raised vegetables for sale, while the vegetarians hunted elephants, but sold the meat and tusks. Distinctive dimensions (again rated for elephantness by other subjects) included heavy–thin, strong–delicate, interesting–boring, and leathery skin-smooth skin. Elephant eaters scored as more elephant-like on all 12 marked dimensions. The correlation (rho) between the rated elephantness of 23 dimensions and the mean difference between elephant eaters and vegetarians on each dimension was .70.

We have extended this work (Rozin, Markwith, & Nemeroff, 1989) to studies using vignettes about American college students. Our data indicate that vegetarian students are seen as more plant-like, and less animal-like. One problem with all of these studies is that there is an inherent confound between "you are what you eat" and "you eat what you are." That is, people may select foods that match their personalities, and this could give rise to the pattern of data that we have obtained. We have collected evidence, using the same Asch paradigm, that indicates an unacknowledged belief that "you eat what you are." For example, people who eat equal amounts of boar and turtle but prefer turtle are rated as more turtle like than those who prefer boar. However, we also have evidence for the separate, unconfounded action of "you are what you eat." For example, students described as on a no-meat diet for medical reasons are rated as more plant like than students on another type of restricted diet.

We do not know, at this point, whether such beliefs significantly influence food decisions in our culture, nor do we know what factors make the belief more salient. For example, are animal foods more potent in the transfer of properties? Are raw/unprocessed foods more potent than cooked/processed foods? Is this belief more prominent in children (especially since it is more prominent in traditional cultures)? Our conclusion is simply that, at some level, "you are what you eat" may be a universal belief.

CONTAGION

A second belief, which subsumes "you are what you eat," is the law of contagion, one of three laws of sympathetic magic, which was originally stated by Edwin Tylor (1871/1974), and richly elaborated by Sir James Frazer (1890/1959) and Marcel Mauss (1902/1972). It was described as a belief, very common in traditional societies, that when two entities make physical contact, a permanent transfer of properties occurs. This can be summarized as: once in contact, always in contact. The psychological aspects of the law of contagion are discussed at some length by Rozin & Nemeroff (1989). A critical feature of contagion is that it is more or less dose independent; that is to say, minimal contact is sufficient to transfer enough of the "essence" in question to transform the contacted object. This can be appreciated intuitively by imagining the reaction to wearing a shirt that was worn by Adolph Hitler for 5 minutes 50 years ago. Most people find this prospect very unpleasant, and not much less unpleasant than the prospect of wearing the same shirt after it had been worn for a day by Hitler.

The implication of contagion is that every object carries an invisible and perhaps insensible record of its past contacts. For the case of food, this includes contacts of food with nonhuman entities (such as insects) and human contacts occurring in the gathering, preparation and serving of food. Contagion is particularly salient in the domain of food, simply because oral contact/incorporation is probably, with the exception of vaginal contact (the vagina being a second entry point into the body), the most intimate and affectively laden form of contact.

We (Rozin, Millman, & Nemeroff, 1986) have demonstrated the operation of the law of contagion in Americans in a number of domains. People refuse foods that have contacted offensive entities, such as insects, on the grounds that some properties have been passed in the contact. Indeed, a defining feature of disgusting entities is that they render acceptable foods inedible by contact (see below; Rozin & Fallon, 1987). Contagion beliefs are very salient in Americans outside of the domain of food. In such cases, the principal sources of contagion are other persons. Thus, most people are reluctant to wear clothing that had previously been worn by people they dislike or people they find unsavory (Rozin, Nemeroff, Wane, & Sherrod, 1989). There is some evidence for positive contagion as well, in that for some Americans, the value of a piece of clothing is enhanced if it had been worn by a loved or admired person, but this effect is much weaker and more variable than the negative effect.

As indicated in the brief description of the way Americans relate to food at the beginning of this paper, industrialization has separated food from its origins, and thus broken the personal chain of contagion that accompanies food in traditional culture. For this reason human source contagion is not very salient in American's responses to food, in contrast to India and to traditional cultures. However, we see strong effects in appropriate contexts, as in the great reluctance people have to eat a piece of food after a bite has been taken from it by a disliked or unsavory person (Rozin, Nemeroff, Wane, & Sherrod, 1989).

FOOD AS A MORAL SUBSTANCE

The principle of contagion (including "you are what you eat") concerns the transmission of properties from source to recipient. The law of contagion does not specify what determines whether a source is negative, positive or neutral. This involves moral issues. I discuss here two aspects of this morality, specifically in relation to food. One is the sense that being animal-like is immoral (inferior, nonspiritual), and the second is the confusion between physical and moral explanations.

The Human/Animal Distinction

Cross-culturally, humans see themselves as different from and above all other animals, and make efforts to distinguish themselves from animals (e.g., Ortner, 1973). For example, animal names are commonly used as insults (Leach, 1964); in our culture, being called a generic *animal* is insulting. Intimate relations with animals, including the ingestion of animal flesh, tend to blur this distinction, with consequent moral implications. One trend in western European history, since the middle ages, has been to remove both the appearance and the reality of an animal nature of humans (Elias, 1978; Thomas, 1983). Elias (1978), in accounting for the evolution of table manners, beginning with Medieval Europe, states that ". . . people, in the course of the civilizing process, seek to suppress in themselves every characteristic that they feel to be animal." I have already referred to the Old Testament view that being animal-like is immoral (Grunfeld, 1972/1982), and that ingestion of animals can produce this undesirable effect.

The Moral/Physical Confusion

Food is by its nature a biologically necessary substance; the moral side is optional. As a biological entity, a source of nutrients and toxins, food relates directly to health. But health itself has a complex relation to morality. Piaget (1965) notes that the predominant theory of illness in preschool children is that it results from moral transgressions. The same notion is the most frequent theory of illness in traditional cultures (Murdock, 1980). Although American adults seem to prefer physical to moral accounts of disease, there are clear moral overtones in their attitudes to disease. This is particularly clear in the case of AIDS, but it has a long history (Sontag, 1977). Thus, in 19th-century America, cholera was seen as a product of living in crowded and unclean quarters, a situation which was framed in moral terms. Before the rise of germ theory at the end of the 19th century, the American medical profession held to such a moral explanation for cholera (Rosenberg, 1962).

In the domain of food, there is a tendency in American and European culture to interpret food habits in physical as opposed to moral terms. Examples are efforts to explain the Hebrew pork taboo, which almost certainly has moral/social origins, in terms of avoidance of trichinosis, or explanations of modern table manners (such a not eating from a common pot, or using silverware) as hygienic, when they appear to have arisen as attempts to be less animal like and more distinct from lower class people (Elias, 1978). Similarly, Westerners may try to justify the Hindu food handling rules in terms of minimization of microbial transfer. But the facts are that higher caste people can consume raw food purchased from lower class people, but they cannot consume the microbially much safer cooked food from these same people; the cooked food has more of the persona of its maker than does the raw food.

Moral/physical confusions about food appear frequently in American culture. Attitudes to meat among vegetarians are often a complex mixture of moral and health concerns. Attitudes to supposed unhealthy foods such as sugar have a distinct moral character. Historically, American health movements have been inextricably intertwined with the good, moral life (Whorton, 1982).

DISGUST: THE FOOD-RELATED, MORAL EMOTION

Disgust, one of the basic and universal emotions, encompasses the basic issues raised in this paper. Disgust is the only emotion explicitly related to food. Although in American and other cultures it is also expressed in nonfood situations, there is much to indicate that at its core this emotion is about food (Rozin & Fallon, 1987). The distinctive facial expression of disgust is functionally related to movements that would expel food from the mouth. The name, "disgust,'' itself means bad taste, and the characteristic physiological concomitant of disgust is nausea, a state which is very effective in suppressing ingestion.

Following up on the seminal paper by Angyal (1941) on disgust, Fallon and I (Rozin & Fallon, 1987) defined disgust as: ''Revulsion at the prospect of (oral) incorporation of an offensive object. The offensive objects are contaminating; that is, if they even briefly contact an acceptable food, they tend to render that food unacceptable.'' Disgust, as we use the term, is to be distinguished from distaste, a dislike for the sensory qualities of a potential food (Rozin & Fallon, 1980). Disgusting foods are offensive; the idea of the food, its nature or origin, are involved in the rejection. This is a much more cognitive and moral base than simply rejection because of bad taste.

The principle of contagion is contained within our definition of disgust. It was through the study of disgust that we came upon the literature on the law of contagion. ''You are what you eat,'' as well, is at the center of disgust, since oral incorporation is a defining aspect of disgust. Concern about consumption of animals is probably at the heart of disgust. Angyal (1941) pointed out that almost all objects of disgust are of animal origin, with feces as the universal disgust. We have confirmed this claim, and suggest that the basic category of disgusting things is all animals and their products (Rozin & Fallon, 1987). The small number of animals or animal products that are considered edible in most cultures can be thought of as exceptions to this general principle. It is notable that in our culture and many others, some care is taken to disguise the animal origin of foods. We rarely eat whole animals, or animal heads, and sometimes have a flash of disgust when reminded of the animal origins of something we are eating (Angyal, 1941).

Disgust seems to reflect a moral concern, with a veneer of physical concern. We ask subjects if they would consume a glass of juice after a cockroach was dipped into it for a moment. All American subjects say ''no,'' pointing out that cockroaches are disease vectors. When we repeat this question, but now specify that the cockroach is dead and sterilized, we find just about the same negative response. Subjects, somewhat embarrassed that what looked like a good reason has little force, eventually come to the position that it is the cockroachness itself that bothers them. Cockroaches are offensive creatures, and people don't wish this to be transmitted to them.

We suspect that disgust is the emotion that maintains and expresses the extensive avoidances of foods in specific contexts in India, and is the emotion most associated with pollution and purity. It is intimately associated with toilet training, and can be seen as a powerful cultural vehicle to internalize strong rejections, including culturally abhorrent activities outside of the food domain, such as incest or bestiality. Disgust is one of the powerful emotions that are engaged in the process of socialization. In a sense, disgust, originally a food-related emotion, is also the moral emotion that protects the soul from threats, just as fear primarily protects the body.

CONCLUSION AND SUMMARY:

I have argued that food is, in many ways, a quintessentially social substance. The existence of cuisines, including elaborate preparation of food, guarantees that the foods we eat pass through the hands of others, and are shaped by others. The contagion principle, amplified by the belief in "you are what you eat," makes of food an intimate interpersonal message. The almost complete absence of discussions about food in American social psychology probably follows from the decontextualization of food in Western industrialized cultures. A Hindu Indian would be astounded by the fact that a South African White, who considers South African Blacks a lower form of human and refuses to associate with Blacks in many contexts, may employ a Black cook or otherwise eat foods prepared by Blacks. Clearly, it is possible to take food out of the social context that I have presented here. But for most people in the world, it is embedded in this context, and is a major vehicle of interpersonal traffic. My aim has been to call this fact to the attention of psychologists, and hopefully engage their interest in it.

ACKNOWLEDGMENTS

Preparation of this paper was supported by a grant from the University of Pennsylvania Research Fund and by funds from the Mental Health Research Network on Determinants and Consequences of Health-Promoting and Health-Damaging Behaviors of the John D. and Catherine T. MacArthur Foundation. Thanks to Carol Nemeroff for collaboration on some of the work presented, and to Arjun Appadurai and Carol Nemeroff for critical readings of this manuscript. Thanks to Solomon E. Asch for providing an inspiration and a model for my research, and for indirectly providing the opportunity to compose and present this paper.

REFERENCES

Altorki, S. (1980). Milk-kinship in Arab society: An unexplored problem in the ethnography of marriage. *Ethnology, 19*, 233–244.

Angyal, A. (1941). Disgust and related aversions. *Journal of Abnormal and Social Psychology, 36*, 393–412.

Appadurai, A. (1981). Gastro-politics in Hindu South Asia. *American Ethnologist, 8*, 494–511.

Asch, S. E. (1946). Forming impressions of personality. *Journal of Abnormal and Social Psychology, 41*, 258–290.

Breckenridge, C. A. (1986). Food, politics and pilgrimage in South India, 1350–1650 A.D. In R. S. Khare & M. S. A. Rao (Eds.), *Food, society, and culture: Aspects in South Asian food systems*. Durham, NC: Carolina Academic Press.

Crawley, E. (1902). *The mystic rose. A study of primitive marriage*. London: Macmillan.

Dettwyler, K. A. (1988). More than nutrition: Breast feeding in urban Mali. *Medical Anthropology Quarterly, 2*, 172–183.

Dombrowski, D. A. (1984). *The philosophy of vegetarianism*. Amherst: University of Massachusetts Press.

Elias, N. (1978). *The history of manners. The civilizing process: Vol. I* (E. Jephcott, Trans.). New York: Pantheon Books. (Original work published 1939).

Frazer, J. G. (1890/1959). *The golden bough: A study in magic and religion*. New York: Macmillan. (Reprint of 1922 abridged edition, edited by T. H. Gaster; original work published, 1890).

Grunfeld, D. I. (1982). *The Jewish dietary laws. Volume One. Dietary laws regarding forbidden and permitted foods, with particular reference to meat and meat products (3rd edition)*. London: Soncino Press. (Original edition, 1972).

Khare, R. S. (1976). *The Hindu hearth and home*. Durham, NC: Carolina Academic Press.

Leach, E. (1964). Anthropological aspects of language: Animal categories and verbal abuse. In E. Lenneberg (Ed.), *New directions in the study of language* (pp. 23–64). Cambridge, MA: MIT Press.

Marriott, M. (1968). Caste ranking and food transactions: A matrix analysis. In M. Singer & B. S. Cohn (Eds.), *Structure and change in Indian society* (pp. 133–171). Chicago: Aldine.

Marriot, M. (1976). Hindu transactions: Diversity without dualism. In B. Kapferer (Ed.), *Transaction and meaning: Directions in the anthropology of exchange and symbolic behavior* (pp. 109–142). Philadelphia: Institute for the Study of Human Issues.

Mauss, M. (1902/1972). *A general theory of magic* (R. Brain, Trans.). New York: W. W. Norton. (Original work published 1902).

Meigs, A. S. (1978). A Papuan perspective on pollution. *Man, 13*, 304–318.

Meigs, A. S. (1984). *Food, sex, and pollution: A New Guinea religion*. New Brunswick, NJ: Rutgers University Press.

Meigs, A. S. (1988). Food as a cultural construction. *Food & Foodways, 2*, 341–358.

Murdock, G. P. (1980). *Theories of illness. A world survey*. Pennsylvania: University of Pittsburgh Press.

Nemeroff, C. J., & Rozin, P. (1989). An unacknowledged belief that ''you are what you eat'' among college students in the United States: An application of the demand-free ''impressions'' technique. *Ethos, 17*(1), 50–69.

Ortner, S. B. (1973). Sherpa purity. *American Anthropologist, 75*, 49–63.

Piaget, J. (1965). *The moral judgment of the child* (trans. M. Gabain). New York: Free Press. Original work published.

Rosenberg, C. E. (1962). *The cholera years*. Illinois: University of Chicago Press.

Rozin, P., & Fallon, A. E. (1980). Psychological categorization of foods and non-foods: A preliminary taxonomy of food rejections. *Appetite, 1*, 193–201.

Rozin, P., & Fallon, A. E. (1987). A perspective on disgust. *Psychological Review, 94*, 23–41.

Rozin, P., Markwith, M., & Nemeroff, C. J. (1989). *''You are what you eat'' or ''you eat what you are''; clarifying the nature of ''magical beliefs'' in Americans*. (manuscript in preparation)

Rozin, P., Millman, L., & Nemeroff, C. (1986). Operation of the laws of sympathetic magic in disgust and other domains. *Journal of Personality and Social Psychology, 50*, 703–712.

Rozin, P., & Nemeroff, C. J. (1989). The laws of sympathetic magic: A psychological analysis of similarity and contagion. In J. Stigler, G. Herdt & R. A. Shweder (Eds.), *Cultural psychology: The Chicago symposia on human development*. New York: Cambridge University Press (in press).

Rozin, P., Nemeroff, C. J., Wane, M., & Sherrod, A. (1989). Operation of the sympathetic magical law of contagion in interpersonal attitudes among Americans. *Bulletin of the Psychonomic Sciences, 27*, 367–370.

Shweder, R. A., Mahapatra, M., & Miller, J. G. (1987). Culture and moral development. In J. Kagan & S. Lamb (Eds.), *The emergence of moral concepts in young children* (pp. 1–82). Illinois: University of Chicago Press.

Sontag, S. (1977). *Illness as metaphor*. New York: Farrar, Straus & Giroux.

Thomas, K. (1983). *Man and the natural world*. New York: Pantheon Books.

Tylor, E. B. (1871/1974). *Primitive culture: Researches into the development of mythology, philosophy, religion, art and custom*. New York: Gordon Press. (Original work published 1871).

Watson, J. (1983). *Tairora culture: Contingency and pragmatism*. Seattle: University of Washington Press.

Whorton, J. C. (1982). *Crusaders for fitness*. Princeton, NJ: Princeton University Press.

III COGNITION

7 Perceptual Organization Affects Both the Learning and Integration of Object Properties

John Ceraso
Institute for Cognitive Studies, Rutgers University

ABSTRACT

In this study we investigated the learning of four different kinds of pairs: form and color, form and mode, letter and color, and letter and letter. The members of each pair were either conjoined in one object (unitary condition), or were separately placed in different objects (separate condition). Half the subjects learned under intentional instructions, while the others were given incidental instructions. Asch has shown that items are more easily associated in the unitary condition as compared to the separate condition. We found that with intentional learning there was no difference between unitary and separate conditions. With incidental learning, however, we found a strong unitary to separate superiority. I take the results to mean that with intentional learning, mnemonic transformation of the material may obscure the role of perceptual organization in memory, while incidental learning will highlight it. Analyses of the incidental learning results suggested that the properties which constitute an object are available before integration, but that perceptual organization affects the availability of the properties themselves, and also the ease with which they are integrated.

INTRODUCTION

This project originated when the author was research assistant to Professor Asch at Swarthmore in the late 1950s. At that time Asch had begun to study the role of perceptual organization in memory. He conceived of studying the formation of an association under two conditions; one in which the properties to be associated were aspects of the same visual object, and the other in which these same properties were aspects of two different objects. The paradigm was expressed in several different forms, one of which is shown in Fig. 7.1a, where the two properties to be associated are form and color. In the unitary condition the form and color make up the colored object, while in the separate condition the top item has a distinctive form but is always the same color, and the bottom item has a distinctive color but always the same shape. In these experiments (Asch, Ceraso, & Heimer, 1960) we found substantially more correct pairing of the two properties in the unitary condition than in the separate condition. An additional finding was that the difference between unitary and separate conditions was greater with incidental learning than it was with intentional learning, suggesting that the subject's spontaneous apprehension of the visual scene leads to a representation which is easier to learn in the unitary condition than it is in the separate condition.

The experiments I report had their beginnings in a doctoral dissertation by Robert Velk (Ceraso, 1985). Velk studied the case where a letter was used instead of a form (see Fig. 7.1b). A letter printed on a card is, of course, itself a form, and if we used letters with subjects who did not know their meaning, then there would be no reason to expect memory differences between forms and letters. But our subjects are familiar with these letters, and each letter has a corresponding sound and meaning. Velk's question was whether the meaning given to the stimuli by the subjects would alter the way in which the stimuli were encoded and recalled.

Velk ran several studies with letters; in some he used letters combined with colors, and in others he used letters combined with letters, as in Fig. 7.1c, and Fig. 7.1d. In all his studies the result was the same; no difference between unitary and separate stimuli when letters were properties of the stimuli. His

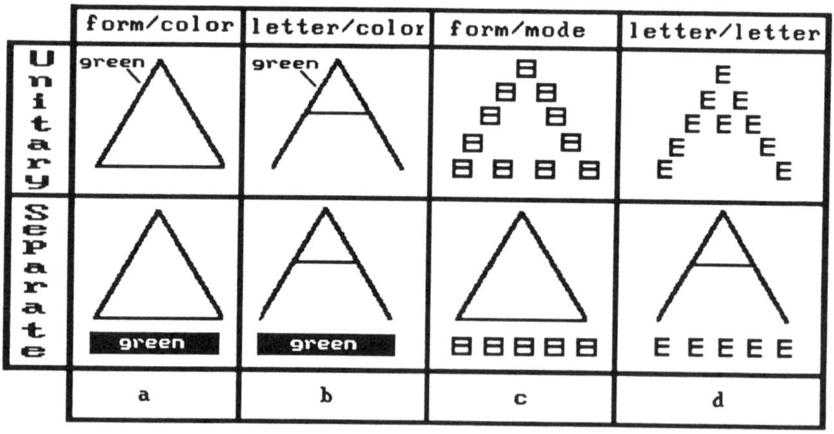

	form/color	letter/color	form/mode	letter/letter
Unitary				
Separate				
	a	b	c	d

FIG. 7.1. Unitary and separate stimuli. All figures are drawn in black unless otherwise indicated.

results show that a unitary-separate perceptual difference does not necessarily generate a corresponding memory difference.

Velk's experiments suggest that memory for a visual array is not solely determined by the physical properties of the array since the physical structure of a form/color stimulus is no different from the physical structure of a letter/color stimulus. The difference in memory between them would seem to be due to the different ways in which they are encoded, with forms encoded as visual objects, and letters encoded as linguistic entities.

When shapes are regarded as visual objects it is reasonable to suppose that the graphic properties of the stimuli are pertinent to their representation in memory. The unitary display should be represented as one object comprising the properties of form and color. The separate display should be represented as two objects with form a property of one object and color a property of the other. The difference in the way in which these stimuli are remembered I would attribute to the difference in the way in which they are represented.

When the shapes are regarded as letters, however, the properties are in different domains; that is, the letter is an abstract linguistic entity, the color a visual entity. I propose that in order to integrate these properties some transformation of the material is necessary. For example, if the letter B were presented, and it were colored blue, then the subject could conceive of the mnemonic "bluejay" as a vehicle by which the two could be integrated. That mnemonic (or one comparable) should be derived as easily for the separate as the unitary condition. If the unitary and separate displays in the letter/color condition are represented by the same kind of mnemonic, then one can understand why they do not differ in memory. The implication of this analysis is that memory for a visual array is tied to the way in which it is represented, and that the representation is constructed after the physical properties of the array have been apprehended.

EXPERIMENTS: RATIONALE AND PROCEDURE

In the experiments reported in this chapter we attempted to influence the way in which subjects encode the presented material. Of special interest were the stimuli that have a letter as part of the display. Two conditions of this kind were studied: letter/color, and letter/letter (see Fig. 7.1b, and 7.1d). The aim of the experiment was to have the subjects regard the *letters as shapes* and not as *linguistic entities*. We hypothesized that if the letters were encoded as shapes then the physical differences between unitary and separate stimuli would be relevant to the way in which these stimuli are represented, and therefore we should find a memory difference between them, just as in the case of form/color combinations. That outcome would support the hypothesis that in earlier studies, where no unitary-separate difference was found, subjects had encoded the letters as linguistic entities. Two comparison conditions, form/color, and form/mode (Fig. 7.1a and, 7.1c) were also studied. The stimuli constructed for these conditions matched the first two conditions structurally, but differed in that letters were not present. To construct the forms and modes we began with the letter shapes and altered them so that, in our estimation, they would not remind the subjects of letters. Figure 7.1 shows one illustrative pair for each condition of the experiment. The triangle in Fig. 7.1c is, *qua* shape, very similar to the letter A in Fig. 7.1a; the element (mode) in Fig. 7.1c is very similar, *qua* shape, to the letter E in Fig. 7.1d.

Two sets of instructions were given: The intentional instructions directed the subjects to try to associate the two properties given on each card so that at recall they could remember how these properties went together. The instructions were explicit in naming the two properties to be associated. We alternated the order in which the properties were named (e.g., form and color, or color and form), so as not to emphasize one property over the other. The incidental instructions stated that the experimenters were preparing material for use in an experiment and that we wanted to be sure that the materials were visually clear. The subjects task was to rate each card, on a scale from 1 to 5, for visual clarity. It was our hope that these instructions would emphasize the visual properties of the stimuli and would minimize verbal encoding. As in the intentional condition, the relevant properties were named. There were eight pairs in each condition of the experiment and each pair was seen for 5 seconds. After presentation of the list the subjects were given a 5 minute arithmetical series completion task, and they were then tested for recall. The subjects were given a blank answer booklet and asked to reproduce the cards as they had seen them, one pair to a page with order of presentation not important. When the subjects had remembered as many pairs as they could, they were also asked to reproduce any isolated items they recalled, which they had not already given as pair members. The subjects drew the shapes or letters, and wrote the names of the colors.

To summarize: There were four types of material used—form/color, letter/color, form/mode, and letter/letter. Each of these was presented as a unitary or separate structure, and the instructions were either intentional or incidental. These factors yielded 16 groups, with 15 subjects per group. The subjects were recruited chiefly from the undergraduate population of Rutgers University in Newark, but other subjects outside the university, comparable in age and education, were also included.

RESULTS

Table 7.1 shows the number of pairs correctly recalled by each group. The results are very consistent, though in some ways at odds with previous results. For none of the intentional groups is there a significant difference between

TABLE 7.1
Mean Number of Correct-Pairs

	Incidental	Intentional
form/color		
unitary	4.43	4.57
separate	2.50	4.71
form/mode		
unitary	1.36	2.93
separate	.14	3.50
letter/color		
unitary	2.93	4.00
separate	1.14	3.14
letter/letter		
unitary	2.71	4.21
separate	.43	3.93
Maximum number correct = 8		

unitary and separate arrangements, while for the incidental groups, unitary displays are consistently superior to separate displays. I had predicted exactly this result for the letter displays since I thought the letters would foster mnemonic encoding under intentional instructions, and override the perceptual difference that would reveal itself under incidental instructions. The unexpected result was that there was no unitary-separate difference for form/color and form/mode with intentional instructions. Because this result has been repeatedly obtained, the outcome was a surprise. After reviewing the experiment I believe the most plausible explanation for the unexpected finding is that the form stimuli we used were very familiar and nameable shapes. In attempting to draw shapes that were structurally similar to the letters we produced familiar forms. The eight forms were: circle, triangle, square, diamond, cross, semicircle, a shape which looked like a house, and an x with lines connecting the top and bottom (these forms corresponded to the following letters; O, A, H, X, T, U, M, and Z). Given easily nameable shapes, the subjects may have been encouraged to use verbal mnemonics in the form/color and form/mode conditions as well as in the letter/color and letter/letter conditions. In contrast, the experiments of Asch et al. (1960) had used novel shapes. In any case, I think that we have learned something from the unanticipated result.

I began with the assumption that there was a significant difference in the encoding of displays with letters and those without letters, but the results have made me reconsider that position. It now seems that the difference is a relative matter. Unitary items with letters are more likely to be verbally encoded than are geometric shapes, but the latter may also be encoded by verbal mnemonics. It also seems probable that verbal mnemonics are easier to generate in the separate conditions for the letter stimuli than for the shape stimuli. These factors would make it more likely that the unitary-separate memory difference is eliminated with the letter stimuli than with the shape stimuli, but they do not preclude the possibility of a failure to find a difference with shape stimuli, especially when the forms are nameable and familiar.

In summary, it seems that when given the explicit instruction *to learn* visual material, subjects can use strategies that offset the perceptual structures and render them irrelevant. Originally we believed that effect to be limited to stimuli with letters, but we find that under some conditions the result can also be obtained with geometrical shapes and colors.

If it is true that the learning that occurs with intentional instructions is the result of a complex of factors which include the perceptual nature of the material and the encoding strategies used by subjects, then it should be informative to examine more closely the learning that occurs under incidental instructions. These instructions direct the subjects to regard the stimuli as visual entities and to make a judgment about their visual clarity. Much of the information we acquire in everyday life is obtained without the deliberate attempt to learn. We look, we listen, we understand, and later we can remember what we saw, what we heard, and what we understood. I believe that the incidental condition imitates that kind of learning. Obviously, it is not only through the deliberate mnemonics of the laboratory that we learn. The schemata we use to organize and comprehend our everyday experience are unquestionably the prime shapers of memory. From the results of the incidental condition we may learn something about the effect that the act of looking at objects attentively has on memory.

Several investigators (Nissen, 1979; Stefurak & Boynton, 1986; Treisman, 1986) have argued that, early in processing, the properties of a unit are independently processed and that is taken to support the idea that properties are available first and only then put together to form a unit. It is hard to evaluate this hypothesis as any alternative hypotheses against which it might be tested have not been clearly articulated. Certainly, the converse hypothesis does not make much sense. How could one first put together properties which are not yet available? In its present form the issue seems to based on the old question of whether the parts are prior to the whole, or the whole prior to the parts. Rather than casting my vote on that issue I argue that there is a sense in which both ideas are true. In order to develop the argument I have evolved two measures of a unit, one of which emphasizes the items, while the other emphasizes their integration. I call the first measure available-item pairs, and the second, correct-pairs.

An available-item pair is a pair both of whose members have been recalled, but not necessarily correctly paired. For example, if one of the presented pairs is a green triangle and the subject recalls a green circle and also recalls triangle as an isolated property, green triangle would qualify as an available-item pair. If items have priority, and the available-item pairs are derived from the independently processed available items, then we should be able to predict available-item pairs from available items. If the pairs are in some sense prior then there should be more pairs then would be expected, given the number of available items.

Tables 7.2 and 7.3 give the following information: first, the mean number of items recalled for each property. Second, the predicted number of available-item pairs, and third, the number of available-item pairs actually obtained. The data were compiled in the following way: First, for each subject we obtained the probability of recall for each property. For example, if a subject recalled six forms and four colors then, since there are eight possible items in each case, the recall probabilities of form and color would be .75 and .50, respectively. The joint probability of recalling both the form and color of a particular pair would be .375, and, given that there are eight possible pairs, the predicted number of available-item pairs for that subject would be three. These predicted values are compared to the values actually obtained. The values in Tables 7.2 and 7.3 are the means for the 15 subjects in each condition. Table 7.2 presents the data for the incidental condition and Table 7.3 presents the corresponding data for the intentional condition. For the reasons given earlier I am mainly concerned with the incidental condition.

There are two aspects of the data of Table 7.2 which I believe to be important. First, there is the good agreement between the predicted scores and the obtained scores. I should mention that very good agreement is also found at the level of the individual subjects. Furthermore, the agreement between predicted and obtained scores is of roughly the same magnitude for unitary and separate stimuli.

TABLE 7.2
Mean Items and Available-Item Pairs for the Incidental Condition

	Obtained Available-Items		Predicted Available-Item Pairs	Obtained Available-Item Pairs
	form	color		
unitary	5.80	5.20	3.78	4.40
separate	4.40	5.13	2.98	3.20
	form	mode		
unitary	4.73	2.67	1.58	1.67
separate	3.00	2.00	.72	.80
	letter	color		
unitary	4.40	4.93	2.85	3.06
separate	3.53	4.27	1.90	1.93
	letter	letter		
unitary	4.73	3.80	2.32	3.13
separate	4.07	2.27	1.24	1.60

Maximum correct = 8

TABLE 7.3
Mean Items and Available-Item Pairs for the Intentional Condition

	Obtained Available-Items		Predicted Available-Item Pairs	Obtained Available-Item Pairs
	form	color		
unitary	5.80	5.47	3.96	4.70
separate	5.53	6.13	4.32	4.80
	form	mode		
unitary	5.93	3.66	2.67	3.20
separate	5.73	4.53	3.33	4.00
	letter	color		
unitary	5.47	5.80	4.12	4.47
separate	5.33	5.93	4.02	4.13
	letter	letter		
unitary	5.53	4.80	3.40	4.40
separate	5.53	4.60	3.25	4.13

Maximum correct = 8

Second, an analysis of variance of the obtained available-item pairs shows a significant difference for unitary and separate stimuli. When we ran an analysis of covariance for these pairs, however, using the total number of items available as the covariate, that difference evaporated. The reader may have noticed that the obtained scores tend to be a bit higher than would be expected by chance, but, as Nissen (1979) has pointed out, these are probably due to certain artifacts such as occasional loss of attention during exposure.

The two facts that I glean from the data may seem at first to be somewhat contradictory. On the one hand, the number of available-item pairs recalled can be completely accounted for by the number of items the subject recalls, and this is equally true for both unitary and separate stimuli. From this perspective, items come first in that the available-item pairs are generated by the independent recall of the individual items. On the other hand, the pair comes first in that the number of items recalled is significantly greater for unitary stimuli than it is for separate stimuli, and this shows that the way the pairs are organized determines the rate with which *the items themselves* are available for recall. Although many details need to be filled in, I believe there is no real contradiction between these findings.

I propose that at a first level of processing, resources can be simultaneously brought to bear on both properties of a visual unit, whereas properties that are aspects of different units are processed separately. I assume that this is the basis of the unitary item recall superiority. Second, the data suggest that the members of both unitary and separate pairs are independently processed. That is, I propose that unitary stimuli are simultaneously *and* independently processed, and that separate stimuli are successively *and* independently processed. As far as I can see there need be no necessary relation between simultaneous-successive processing and independent-dependent processing. The data we have obtained in the present experiment can be taken as evidence for this conclusion. In previous studies of the *perception* of unitary and separate stimuli (Ceraso, 1985), we also found that while the properties of unitary and separate stimuli were detected independently, divided attention had no adverse effect on the detection of properties of the unitary display, but did impede the detection of separately organized properties. Again, the evidence points to simultaneous processing of unitary stimuli, successive processing of separate stimuli, but independent processing of both.

The preceding analysis has dealt with the relation between item recall and available-item pair recall. I turn now to a discussion of correct-pairs. Table 7.1 shows a substantial superiority of unitary correct-pairs to separate correct-pairs with incidental instructions. Considering the corresponding superiority of available-item pairs we asked whether the unitary-separate difference in correct-pairs could be accounted for by the difference in available-item pairs. One way in which we examined that question was to try to correct for differences in available-item pairs by obtaining the ratio of correct-pairs to available-item pairs. We derived this ratio for each subject and based on those scores we obtained the mean ratio for teach group. These data are given in Table 7.4.

One can see that even when the difference in number of available-item pairs is taken into account, the unitary correct-pairs in the incidental group are still superior to the separate correct-pairs. We also ran an analysis of covariance on correct-pairs where total number of items recalled was the covariate. The analysis showed that for the incidental group, recall of the unitary correct-pairs remained significantly greater than recall of the separate correct-pairs. An interest-

TABLE 7.4
Mean Ratios of Correct-Pairs
to Available-Item Pairs

	Incidental	Intentional
form/color		
unitary	.95	.88
separate	.77	.92
form/mode		
unitary	.76	.83
separate	.28	.82
letter/color		
unitary	.89	.74
separate	.62	.69
letter/letter		
unitary	.88	.88
separate	.15	.87

ing finding is that ratio of correct-pairs to available-item pairs is about the same for incidental and intentional unitary stimuli even though the latter enjoy an advantage in available-item pairs. The ratio for separate stimuli show a striking decrement with incidental instructions.

To summarize: The incidental condition allows us to observe the effect of perceptual organization uncontaminated by the deliberate use of mnemonic strategies. The analysis of this condition suggests that perceptual unity has two separate effects; an effect on *item availability,* and an effect on *correct pairing.* The availability of an item in both the unitary and separate conditions was independent of the availability of its pair-mate, and the number of available-item pairs a subject recalled was accounted for by the number of items available and not vice versa. These facts support the hypothesis that items are available before pairs. The first effect of perceptual organization, however, can be seen in that more items are available in the unitary condition than in the separate condition. The second effect of perceptual organization is seen in the superiority of the unitary condition to the separate condition in the number of correct-pairs. The superiority of the unitary condition holds even when differences in item availability are taken into account. The perceptual schemata that are operative in attentive viewing of a scene lead to a memory trace which integrates unitary stimuli more effectively than separate stimuli. In fact, we regard it as a challenge to account for *any* integration that occurs in the separate displays. Without intention and the use of mnemonic strategies, and without perceptual unity what is it that integrates the properties of separate units? Of course, one cannot rule out the possibility of verbal encoding of these displays. A second possibility is that subjects in the separate condition attempt to encode the whole card with all its properties. That encoding would be more complex, put more demand upon the subjects and might, therefore, be successful less often.

DISCUSSION

Related Literature

In recent years there has been growing interest in perceptual organization in studies of both memory and perception. An important force in this direction has been the work of Treisman (1986). From her work Treisman has come to the Lockean conclusion that in perception one first detects simple features and then puts these together to construct the objects which constitute the visual world. For example, in studies of target detection she has shown that simple colors and shapes are found as quickly when embedded in arrays with many distractors as when only few distractors are present. Conjunctions of these same properties, however, are detected more slowly as the number of distractors is increased. This finding is compatible with the idea that perceptual elements are registered in an early, parallel analysis of the visual array, while conjunctions are only apprehended after attention has been directed to successive portions of the visual array.

Nissen (1979) has attempted to explicate the notion of integration. In her experiments subjects are shown four simultaneously presented colored shapes. One can regard each stimulus as having three distinctive properties, i.e., shape, color, and location. Then subjects are given one of these properties as a cue and asked to recall the other two. Nissen's results are quite striking. When location is given as a cue, recall of color and shape are independent; that is, the probability of recalling a given property (shape or color) is the same when its companion property is recalled as when it is not. This finding is compatible with the findings we presented earlier regarding available-item pairs. What is surprising, however, is that when either shape or color is the cue than there is a dependence on location, and it is rare for a subject to recall the associated color or shape without also recalling location. These findings suggest that color and shape are never directly integrated and that it is only through the link to a common location that they are known to belong together. If I interpret Nissen correctly, then I think there is a problem with this formulation as a general statement about integration. In many experiments, for example, the ones we reported earlier, the pairs are presented successively and in the same location. Under these conditions one observes correct pairing of shape and color without a distinctive location to mediate the pairing. It is not that we question Nissen's findings, indeed, we have confirmed them in our laboratory. The interesting question is why direct pairing of shape and color are not observed with her procedures when direct pairing does occur with list learning procedures.

A related set of findings have been presented by Stefurak and Boynton (1986). These investigators used a procedure similar to that used by Nissen. Subjects were presented with five color/shape pairs presented simultaneously for 5 seconds. The critical variable in their experiment was the subject's activity during the presentation period. In the experimental condition subjects were engaged in a demanding arithmetic task and were given respectable monetary rewards for correct answers. When tested for recall with a recognition procedure, subjects were able to distinguish between new and old properties, but were not able to distinguish between new and old conjunctions or properties. In a control condition, where the distractor procedure was not employed, subjects could distinguish between new and old conjunctions. These important findings suggest that items are available for recall before integration occurs and that integration requires some additional activity which is prevented by the distractor task.

These three lines of investigation all point to two stages of learning where properties are apprehended first and are then integrated. The analysis is reminiscent of older theories that postulated item learning and associative learning as distinct aspects of associative learning (Rock & Ceraso, 1964; Underwood & Schultz, 1960). The findings I presented earlier regarding the distinction between available pairs and correct pairs is also consistent with a two-stage formulation of associative learning. The difference between my thinking and the thinking of the investigators who performed the three lines of work reviewed concerns their belief that the unit only comes into existence after item detection. In the present study and in previous work we have shown that the detection and recall of these items is itself influenced by perceptual organization. Studies supporting a feature integration theory of unit formation have usually studied the problem using only unitary stimuli. When both unitary and separate stimuli are included in the investigation, however, the unique effects of the perceptual organization of units can be observed.

SUMMARY AND CONCLUSIONS

The experiments I have reported lead to the following conclusions:

1. Differences in the perceptual structure of properties are not necessarily depicted in the memory representations of those properties. Rather, the representation can take many forms depending on the activity of the learner. At one extreme, we have the finding of Stefurak and Boynton (1986), which shows that with distraction, the forms and colors of an array of colored objects can be recognized, but that the conjunctions of color and shape cannot be recognized. At the other extreme, we find that with an attitude of careful visual inspection, but with no attempt to learn, subjects recall more unitary conjunctions than they do separate conjunctions. Finally, when intentional learning instructions are given, unitary and separate conjunctions may be recalled equally well. I take the last mentioned finding to mean that with intention to learn, mnemonic strategies determine the way in which the material is encoded and make the perceptual structure of the array irrelevant.

2. We conducted analyses of the incidental conditions since it was in those conditions that substantial memory differences were found between the unitary and separate displays. Of major concern was the effect of perceptual structure on item recall and associative recall. Independence of recall of items was found for both unitary and separate displays. That is, the recall of one member of a pair was independent of the recall of the other member. The number of items recalled, however, was a function of the nature of the display since more items were recalled in the unitary condition than in the separate condition. This result was consistent with findings from our previous studies of perception where we found independent detection of the properties of both unitary and separate displays, coupled with the finding that divided attention had no adverse effect on unitary displays, but did impede the detection of separately organized properties. The important point here is that the difference in the way attention is distributed over the properties of unitary and separate stimuli results in a clear difference in the degree to which these properties are recalled.

3. Associative recall, that is, the correct pairing of the properties of a display, is also a function of the way in which the properties are organized. Pairing in the unitary condition was superior to pairing in the separate condition, and furthermore, that superiority in pairing was over and above what could be accounted for by the unitary superiority in item learning. We believe one can most directly observe the effect of perceptual encoding on memory in the incidental condition, where subjects are carefully looking at the objects as visual entities and are not actively trying to learn. We believe that the memory difference between unitary and separate displays under incidental conditions reflects the relative ease of constructing a representation of a single object compared with constructing a representation of a scene consisting of two objects.

In summary, the results suggest that there is a sense in which the whole is prior to the parts, and a sense in which the parts are prior to the whole. The detection and recall of the properties of visual objects is greatly affected by structure. Properties which are part of the same structure are more readily detected and recalled than properties which are components of different structures. But these properties are treated independently and require further processing before they are integrated.

ACKNOWLEDGMENT

I would like to acknowledge the contributions of Frank Gengaro, Joy Layng, and Kathleen Lucas, who are graduate students at the Institute for Cognitive Studies. They helped in designing the studies and they ran the experiments.

REFERENCES

Asch, S. E., Ceraso, J., & Heimer, W. (1960). Perceptual conditions of association. *Psychological Monographs, 74*. whole No. 3.

Ceraso, J. (1985). Unit formation in perception and memory. In G. H. Bower (Ed.), *The psychology of learning and motivation* (Vol. *19*). Orlando, FL: Academic Press.

Nissen, M. J. (1979). Identification, localization, and the processing of conjunctions. *Talk presented to the Psychonomic Society,* Phoenix, Arizona. November.

Rock, I., & Ceraso, J. (1964). Toward a cognitive theory of associative learning. In C. Scheerer (Ed.), *Cognition: Theory, research, promise.* New York: Harper & Row.

Stefurak, D. L., & Boynton, R. M. (1986). Independence of memory for categorically different colors and shapes. *Perception and Psychophysics, 39,*(3), 164–174.

Treisman, A. (1986). Features and objects in visual processing. *Scientific American, 255,* 114–125.

Underwood, B. J., & Schultz, R. W. (1960). *Meaningfulness and verbal learning.* Chicago: Lippincott.

8 Some Reflections on Drama and the Dramatic Experience

Henry Gleitman
University of Pennsylvania

ABSTRACT

While the dramaturgical metaphor has become a commonplace among social scientists, rather little is known about the psychological processes that underlie the dramatic experience in the theater. This paper sketches a few of the problems that a psychology of the drama must address. (1) Some grow out of the fact that while drama is necessarily based on pretense, it nevertheless can move us very deeply. The paper argues that the emotion felt by the audience (or by the actor who portrays it) has an as-if character whose quality may be derived by cognitive reinterpretations similar to those which Schachter and Singer proposed to explain "real" emotions. This as-if character can become very complex, for the cognitive context can become embedded in a further cognitive frame, of which the play-within-a play is an example. (2) Other issues derive from the fact that the drama is a temporal art form which trades on the arousal and betrayal of expectations. The paper describes some attempts to study possible precursors of the dramatic experience by looking at expectations about inanimate events in adults and the enjoyment of the peak-a-boo game in infants. (3) The paper ends with a classical problem, the enjoyment of tragedy, and discusses several interpretations of this phenomenon.

Since Shakespeare, the dramaturgical metaphor has become a commonplace among both playwrights and social scientists (e.g., Buss & Briggs, 1984). Shakespeare told us that "All the world's a stage and all the men and women on it merely players." Similarly, various modern sociologists and social psychologists insist that much of ordinary life is spent in playing roles—in taxi cabs whose passengers are afraid to give the impression of being cheap while waiting as the driver adroitly fumbles for change (Davis, 1959), or at cocktail parties, in which husband and wife carefully stage manage the event so all possible mishaps are relegated to a hidden backstage area (Goffman, 1959), or in wards for the terminally ill in which doctor and patient conspire to maintain the fiction that ultimately all will be well (Glaser & Strauss, 1965). While such descriptions have a certain sardonic aptness reminiscent of an unusually biting Comedy of Manners, one may wonder whether we as psychologists really understand the life-is-a-stage metaphor well enough to use it as confidently as we sometimes do. Just what is it that a play—or a film or television drama—evokes in the audience that beholds it? What goes on in the actors as they perform their roles? Why is it that we as audience submit ourselves to watching staged events in which people voluntarily take out their own eyes or exit, pursued by a bear?

These and similar questions go back to Aristotle's *Poetics,* but we psychologists haven't answered them. We haven't, because to date we have nothing that even begins to approach a psychology of drama or the dramatic experience. This is unfortunate, for drama is an enormously powerful art form. It has primitive roots that go back to ancient rituals (e.g., Hardison, 1968); it is widespread and some forms of it are found in many, perhaps all, cultures (e.g., Havemeyer, 1916); it is immediate and gripping, and is built out of basic social interactions and touches on fundamental emotions and urges that all of us share.

Under the circumstances, it is a pity that apart from some psychoanalytical speculations there has been so little work on the psychology of drama and the dramatic experience.

What I do here is to sketch a few of the problems and present a few of my own speculations and observations (as an amateur actor and director) together with some pilot studies using audience questionnaires or laboratory analogues of suspense or humor.

Let me begin by asking how drama relates to other art forms. I see two relevant characteristics by which art forms might be classified. One is whether the art form is or is not representational. Drama clearly is, as is much of visual art. Another distinction is whether the art form is essentially spatial or temporal. Since drama depends on actions on events that unfold over time, it is necessarily temporal, as is music and dance. I start out by considering some of the ways in which drama represents reality.

PRETENSE AND MAKE-BELIEVE

One of the most basic attributes of a stage performance is that it is based on pretense. On the stage, champagne is ginger ale, bullets are blanks, and no Desdemona ever suffers permanent pulmonary damage at Othello's hands. It is all make-believe and illusion—and we all know it. And yet this illusion sometimes grips us, keeps us on the edge of our seats, caught up in the emotions of the play which at the time seem almost more real than our everyday world. The

general question about what's appearance and what's reality has occupied dramatists and drama critics since the days of the Greeks. But do we as psychologists
have anything to say about it?

Emotion In the Theater

More specifically, what can we say about the "dramatic emotion" of the spectator who says he is involved in a dramatic performance? What kind of emotion
does he experience? And what can we say about the emotion felt by the actor
who plays the part?

Dramatic emotion and the audience.   Many of us would insist that while
watching some play or film we were "really in it" and had come to accept the
characters' joys and sorrows as if they were real. Our reactions often include
appropriate bodily indices: clenched fists, pounding hearts, and sometimes genuine tears. On the fact of it, everything suggests that we felt a *real* emotion. But
did we really? Consider the scene in which King Oedipus blinds himself. We
may say that while watching the play we believed that what happened on stage
was reality. But in fact, we surely did no such thing. For if we had, we would
have felt horror, not awe, might well have rushed for help, perhaps shouting "Is
there an ophthalmologist in the house?" We did not really believe that the stage
Oedipus was real. In Samuel Coleridge's well known phrase, all we did was to
suspend our disbelief. For however we may be moved by the events in Thebes,
on the fringes of our consciousness we are always aware that we're sitting in a
comfortable arm chair. We accept the make-belief *as if* it were real, but we never
quite lose sight of the fact that it is *as if*. To quote Coleridge (1836):

> These, and all other stage presentations, are to produce a sort of temporary half-
> faith, which the spectator encourages in himself and supports by a voluntary
> contribution on his own part . . . (Or, in talking about some painted sce-
> nery) . . . The true stage illusion in this and in all other things consists—not in the
> mind's judging it to be a forest, but in its remission of the judgement that it is not a
> forest. . . . (p. 37–38)

Dramatic emotion and the actor.   Many of the questions that can be asked
about the spectator who watches a play, can also be raised about the actors who
perform in it. What is their emotion as they portray the jealousy of the Othello or
the rage of a Lear? According to some schools of acting, the actor's job is to
bring emotional reality to his role. In practice, this is accomplished by vividly
recalling some emotion-filled fragments of his own life that are appropriate to his
present role and scene. The result is often a sense of genuine dramatic truth,
experienced as such by both actor and audience. But admirable as this may be, is
it real in the sense in which everyday emotion is real? Again, the answer is

almost surely "no." Numerous anectodes in the theatrical literature bear this point out. Actors may assert that they are caught up in the passion of a love scene but they won't forget how to move where the lights are placed so that the scene shows up to maximum effect. Or how to ad lib when a fellow actor forgets a line, or how to lean on a balcony railing when you know it won't support your weight. To quote from Fanny Kemble (cited in Archer, 1888), a member of a famous 18th century acting family:

> The curious part of acting, to me, is the sort of double process which the mind carries on at once, the combined operations of one's faculties—so to speak, in diametrically opposite directions. For instance, in that last scene in which I was half dead with crying in the midst of the *real* grief created by an entirely *unreal* cause, I perceived that my tears were falling like rain over my silk dress and spoiling it; and I calculated and measured most accurately the space that my father would require to fall in, and moved myself and my train accordingly in the midst of the anguish I was to feign, and absolutely did endure. . . . (p. 151).

It would seem then that the actor's experience is not all that different from the spectator's. He too has an as-if experience—an emotion that is—and yet is not—the one he would have had if he had really been the character and really found himself in the situation he portrayed.

Dramatic Emotion and the Schachter-Singer Theory

If the emotion we experience in the theater—as spectators or as actors—is not identical to that which we feel in the real world, what then is it? One possibility is suggested by the Schachter-Singer theory of emotion (Schachter & Singer, 1962). For my present purposes, I'm only concerned with their basic idea, ignoring the many aspects of their theory that have been questioned (for review and discussion, see Mandler, 1984; Reisenzein, 1983; Leventhal & Tomarken, 1986). As I understand it, their fundamental claim is that emotional experience is produced by an amalgam of sensed bodily (especially autonomic) arousal and the interpretation of the conditions that produce (or seem to produce) that arousal. Given this approach, it's clear why the injection of epinephrine will not produce rage or fear, contrary to what the James-Lange theory might incline us to believe; since the subject knows that he was injected with a drug, and knows that the drug will lead to increased heart rate and the other signs of sympathetic arousal, he will necessarily attribute his bodily arousal to the drug, experiencing a sense of "cold fear" rather than the real thing (Marañon, 1924).

I would suggest that the dramatic experience is in one sense analogous to this experience of cold fear. Let us assume that we witness certain events that befall others in real life—say, a tearful reunion, or a fistfight, or a death scene. Such events will produce a number of relevant bodily concomitants and physiological arousals. When analogous events happen on stage, they are likely to evoke a similar arousal. But the cognitive context is now quite different, for we surely know that whatever terrible events we might see and hear *on* stage, we see and hear them while sitting in a perfectly comfortable chair in a darkened theater hall. As a result, the resulting emotion has an ''as if'' quality.

A somewhat similar story can probably be devised to account for the emotional experience of the actor. He too induces various concomitants of emotional states in himself. Some are induced by the character's situation and by the actor's efforts to relate this to events in his own life. Some others may be induced by the actor's physical stage exertions—his clenched fists, heavy breathing, and so on. The belief that these will affect his emotions, as it were, from the outside-in, was part of theatrical lore which predates James and Lange by at least a century. Here is a quote cited by Robertson (1939) from the 18th century German playright Lessing:

> I believe that when the actor properly imitates all the external signs and indicators and all the bodily alterations which experience taught him are expressions of a particular (inner) state, the resulting sense impressions will automatically induce a state of his soul that properly accords with his own movements, posture and vocal tone. . . (Lessing, in *Theatrische Bibliothek* 1767; (p. 475; Transl. mine)

A number of factors will then lead to general arousal in the actor. The resulting emotional experience is again based on a cognitive interpretation of this arousal, and will again lead to an ''as if'' experience, for the actor knows that he's acting no matter how truthfully and sincerely he may act.

The Poles of "As If"

The special aesthetic flavor of the theatrical experience probably depends on just this ''as if.'' But this quality requires a delicate balance between belief and disbelief, between too little arousal and too much. On the one hand, there must be some sense of being ''in it,'' or the experience will be cold and dispassionate, like that of the bored usher who has seen the same show over and over again. On the other hand, too much of a sense of reality will also defeat the aesthetic goal for the ''as if'' feeling may be lost altogether.

Too much reality. A theatrically naive audience sometimes believes that what happens on stage is truly real. There are stories of 19th century Shakespeare troupes that performed before Gold Rush miners who took pot shots at Macbeth, and of spectators who ran on stage to stop Othello from strangling Desdemona. One night, when a famous 18th century actor (I believe it was David Garrick) shouted Richard's ''My kingdom for a horse,'' a sympathetic peasant in the audience offered him his own. According to the anectode, Garrick responded: "Come up yourself. An ass will do" (Esslin, 1978).

In these cases, *suspension of disbelief* had turned into real *belief* and the aesthetic experience that is peculiar to the drama had disappeared.

Similar effects are found in children's theater. Its performances are very much worth watching—not so much for what happens on the stage (unless you have a secret passion for Snow White or identify with one of the dwarfs). What's interesting is what goes on in the young audience. The little 4- and 5-year-olds shout warnings at Snow White when the evil old witch approaches. But their 7-year-old cousins are less naive and thus more capable of enjoying a genuine dramatic experience. They feel aroused and excited, but can nevertheless reassure their younger friends with an air of sophisticated superiority: "Don't worry! It's not really real."

To take another example from children's theater. I once saw a play with a rather involved plot that features a bad witch, a number of imps who wanted to steal her various treasures, and a hat which made its wearer invisible to one and all. When someone wore the hat, everyone on stage acted as if he weren't there. And the young audience accepted this readily enough, even though they themselves could see what the actors evidently did not. But there was more. The littlest and most lovable imp had a tragic flaw—he was incurably absent-minded. There were several scenes in which he sneaked into the witch's house, wearing the hat, and then took it off to scratch his head and forgot to put it on again. At this point, the younger children became greatly excited and exhorted their hero with loud warnings" "Put it on! Put it on!"

Consider what these children did. They had evidently forgotten that it was all make-belief and that imp, witch, and all were only actors on a stage. As a result, they accepted what they saw as real. But what about the invisibility hat? To accept this too, they had to ignore the evidence of their own eyes. Somehow the children did not seem aware of the contradiction in their own behavior. In part, this probably stems from the level of cognitive development of these young children. But in part, it may also reflect something about the nature of the theatrical experience itself whose as-if quality readily lends itself to contradiction and paradox.

An Optimum Aesthetic Distance

A theatrical experience may be too real because of a lack of audience sophistication. But a related phenomenon may occur even in well-schooled adults. A performance sometimes threatens to become too real and then even sophisticated playgoers may protect themselves by laughing nervously, thus breaking the spell altogether. This reaction to the loss of what is sometimes called "psychical distance" (Bullough, 1912) is sometimes seen in in-the-round theaters where the audience surrounds the playing area and those in the front row can almost touch the actors. If the play is a blood-and-guts melodrama, in-the-round staging may become too close for comfort. I once stage-managed a play whose climax was a very well-acted scene in which a man nearly ax-murders his wife. I was watching the audience and saw that those who were within two or three feet of the action averted their eyes. The scene had become too real and the emotion too genuine and so the audience reacted by breaking contact.

Similar conclusions come from some informal studies I've conducted on the effect of physical viewing distance. I questioned members of the audience on their reaction to several plays seen on a proscenium stage. These pilot studies had serious methodological flaws—seating was by self-selection and there was no adequate sampling of plays. But for what it's worth, there was a psychical distance effect. Mean involvement was maximal when the distance to the stage was intermediate—about 8 to 10 rows back. When the distance became greater or lesser than this, the audience reported that they were less involved.

In summary, it seems that the dramatic experience involves a state that's midway between genuine reality and cold, detached disbelief. It may be that this "as if" experience is an important ingredient, not just of drama but of several other art forms as well. In the drama, it is the awareness of events that move us deeply and are simultaneously known to be unreal. In the representational visual arts, it is the awareness of a scene that looks real and lifelike, but is simultaneously seen to be a flat, painted canvas.

The Complexities of "As-If"

Multiple frames. In the as-if phenomenon, there are two levels. One is the focal reaction (prompted by what happens on stage). The other is the cognitive context (the awareness that what happens occurs on a stage). To use Erving Goffman's terms, this context serves as a *frame* for the focal reaction and transforms it. Such frames may be analogous to the perceptual frameworks studied by students of visual perception. As in perception, a theatrical experience—as well as many that occur in real social life—can be framed by multiple context. Thus frames can be embedded in other frames, as in the play-within-a-play.

To a large extent, these dramatic complexities are based on what we already know about the theater before we ever take our seats. The play-within-a-play can have a powerful effect—as witness *Hamlet*—but this effect depends on our prior knowledge of what a play is supposed to be. The same holds for various modern manipulations of the dramatic form itself. The obvious example is Pirandello in whose hands the play-within-a-play evolved into a play-on-being-a-play as in *Six Characters in Search of an Author* in which some characters in an as yet unwritten play enter a theater and insist that they are more real than the actors who are presently rehearsing there. In other cases, what is manipulated is the nature of the as-if experience itself. Some authors, such as Brecht, want to push the experience toward detachment. Certain other theatrical figures, such as the members of the *Living Theater* of the 60s, try to decrease the aesthetic distance between audience, actors and play.

It is very likely that none of these dramatic modernities would have their desired effect without the spectators' knowledge of the very form that is being violated. Because what's involved is an experience with multiple frames. Our reaction to the Brechtian detachment is affected by the cognitive framework we bring to it; by what we know about most preBrechtian theater with *its* emphasis on empathy and involvement. Our reaction to being talked to directly by a member of the *Living Theater*—or being shouted at or touched— is shaped and framed by our knowledge that actors just don't do this sort of thing. This effect of prior knowledge of the art form on present experience has been repeatedly documented for music, drama, literature, and the visual arts. Let me illustrate it by reference to one of the lesser art forms: the joke. There is a kind of joke with the generic name *The shaggy dog story,* which is usually rather long, repetitive, and then ends abruptly, with neither point nor punch line. If well told, it can be very funny. But it is only funny if you know what a joke is supposed to be, for its very point is that it has no point.

Over and over again, we encounter the complexities of the as-if experience in which multiple framings are the rule, not the exception. With due deference to Pirandello, Genet, and Ionesco, it's worth noting that multiple framings are not exactly new to dramatic art. Shakespeare delighted in them. In *As You Like It,* the heroine is disguised a boy, who then plays several scenes (with a boy who doesn't see through her disguise) in which both pretend that she is a girl (actually, herself). Add the Elizabethan use of boy actors, and you have a boy playing a girl, playing a boy, playing a girl, making for a triply embedded dramatic event.

Stage Props and Multiple Frames

An interesting example of the complexity of the as-if phenomenon is the use of various mechanical stage contrivances—props, scenic devices, make-up, and the like. On the face of it, the point of such devices is to help create some semblance of reality—as in using wigs and beards to age a younger man. But in modern theatrical practice, their effect is often quite a bit more subtle. Let me use two examples from a recent season of the Royal Shakespeare Company's repertory.

One is a modern dress production of the *Merry Wives of Windsor* in which two stage platforms revolved adjacent to each other, changing scenes quickly and efficiently in full view of the audience. The characters took many exits and entrances by stepping from one to the other of these revolving platforms. They did so with a minimum of fuss, and acted as if these platforms weren't really there. The one exception was Mrs. Quickly, a rather likable busybody, much given to various forms of liquor. As time and alcohol wore on, her exits changed.

Before stepping from one rotating stage to another, she paused. On a later occasion, she hesitated and staggered, then took a wobbling little leap. This changed the nature of the "as if." The device was presumably designed as a mere mechanical underpinning to the physical illusion and as such was not noticed. By making a show of crossing from one platform to the other, the actress who played Mrs. Quickly undercut this physical illusion. But while doing so, she strengthened another illusion: She might be on a stage rather than in a house in Windsor, but she was Mrs. Quickly and not the actress Sheila Steafel.

Another example concerns a brilliant production of *As you like it,* in which an enormous white sheet served many purposes: In the first act, it covered the entire stage to give a sense of winter and desolation. It was later bunched together and pulled up so that it served as a very tall tree trunk on which the young hero pinned dozens of love notes. Eventually the heroine, disguised as a boy, played a girl to show the folly of love to the hero. At one point, she lifted the bottom of the sheet—hitherto, part of the tree trunk—and pulled it around herself to serve as a bridal gown. She then accidentally dropped the sheet, looked down on herself and quickly pulled the sheet up again to cover her "nakedness"—a hilarious bit of stage business in which a pretend tree trunk had become a pretend gown that covered a pretend nudity of a pretend female who was really what she pretended to pretend. Here the framings included the prop which raised the complexity of the framings to a new level of magnitude.

DRAMA AS A TEMPORAL ART FORM

Thus far, we've talked entirely about drama as an art form that trades in representation and "as if." But it is also an art form that is temporal by its very nature. What can we say about this temporal aspect of the drama?

Theater is normally about people and their actions, especially as these come into conflict with each other. As the spectator watches, he forms expectations about what X will do to Y, and a good playwright will manipulate these expectations—establish them, develop them, and betray them. The result is suspense. It's clear that this suspense may still be present even if we have explicit knowledge about what will happen at the end, for we can see a play or a film and enjoy it even if we have seen it before. The same is true of other art forms that depend on temporal progression such as narrative fiction or music. My best guess is that the kind of suspense that all of these forms trade in depends on the immediate rather than the more extended temporal context. We see Hamlet stab Polonius through the arras, and are aroused and held in suspense by the sheer vehemence of his act—for the moment losing sight of the plot structure as a whole even though we know it perfectly well. I suspect that if we could recall the local events of the scene—every word, every inflection—as well as we can recall the larger structure, suspense and enjoyment would disappear. The child who insists on being read the same story night after night, may be an example of the same phenomenon.

My own efforts to get at the expectation arousals that might underlie the dramatic experience, amount to little more than tentative stabs. Let me nevertheless tell you a bit about them.

Expectations About Inanimate Events

Some of my work involved expectations about inanimate events. Three or four clicks (or various forms on a computer screen) were presented in succession at a fixed interval, followed by a longer pause after which there was a final click: Click, click, click. . . . click. If the pause was just right, he subjects laughed. An expectation was aroused, betrayed, and then satisfied. In this instance, the result was humor. But we found that we could sometimes shift the resolution to the dramatic. We presented several set-up sounds of medium intensity, than a longer pause followed by a sound that was not identical to the first three or four. For some subjects, it was much softer and of higher pitch: Boom—boom—boom——bing. This was rated as funny. For other subjects the terminal sound was much louder: Boom—boom—boom——BANG! Now the subjects rated the experience as dramatic rather than funny. In some ways, this result fits some of our preconceptions of what comedy and tragedy (or melodrama) are all about. In both cases, we expect A, but encounter B instead. In comedy, B will be of lesser import than A, as in Oscar Wilde's remark that to have lost one parent is a misfortune—to have lost two amounts to carelessness. In melodrama and tragedy, B has a greater import: as in the movie *Godfather* in which a smiling toll booth attendant turns out to be a gangster who suddenly pulls a gun and splashes the driver's face all over the screen.

Infants and the Peek-A-Boo Game

More recently, Jerry Parrott and I have tried to find some primitive precursors of the suspense phenomenon in 6- to 8-month-old infants. We decided that a good candidate was the peek-a-boo game. An experimenter served as the stimulus that was peek-a-booed at (let's call him the peek-a-boondum). He or she peered over a screen, disappeared for a number of seconds, and then reappeared. During all this, the infant's facial expressions were photographed as they sat on their mother's lap and were rated by several independent judges. The results—which are pretty much the same for 6- and 7-month-olds—are shown in Fig. 8.1 in which the undotted line shows the means of the smile rating (0 = no smile and 5 = laughter) during the 3 seconds when the peek-a-boondum appeared, the 3 seconds when he or she disappeared behind the screen, and the 4 seconds when he or she reappeared. There is a slight suggestion that the degree of reappearance

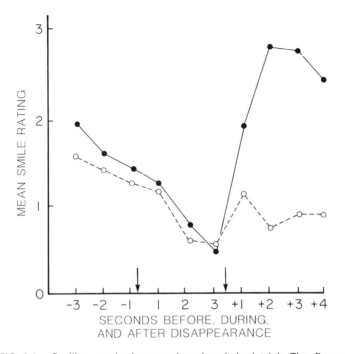

FIG. 8.1. *Smiling on both normal and switched trials* The figure shows mean smile rating of seven-month olds during trials on which there was no switch of the person (unbroken line) and trials on which there was (broken line). The second-by-second ratings are shown for the period prior to the disappearance of the person playing peek-a-boo, after his or her disappearance, and after his or her reappearance (or the appearance of a different person). The arrows indicate the beginning and end of the disappearance interval). Smiling was rated on a five-point scale in which "0" denotes no smile, "2" a small smile, "4" a large smile, and "5" denotes laughter. From Parrott (1984).

smiling increases with a moderate increase in the disappearance interval. It looked as if an expectation was set up, and that its confirmation was somehow satisfying.

Would this satisfaction be increased when the expectation was betrayed in a mild and presumably unthreatening manner? We hoped that experience with the game might make the infants able to enjoy variations from the expected routine. To determine whether this is so, we switched peek-a-boonda. After several trials of the usual manner, there was a switch: One experimenter appeared initially, but another one reappeared after the usual interval. To us, this seemed rather amusing. But the infants evidently felt otherwise.

As shown by the dotted line in Fig. 8.1, there was a decline in the postreappearance smile when the peek-a-boondum is altered. (Again, the same effect was found in 6- and 7-month-olds.) It appears that 6-month olds have peek-a-boon-dum constancy, a result that may have some relevance to Piagetian claims about the lack of object permanence at that age. But it also shows that infants of that age don't yet enjoy the kind of deviation from the expected that underlies dramatic appreciation. Jerry Parrott performed a number of variations on the same theme—using inanimate peek-a-boonda (which don't work well at all), switching the location at which the peek-a-boondum reappears, and so on. All to no effect. Most recently he tried to use older infants—from 10- to 12-months-of-age—in the hope that some further refinements of dramatic appreciation might show up there. They may be there, but the peek-a-boo method didn't show it. The trouble was that at that age, the infants prefer hide-and-seek to peek-a-boo. When the experimenter disappeared behind the screen, the infants were not content to sit passively during the interval and wait for him to reappear. Instead, they squirmed out of their mother's lap and crawled over to get behind the screen (Parrott, 1985).

Despite our inability thus far to find signs of advanced theatrical sophistication in infants, we believe that we've at least shown a rudiment of suspense and the enjoyment that comes with its resolution—a first ingredient of the dramatic experience.

THE MOTIVES FOR WATCHING DRAMA

I've sketched a few of the characteristics of the dramatic experience. It's a difficult job, for the phenomenon is so very elusive. The difficulty becomes even greater when we ask why people seek out this dramatic experience, especially in the form of tragic drama.

Here's how David Hume (1980) stated the puzzle:

> It seems an unaccountable pleasure, which the spectators of a well-written tragedy receive from sorrow, terror, anxiety, and other passions that are in themselves disagreeable and uneasy. The more they are touched and affected, the more they are delighted with the spectacle; and as soon as the uneasy passions cease to operate, the piece is at an end.

In short, we pay good money to see lives shattered and minds and bodies broken. Why?

There are probably several answers, many of which go back to Aristotle's *Poetica*. Let me briefly sketch a few:

Hedonic Factors

Some authors argue for a hedonic factor. They hold, that paradoxically, the passions of sorrow, terror, and anxiety that Hume described as disagreeable, are in fact not really so when encountered in the as-if atmosphere of the theater. The foremost modern advocate of this position was Berlyne who argued that we often seek to increase arousal. On some occasions, we do so because our present arousal level is below some hedonic optimum; on others, we push our own arousal to an over-intense level because of the pleasurable feeling when it comes down again. Something of this sort may well be part of the motive for watching tragedy and melodrama. We seek an emotional *rush,* a thrill, but one whose make-belief nature guarantees that it is perfectly safe. If so, one of the motives for watching a tragedy has something in common with whatever impels people to ride in a roller coaster (Berlyne, 1966, 1971).

Psycho-dynamic Factors

Other authors (Hardison, 1968) stress what might be called "psycho-dynamic" factors. The first version of this position was Aristotle's famous statement about *catharsis:*

> Tragedy is an imitation of a noble and completed action . . . which achieves through the representation of pitiable and fearful incidents, the catharsis of such pitiable and fearful incidents. (p. 11)

One interpretation of this statement is that *catharsis* as here used means "purgation." The emotions aroused in the theater act like a purgative, and expel the spectator's unhealthy passions. According to some commentators, Aristotle was simply reflecting the ancient homeopathic theory of medicine according to which like drives out like. Heat was applied to cure fever, cold to cure a chill, and by the same reasoning, pity and fear in the theater would drive out fear and unwanted pity in ordinary life. Seen in this light, weeping is to the soul as vomiting is to the body, a position not unrelated to some 19th and 20th century conceptions of psychotherapy (Hardison, 1968).

In some ways, the psychoanalytic theory of the effect of tragedy can perhaps be considered as a distant descendant of Aristotle's. To Freud, as to Aristotle, the tragic events on stage touch emotional chords in the spectator and this has various beneficial effects (Freud, 1961; Jones, 1954). While Aristotle would not have shared Freud's interest in tragedy as a vehicle for the disguised expression of unconscious impulses, he might well have agreed to Freud's further point that exposure to the disturbing work of art helps the spectator to master his own anxieties by "working them through."

Cognitive-structural Factors

Still other authors emphasize the cognitive and structural aspects of the experience one obtains when watching a tragedy. When Oedipus finally recognizes the truth, the emotional impact is overwhelming. But this impact is accompanied and amplified by the intellectual insight that makes us see the poet's vision as a whole—as we share Oedipus' recognition that the cause of the plague he sought is he himself, that all of the precautions of his parents only served to bring about the tragedy they tried to prevent, that the blind Tiresias could see what the sighted Oedipus could not, and that when Oedipus finally *does* see the truth he loses his eyes. The recognition of how the parts of a whole fit together is yet another factor that contributes to aesthetic feeling and enjoyment. This holds for drama, literature, music and the visual arts, and may even relate to the lowlier joy that comes from finding the last word in a crossword puzzle.

Social-moral Factors

There is yet another factor, which may well be the most important one. Tragedy has a social and moral function. After all, it grew out of religious ritual—in Greece, and then again in medieval times. Aristotle's *catharsis* theory is often interpreted in just this light, for *catharsis* can be translated as "purification" or "clarification." Aristotle probably meant that the spectator at a tragedy would become morally enlightened by what he saw and felt. Whether watching a tragedy makes us better persons is rather doubtful. What is likely is that it temporarily leaves us with a heightened perception of our own place in the social and moral order. This perception may be grim, as in Oedipus's "Judge no man happy until he is dead" or Lear's "As flies to wanton boys are we to the gods. They kill us for their sport." Or it may be resigned, as in the plays of Chekhov that end with a sigh. What matters is that it—sometimes—leaves us with a brief sense of the human condition, taking us outside of our own selves. Sometimes, after a great performance, the audience doesn't applaud immediately. There is a momentary hush, a silence, before the clapping starts. And sometimes one doesn't want to talk immediately after leaving the theater. One doesn't want to break the mood, at least for a while.

I suppose that in 1988 that's about the closest we can come to Aristotle's purification.

SUMMARY

To sum up. I've described a few of the phenomena of the dramatic experience and of the problems which they raise. Hamlet called the players the "abstract and brief chronicles of the time." But they are even more than that. They and the theater traffic in as-ifs, but those as-ifs contain all the richness of human experience and social intercourse. If we psychologists can somehow study this subject without squeezing out its lifeblood in the process, without losing the phenomena we are after as we so often do—we may then find the drama a mirror in which we can see ourselves.

REFERENCES

Archer, W. (1888). *Masks or faces.* London: Longmans, Green.

Berlyne, D. E. (1966). Laughter, humor, and play. In G. Lindzey & E. Aronson (Eds.), *The handbook of social psychology,* 2nd edition. Addison-Wesley Publishing Co.: Reading, Mass., 795-852. Doubleday and Co.: New York, 1966.

Berlyne, D. E. (1971). *Aesthetics and psychobiology.* New York: Appleton-Century-Crofts.

Bullough, E. (1912). "Psychical distance" as a factor in art and an aesthetic principle. *British Journal of Psychology, 5,* 87–118.

Buss, A. H., & Briggs, S. R. (1984). Drama and the self in social interaction. *Journal of Personality and Social Psychology 47,* 1310–1324.

Coleridge, S. T. (1836). Progress of the drama. In H. N. Coleridge (Ed.), The literary remains of Samuel Taylor Coleridge (Vol. 2, pp. 24–34). London: Pickering.

Davis, F. (1959). The cab driver and his fare: Facets of a fleeting relationship. *American Journal of Sociology, 65,* 158–165.

Esslin, M. (1978). *An anatomy of drama.* London: Sphere Books.

Freud, S. (1961). *Beyond the pleasure principle* (tr. J. Strachey) New York: Norton (original German edition, 1920, Leipzig: Internationaler Psychoanalytischer Verlag).

Glaser, B., & Strauss, A. (1965). The ritual drama of mutual pretense. In B. Brissett & C. Edgley (Eds.), *Life as theater: A dramaturgical sourcebook* (pp. 358–364). Chicago: Aldine Publishing.

Goffman, E. (1959). *The presentation of self in everyday life.* New York: Doubleday.

Hardison, O. B., Jr. (1968). *Aristotle's poetics: A translation and commentary for students of literature* (transl. by Golden, L.) Englewood Cliffs, NJ: Prentice-Hall.

Havemeyer, L. (1916). *The drama of savage peoples.* New Haven, CT: Yale University Press.

Hume, D. (1980). Of tragedy. In R. P. Draper (Ed.), *Tragedy: Developments in criticism* (pp. 92–98) London: Macmillan. (Originally published in 1757, as part of *Four Dissertations*).

Jones, E. (1954). *Hamlet and Oedipus* (pp. 51–103). New York: Doubleday Anchor. Pages 51–103.

Leventhal, H., & Tomarken, A. J. (1986). Emotion: Today's problems. In M. R. Rosenzweig & L. W. Porter (Eds.), *Annual Review of Psychology, 37,* 565–610.

Mandler, G. (1984). *Mind and body. Psychology of emotion and stress.* New York: W. W. Norton.

Marañon, G. (1924). Contribution à l'ètude de l'action émotive de l'adrénaline. *Revue Française d'Endocrinologie, 2,* 301–325.

Meyer, L. B. (1956). *Emotion and meaning in music.* Illinois: University of Chicago Press.

Parrott, W. G. (1985). *Cognitive and social factors underlying infants smiling and laughter during the peek-a-boo game.* Unpublished doctoral dissertation, University of Pennsylvania.

Reisenzein, R. (1983). The Schachter theory of emotion: Two decades later. *Psychological Bulletin, 94,* 239–264.

Robertson, J. G. (1939). *Lessing's dramatic theory.* London: Cambridge University Press.

Schachter, S., & Singer, J. (1962). Cognitive social and physiological determinants of emotional state. *Psychological Review, 69,* 379–399.

9 The Cooperative Synthesis of Disparate Points of View

Howard E. Gruber
University of Geneva and Teachers College, Columbia University

ABSTRACT

The synthesis of information gained from different points of view is an essential feature of scientific work. When the different viewing points are occupied by different individuals, the cooperative synthesis of points of view is required, and this entails successful dialogue among the participants. In such situations, a difference among observers does not necessarily imply a disagreement: It may present an opportunity for going beyond the limitations of a single point of view.

The research reported here presents the observers with a situation, a "shadow box," inviting and permitting dialogue and synthesis of information gained from different perspectives. To solve the problems presented, the subjects must take account of two points of view.

INTRODUCTION

The Perplexities of Truth

In Plato's *parable of the cave* the prisoners are chained to a single station point and see nothing but shadows on a wall. They have no way of distancing or decentering themselves from this one limited view of the world. It is all they know. Limited and distorted as it may be, that is their "reality." Plato's point is that this is the normal situation of ordinary mortals.

The classic studies of conformity by Sherif (1936) and by Asch (1952, 1956, 1961) stemmed from rather different perspectives about the truth-value of beliefs. Sherif thought that the function of social norms can be appropriately

143

studied with highly ambiguous stimulus situation, notably the autokinetic effect, and that this ambiguity corresponds well to real-world conditions. In response to this work, Asch was concerned with the suggested image of human nature as passively yielding to the group; he believed that when confronted with unambiguous stimuli, notably easily discriminated lines, observers would see things accurately, would resist conformity pressures, and would report faithfully what they saw: People can be vigorously truthful. I believe that Asch was taken by surprise at the discovery that, under such unequivocal conditions, there was any yielding at all.

In spite of important differences in their methods and in their world views as expressed in their experiments, Sherif's work on the formation of social norms and Asch's work on group pressures have certain points in common. First, the subjects are all looking at the scene to be judged in essentially the same way and from the same point of view. Thus, a difference in the report of what is seen *must* mean a disagreement. Second, there is no opportunity for dialogue among the observers; each one is limited to looking at the stimulus, listening to the others' judgments, and making his or her own report. Third, the subjects are limited to looking and listening; they have no opportunity for a more active exploratory or manipulative approach to the material to be apprehended. Fourth, the situation invites only judgment on a single variable, not the construction of a complex idea or object. Under such conditions, intersubjective differences become disagreements that can only be resolved by yielding, domination, and compromise—all of which occur.

Synthesis of disparate points of view. The approaches outlined above are, within limits, impeccable. Each reflects some experimental findings and corresponds to some of our nonexperimental knowledge of the world. But they do not give us much guidance as to how people, sometimes at least, struggle toward the truth. In this regard there is at least one type of situation that is not covered by previous research, situations requiring the synthesis of different points of view.

It is possible to imagine conditions in which different observers have different information about the same reality but have no need to disagree with each other. Moreover, if they are fortunate enough to discover each other, they may be able to transcend their individual limitations and together arrive at a deeper grasp of the reality in question than would be possible for either one alone. We have embodied this type of situation in the microcosm of a "shadow box" (see Fig. 9.1). This is an arrangement in which an object concealed in a box casts two different shadows on two screens at right angles to each other. The subjects' task is to combine or synthesize these shadows in order to work out the shape of the hidden object. In what follows, I will refer mainly to situations with two points of view and two participants, although other arrangements are obviously possible.

When we refer to the different points of view as *disparate* it is to emphasize the analogy of the shadow box with binocular vision. In both cases two different images give rise to a single psychological object, in one case through direct perception, in the other through problem solving and creative synthesis. Were it not for the synthesis, the multiple images might lead to confusion rather than to improved knowledge of the world.

The cooperative synthesis of disparate points of view in the shadow box situation is not a simple matter: A prior assumption must be made that the participants' observations correspond to the same entity. Each participant must convey his or her knowledge to the other clearly and correctly; this may required the invention of a scheme for representing the information in question. When difficulties of communication arise, the problem of trusting the other person must be dealt with. Often, too, the subject must overcome a common tendency to ignore or underemphasize the other person's contribution, and to center attention on one's own point of view.

While these problems are being solved, the actual work of synthesis goes forward: How exactly can we put *this* configuration together with *that* one to form a coherent whole? Once again there are interacting problems of cognition and communication to be resolved.

Up to this point, I have presented the problem of synthesis in a social guise: the *cooperative* synthesis of different points of view. But clearly, there will be some situations where, in principle, one person can move back and forth between different points of view. Experimentally, the two point of view situation permits us to compare the performance of an individual with that of a pair. A priori, one can think of good arguments for the superiority of either arrangement. On the one hand, the individual perceptual apparatus is admirably organized for synthesizing disparate inputs: binocular vision, the kinetic depth effect, and all sorts of inter-modal phenomena testify to this capability. On the other hand, although the literature on group problem solving is ambiguous about this, there are at least some situations in which two heads are better than one.

From a practical point of view, the question of one head or two may not always be germane. There are, after all, situations in which shuttling back and forth between station points is not feasible, so there must be an observer at each point. For example, this may be the case with two astronomers viewing the heavens from different points on the earth. And if we generalize the idea to negotiating situations, the number of heads will be determined by socio-political realities. The processes involved in the cooperative synthesis of points of view are therefore interesting in their own right.

Reichenbach's "cubical world". .In certain respects our shadow box resembles Reichenbach's (1938) philosophical examination of a hypothetical "cubical world." In this world, the inhabitants are enclosed within a very large hollow cube, made with translucent walls and ceiling. Outside, birds fly around and cast shadows on the walls and ceiling, but the inhabitants know nothing of birds. They see only dark spots moving haphazardly. Here Reichenbach introduces a complication. There is a very large mirror, so placed that at some moments a single bird may cast two shadows, one on the ceiling and another on the wall opposite the mirror. But the inhabitants are not aware of these coincidences or of their significance. One day, among the inhabitants there appears a "Copernicus"—a genius who notices the coincidences, reflects upon their meaning, and deduces the existence of the world outside and of the creatures casting the shadows.

Reichenbach's cubical world is interesting to us both for its similarities and dissimilarities to the shadow box world. Evidently, the mirror produces the equivalent of two points of view, but this fact must be discovered; in our shadow box work, for the most part, we have shown the subjects directly how the two viewing points make two different shadows visible. Reichenbach's "Copernicus" solves only what we have come to call *the correspondence problem:* He recognizes that a given pair of shadows, projected onto different surfaces, are produced by the same object. But Reichenbach does not raise the *construction problem*—how to put the specific shapes of the shadows together to form a definite 3-dimensional object; this constructive synthesis of points of view is the heart of our shadow box experiments. Finally, Copernicus makes his discovery alone. In fact he could do it standing still and silent, since both projections are visible from one point; in the shadow box world, the subject working alone must move from one station point to another, or if two subjects are working together they must communicate—and effectively. Dialogue thus becomes an integral part of the process of synthesis.

Perspective-taking and the three-mountain problem. In the research approaches already discussed the thrust has been reality-oriented. The subject is asked, in effect, "what is out there?" In contrast, in the three-mountain problem studied by Piaget and Inhelder (1956), what is out there is completely visible. The subject sees the scene, an array of objects on a table, from one vantage point. The question put is not "What is there?" but "What would another person see?", looking at the same scene from a different vantage point.

In this well known and often repeated experiment, Piaget and Inhelder found that young children were unable to "decenter" correctly from their own point of view. Piaget and Inhelder labeled this characteristic "egocentrism."

There is little dispute over the difficulty of the three-mountain problem for children. But there are important differences in interpretation of the results. By now there seems to be widespread agreement that in some sense very young children sometimes behave in ways implying a grasp of the other person's point of view. For example, the child of 16 months looks appropriately where others point, and points at objects correctly, coordinating the act with vocalizations that appropriately attract another's attention (Leung & Rheingold, 1981).

At the other extreme, there is little doubt that in some situations mature and sophisticated adults fail to see the other person's point of view. Probably, whenever the task is difficult enough, or emotion intense enough, one common form of error is the lapse into egocentrism.

With regard to the three-mountain problem itself, it has been argued, with some experimental support (Liben, 1978; Liben & Belknap, 1981), that the child's most typical error is not to predict that the other will see what it sees, but rather to predict that the other will see the view that best represents what the child *knows* about the scene. It seems to me that these findings could be described as another form of egocentrism: confusing one's immediate experience with what one knows to be the case.

In spite of their evident differences, the past research discussed earlier (Sherif, Asch, Piaget, etc.), have one key point in common: the emphasis is on judgment. The subject engages in little or no active exploration, discussion, and construction. (To be fair, this is not true of Piaget's other work. Moreover, Doise and Mugny (1979) studied children cooperating in working on the three-mountain problem; their focus, however, was not on the process of synthesis of different points of view, but on the effects of cooperation on the later cognitive level of the child working alone.)

Peculiarly, in a number of studies of cooperation (e.g., Doise & Mugny, 1979, 1981; Emler & Valiant, 1982) the investigators' emphasis has been on the growth-potentiating value of *conflicts* engendered within the cooperative situation, rather than on more obviously positive processes, such as helping behavior.

There is a need, therefore, for some study of the cooperative synthesis of different points of view in tasks requiring active discussion, exploration of possibilities, and construction. It seems to me that such studies are entirely in the spirit of Asch's own thinking about these matters.

STUDIES OF THE SYNTHESIS OF DISPARATE POINTS OF VIEW

Our main aim was to study the *cooperative* synthesis of different points of view, but in order to pursue this aim we also studied individuals working alone. This had unexpected results.

In the experiments summarized here we followed a common pattern. The subject or subjects were first familiarized with or reminded about the general nature of shadows. Then they were introduced to the shadow box: they looked inside, saw the two light sources and the two screens, and saw how an object could be mounted on a vertical stalk in such a position that it cast a shadow on each screen. From each of the two viewing points only one shadow was visible.

In conditions with pairs of subjects, they were asked to communicate with each other about what they saw, and to try to work together to come to an agreement as to what shape of object inside the box would account for the two shadows. They were given paper, pens, and scissors, modeling clay, and where

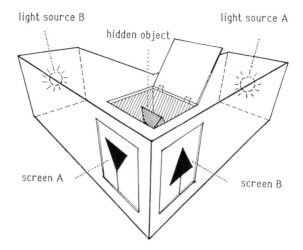

FIG. 9.1. The shadow box. The synthesis of disparate points of view. The task is to use the two shadows to work out the shape of the hidden object.

appropriate, Lego blocks with which to construct an object like the concealed one. In conditions with a single subject working alone, he or she was given the same materials and asked to go back and forth between the two station points as often as desired in order to solve the problem. There were no time pressures put on the subjects.

Experiment 1: Interaction of Social and Cognitive Factors

In this study we compared subjects working in pairs with subjects working alone. There were 12 single subjects and 12 same-sex pairs of both sexes in each of 3 age groups; thus 36 children (7–9 years), 36 adolescents (14–16 years), and 36 adults (20–53 years). Each single or pair worked on two Lego objects and two geometrical objects (Fig. 9.2). The order of presentation of objects was counterbalanced. There were always two experimenters present and all sessions were videotaped.

The subjects almost invariably found the task challenging and interesting, and willingly worked on it for as long as an hour. The task can be very difficult, as shown by the length of time taken; also, as shown in Fig. 9.3, among the children the majority failed to solve any of the objects, and among the adolescents and adults there were still some who failed completely.

As shown in Fig. 9.4 the subjects used three main strategies: recognition, addition, and transformation (or multiplication). Recognition of a familiar object can play a role even with the seemingly abstract shapes, since, for example, a

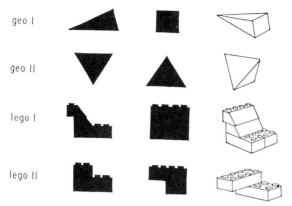

FIG. 9.2.   Objects and shadows in Experiment 1: Different kinds of
material.

square shadow and triangular shadow can be additively composed into a "house"
(with square as the building and the triangle as the roof. Or the triangular shadow
can (presumably with a little help from the other shadow) evoke the response,
"piece of cheese." The addition strategy consists in simply juxtaposing two
planes, which can be done either correctly or incorrectly. Mixed strategies occur,
such as combinations of recognition and juxtaposition.

Among the children, use of the recognition strategy was quite frequent (often
incorrectly). Among adolescents and adults, the work of synthesis usually led to
the understanding that the shape of the shadow does not necessarily correspond

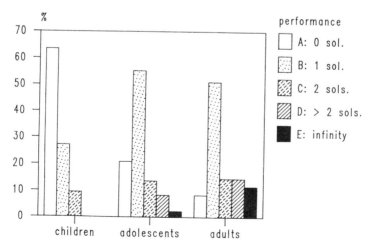

FIG. 9.3.   Developmental differences in synthesis of points of view.
Percent of subjects in each age group exhibiting different performance
levels in solving shadow box problems.

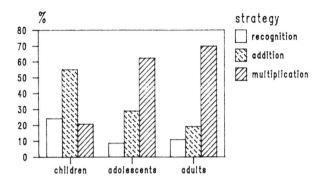

FIG. 9.4.   Use of different strategies in solving shadow box problems.

to any face of the object; and similarly that, even though the planes of the shadows were vertical, the planes of the surfaces of the object might or might not be so. Among the adults, most subjects began the process of construction and transformation immediately.

We speak of "transformation" or "multiplication" because taking both shadows into account at once can lead the subject to move from identifying the shadow with a face of the sought-for object to some other way of viewing the whole object. For example, in "Lego 2" (Fig. 9.2), a correct solution requires the subject(s) to grasp the way in which the two pieces are offset from each other, so that a region which appears on the screen as "up front" in the shadow may correspond to a rearward part of the object. The difficulty of recognizing this point led to characteristic errors among the children, and to quite a struggle for the adolescents and even for some adults.

The task requires at least a double and, for what we came to consider optimal performance, a triple decentration on the subject's part. First, the subject must avoid basing his efforts on a single shadow; this can happen even to a subject working alone, much as the solitary chess player playing both sides of the board has difficulty in remaining decentered. Second, the subject must separate the plane of the shadow from the various possible planes of the object. Third, for an optimal performance, recognizing the multiplicity of possible solutions, the subject must distance himself or herself from the first solution discovered. In the case of pairs, this may mean acknowledging that the other person's solution is good, too. Figure 9.5 shows some examples of possible solutions for two of the objects used in the experiment.

For each object, the performances of the singles and pairs were coded into one of five categories: (A) zero correct solutions; (B) one correct solution; (C) two different correct solutions; (D) more than two correct solution for a given pair of shadows; (E) the concept of an infinite number of possible solutions. This last category was only used for performances where the subjects had already achieved at least one correct solution. In other words, it would not have been used for an "anything goes" reaction to the task.

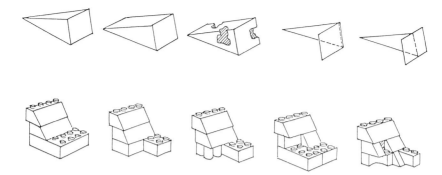

FIG. 9.5.   Alternative solutions compatible with shadows presented.

An analysis of variance (3 ages × 2 kinds of object × 2 social conditions—singles and pairs) was performed on these data. For this analysis the scores for the two objects of a given type were combined. The main effects of age and kind of object were highly significant. The effect of social condition was insignificant. The main difference between children and the other two groups was that most of the children failed to produce any correct solutions. The main difference between the adolescents and the adults was in the greater number of adults who found two or more correct solutions for a given pair of shadows and who recognized the possibility of an infinite number of solutions. See Fig. 9.3.

The pattern of responses was different for the Lego objects and the geometrical objects. The Lego objects were more difficult both in the sense that there were more total failures and in the sense that there were fewer instances of multiple solutions (categories D, and E). These results permit only a cautious conclusion, that the particular nature of the object and the shadows it generates have a considerable effect on performance.

Based on our exploratory work we undertook this study with two questions about the difference between singles and pairs: First, would there be an important difference in success between the two conditions? Second, would the pairs produce a larger number of multiple solutions (categories D and E)? Both questions must be answered in the negative. It may be that the processes involved are different, but happen to lead to similar results under the particular conditions of this experiment. On the other hand, it is also true, in spite of the evident differences in behavior between singles and pairs, that there are moments when, within a pair, an individual is in effect working alone. To support the claim that cooperative work is effective, there is no need to insist that working alone is ineffective. We need a more differentiated view of the process of cooperation, taking account of the ebb and flow of interaction. It should be added that working alone is not entirely an asocial process.

Initially, the basic shadow box situation, even with a single subject, was understood as a simulation of the cooperative synthesis of points of view. But we soon came to think that the pair condition would yield better results, because two heads are better than one. To our surprise, in a number of different experiments there was little difference in problem solving success between the single and pair conditions. In only one respect was the pair condition clearly superior to the single: the frequency of multiple solutions. And this superiority was more pronounced in adult pairs than in adolescent pairs.

Experiment 2: Comparison of Cooperative and Individualistic Orientations

Reflecting on our work thus far we came to realize that the distinction between working alone and in pairs is too crude. Within pairs there may be all sorts of relationships. Our next goal was to examine this question by comparing the effects of different social orientations within pairs on the synthesis of points of view. To this end, we used three different kinds of instruction to the pairs. The *cooperative* instruction encouraged the pair to work together throughout the whole experiment, indicating that their performance would be evaluated as a pair compared with other pairs, not as individuals. The *individualist* instruction asked the subjects to exchange information as to their respective shadows and then to work alone in solving the problem, indicating that their performance would be evaluated as individuals. The *neutral* instruction did not specify any mode of working together and did not mention evaluation.

The subjects were 24 pairs of adolescents (14½–16½ years old) and 24 pairs of adults (23–58 years old). All pairs were same-sex, and the subjects knew each other as friends, classmates, and colleagues. Within both age groups the number of males and females were equal. In the results, there were no consistent or striking differences between the sexes, so that variable is ignored in what follows.

Each pair was given a single problem, a tetrahedron fixed on an edge in such a position that each subject saw a triangular shadow, one with apex up, the other with apex down (see Fig. 9.2, II). We chose this rather difficult task in order to avoid a ceiling effect and to keep the pairs working long enough for the observations we hoped to make. As before, all performances were videotaped, and there were two experimenters present at every session.

The resulting patterns of social behavior could be classified as individualist, cooperative, or competitive. We categorized the individual performances rather than the pairs, since the members of a pair did not necessarily act the same way. As shown in Table 9.1, subjects by no means followed the instructions we gave them. Among the adults, the predominant behavior was cooperative, both in the groups given cooperative and neutral instructions; even in the group given individualist instructions, almost half the subjects were cooperative. It seemed almost as though the shadow box situation, presenting two perspectives bearing on a single object, naturally evoked cooperation as the appropriate response mode.

Nevertheless, among the adolescents given the individualistic instruction, the

TABLE 9.1
Developmental Differences in Social Behavior

Adults

Social Behavior

		coop	ind	comp
	coop	13	2	1
instruction	indiv	7	8	1
	neutral	13	3	0

Adolescents

Social Behavior

		coop	ind	comp
	coop	8	6	2
instruction	indiv	2	14	0
	neutral	10	5	1

Number of subjects in each of three instruction conditions exhibiting each of three behavioral tendencies: cooperative, independent, or competitive.

predominant response mode was individualistic, with divided results in the other two groups. In both age groups and all conditions, competitive relationships were quite rare.

We arrived at a composite score for each subject, based on the number of correct solutions produced during the problem solving phase of the experiment and on responses during a post experimental interview to questions about the possibility of alternative solutions. The highest score, 6, would be achieved by a subject who produced multiple solutions during the problem solving phase and who could, during the interview, elaborate the idea of an infinite number of possible objects producing the same projections.

For an age × social behavior × total performance analysis of variance, we combined the individualist and competitive subjects (classified according to their actual behavior, not the instructions they had received). Adults performed significantly better than adolescents ($p < 0.002$). But neither the effect of social behavior nor the interaction of social behavior and age was significant. The difference between age groups is due to differences both during the problem solving phase and the interview. Failure to construct at least one correct solution was more frequent in adolescents, and adults were clearly more sophisticated in handling the idea of multiple solutions. The idea of an infinite number of solutions occurred only in adults (8/48 subjects).

Most of the best adult pairs were ones in which both members were cooperative. Moreover, in six of the eight best pairs, the partners had *different* problem solving strategies, one working mainly by addition of planes and the other by constructing volumes. In exchanging information the adults were more precise and detailed than adolescents, giving information not only about shape but also about orientation, size, and position on the screen. In solving the problems, the adults give equal weight to both shadows, whereas the adolescents tend to focus on their own viewpoint. Adults were more attentive to their partner's suggestions, and they profited from their differences by improving the quality of their solutions and of their comprehension of the task. The adolescents were less interested in the other's ideas. They were also more concerned about whose solution is correct, as if only one were possible.

DISCUSSION AND CONCLUSIONS

Cooperative synthesis of different points of view.   With the shadow box task we created a situation in which syntheses of disparate points of view could be accomplished either by an individual with full access to both perspectives or by a pair of communicating subjects. The most important result is that such syntheses are possible and that they are, for the most part, difficult. We were not able to demonstrate any conclusive superiority of cooperating pairs over individuals with full access. On the other hand, we were able to create a situation in which cooperation was necessary for successful task resolution. Finally, in this regard, full cooperation with adequate attention to and respect for the other was distinctly more characteristic of adults than of adolescents, and led to more sophisticated performances.

In a sense, comparing individual and cooperative performance is asking the wrong question. In order to make such comparisons it is necessary to study situations where the choice of either kind of behavior is within reason. But if we are interested in cooperation, it should be studied primarily in situations where it is essential, and the question should be "how does it work?"

The process of synthesis of disparate points of view is extremely complex. In the sense that it requires the construction of something new, it has some of the properties of creative work (Gruber, 1989; Wallace & Gruber, 1989). A kindred point was recognized by Crutchfield (1964) in his study of conformity and creativity.

Self and other.   In some respects, of course, the synthesis of disparate points of view appears early in life, with binocular vision. But there is a long developmental road from such perceptual beginnings to successful performance in the shadow box task. Few children between the ages of 7–9 could do it. We have additional evidence suggesting that the cognitive level reflected in successful performance in the three-mountain problem is a necessary but not sufficient prerequisite for success in the shadow box task (Giacomini-Biraud, 1988). In other words, the ability to understand correctly what will be seen from another perspective is a prerequisite to being able to "turn around" and use two perspectives to construct an unknown object.

It would seem reasonable to suppose a distinct interaction between self-awareness and other-awareness. This idea is dramatically illustrated by the account (Degand, 1911) of a deaf child who could lipread and speak, but who had no idea that he was deaf. At the age of eight, he noticed with astonishment that his teacher could understand him without her seeing his lips. From then on he was attentive to other children, interested in classifying them according to their perspectives on the world: Could they understand without seeing (i.e., hear) or not? Although the interaction between self-concept and other-awareness may seem reasonable, there is an almost complete separation of the psychological literatures dealing with these topics (Ford, 1979; Baumeister, 1987).

Appearance and reality.   The synthesis of different points of view must depend on some grasp of the distinction between appearance and reality. If the subject does not posit a unifying object or real world, then each scene is just a scene, more or less like other moments of experience. In order to interact with each other, both cooperating subjects must assume the distinction between appearance and reality, and further, they must both assume that their different perspectives bear on the same reality. In other words, the subjects must have at least a tacit agreement as to the solution of the correspondence problem.

Although there has not been much research with adult subjects on the relation between appearance and reality (but see Brunswik, 1956; Gruber & Dinnerstein, 1965), there has been a recent spate of research on the child's growing comprehension of the distinction between them (Flavell, 1986). Flavell, Flavell, and Green (1987) have carried the argument further and attempted to demonstrate that there is a "pretend-reality" distinction that emerges in 3–4 year olds, or about a year before the appearance-reality distinction. For an example, the child of 3, playing with a wooden block and pretending it is a car, knows perfectly well that it is both a real block and a pretend car. Flavell et al. argue that the pretend-reality distinction not only precedes but leads to the appearance-reality distinction: What the child first constructs he later confronts.

Although it is tempting and plausible to elaborate such neat sequential taxonomies, I doubt if they will stand up very long. Peek-a-boo and other hiding games emerge in babies very early. They involve some grasp of the point of view of the other, some knowledge of pretend–appearance–reality distinctions, and even some cooperative effort. It is equally plausible to conceive of approaches to reality as developing in a spiral of increasing complexity, with each of many schemata becoming more and more powerful.

The correspondence problem.   In the experiments reported here we solved the correspondence problem for the subjects. That is, we showed them in advance exactly how the two shadows correspond to the same object. But as we have seen, in Reichenbach's cubical world, it takes a "Copernicus" to solve the correspondence problem. We have now invented a situation in which our subjects can confront that issue. There are two objects in the shadow box, producing four shadows, two on each screen. The subjects must first work out how to pair off the shadows—which goes with which?—(the correspondence problem) before they can arrive at a cogent proposal as to the shapes of the objects. At the same time, preliminary glimmerings about possible shapes affect the decision as to how to pair the shadows.

The discovery that adults are more keenly aware than adolescents of multiple solutions is one of the most interesting findings of our work thus far. We thought that the 4-shadow situation would make this kind of solution more salient. To our surprise, preliminary findings suggest that the opposite is the case. Subjects who exert themselves to solve the correspondence problem both ways are then satisfied with one solution of the object shape problem for each correspondence, and do not go on to discover that there are alternative solutions for a given choice of correspondences.

The Copernicus question.   Does it really take a Copernicus to perform excellently on the shadow box problems? Our initial expectation was quite the contrary. Part of the motivation for the construction of the shadow box was the idea that it is the point of view that counts: Endow subjects with access to multiple perspectives and they will be able to transcend their individual limitations. Our research has shown that this idea is only partially substantiated. There are both wide individual differences and strong developmental trends in the synthesis of disparate points of view. Apart from our experimental subjects we have tested a few individuals, including a distinguished mathematician and a physicist, who seem to function at a much higher level.

We undertook this work as part of an approach that recognizes the social construction of knowledge without falling into the morass of extreme relativism: Exploiting multiple perspectives is one form of acquiring an enlarged vision. We can now see that such an approach does not require everyone to make equally good use of such possibilities. It is enough that those few who see the furthest can successfully communicate what they see to others.

ACKNOWLEDGMENTS

This research was supported by a grant to Howard E. Gruber from Le Fonds National Suisse de la Recherche Scientifique, project No. 1.043-0.84 and 1.738-0.87.. Collaborators in the research are Danielle Maurice, Emiel Reith, Isabelle Sehl, and Anastasia Tryphon. The author thanks them and Doris Wallace for help in writing this essay, and grants them the usual absolution. I thank also the Institute for Advanced Study for my stay in Princeton during which some preliminary work for this project was done.

REFERENCES

Asch, S. E. (1952). *Social psychology*. Englewood Cliffs, NJ: Prentice-Hall.
Asch, S. E. (1956). Studies of independence and conformity: 1. A minority of one against a unanimous majority. *Psychological Monographs, 70*(9), 1–70.

Asch, S. E. (1961). Effects of group pressure upon the modification and distortion of judgments. In M. Henle (Ed.), *Documents of Gestalt psychology* (pp. 222–236). (Original work published 1951).

Baumeister, R. F. (1987). How the self became a problem: A psychological review of historical research. *Journal of Personality and Social Psychology, 52*, 163–176.

Brunswik, E. (1956). *Perception and the representative design of psychological experiments.* Berkeley: University of California Press.

Crutchfield, R. S. (1964). Conformity and creative thinking. In H. E. Gruber, G. Terrell, & M. Wertheimer (Eds.), *Contemporary approaches to creative thinking.* New York: Atherton Press.

Degand, J. (1911). Observations sur un enfant sourd. *Archives de Psychologie, 10*, 378–389.

Doise, W., & Mugny, G. (1979). Individual and collective conflicts of centrations in cognitive development. *European Journal of Social Psychology, 9*, 105–108.

Doise, W., & Mugny, G. (1981). *Le development social de l'intelligence.* Paris: Intereditions.

Emler, N., & Valiant, G. L. (1982). Social interaction and cognitive conflict in the development of spatial coordination skills. *British Journal of Psychology, 73*, 295–303.

Flavell, J. H. (1986). The development of children's knowledge about the appearance-reality distinction. *American Psychologist, 41*, 418–425.

Flavell, J. H., Flavell, E. R., & Green, F. L. (1987). Young children's knowledge about the apparent-real and pretend-real distinctions. *Developmental Psychology, 23*, 816–822.

Ford, M. E. (1979). The construct validity of egocentrism. *Psychological Bulletin, 86*, 1169–1188.

Giacomini-Biraud, V. (1988). *Synthèse de points de vue et coordination de perspectives.* Unpublished recherche de diplome, University of Geneva.

Gruber, H. E. (1989). The evolving systems approach to creative work. In D. B. Wallace & H. E. Gruber (Eds.), *Creative people at work: Twelve cognitive case studies.* New York: Oxford University Press.

Gruber, H. E., & Dinnerstein, A. J. (1965). The role of knowledge in distance perception. *American Journal of Psychology, 78*, 575–581.

Leung, E. H. L., & Rheingold, H. L. (1981). Development of pointing as a social gesture. *Developmental Psychology, 17*, 215–220.

Liben, L. S. (1978). Perspective-taking skills in young children: Seeing the world through rose-colored glasses. *Developmental Psychology, 14*, 87–92.

Liben, L. S., & Belknap, B. (1981). Intellectual realism: Implications for investigations of perceptual perspective taking in young children. *Child Development, 52*, 921–924.

Piaget, J., & Inhelder, B. (1956). *The child's conception of space.* London: Routledge & Kegan Paul. (Original publication 1948).

Plato (1928). *The Republic.* New York: Scribner. (Original work published about 400 B.C.).

Reichenbach, H. (1938). *Experience and prediction.* Chicago: University of Chicago Press.

Sherif, M. (1936). *The psychology of social norms.* New York: Harper.

Wallace, D. B., & Gruber, H. E. (1989). *Creative people at work: Twelve cognitive case studies.* New York: Oxford University Press.

Other Works Consulted

Archer, M. S. (1987). Resisting the revival of relativism. *International Journal of Sociology, 2*, 235–250.

Asch, S. E. (1948). The doctrine of suggestion, prestige and imitation in social psychology. *Psychological Review, 55*, 250–276.

Bok, S. (1978). *Lying: Moral choice in public and private life.* New York: Vintage.

Gibson, J. J. (1966). *The senses considered as perceptual systems.* Boston: Houghton Mifflin.

Giere, R. N. (1984). Realism in the laboratory. In *George Sarton Centennial, University of Ghent*, 15–21.

Hanson, N. R. (1958). *Patterns of discovery: An Inquiry into the conceptual foundations of science.* Cambridge, England: Cambridge University Press.

Henle, M. (1974). On naive realism. In R. B. MacLeod & H. L. Pick (Eds.). *Perception: Essays in honor of James J. Gibson.* Ithaca, NY: Cornell University Press.

Latour, B., & Woolgar, S. (1979). *Laboratory life: The social construction of scientific facts.* Beverly Hills, CA: Sage Publications.

Milgram, S. (1963). Behavioral study of obedience. *Journal of Abnormal and Social Psychology, 67,* 371–378.

Milgram, S. (1977). *The individual in a social world: Essays and experiments.* Reading, MA: Addison-Wesley.

Postman, L., Bruner, J. S., & McGinnies, E. (1948). Personal values as selective factors in perception. *Journal of Abnormal and Social Psychology, 43,* 142–154.

Rock, I. (1983). *The logic of perception.* Cambridge, MA: The MIT Press.

10 Associative Learning in Animals: Asch's Influence

Robert A. Rescorla
University of Pennsylvania

ABSTRACT

Three aspects of Asch's studies of associative learning are emphasized: the importance of regarding associations as the learning of relations, the possibility of different associative processes at different levels of learning, and the involvement of features of the elements in associative recall. Each of these has a parallel in contemporary studies of associative learning in animals. First, modern descriptions of Pavlovian conditioning stress the importance of relations beyond contiguity in the formation of associations. For instance, it is common to acknowledge a role for both informational and perceptual relations. Second, recent studies of conditioning point to a hierarchical organization in which associations are formed among elements that themselves are constructed by learning. Third, the importance of features of the elements to performance based on associations is routinely exploited by a highly useful technique, post-learning manipulation of value. Each of these is illustrated by experiments from the laboratory of the author, who counts Asch as one of his major intellectual mentors.

INTRODUCTION

In the early 1960s Asch turned his attention to the problems of learning and memory. He brought to that study a new perspective, based on his background in Gestalt psychology but molded by his own views. Asch's concern was with the representation of the coherence of experience—how elements in the world are learned to go together. This naturally led him to the study of what is conventional called associative learning. But his views differed in many respects from those advocated by associationists. I want to emphasize three such differences because they have particular relevance to work that has been done in my own laboratory.

First, Asch preferred to describe associations as arising from the experience of relations among events in the world. He particularly emphasized that relations beyond simple contiguity are important to the formation of associations. Second, Asch suggested that there are different kinds of coherence among experiences; he rejected the view that there is a single associative mechanism that is responsible for representing all joint occurrences. In particular he called attention to the coherence that is acquired within a unit, suggesting that it differs from that formed between units. Third, Asch argued that associative recall, performance based on associative learning, depends upon features of the elements associated; he noted that variations in performance might have sources in the elements themselves rather than in the association.

Each of these propositions constitutes a rejection of classical thinking about associations. Each affected my own thinking about the nature of associations and, in retrospect, seems to have changed the direction of my research. These propositions have implications for what I have repeatedly described as the three basic questions to be asked about learning: What is the content of the learning, what are the circumstances for its occurrence, and how does that learning map into performance. I want to comment on each in turn.

CIRCUMSTANCES OF LEARNING: RELATIONS BEYOND CONTIGUITY

Asch's View.   Asch (1969) argued that . . . "the problem of associations is part of the general psychology of relations and the study of associations is in large part the study of the properties and effects of experienced relations" (p. 92). He agreed with Kohler (1941) that associations are the products of perceptual relations and are influenced by a broad range of relations beyond contiguity. Thus Asch (1969) claimed that "What is most important about contiguity is that it is a condition for the emergence of relations. All the relations we have studied, and most others, presuppose contiguity and go far beyond it" (p. 98).

In support of these claims, Asch described various instances in which perceptual relations beyond contiguity promoted the formation of associations. Such traditional Gestalt principles of grouping as similarity (Kohler, 1941), whole-part (Asch, 1969), and good continuation (Prentice & Asch, 1958) appear to have facilitative effects on learning to associate two items. But the most dramatic evidence in support of this view comes from Asch's investigation of the "constitutive relation." Asch, Ceraso, and Heimer (1960) reported an extensive series of investigations in which human subjects were asked to associate outline geometric forms with the line patterns (so-called modes) used to draw those forms. They found dramatically superior learning when a form was drawn in its to-be-associated mode compared with a condition in which a form was drawn in a standard mode but presented adjacent to its to-be-associated mode (see also Ceraso, 1985). Asch (1962) similarly reported that form-color associations are better learned when a form is filled with a color rather than simply presented adjacent to or superimposed upon a colored patch. In both papers, Asch argued that the "constitutive" relation between form and mode was a condition beyond contiguity that promoted the formation of associations.

In recent years the study of associations with Pavlovian conditioning has also moved from an emphasis on contiguity to one on the learning of relations. Increasingly, conditioning has been seen as the means by which organisms represent relations among events in their environment. As a consequence there has been increasing attention to the variety of interevent relations to which the organism must be sensitive in order to have a rich representation. I mention here several instances.

Informational Relations.   Perhaps the clearest example of the general trend to place Pavlovian conditioning in the context of the learning of relations comes from the modern emphasis on informational relations. Many authors have suggested that a signaling conditioned stimulus (CS) and its consequent unconditioned stimulus (US) develop an association when the CS provides information about the US. The informational relation goes beyond simple contiguity because it takes into account the context in which contiguities occur. The same CS/US contiguity can yield a CS that is informative or noninformative about the US, depending on the context in which that contiguity occurs. One experiment that makes this point clear was reported by Rescorla (1968). In that experiment, rat subjects received extended tone CSs in the presence of which brief, mild footshock USs could occur with various probabilities. In addition, footshocks also occurred with various probabilities in the absence of that tone CS. The question of interest was the degree to which the CS and US would become associated, as a joint function of the US likelihood in the presence and absence of the CS.

Figure 10.1 shows the data of primary interest, the amount of conditioning, as indexed by the ability of the separately presented CS to evoke a fear response (i.e., to interrupt ongoing behavior). The data are plotted in terms of a suppression ratio, as a function of the likelihood of the US during the CS; individual curves differ in the likelihood of the US in the absence of the CS. The result of interest is that conditioning was determined jointly by the likelihood of shock in the CS and in its absence. Not surprisingly, conditioning was an increasing function of the shock rate during the CS, as indicated by the observation that all curves are rising. However, the more interesting observation is that conditioning was an inverse function of the shock likelihood in the absence of the CS, as indicated by the ordering of the curves on the graph. With the likelihood of shock during the CS (i.e., the contiguity) fixed along the abscissa, the success of

FIG. 10.1. Dependence of conditioning on the information that the conditioned stimulus (CS) gives about the unconditioned stimulus (US). Conditioning is plotted as a function of US likelihood during the CS. The parameter is the likelihood of the US in the absence of the CS. Conditioning increases as the US likelihood increases during the CS; conditioning decreases as the US likelihood increases in the absence of the CS. From Rescorla (1968). Copyright (1968) by the American Psychological Association. Reprinted by permission of the publisher.

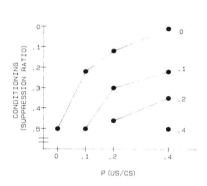

conditioning varies from excellent to negligible, depending on the likelihood of shock in the absence of the CS. Indeed, when the shock rate is the same in the presence and absence of the CS, as it is for the initial point of each curve, there is little evidence of any conditioning, despite quite a substantial number of CS/US contiguities in some cases.

These results suggest that simply knowing the likelihood of a CS/US contiguity is insufficient to determine the degree to which a CS–US association will form. Rather, that contiguity must be interpreted in the context of the baserate of occurrence of the US. It appears as though conditioning depends not on the simple contiguity but rather on the degree to which that contiguity represents a deviation from baserate, i.e., provides information about the US. These results make the general point that one should think about conditioning as the learning of a relation between two events. Moreover, they emphasize that the relation of contiguity is not rich enough to capture the conditions that produce Pavlovian associations.

In retrospect, Rescorla (1985b) argued that one can conceptualize data such as these as temporal analogues of the perceptual variable of relative spatial proximity. The organism can be seen as perceptually grouping the tone and shock, with that grouping being undermined by the addition of shocks that occur in the absence of the tone. Rescorla (1985b) has shown how that analogy can be extended to make understandable certain more detailed results from such paradigms.

Similarity.   More recently, we have also conducted several experiments that more deliberately attempt to explore perceptual variables like those that have influenced Asch's thinking. In particular, we have looked at the influence of the similarity and constitutive relations.

Kohler (1941) reported that human paired-associate learning is promoted by a similarity relation between the items to be associated. He presented one group of subjects with homogeneous pairs of items in which numbers were paired with numbers, syllables with syllables, and figures with figures. Another group received the same items but arranged so as to yield heterogeneous pairs. He found superior recall for the homogeneous group, a result that he interpreted in terms of a perceptual relation promoting the formation of associations. Although the details of Kohler's experiments have been criticized (e.g., Postman & Riley, 1957), Asch (1969) viewed them as suggesting that something beyond the ability of the individual items to enter into associations as a result of a contiguity must be at work. Rather he noted that "A relation cannot be resolved into a fact about one term plus a fact about another term; it is not a property of either term taken singly. It was precisely facts of interdependence of this kind that the psychology of association excluded." (Asch, 1969, p. 94).

Exactly the same claim has been made about the role of similarity in Pavlovian associations, based on a series of experiments conducted in our laboratory. There too, the results had to be understood in terms of a relation that could not be resolved into a property of either term taken singly. One such experiment used a Pavlovian preparation in which a localized disc of light (e.g., blue) signaled food for pigeon subjects. As pigeons learn the association between the color and food, they come to peck at that color. Moreover, they will learn to peck at another color or pattern that itself signals blue; that is, they will show what has been called second-order conditioning. This experiment exploited the flexibility of second-order conditioning to conduct an experiment highly analogous to that carried out by Kohler. Two groups of pigeons were first given conditioning in which a blue light (B) and a horizontally oriented grid pattern (H) separately signaled food. Then for both groups a green color (G) and a vertically oriented grid pattern (V) were paired with B and H, in order to produce second-order conditioning. However, for half the animals the pairings were homogeneous (i.e., of similars), Green with Blue and Vertical with Horizontal. The other half of the animals received the same elements in a heterogeneous pairing, Green with Horizontal and Vertical with Blue. Figure 10.2 shows the course of second-order conditioning under these two kinds of pairings. It is clear that conditioning proceeded more rapidly when similars, rather than dissimilars, were paired. This result entirely parallels that described by Kohler. The perceptual relation of similarity clearly affects the development of Pavlovian associations. Because the same elements were used for both groups it is clear that this similarity relation "cannot be resolved into a fact about one term plus a fact about another term; it is not a property of each term taken singly."

More generally, much of the literature that goes under the rubric of "con-

FIG. 10.2. Dependence of conditioning on the similarity of the signal and consequence. Responding is shown to two second-order stimuli, green and vertical, when they signaled either similar or dissimilar stimuli, blue and horizontal. The data points to the left show responding during a discrimination session prior to conditioning. From Rescorla (1980). Copyright (1980) by the American Psychological Association. Reprinted by permission of the publisher.

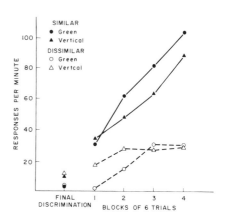

straints on learning" has the same implication. For instance, in the work of Garcia and his collaborators, certain preexisting intrinsic relations between events importantly influences the degree to which they enter into associations. Consequently, this theme in the work of Asch and Kohler has important parallels in Pavlovian conditioning.

Constitutive Relation. There is also evidence that the constitutive relation studied by Asch, Ceraso, and Heimer has an impact on the associations formed in Pavlovian conditioning. In one recent experiment (Rescorla, 1986) we explicitly examined the impact of that relation. For this purpose, pigeons were exposed to four perceptual displays, each containing a color (red or green) and a form (square or triangle). However, the displays differed in whether the color and form bore a constitutive relation (i.e., a red square) or not (i.e., an outline square on a red ground). As illustrated in Figure 10.3, each form was presented in a constitutive relation with one color and in a nonconstitutive relation with the other. The question of interest was whether the form would become better associated with the color to which it bore a constitutive relation. In order to detect the relative strength of these associations, we employed a technique discussed in more detail below: One of the colors was paired with food and then the two forms were tested for responding. The intention was to establish pecking at one color, but not the other, and then detect the color-form association by inspecting which form evoked more pecking. If the constitutive relation produces a better association, the form that bore that relation to the now-valued color should evoke more pecking. That was precisely the outcome observed: pigeons pecked at three times the rate to that stimulus. Clearly the constitutive relation was important to the formation of associations.

These results provide clear evidence that the sorts of perceptual relations envisioned by Asch to affect associations also affect Pavlovian conditioning. They illustrate not only the particular value of considering perceptual relations

FIG. 10.3. Design of an experiment using the constitutive relation. Birds were exposed to four keylights consisting of a triangle or a square and one of two colors. Each color was an interior color of one figure and a background color for the other figure. Then the colors were paired with food (+) and the figures were tested.

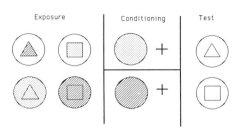

but also the more general value of placing conditioning in the context of learning about relations. Although there are several intellectual bases for such a reorientation within Pavlovian conditioning, it is clear that the ideas of Asch constitute an important impetus for some of that work.

DIFFERENT LEVELS OF COHERENCE: THE CONTENT OF LEARNING

For Asch the impact of different relations went beyond their differential success in producing a common associative connection. Instead he argued that different relations might well produce different contents of learning. "The question I propose to examine is whether there are distinct kinds of functional connections, of which the phenomena today called associative are only one" (Asch, 1962, p. 553). He was especially interested in the possibility that the mechanisms by which perceptual units are formed differ from those by which those units might be further joined by associative connections. Thus in referring to the work on the constitutive relation he wrote "The typical associative situation . . . begins with the apprehension of unrelated data that are *subsequently* joined. The situation is importantly different when the data are *from the start* apprehended as members of one unit" (Asch, Ceraso, & Heimer, 1960, p. 39). Although the primary data from this work are that the constitutive relation produces greater level of recall, Asch thought of the learning within a unit as qualitatively different from that between units.

The notion that associations are formed between units that are themselves complexly constructed and learned by the organism has also found its way into the Pavlovian conditioning literature. Our own thinking on this possibility has been importantly influenced by Asch's writings. It has encouraged us to explore the learning that occurs within both of the elements of the Pavlovian association. For both the CS and the US, we have found evidence for a representation with a coherent internal structure. Indeed, one recent experiment with second-order conditioning in pigeons displays evidence of such a structure for both a signal and a consequent event.

The design for this experiment is shown in Fig. 10.4. One stimulus (X) signaled the occurrence of a compound stimulus composed of a keylight that was red (R) on one half and had horizontal stripes (H) on the other half. The R and H stimuli had each had a separate history of signaling the occurrence of food. We knew from earlier second-order conditioning experiments that the birds would come to peck X when it was followed by the RH compound. The question of interest was whether that compound would become a unit that entered into the association with X or whether R and H would develop separate associations. As will be discussed in the next section, one way to determine whether or not X is associated with a stimulus is to change the value of that stimulus after conditioning has been completed. When an associate of X changes its value, the response to X will change. As a result, one may separate these alternatives by giving the RH compound a different value from R and H individually. Consequently, after X had been paired with RH, some birds received a discrimination of the form RH+, R−, H− whereas others received the reverse RH−, R+, H+ discrimination. If X is associated with the RH unit, we should expect it to continue to evoke pecking when RH is reinforced but the elements extinguished; on the other hand, if X is associated with the individual R and H elements, it should evoke responding when they are reinforced even though RH is extinguished. In order to compare the results of X with those from an associative structure known to represent simple associations with the elements, we also used R and H to condition another stimulus (Y). Like X, Y was followed by R and H, but unlike X, Y received R and H on separate trials, thereby insuring its having separate associations with the elements. Consequently, we should expect responding to Y to track the current value of R and H, rather than of the RH compound.

Figure 10.5 shows the results of various stages of this experiment. The first

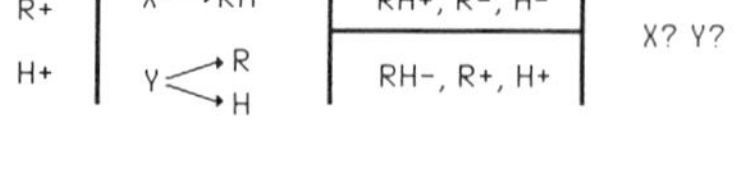

FIG. 10.4. Design of an experiment showing hierarchical organization. Birds received first-order Pavlovian conditioning of two keylights (R and H) with a food (+) unconditioned stimulus (US). Then one second-order stimulus (X) signaled the RH compound, whereas another (Y) signaled the elements. Then the birds received one of two conditional discriminations between the RH compound and its elements and were tested for the response to X and Y. From Rescorla (1988). Copyright (1988) by the American Psychological Association. Reprinted by permission of the publisher.

| R+ | X →RH | RH+, R−, H− | X? Y? |
| H+ | Y ⤜ R H | RH−, R+, H+ | |

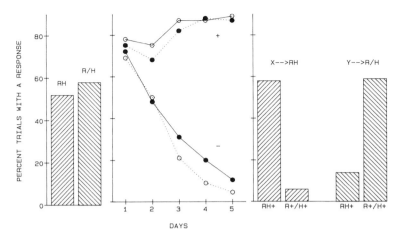

FIG. 10.5. Results of an experiment showing hierarchical organization. The left panel shows asymptotic second-order conditioning of X
and Y by the RH compound and the R and H elements, respectively.
The middle panel shows learning of a conditional discrimination of the
form RH+, R−, H− (solid symbols) or RH−, R+, H+ (open symbols).
The right panel shows responding to X and Y as a function of the most
recent treatment of the RH compound and its elements. In both cases,
responding to X and Y tracked the current value of the stimulus that it
had signaled. From Rescorla (1988). Copyright (1988) by the American
Psychological Association. Reprinted by permission of the publisher.

panel shows the level of responding to X and Y at the end of their second-order
conditioning by the RH compound and the R/H elements. These two treatments
produced similar levels of conditioning; consequently, on that basis one could
not identify differences in the associations of X and Y. The middle panel shows
the course of the discrimination when RH and its elements differentially signaled
food. The fact that the birds readily solved that discrimination is itself of considerable interest. During this phase, R, H, and the RH compound are serving as
signals of other outcomes. The discrimination pattern suggests that such signals
can become complexly coded; that is CSs have a learned internal structure.

But the data of most interest are from the final panel, when the events
signaling RH and its elements were themselves tested. The results for the Y
stimulus are unsurprising. Responding to Y, the stimulus that had signaled R and
H individually, tracked the value of those elements, not of the compound.
Apparently, the anticipated individual associations with R and H were formed.
Quite different are the results of testing the X stimulus that signaled the RH
compound. Responding to X reflected the current value of the RH compound
rather than of its elements. Clearly the animals had coded the consequent RH
event differently than they coded its elements. These results suggest that a
representation of the compound had been formed and itself entered into further

associations, both when it was the signal of food and when it was signaled by other events. Apparently, learned units can enter into associations.

Further evidence for learning of the internal structure of the elements of an association comes from a recently explored paradigm, facilitation or occasion-setting (Holland, 1983; Rescorla, 1985a). In such a paradigm, one stimulus signals the relation between two others. For instance, pigeon subjects might be exposed to a blue keylight that is followed by food on half its occurrences. However, trials on which blue is followed by food are signaled by the prior occurrence of a diffuse tone. Under those circumstances, the bird comes to peck only at those blue lights preceded by the tone.

Detailed experimental analysis reveals that the ability of the tone to augment responding to the light does not result from the tone's having a simple conventional association with either the light or the food. Rather it seems to take on the ability to signal that the light signals food. The evidence for this assertion comes from various sources. For instance, straightforward Pavlovian conditioning of the tone does not give it the power to promote pecking at a lighted key; nor do operations known to remove Pavlovian associations remove that power. Moreover, a tone trained in such a facilitation paradigm exhibits relatively little evidence of being a Pavlovian excitor. Indeed, a tone can be made a facilitator with procedures known to be inadequate to establish a Pavlovian association. For instance, in one recent experiment pigeons received half-hour sessions composed of alternating 30-sec periods with and without a tone. A 5-sec keylight and a 5-sec food presentation occurred with equal likelihood during both these periods. However, in the presence of the tone the keylight and food were positively correlated (i.e., presented sequentially) whereas in the absence of the tone they were equally often but in an unpaired fashion. We know from experiments like those described in the first section that under these conditions the tone is uninformative about both the light and food and hence will become associated with neither. In particular, the tone will not become a simple Pavlovian signal of food. However, the tone is informative about the relation between the two events—it signals the positive correlation between light and food. Under these circumstances, the tone nevertheless becomes a facilitator, promoting responding to the light, as illustrated in Fig. 10.6. That result implies the learning of a hierarchical associative structure in which the tone takes as its associate the light-food association.

Both of these experiments suggest that indeed the units that enter into associations can themselves have learned internal structure. That conclusion is supported by experiments from several other Pavlovian paradigms (e.g., Rescorla & Durlach, 1981). However, these experiments also leave unanswered a basic question of central interest to Asch—whether the nature of the learning within a unit is the same as that between units. On the one hand, there is evidence that many of the same variables that promote learning to associate units also promote the learning within units. On the other hand, some instances of within unit

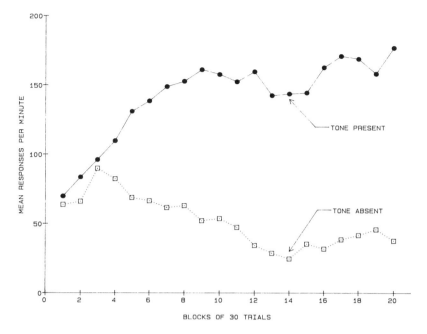

FIG. 10.6.   Facilitation of keypecking by a tone that signals the relation between keylight and food. In the presence of the tone a keylight was followed by food; in the absence of the tone they were presented in an unpaired fashion. Data are the rates of pecking the keylight when it is given in the presence and absence of the tone.

learning appear to involve elements not initially perceived as separate elements. As discussed elsewhere (e.g., Rescorla & Durlach, 1981), the available techniques are probably still too crude to permit a decision in many cases. Nevertheless, it is clear that, as Asch suggested, units are formed and serve as the basis for further associative learning.

DETERMINANTS OF PERFORMANCE

One theme that has run through Asch's study of memory is that performance is not based solely on the presence of an association. He repeatedly emphasized that our ability to use associations to govern behavior is heavily dependent on other determinants of performance. Of course, it is common enough to argue for a separation of learning and performance, with a particular appeal to motivational variables. But in Asch's thinking the properties of the associated elements themselves played a central role in governing performance.

This emphasis on the properties of the associated elements is especially clear in his discussion of the role that associations play in recall of past experience. According to Asch, simply having an association between a and b is inadequate to allow a to lead to the recall of b; in addition, b must have the property of being available. In Asch's view, availability is a property that a single item may possess independently of any associative connections it has with other items. Thus variations in the ability of a to yield recall of b might result from variations either in the strength of the $a-b$ association or in the recallability of b per se. Of special interest, failure of a to produce recall of b can occur even in the presence of a strong $a-b$ association, if b is unavailable. Asch and Ebenholtz (1962) argued that just such a case arises in many studies of "backward" recall, in which subjects are taught an $a-b$ pair and then asked for recall of a when presented with b. They found that much of the superiority in recall in the forward, as compared with the backward, direction is attributable to differences in the availability of the a and b items, rather than to any associative differences. They manipulated the separate recallability of the a and b items by presenting them independently for recall practice. Such separate presentation had a dramatic positive effect on backward recall of a given b. Indeed, it virtually eliminated the commonly observed asymmetry of associative recall.

It is striking to note that modern studies of Pavlovian conditioning heavily exploit a very similar logic in analyzing associations. One standard procedure for revealing the presence of an association between two stimuli, a and b, is to present b separately with the intention of changing some of its properties. The question of interest is whether that separate treatment of b affects performance to a. The observation that variations in stimulus b have specific consequences for performance to a is often used as the basis for inferring an $a-b$ association. It is especially common to use this technique under circumstances where one otherwise cannot detect the presence of an association.

Previous sections of this chapter, in fact, have described several examples of this technique. It was used to assess the impact of the constitutive relation and to detect organizational structure within the second term of an association. In both cases we uncovered the presence of an association of a with b by changing the response to b and inspecting the response to a. More generally, within the Pavlovian conditioning literature, such manipulations have been used to detect the presence of many types of associations that are otherwise undetected, such as associations between neutral elements, associations between a stimulus and the context in which it occurs, and associations among the elements within a stimulus (e.g., Rescorla, 1980). They have also been used to determine which of several features of a stimulus actually enter into associations with other elements. Indeed, Rescorla (1982) has argued that such techniques may be the procedures of choice for analyzing associations.

An especially important recent application of this technique has been highly informative about the associative structure of instrumental goal-directed learning. In instrumental learning situations, an outcome (O) of some importance to the organism is contingent upon its making a response (R) in the presence of some stimulus (S). Discussions of instrumental learning have frequently contrasted two alternative associative structures that might be learned: (a) An association might be formed between S and R, with O serving as a reinforcing event that promotes the S-R association; (b) An association might be formed between R and O, with S serving as the occasion on which the R-O association is functional. One important way in which those accounts differ is that the latter, but not the former, sees the outcome as part of the associative structure that is acquired. Although intuitively that seems like a reasonable possibility, in fact the S-R alternative has been historically dominant and it has proved quite difficult to obtain evidence for the presence of an R-O association. However, the technique of manipulating one stimulus and detecting associations through the resulting variations in performance has proven very powerful for this case.

A recent experiment by Colwill and Rescorla (1985) illustrates the point. In that experiment, rat subjects were trained to make two different responses (lever pressing and chain pulling) each leading to a distinctive outcome (liquid sucrose or a pellet). Then the value of the outcomes was differentially manipulated by pairing one, but not the other, with a mild toxin, LiCl. It is well known that such a treatment will have a dramatic adverse effect on the organism's evaluation of the food. The question of interest was whether devaluation of an outcome after it has been used to train a response will have a specific depressive consequence for future occurrences of that response. If so, one might infer the presence of a particular R-O association.

Figure 10.7 shows the results of that experiment, plotted in terms of the rate of two responses, one whose outcome had been devalued and one whose outcome had been left valuable. It is clear that during this extinction choice test between the two responses, behavior was very sensitive to the current value of the outcomes. That provides strong evidence for the presence of an R–O associa-

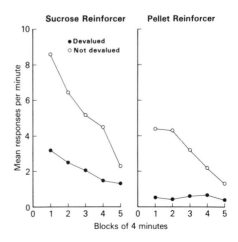

FIG. 10.7. Use of a postconditioning devaluation procedure to demonstrate response-outcome association. Responding is shown for two instrumental behaviors previously paired either with sucrose or with pellets after that outcome had been either devalued or not. From Colwill & Rescorla (1985). Copyright (1985) by the American Psychological Association. Reprinted by permission of the publisher.

tion in instrumental learning. Additional use of this technique exposes even further the richness of associations in instrumental behavior. This procedure has revealed the presence of associations between S and O as well as an association between S and the R–O association (Colwill & Rescorla, 1986). That is, this technique helps to reveal the kind of hierarchical organization for instrumental learning that we described earlier for Pavlovian conditioning.

This experiment is one illustration of the way in which modern studies of learning in animals often detect the presence of associations. The insight by Asch that associations can be measured by manipulating the properties of one element and testing the other has been put to extensive use in that arena.

CONCLUSION

There seem to me to be some striking parallels between techniques and ideas that Asch developed in the 1960s and those currently in use in our own studies of Pavlovian conditioning. Asch's notions of associations as the learning of relations, within unit learning, and how event properties affect recall, all seem to have surfaced in our Pavlovian experiments. Although I cannot claim to have always been aware of the parallels when our own work was conducted, it is difficult to believe that my earlier contact with Asch was not a major source. It seems clear to me that I owe him a substantial intellectual debt and it is one that I gladly acknowledge.

ACKNOWLEDGMENTS

The research described in this chapter was supported by grants from the National Science Foundation.

REFERENCES

Asch, S. E. (1962). A problem in the theory of associations. *Psychologische Beitrage. 6.* 553–563.
Asch, S. E. (1969). Reformulation of the problem of Association. *American Psychologist, 24,* 92–102.
Asch, S. E., Ceraso, J., & Heimer, W. (1960). Perceptual conditions of association. *Psychological Monographs, 74* (3, Whole No. 490).
Asch, S. E., & Ebenholtz, S. M. (1962). The principle of associative symmetry. *Proceedings of the American Philosophical Society, 106,* 135–163.
Ceraso, J. (1985). Unit formation in perception and memory. In G. H. Bower, (Ed.), *The psychology of learning and motivation,* (Vol. *19,* pp. 179–210). New York: Academic Press.
Colwill, R. M., & Rescorla, R. A. (1985). Post-conditioning devaluation of a reinforcer affects instrumental responding. *Journal of Experimental Psychology: Animal Behavior Processes, 11,* 120–132.

Colwill, R. M., & Rescorla, R. A. (1986). Associative structures in instrumental learning. In G. H. Bower (Ed.), *The psychology of learning and motivation* (Vol. *20*, pp. 55–104). New York: Academic Press.

Holland, P. C. (1983). "Occasion-setting" in Pavlovian feature positive discriminations. In M. L. Commons, R. J. Herrnstein, & A. R. Wagner (Eds.), *Quantitative analyses of behavior: Vol. IV. Discrimination processes* (pp. 183–206). Cambridge, MA: Ballinger.

Kohler, W. (1941). On the nature of associations. *Proceedings of the American Philosophical Society, 84*, 489–502.

Postman, L., & Riley, D. A. (1957). A critique of Kohler's theory of association. *Psychological Review, 64*, 61–72.

Prentice, W. C. H., & Asch, S. E. (1958). Paired association with related and unrelated pairs of nonsense-figures. *American Journal of Psychology, 71*, 247–254.

Rescorla, R. A. (1968). Probability of shock in the presence and absence of CS in fear conditioning. *Journal of Comparative and Physiological Psychology, 66*, 1–5.

Rescorla, R. A. (1980). *Pavlovian second-order conditioning: Studies in associative learning.* Hillsdale, NJ: Lawrence Erlbaum Associates.

Rescorla, R. A. (1982). Comments on a technique for assessing associative learning. In M. L. Commons, R. J. Herrnstein, & A. R. Wagner (Eds.), *Quantitative analysis of behavior, Vol. IV.* (pp. 41–63). Cambridge, MA: Ballinger.

Rescorla, R. A. (1985a). Conditioned inhibition and facilitation. In R. R. Miller & N. S. Spear (Eds.), *Information processing in animals: Conditioned inhibition.* Hillsdale, NJ: Lawrence Erlbaum Associates.

Rescorla, R. A. (1985b). Pavlovian conditioning analogues to Gestalt perceptual principles. In F. R. Brush & J. B. Overmier (Eds.), *Affect, conditioning and cognition: Essays on the determinants of behavior* (pp. 113–130). Hillsdale, NJ: Lawrence Erlbaum Associates.

Rescorla, R. A. (1986). Two perceptual variables in within-event learning. *Animal Learning and Behavior, 14*, 387–392.

Rescorla, R. A. (1988). Pavlovian conditioning: It's not what you think it is. *American Psychologist, 43*, 151–160.

Rescorla, R. A., & Durlach, P. J. (1981). Within-event learning in Pavlovian conditioning. In R. R. Miller & N. E. Spear (Eds.), *Information processing in animals: Memory mechanisms* (pp. 81–111). Hillsdale, NJ: Lawrence Erlbaum Associates.

11 "Say, That Reminds Me!" A Study of Spontaneous Recall

William F. Walsh

ABSTRACT

The research presented here focuses on some of the structural factors affecting spontaneous or unintentional recall. The investigation of this neglected phenomenon was carried out by means of a novel method in which both the encoding of a visual pattern and its recall by cues corresponding to some of its parts occurred under incidental conditions. The set of critical patterns was interspersed among a series of other shapes, with spontaneous recall occurring over relatively brief intervals. Experimental results indicated that the evocativeness of a cue was a function of such factors as the perceptual organization of the incidentally encoded whole, the structural attributes intrinsic to a cue itself, the characteristics of the series and figural relations between cues. Comparison of incidental encoding and spontaneous recall with their intentional counterparts revealed that the former may be far more sensitive to the influence of perceptual organization than the latter, providing an empirical basis for a psychological distinction between these two types of memory.

INTRODUCTION

Every person has experienced the unexpected or spontaneous recall of a past event. While attention is directed elsewhere, a memory surfaces, its evocation often triggered by a chance encounter with a stimulus resembling the whole or perhaps only a part of it. If not dismissed as a mere distraction, the unsolicited memory may give rise to fertile associations and novel reinterpretations of the past.

The evocativeness of a part for a whole is a pivotal feature of one of the best known literary examples of spontaneous recall. In *Remembrance of Things Past* (Proust, 1913/1981), the protagonist at one point tries in vain to retrieve memories that would explain why the eating of a tea drenched madeleine should seem so intensely and provocatively familiar. In this case, the aura of familiarity accompanied by feelings of surprise and chagrin represents a partial spontaneous evocation which hints tantalizingly of memories to come—memories which, by the way, may very well have been acquired incidentally. Although refractory to intentional search, these recollections eventually emerge spontaneously, providing a rich context which illuminates the gustatory event as a significant part of a poignant childhood episode.

The steps highlighted in Proust's artful paradigm of remembrance point to the fact that cued recall begins with an act of recognition wherein a percept elicits a memory trace on the basis of their mutual similarity. This step underlies the feeling of familiarity we have on encountering the evocative stimulus. Other information associated with the evoked trace may then emerge in consciousness, elaborating the significance of the original stimulus. This biphasic account of the recall process, first proposed by Höffding (1891), became a cornerstone of the Gestalt theory of memory (Koffka, 1935/1963; Köhler, 1965). Its assimilation by cognitive theories of memory processing has been explicit in some cases (Asch, 1968; Rock, 1962; Rock & Ceraso, 1964) and implicit in others (Mandler, 1980).

In keeping with the theme of our work, we note that the steps of recollection may occur as either intentional or spontaneous memory events. Correspondingly, the specific memory traces—those which contribute to our feeling of familiarity and those which when recalled help place the familiar object or event in a meaningful context—also may be formed or encoded either intentionally or incidentally. The research reported here focuses on the spontaneous recall of incidentally acquired memories.

The technique used in this research involved the presentation under incidental conditions of a moderately complex pattern, designated parts of which later served as cues to its spontaneous recall. Both the whole and the parts which served as cues were interspersed in a short series of patterns which was shown to naive observers. This arrangement not only provided a means for studying how the perceptual organization of the whole affects the evocativeness of cues, but it also enabled us to investigate other matters such as how the evocativeness of a prior cue might influence that of a later one.

As Bower and Glass (1976) have pointed out, the use of parts of a visual pattern as cues in the recall of an inclusive whole is a somewhat novel method in the field of memory. Both the method employed here and the one used by Bower and Glass were derived with adaptive variations from a common intellectual ancestor, Köhler (1947). Essentially, Bower and Glass confirmed what Köhler had earlier demonstrated, which is that parts derived from wholes in accordance with certain Gestalt principles are more effective as recall cues than parts derived by means of arbitrary rules.

The present investigation, which actually predates that of Bower and Glass,[1] differs from it through its focus on spontaneous recall of incidentally acquired memories and its search for serial order effects. The fact that both the encoding and recall phases were conducted under incidental conditions also distinguishes this study from conventional investigations of incidental learning in which intentional tests are typically used to measure the amount of material inadvertently acquired by naive learners (Eagle & Leiter, 1964; Neimark & Saltzman, 1953; Postman, Adams, & Phillips, 1955; Postman & Phillips, 1954; etc.).

The influence of perceptual organization on memory and learning has been widely demonstrated (Arnold & Bower, 1972; Asch, 1969; Asch, Ceraso, & Heimer, 1960; Kaswan, 1957; Prentice & Asch, 1958; etc.). The primary emphasis of these studies, however, was on the perceptual conditions of association and not on recall per se. Contemporary students of memory, even those within the Gestalt tradition, have seemingly neglected the investigation of spontaneous memory first explored by Köhler and von Restorff (1935). Their pioneering work examined the occurrence of spontaneous recall as a function of the characteristics of activities performed between the time when a target memory was encoded and subsequently evoked by a critical percept. Intervening activities which intensified the distinctive similarity of a percept to a trace increased the likelihood of spontaneous recall. The present investigation extends the work begun by Köhler and von Restorff.

Experiment 1: Spontaneous Recall of a Whole by Its Parts

We began our research on the assumption that the evocativeness of isolated parts encountered subsequent to the presentation of a pattern in which they were integral features would depend to a large degree on the perceptual organization or structure of the inclusive whole. Gottschaldt's work (1926/1969a & 1929/1969b) on the visual perception of complex patterns demonstrates, for example, that the distinctiveness or perceptibility of parts depends on structural factors involved in the visual organization of the whole. Accordingly and with regard to the patterns used in condition 1 of this experiment (see Fig. 11.1, where item number also signifies

---

[1]This chapter is based in large measure on research carried out as part of the author's doctoral dissertation (Walsh, 1973) which was conducted under the supervision of Professor S. E. Asch, whose suggestion of the problem, inspiration, wisdom and patient guidance are gratefully acknowledged. The presentation of this work in this special volume achieves a professionally and personally meaningful closure effect. For their assistance in collecting data, appreciation is extended to: Stephen Konscol, Sandra Blazek, and Carolyn Thoburn.

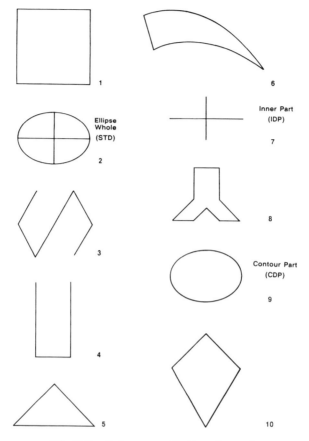

FIG. 11.1. Patterns used in Experiment 1.

serial position), it was predicted that the incidentally acquired trace of the ellipse whole (item 2) would be spontaneously recalled more frequently by a cue corresponding to its more salient contour part (item 9) than by one matching its less conspicuous inner part (item 7). In condition 2, the structure of the ellipse whole was modified by separating its component parts, thereby making each more distinctive and presumably increasing the evocativeness of their respective cues.

The parts were inserted as cues in the series used in each condition in order to examine how the evocativeness of the first might affect that of the second. As the cues were dissimilar, we wondered whether spontaneous recall of the trace of the whole by the first might alter the encoded structure of the whole so as to make it less accessible to a second. We refer to this hypothetical outcome as the trace preemption effect in order to distinguish it from other forms of memory interference derived from associative as opposed to structural factors.

Procedure.   For obvious reasons, the purpose of the experiment had to be disguised. Accordingly, preliminary instructions defined the task for observers (*O*s) as a screening procedure. The relevant portion of the instructions follows: "As you look at each figure, I would like you to comment on it. You might for example say what a figure is, or what it might be, or what it could be. Please feel free to mention anything of interest that comes to your mind as you are looking at each of the figures." Because of space limitations, only an abbreviated account of the procedure will be provided here.[2]

Following the opening instructions, the 10 patterns shown in Fig. 11.1 were presented manually and in serial fashion to individual *O*s in condition 1. For presentation, each pattern was drawn in black ink, photocopied, and mounted on a 6″ × 8″ posterboard. Display time was 4 seconds per pattern with a 6-second interstimulus interval during which time *O* viewed a blank card. *O*'s comments were jotted down during the intervals.

The set of three critical patterns (CPs) used in condition 1 included a moderately complex whole or standard pattern (STD), the major and minor axes of which measured 2″ and 1⅜″, respectively. Two designated parts (DPs), one corresponding to the STD's contour (CDP), the other to its inner cross (IDP), were used as cues. The DPs were identical in shape, size, and location to the corresponding regions of the STD. The serial positions of the DPs varied, while those of each of the other eight patterns were constant: half of the *O*s encountered the CDP in position 7 followed by the IDP in position 9 (group 1); DP order was reversed for the remaining *O*s (group 2).

In condition 2, the principal parts of the STD were separated (see illustrations in Table 11.1). This was accomplished by shortening each of the arms of the inner part by ¼″. Thus, the restructured STD consisted of an elliptical outer part surrounding but not touching the inner cross part. This modification preserved the topological relationship between the parts of the original STD used in condition 1, while altering only their articulation. The size of the IDP was adjusted accordingly. In all other respects the procedure used in condition 2 was the same as that of condition 1.

For the most part information about spontaneous recall (SR) was obtained during a comprehensive interview which began immediately after presentation of the series. Variations on the following question were used in a relaxed, conversational manner to obtain information about recall occurrences: "Did it happen that a particular figure in the series reminded you of one or more of the figures that preceded it—that is, while looking at a particular figure did you ever think back to one or more of the figures that had preceded it in the series for any reason whatsoever and with any degree of intensity."[3]

---

[2]See Walsh (1973) for a more comprehensive account of the experimental method.

[3]Ironically, the incidental instructions established a set which caused most *O*s to treat instances of SR as irrelevant to the study. Hence, they were seldom mentioned at the time of their occurrence.

For each such report, O was asked to describe the patterns, to indicate their relative order and to state whether the instance mentioned had occurred on exposure to the evocative pattern or whether it was only induced by the interview question. Further, each O was also asked if, during the initial presentation of the series, he or she had deliberately searched for interpattern relations or had attempted to learn the series. A positive response in either case disqualified O and the data he or she provided. A report was, thus, treated as an instance of SR only if it was reported by a naive O to have occurred at or shortly after the time of the initial viewing of the evocative pattern. Reports of groupings induced by the interview are discussed in a later section of this chapter.

If O initially failed to mention recall of the STD by one or both DPs, a portion of the series, including the DPs but not the STD, was reexposed—the patterns being placed before O at the same time—while he or she was asked, indirectly and, if necessary, directly, whether the DPs reminded him or her of patterns from the unexposed portion of the series.

Near the end of the interview, a check was made to determine if Os who had not mentioned the STD could recognize it. Os who did not recognize the STD were disqualified on the grounds that their apparent failure to register and/or store the STD accurately did not afford an opportunity to measure the differential evocativeness of the DPs.[4] Finally, with the three CPs present, all reports of occurrences of cued recall, spontaneous or induced, together with those nonoccurrences involving the CPs, were double checked to insure for accuracy.

Os in this and the following experiments were volunteers drawn from the graduate and undergraduate populations at Rutgers University (Newark), Seton Hall University and Teachers College, Columbia University. For the experiments on spontaneous recall, a total of 370 Os were interviewed; of these 330 (90%) met our criteria for being incidental encoders and recallers. An additional 48 Os were included in experiments on intentional encoding and recall.

Results and Discussion.   The data in Table 11.1 reflect reports in which the entire STD was spontaneously recalled. There were, however, five reports of partial SR (three in condition 1 and two in condition 2). In four of these the IDP was involved, while the CDP triggered only one instance of partial SR. In each case, O reported that the DP had appeared familiar, but had not spontaneously recalled the STD. Nevertheless, these Os were eventually able to retrieve the entire STD. Thus, in each condition, both parts tended when evocative to spontaneously recall the trace of the complete STD. Indeed, Os frequently reported that evocative DPs were perceived as being incomplete, suggesting that the recalled trace of the STD influenced the perceptual qualities of evocative DPs.

Inspection of the evocativeness of the DPs in condition 1 shows that overall

---

[4]Disqualifications based on recognition failures seldom occurred, involving no more than one or two Os per condition when they did.

TABLE 11.1
Experiment 1: Spontaneous Recall of the Ellipse Whole by Its Parts

Condition	Order of CPs			N	SR Types		
	2	7	9		7-2 F(%)	9-2 F(%)	9-7 F(%)
1. Intact Whole							
Group 1	⊕	○	╫	18	16(89)	4(22)	1(6)
Group 2	⊕	╫	○	18	7(39)	8(44)	2(11)
2. Segmented Whole							
Group 3	⊕	○	╫	18	13(72)	13(72)	5(28)
Group 4	⊕	╫	○	18	12(67)	11(61)	2(11)

the CDP was about twice as evocative of the STD than was the IDP ($p < .005$, $\chi^2 = 8.01$).[5] In condition 2, however, where the STD was segmented, the DPs were nearly equally evocative. Clearly, structural modification of the STD benefited the IDP, the evocativeness of which more than doubled ($p < .005$, $\chi^2 = 9.39$), while that of the CDP remained unchanged.

It seems, thus, that the intact structure of the STD used in condition 1 tended to deprive its inner part of perceptual salience. While the cross was objectively present in that STD (indeed, its dimensions were even larger than they were in the segmented STD), it was merely a subsidiary part, the nature or identity of which depended on the structure of the whole (Wertheimer, 1923/1969). Appearing in isolation, the IDP, therefore, was unlikely to remind a naive O of the intact STD. The outer contour, however, being a relatively conspicuous feature of the STD to begin with, provided a strong basis for the CDP to be an effective cue in both conditions.

There was a general tendency in both conditions for SR of the STD by the second DP to occur in conjunction with SR of the STD by the first DP: 67% (8 of 12) in condition 1 and 79% (19 of 24) in condition 2. This trend contradicted our preemption hypothesis which called for SR of a STD by two dissimilar DPs to be mutually exclusive. That the DPs were perceived as dissimilar, however, is suggested by the infrequency with which SR of the first DP by the second was reported: 8% in condition 1 and 19% in condition 2. Even when both DPs spontaneously evoked the STD, SR of the first DP by the second occurred in only 25% of such cases in condition 1 (2 of 8) and 32% in condition 2 (6 of 19). Apparently, the trace of the STD, although jointly evoked by both DPs, seldom acted as a mediator between its dissimilar parts.

Whereas in condition 1, each DP was about twice as evocative in position 7

---

[5]Levels of significance were determined on the basis of one-tailed tests. Decisions for using either the Chi-square test or the Fisher test were guided by rules presented in Siegel (1956).

than it was in position 9, serial position had no affect on the evocativeness of the DPs in condition 2. This comparison suggests that the structure of the STD played a part in the observed order effect. To determine whether the interposition of a first DP between the STD and a second DP contributed at all to this result, a control for condition 1 was carried out. Accordingly, 36 naive Os were evenly divided into two groups; for each, a substitute pattern replaced the DP in position 7, leaving only two CPs in the series with the STD in position 2 and either the IDP or the CDP in position 9. Evocativeness of the lone DP rose for each control group: eight Os (44%) reported SR of the STD by the IDP vs. four (22%) in group 1 of condition 1; 12 Os (67%) reported SR of the STD by the CDP vs. eight (44%) in group 2 of condition 1. The overall difference between experimental and control conditions was statistically significant ($p < .05$, $\chi^2 = 2.76$). Evidently, the observed order effect was a function of both the structure of the STD and the presence of an intermediate DP.

Comparison of the main results of conditions 1 and 2 supports the initial assumption that the perceived structure of a pattern plays a major role in its SR by its isolated parts. One might ask, however, whether the comments or verbal descriptions which Os mentioned while inspecting the patterns contributed in a significant way to the recall process under investigation. To answer this question, the protocols of Os in both conditions were examined. For both conditions, subgroups of Os were found whose comments while viewing the STDs were similar in that they made reference to both parts, e.g., "egg with a cross in it," "a gun sight," etc. Of the 8 such Os in condition 1 only 3 (38%) reported spontaneous evocation of the STD by the IDP, whereas 17 of the 19 Os (89%) in the corresponding subgroup of condition 2 made such reports ($p < .01$, $\chi^2 = 5.44$). Using a different mode of analysis, Bower and Glass (1976) found that the frequency with which highly evocative parts and wholes received similar verbal labels was insufficient to account for the rates at which parts recalled wholes in their study. Given these two sets of results it seems that SR of a whole by its parts was influenced primarily by perceptual rather than linguistic structures.

Experiment 2: A Further Look at SR of a Whole by Its Parts

Introduction and Procedure. Condition 1 of this experiment was designed to explore further the relative evocativeness of structurally dissimilar parts for the memory trace of an incidentally acquired whole. In addition, we wished to examine the contribution of certain nonstructural features to the occurrence of SR. For this reason, a series of punctiform patterns was used (see Fig. 11.2). These were delineated by means of dots which were $\frac{3}{32}$" in diameter; the CPs appear in positions 2, 7, and 9. The DPs were derived from the STD ($1\frac{1}{4}$" per side) by the deletion of a component dot.

There were two principal nonstructural or modal features which the CPs

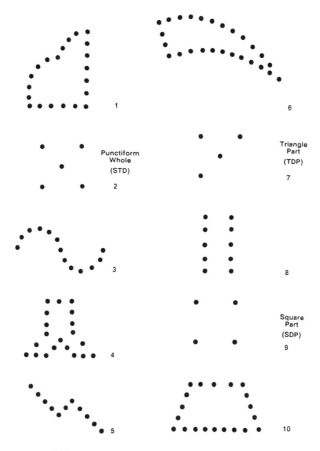

FIG. 11.2.   Patterns used in Experiment 2.

shared. In contrast to the other patterns in the series, the CPs were composed of just a few widely spaced dots. Thus, they shared the modal features of relative density and numerosity. With respect to the arrangement of the dots in the DPs, however, the square DP (SDP) appeared to have a distinct advantage over the triangular DP (TDP), the former corresponding to a salient natural part of the STD while the latter matched only an obscure arbitrary region, made up of segments of the "X" and "square" components of the STD. We had assumed that, while the modal similarities might benefit both DPs, the evocativeness of the SDP would, nevertheless, exceed that of the TDP, the difference between the two reflecting the contribution of perceptual organization effects. The series was presented under incidental conditions to two groups of 12 naive Os each to counterbalance the order of the DPs.

Results and Discussion.   The results of condition 1 are obtained in the first two rows of Table 11.2. Surprisingly, neither DP was very effective as a cue; further, differences between them were negligible (29% for the TDP vs. 38% for the SDP). The issue of why the TDP was almost as evocative as the SDP is discussed shortly. First, however, attention is given to a few other findings.

SR of one DP by the other was rare, suggesting that modal similarity was not a potent factor. Further, only one report of partial SR was obtained. Evidently, a pattern, even when composed of discrete elements, is more likely to be recalled *in toto* than in a piecemeal fashion, provided, of course, that the elements can be organized into a unified gestalt.

As to the affect of order on evocativeness of the DPs, we note that, while the DPs were somewhat more evocative in position 7 than in position 9 (42% vs. 25%), the magnitude of the presumed order effect measured in absolute values was modest and seemed to have a greater impact on SDP than on TDP. Also, examination of the distribution of SRs revealed no support for the assumption that evocativeness of the second DP for the STD was inversely related to that of the first DP. Of the six instances in which SR of the STD was produced by a second DP, three (50%) were associated with SR of the STD by the first DP.

Condition 2 of this experiment addressed the matter of the paradoxical evocativeness of the TDP. The main results of condition 1 indicated that a factor other

TABLE 11.2
Experiment 2: Spontaneous Recall of the Punctiform Whole by its Parts

Condition	Order of CPs			N	SR Types		
					7-2	9-2	9-7
	2	7	9		F(%)	F(%)	F(%)
1. Natural vs. Arbitrary Part							
Group 1				12	4(33)	3(25)	0(0)
Group 2				12	6(50)	3(25)	1(8)
2. Orientation							
Group 3				12	0(0)	6(50)	0(0)
Group 4				12	0(0)	8(67)	0(0)
Group 5				12	6(50)	10(83)	0(0)
3. Distinctive Similarity							
Group 6				12	9(75)	9(75)	2(17)
Group 7				12	11(92)	9(75)	5(42)

than the perceptual organization of the STD was involved. In this regard, comments made by Os suggested that some of them tended to perceive the TDP as an unbalanced or lopsided right triangle resting precariously on its apex. For these Os the TDP appeared incomplete, as though it were missing a crucial dot, even before it evoked the STD. This raised the possibility that visual features stemming from the phenomenal orientation of the TDP contributed to its ability to spontaneously elicit the STD. The effect of phenomenal orientation on figural appearance has been well documented (Rock, 1973).

To test this possibility, information on the relative evocativeness of the three other right triangles contained in the STD was obtained under circumstances similar to those of condition 1. One of these TDPs had the structural feature of lopsidedness, while the other two appeared stable as they rested on their bases (see the illustrations for groups 3, 4, and 5 in Table 11.2). For each new group ($N = 12$ naive Os), a different TDP appeared in position 7; the STD and SDP were fixed in positions 2 and 9, respectively.

All evocations of the STD in condition 2 involved SR of the STD as a whole. As to the main issue, examination of the results for groups 1, 3, 4, and 5 in Table 11.2 reveals that, as recall cues, the lopsided and stable TDPs differed markedly and consistently; overall the former produced SR of the STD in 42% of the cases; in contrast, the latter were entirely unevocative ($p < .005$, $\chi^2 = 10.23$). Left-right orientation differences of the TDPs had no influence on the outcome. Further, the stable TDPs were no more likely than their lopsided counterparts to spontaneously recall or to be recalled by nonCPs.

Differences in cue efficacy among the TDPs are certainly incompatible with any explanation of SR based on the modal similarity of the critical patterns. Across all four conditions, there was only one instance of SR of the first DP by the second. Apparently, the nonstructural features shared by the CPs contributed little to the evocativeness of the lopsided TDPs. We were thus led to conclude that the perceptual feature of ''lopsidedness'' which derives from the relation of the perceived top and bottom parts of the TDPs to the vertical axis was the principal factor responsible for their evocativeness. Evidently, the organization of the trace of a whole is not the sole determinant of its accessibility to a cue. Structural features of a cue—even one corresponding to an arbitrary part—can make it more or less capable of eliciting the memory of a whole.

Conditions 1 and 2 found that modal similarity contributed little, if anything, to the evocativeness of the DPs. In condition 3, the relative density and the punctiform composition of the CPs were made highly distinctive by replacing the nonCPs in the series shown groups 1 and 3 with patterns drawn with continuous lines. Each new series was shown to a different group of 12 naive Os.

Distinctive modal similarity enhanced the evocativeness of the DPs for the STDs (compare the data for groups 6 and 7 with those of groups 1 and 3, respectively, in Table 11.2). Reports of SR of the STD by the DPs rose markedly from 27% without distinctive similarity to 79% with it ($p < .001$, $\chi^2 = 24.1$). In condition 3, the previously nonevocative stable TDP even produced slightly more SRs of the STD than the other DPs. Spontaneous evocations of one DP by the other, although somewhat more frequent, still lagged behind SR of the STD by the DPs, suggesting that structural relationships between the CPs continued to play a major role. In terms of design and results, this condition is similar to the studies of Köhler and von Restorff (1935). Further, condition 3 provides a convincing demonstration of the von Restorff effect under incidental circumstances (von Restorff, 1933).

Examination of the results of these experimental conditions provided no consistent support for the occurrence of trace preemption. Evidently, under incidental conditions, evocative parts are not likely to influence the organization of the trace of an evoked whole. Under these circumstances, we turned our attention to other interposition effects.

Experiment 3: DP Order Effects Redux

Introduction and Procedure.   A different perspective on the issue of preemption was suggested by the results of Experiment 2. With a lopsided and a stable TDP in the same series, the percept of the second should recall the trace of the first. We wondered whether such contact would transfer to the later TDP the perceptual characteristics of the earlier one along with its relationship to the STD. In other words, would the trace of the stable TDP preempt the percept of the lopsided TDP and thereby prevent it from evoking the STD? Reciprocally, would the trace of an evoked lopsided TDP enhance the percept of the stable TDP rendering it evocative of the STD?

To test these possibilities, the usual incidental conditions were employed. The punctiform STD in position 2 was followed by a lopsided TDP and a stable TDP, the identity of each of which is shown in Table 11.3. DP positions were 5 and 7, with DP order systematically alternated. The series, which consisted of only seven patterns, was shown to a total of 48 naive Os. The data thus obtained are presented in Table 11.3, where the distribution of reported occurrences ($+$) and nonoccurrences ($-$) of SR involving the evocation of the STD by each of the DPs as well as the evocation of the first DP by the second is detailed. Included in this table are the relevant results from those groups of Experiment 2 which here serve as controls. The number of naive Os in group 1 of Experiment 2 was increased to 24 in connection with research not included in this report.

Results and Discussion.   Comparison of experimental and control groups reveals that the evocativeness of the TDPs in position 7 was impacted decisively by the presence of the TDPs in position 5. Situating the lopsided TDP between the STD and the stable TDP (group 1) did produce a distinct increase in the evocativeness of that DP ($p = .02$, Fisher Test). Further, the interpolation of the stable TDP between the STD and the lopsided TDP (group 2) lowered the

TABLE 11.3
Experiment #: Interposition Effects and Spontaneous Recall

Group	Order of CPs			N	SR Types			
	2	5	7		5-2 F(%)	7-2 F(%)	7-5 F(%)	Totals F(%)
1. Enhancement				24	+	+	+	6 (25)
					+	+	−	1 (4)
					−	+	+	1 (4)
					−	−	+	16 (67)
					7 (29)	8 (33)	23 (96)	
Control (Experiment 2, Group 3)				12	----	0 (0)	----	
2. Preemption				24	+	+	+	2 (8)
					+	−	+	1 (4)
					−	+	+	1 (4)
					−	−	+	20 (84)
					3 (12)	3 (12)	24 (100)	
Control (Experiment 2, Group 1)				24	----	9 (38)	----	

evocativeness of that TDP for the STD ($p < .05$, $\chi^2 = 2.78$). For both groups, Os reporting SR of the STD indicated that it had been evoked in its entirety.

With regard to the hypothesized percept enhancement effect, inspection of the distribution of SR reports shows that seven of the Os in group 1 reporting SR of the STD by the lopsided TDP also reported that the stable TDP had evoked the STD. In contrast, the stable TDP was evocative of the STD in only 1 of 17 instances (6%) when following a nonevocative lopsided TDP, a difference which is highly significant ($p = .001$, Fisher Test). Thus, we conclude that prior SR of the STD by the lopsided TDP facilitated SR of the STD by the base TDP.

As to the hypothesized percept preemption effect, examination of the distribution of SR reports in group 2 reveals that of the three Os reporting SR of the STD by the lopsided TDP, two reported that the stable TDP had evoked the STD; only 1 of 21 Os who reported that the first TDP had been nonevocative indicated that the second TDP had spontaneously evoked the STD (67% vs. 5%, $p = .004$, Fisher Test). Apparently, the interposition of a nonevocative stable TDP between the STD and the lopsided TDP prevented the latter from evoking the former.

To account for both the percept preemption and enhancement effects, we assume: (1) that SR occurred sequentially, and (2) that, because of their greater similarity, the percept of the second DP evoked the trace of the first DP before contacting that of the STD. Once evoked, the trace of the first TDP contributed to the organization of the percept of the second TDP such that the latter was experienced as a variant of the former. As a version of the evocative lopsided TDP in group 1, the stable TDP then tended to spontaneously recall the STD. In contrast, as a version of the inert stable TDP in group 2, the lopsided TDP was blocked from spontaneously evoking the STD. In the preemption condition the trace of the STD was available but not accessible to the second TDP (Tulving & Pearlstone, 1966). The interpretation offered here suggests that a similar process underlines both selective and nonselective SR. The next experiment focuses exclusively on the percept preemption effect.

Experiment 4: Percept Preemption and Selective SR

Introduction and Procedure.   Unlike the previous experiments, the CPs used here were each units (see Fig. 11.3, where the CPs appear in positions 2, 7, and 8). Each was a square measuring 1¼″ per side. The first was rotated 45° impart-

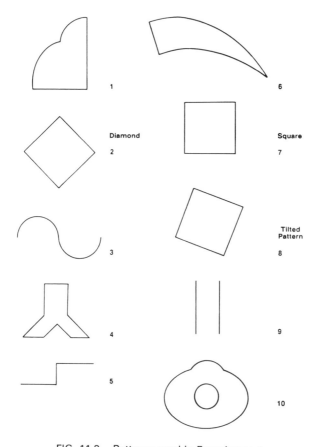

FIG. 11.3.   Patterns used in Experiment 4.

ing to it the appearance of a diamond; the second was in an upright position; the third was tilted 20°. For the purpose of reference, they are termed diamond, square, and tilted pattern, respectively.

The series was shown under incidental conditions to 52 naive Os. For half of them (group 1), the square was in position 2 and the diamond was in position 7; for the other half (group 2), the positions of the square and diamond were reversed. The tilted pattern remained in position 8 for both groups. Provided the CPs preceding it were each encoded as separate and unrelated traces, it was predicted that the tilted pattern would selectively lead to SR of one or the other of the earlier CPs but not both. As a control for each of the experimental conditions, separate groups were shown the two series with a neutral pattern replacing the CP in position 7.

Results and Discussion. The data for each experimental group along with its corresponding control are presented in Table 11.4. In each of the control groups, the tilted pattern was highly evocative of the preceding CP. With the interpolated CP present in each of the experimental groups, however, the evocativeness of the tilted pattern for the first CP declined significantly: from 100% to 62% for group 1 ($p = .001$, Fisher Test) and from 81% to 50% for group 2 ($p < .05$, $\chi^2 = 2.88$).

TABLE 11.4
Experiment 4: Percept Preemption and Spontaneous Recall

	Order of CPs			N	SR Types			
	A	B	C		B-A F(%)	C-A F(%)	C-B F(%)	Totals F(%)
Group 1				26	+	+	+	10(38)
					+	+	−	1 (4)
					+	−	+	1 (4)
	□	◇	▱		−	+	−	5(19)
					−	−	+	8(31)
					−	−	−	1 (4)
					12(46)	16(62)	19(73)	
Control				14	----	14(100)	----	
Group 2				26	+	+	+	7(27)
					+	−	+	3(11)
	◇	□	▱		−	+	+	3(11)
					−	+	−	3(11)
					−	−	+	9(35)
					−	−	−	1 (4)
					10(38)	13(50)	22(85)	
Control				16	----	13(81)	----	

A sizeable proportion of the Os in each experimental group reported that the interpolated CP had spontaneously evoked the first. Under these circumstances, the tilted pattern, should tend to evoke both CPs. Selective SR of the first CP or the second CP by the third should be more likely to occur when the first two CPs are encoded as separate and unrelated events. The data on SR distributions contained in Table 11.5 are analyzed along these lines.

There were 12 Os (46%) in group 1 and 10 Os (38%) in group 2 who reported SR of the first CP by the second. Across these combined subgroups, selective SR of the square or the diamond by the tilted pattern occurred in only five instances (23%), while, conjoint SR of both the square and the diamond by the tilted pattern was reported in 17 instances (77%).

The first two CPs were encoded separately for 14 (54%) of the Os in group 1 and for 16 (62%) of the Os in group 2. For the combined subgroups, selective SR occurred for 25 Os (83%) and conjoint for only three Os (10%). There were two Os (7%), one per subgroup, for whom the tilted pattern evoked neither the diamond nor the square. As expected, selective SR was far more likely when the first two CPs were encoded separately ($p < .001$, $\chi^2 = 22.05$).

Again we assume that, when the percept of the tilted pattern spontaneously evoked either the trace of the square or the diamond, the contact served to identify the former. The identity step fixed or stabilized the organization of the percept such that any relation to the remaining CP was lost. This account accords with the finding that Os who reported selective SR tended to describe the tilted pattern as either a "tilted square" or a "tilted diamond" depending upon which of the two other CPs it evoked.

INTENTIONAL RECALL

In this section we briefly consider the affects of intent on the detection of relationships between CPs. In the preceding experiments, intent was unavoidably introduced during the interview. As a result, Os reporting on SR in those experi-

TABLE 11.5
Experiment 5: Spontaneous Versus Intentional Recall

Condition	Order of CPs			N	Recall Types in Percent		
	A	B	C		B-A	C-A	C-B
1. Spontaneous	⊕	╪	◯	18	39	44	11
Intentional				12	100	100	17
2. Spontaneous	⠒	⠪	⠂⠂	24	38	25	0
Intentional				12	100	100	42
3. Spontaneous	⠒	⠔	⠒	12	0	50	0
Intentional				12	83	83	8
4. Spontaneous	◇	▢	◺	26	38	50	85
Intentional				12	92	92	100

ments also mentioned instances of intentional grouping in which patterns were categorized together in hindsight. Further, several of the original conditions were repeated with a conventional intentional procedure in which Os were instructed just before presentation of the series to search for interpattern relations. How did intent affect the detection of relations between CPs?

When Intent Follows Incidental Encoding

As for the preceding experiments, we note that Os readily distinguished between instances of intentional recall (IR) and SR and that the induction of a set to search for interpattern relations following incidental viewing of a series of patterns generally resulted in an increase in the number of evocations reported, particularly where the CPs were concerned. For example, in Experiment 1, condition 1, total evocations of the intact ellipse STD by the CDP were 32 (24 SR plus 8 IR), whereas total evocations of the STD by the IDP were 30 (11 SR plus 19 IR). Clearly, the IDP benefited more from intentional search than did the CDP, suggesting that intent prompted Os to restructure the trace of the intact ellipse STD in a manner that redressed the imbalance between its primary parts.

The distinction between SR and IR was, thus, crucial to our principal findings. Subtle organizational effects which may govern functioning in the incidental mode would have been completely masked if this distinction had not been made. To further illustrate this point, we note that the character of evocative differences between the lopsided and stable TDPs is substantively changed if SRs and IRs are combined. Neither of the stable TDPs in Experiment 2 produced any SRs, but together they produced a total of 14 IRs (58%) compared with the total of 17 (70%) evocations produced by the two lopsided TDPs (10 SRs plus 7 IRs). Clearly, the major differences between these two sets of cues resided in their capacity to produce SRs. Hence, we agree with Köhler and von Restorff (1935) that the involvement of intent in the recall process introduces analytic factors which may compensate for or even nullify the effects of perceptual organization. We now turn to an examination of those conditions in which intent was introduced before the presentation of a series, where it could impact both encoding and recall phases.

Experiment 5: When Intent Precedes Encoding

The following experimental conditions were repeated under intentional circumstances: experiment 1, group 2; experiment 2, groups 1 and 3; and experiment 4, group 2. The relevant portion of the intentional instructions, which were given prior to the presentation of a series, read as follows: "I would like you to tell me if a figure you are looking at reminds you of one or more of the figures that preceded it. If during the time you are viewing a figure it does remind you of earlier ones, just say 'this one'." Immediately after the series was shown, O was asked to report which shapes he or she had been reminded of in each instance.

The data from both the original incidental conditions and the intentional conditions are presented in Table 11.5 for comparison. Previewing intent raised recall frequencies to maximum or near maximum levels in all of the conditions and blotted out the percept preemption effect seen under the incidental circumstances of Experiment 4. Obviously, the way in which the patterns used in this investigation are grouped depends, to a large extent, on whether they are processed incidentally or intentionally. These preliminary findings suggest an answer to a question posed by Neisser (1982) regarding the relationship between spontaneous and incidental recall. Apparently, these two types of memory are different, and what we learn about one does not necessarily apply to the other.

CONCLUDING REMARKS

Throughout its course our excursion into the realm of spontaneous recall has remained within the parameters of a relatively short time span. Intervals measured in tens of seconds are a far cry from those measured in decades as was the case in the literary example which served as our starting point. Also, our investigation was limited to the study of spontaneous recall of visual memory traces by visual cues. As Salaman (1982) indicates, unexpected memories, varying widely in content, may be elicited by a panoply of stimulus types ranging over all sensory channels. The distinctive taste of the madeleine, for example, which gives rise to Proust's *Remembrances of Things Past* (1913/1981) finds its contemporary reflection in the audible refrains of popular songs from the 30s and 40s which spark the ''instant memory flashes'' of a childhood in Coney Island, New York, so vividly realized in Woody Allen's film *Radio Days* (1987).

From the vantage point of our modest experimental procedures, however, we were able to observe as naive individuals processed information in an incidental mode. While attention was directed elsewhere, they, nevertheless, spontaneously registered relations between patterns in the same series. As we have seen, the detection of such relations was based on the perceptual organization of the patterns involved, which in turn was influenced by serial order effects. As to the latter, under incidental conditions, it was discovered that the primary recognition step may serve to fix or define the structure of an evocative percept in such a way that it either constrains or enlarges the number of items spontaneously recalled. Although we did find data supportive of percept preemption and percept enhancement, we were unable to find uniquivocal evidence of trace preemption. This may reflect differences in the relative ease with which the organization of figural features belonging to an inchoate percept can be influenced compared with those of an already formed trace. At any rate, the naturalness with which Os responded to our questions about their memory experiences suggests that spontaneous recall is a common event and that the human brain is processing in both intentional and incidental modalities much of the time.

The research reported herein along with that of Köhler and von Restorff (1935) establishes that spontaneous recall of incidentally acquired memories is amenable to experimental investigation. While in the present instance the results are based on *ex post facto* reports, the consistency among Os belonging to the same experimental conditions along with the fact that differences between conditions tended to reflect modifications of experimental design combine to suggest that the interview procedure collected reliable data.[6] Further, the independence of the data from experimenter influence may be ascertained from the observation that empirical findings did not always accord with outcome expectancies. Gestalt theory proved to be a fruitful but not unerring guide to the study of spontaneous recall. We hope that the presentation of this work will remove the penumbra of obscurity from this intriguing aspect of memory.

REFERENCES

Allen, W. (1987). *Radio days*. New York: Orion Pictures Corporation.
Arnold, P. G., & Bower, G. H. (1972). Perceptual conditions affecting ease of association. *Journal of Experimental Psychology, 93,* 176–181.
Asch, S. E. (1968). The doctrinal tyranny of associationism: or what is wrong with rote learning. In T. R. Dixon & D. L. Horton (Eds.), *Verbal behavior and general behavior theory* (pp. 215–228). Englewood Cliffs, NJ: Prentice-Hall.
Asch, S. E. (1969). A reformulation of the problem of associations. *American Psychologist, 24,* 92–102.
Asch, S. E., Ceraso, J., & Heimer, W. (1960). Perceptual conditions of association. *Psychological Monographs, 74,* 1–48.
Bower, G. H., & Glass, A. L. (1976). Structural units and the redintigrative power of picture fragments. *Journal of Experimental Psychology: Human Learning and Memory, 2,* 456–466.
Eagle, M., & Leiter, E. (1964). Recall and recognition in intentional and incidental learning. *Journal of Experimental Psychology, 68,* 58–63.
Gottschaldt, K. (1969a). Gestalt factors and repetition. In W. D. Ellis (Ed. and Trans.). *A source book of gestalt psychology* (pp. 109–122). London: Routledge & Kegan Paul. (Original work published 1926).
Gottschaldt, K. (1969b). Gestalt factors and repetition (continued). In W. D. Ellis (Ed. and Trans.). *A source book of gestalt psychology* (pp. 123–135). London: Routledge & Kegan Paul. (Original work published 1929).
Höffding, H. (1891). *Outlines of psychology*. London: Macmillan.
Kaswan, J. (1957). Association of nonsense-figures as a function of fittingness and intention to learn. *The American Journal of Psychology, 70,* 447–450.
Koffka, K. (1963). *Principles of gestalt psychology*. New York: Harcourt, Brace & World.
Köhler, W. (1965). *Dynamics in psychology*. New York: Washington Square Press.
Köhler, W. (1947). *Gestalt psychology*. New York: Liveright Publishing Corp.

---

[6]To allay criticism of our naturalistic method of data collection, separate groups of eight naive Os each—one corresponding to group 1 of Experiment 1, the other to group 1 of Experiment 2—were asked to draw the CPs involved in each report of SR mentioned. There were 14 such reports; all drawing were substantially accurate. SR results were analogous to those originally obtained.

Köhler, W., & von Restorff, H. (1935). Analyse von vorgangen im spurenfeld: II. Zur theorie der reproduktion. *Psychologie Forschung, 21*, 56–112.

Mandler, G. (1980). The judgment of previous occurrence. *Psychological Review, 87*, 252–271.

Neimark, E., & Saltzman, I. J. (1953). Intentional and incidental learning with different rates of stimulus presentation. *American Journal of Psychology, 66*, 618–621.

Neisser, U. (1982). Memory: What are the important questions? In U. Neisser (Ed.), *Memory observed* (pp. 3–19). San Francisco: W. H. Freeman. (Original work published 1978).

Postman, L., & Phillips, L. W. (1954). Studies in incidental learning: I. The effects of crowding and isolation. *Journal of Experimental Psychology, 48*, 48–56.

Postman, L., Adams, P. A., & Phillips, L. W. (1955). Studies in incidental learning: II. The effects of association and the method of testing. *Journal of Experimental Psychology, 49*, 1–10.

Prentice, W. C. H., & Asch, S. E. (1958). Paired association with related and unrelated pairs of nonsense-figures. *The American Journal of Psychology, 71*, 247–254.

Proust, M. (1981). *Remembrance of things past* (Vol. 1) (C. K. Scott & T. Kilmartin, Trans.). New York: Random House.

Rock, I. (1962). A neglected aspect of the problem of recall. In J. Scher (Ed.), *Theories of the mind* (pp. 645–659). New York: The Free Press.

Rock, I. (1973). *Orientation and form.* New York: Academic Press.

Rock, I., & Ceraso, J. (1964). Towards a cognitive theory of associative learning. In C. Scheerer (Ed.), *Cognition: Theory, research, promise* (pp. 110–146). New York: Harper & Row.

Salaman, E. (1982). A collection of moments. In U. Neisser (Ed.), *Memory observed* (pp. 49–63). San Francisco: W. H. Freeman. (Original work published 1970).

Siegel, S. (1956). Nonparametric statistics: for the behavioral sciences (pp. 104–110). New York: McGraw-Hill.

Tulving, E., & Pearlstone, Z. (1966). Availability versus accessibility of information in memory for words. *Journal of Verbal Learning and Verbal Behavior, 5*, 381–391.

von Restorff, H. (1933). Uber die wirkung von bereichsbildung im spurenfeld. *Psychologische Forschung, 18*, 299–342.

Walsh, W. F. (1973). Spontaneous memory for visual patterns. (Doctoral dissertation, Rutgers University, 1973). *Dissertation Abstracts International, 34*, 2893–2894.

Wertheimer, M. (1969). Laws of organization in perceptual forms. In W. D. Ellis (Ed. and Trans.), *A source book of gestalt psychology* (pp. 71–88). London: Routledge & Kegan Paul. (Original work published, 1923).

12 Aspects of Narrative Thinking

Henri Zukier
New School for Social Research

ABSTRACT

A framework of narrative thinking is proposed. The narrative mode is a fundamental way of organizing knowledge around the basic arguments of action. The mode articulates dynamic, sequential relations between components, and considers patterns of goal orientation and agency embedded in context.

PARADIGMATIC THINKING

In the 1987 preface to the Oxford edition of his *Social Psychology,* S. Asch outlined the perspective that animated his work: ". . . a human psychology necessarily had to be a social psychology. In turn it had to be an account of human experience, of beliefs and actions as they appeared to their human agents . . . a phenomenological psychology in which social facts and processes held central place" (Asch, 1987, p. IX). The traditional focus of research in social and cognitive psychology has explored forms of understanding which take rather little account of these dynamics of human action. The prevalent concern has been with rules for categorization and with what may be called "paradigmatic" thinking. From early studies on concept attainment (e.g., Bruner, Goodnow, & Austin, 1956) to current models of decision making (see Abelson & Levi, 1985; Einhorn & Hogarth, 1981), the research has explored strategies for assigning individual events to generic classes and principles for matching new input to preexistent cognitive structures or expectations. Over time, the research considered, alternatively, rectangles, robins, and restaurants; the consistent concern was with the organization of this knowledge in taxonomic and class-inclusion systems.

The paradigmatic research tradition clearly has proved of considerable importance and heuristic value. However, as numerous studies have indicated in passing, there also are other forms of organizing knowledge, which affect all aspects of information processing.

For instance, in *A Study of Thinking,* Bruner and his colleagues employed abstract "nonsense" materials to prevent any recourse to "reasonable" or intuitive solutions possibly suggested by more concrete stimuli. One of the many experimental variations, however, incorporated, rather incidentally, a condition which used thematic materials evocative of a little story on theme. The thematic array of cards depicted an interaction between an adult and a child, and was otherwise identical to a parallel abstract condition. The thematic group, however, evolved very different strategies, resulting in considerable differences in task performance. Thus Bruner et al. (1956) note in passing: "To us, it suggests that much of human reasoning is supported by a kind of thematic process rather than by an abstract logic. The principal feature of this thematic process is its pragmatic rather than its logical structures. . . . One might well call the tendency an effort after empirical verisimilitude" (p. 104). A similar conclusion also emerges from much of current research on decision making. Thus, one major model of judgment under uncertainty (e.g., Tversky & Kahneman, 1983) poses "extensional" (traditional paradigmatic) inference against people's "intuitive reasoning," and "logic versus intuition." The authors note that a basic intuitive cognitive strategy, the representativeness heuristic "generally favors outcomes that make good stories on good hypotheses. . ." They conclude that "A comprehensive account of human judgment must reflect the tension between compelling logical rules and seductive nonextensional judgment" (pp. 311, 314).

NARRATIVE THINKING AND ACTION

The study of narrative thinking (Zukier, 1986) explores another way of structuring knowledge, and proposes a model of coherence linked to the logic of action. While the classic social psychological work emphasized the strong links between perception, motives, and action (e.g., Asch, 1987; Heider, 1944, 1958; Lewin, 1951), such connections have progressively been attenuated in subsequent works, as the focus shifted to the internal representation of the information and to mentalistic models. The focus on action is similar to the perspective articulated by philosophers such as Derrida (1967) and Levinas (1973). In an early work, Levinas noted that Husserl "may have been wrong in seeing the concrete world as a world of objects that are primarily perceived. Is our main attitude towards reality that of theoretical contemplation? Is not the world presented in its very being as a center of action, as a field of activity. . . ?" (Levinas, 1973, p. 119)

Derrida subsequently developed the critical implications of the "ocular metaphor" and of the visual focus in the work of Husserl.

The narrative mode is a way of organizing knowledge, which entails forms of mental activity quite distinctive from paradigmatic processing, and distinctive structural and thematic elements for representation, understanding, and inference. Narrative structuring underlies, for example, many artistic and literary genres; it animates good drama, historical writings that go beyond chronological lists of events, musical compositions, and many other accounts of personal action and human experience. Thus Hayden White (1981) remarks about medieval historiography:

> When we moderns look at an example of a medieval annals, we cannot but be struck by the apparent naivete of the annalist; and we are inclined to ascribe this naivete to the annalist's apparent refusal, inability, or unwillingness to transform the set of events ordered vertically as a file of annual markers into the elements of a linear/horizontal process. In other words, we are likely to be put off by the annalist's apparent failure to see that historical events dispose themselves to the percipient eye as "stories" *waiting to be told,* waiting to be narrated. (p. 6)

The systematic relationships which pull the individual objects together are organized around the basic components of personal action. The intuitive power of the action configuration was illustrated in a series of classic demonstrations (Heider & Simmel, 1944; Michotte, 1946). In the Michotte experiments, subjects were shown several small rectangles in motion, at varying speeds, directions, and distances. Specific patterns of timing and speed evoked "functional relations" between the rectangles and were cast in elaborate accounts: A bumps into B, shoves B forward, carries B off, hits B, or runs away from it. The accounts, moreover, developed narratives which assigned meaning to the motions in the language of social action. In a related study (Heider & Simmel, 1944), people viewed a brief animation film, in which three geometrical figures moved in various directions and at various speeds, in a field that contained a large rectangle. People uniformly interpreted the movements as actions of animate beings, and typically elaborated a connected story to explain the different scenes. In one representative account, for example, "A man has planned to meet a girl and the girl comes along with another man. The first man tells the second to go . . . ," and numerous complications arise. (Heider & Simmel, 1944, pp. 246–247).

Western tradition has long emphasized the role of action forms of understanding and explanation. In *The Poetics,* Aristotle (1973) characterizes narrative as the imitation (mimesis) or representation of human action. The second chapter opens with the insistent remarks that "Artists imitate men involved in action" and that "tragedy is essentially an imitation not of persons but of action and life . . . the end for which we live is a certain kind of activity, not a quality . . . In a play accordingly they do not act in order to portray the characters; they include the characters for the sake of the action. So that it is the action in it, i.e. its Fable or Plot, that is the end and purpose of the tragedy; and the end is everywhere the chief thing'' (p. 678). A similar conviction about the centrality of action concepts animates contemporary literary theory. In the structuralist and the formalist views (e.g., Barthes, 1975; Greimas, 1966; Todorov, 1977; see Ricoeur, 1984, 1986) the characters of a story typically are subordinated to the plot. Thus, Roland Barthes (1966) observes that ''The narratives of the world are numberless . . . narrative is present in every age, in every place, in every society; it begins with the history of mankind and there nowhere is nor has been a people without narrative . . . narrative is international, transhistorical, transcultural: it is simply there, like life itself'' (p 79). Indeed, in psychology and in literary theory there have been suggestions about culturally universal and structurally invariant narrative articulations (e.g., Mandler, 1984; Propp, 1968), which even were linked to deep innate organizing structures (Chomsky, 1972; Levi-Strauss, 1963).

FEATURES OF NARRATIVE THINKING

The narrative framework proposes a broad set of principles to provide coherence to diverse findings in the literature, and to develop an account of various psychological phenomena related to an action-orientation. Some preliminary experimental evidence is available about the basic components of the orientation; the framework, however, does not yet offer a comprehensive and detailed canonical scheme of the narrative mode.

The action configuration of narrative processing organizes the flow of behavior into meaningful and directed patterns articulating connections between individual events. The narrative and the paradigmatic modes act together in inference: Each may be deployed alone or in combination, in interaction or in competition with the other. The logic of the two modes is, in some way, complementary: The paradigmatic mode articulates the categorical structures and vertical hierarchies inherent in all thinking, and the narrative mode develops the horizontal, sequential relations *between* categories or elements. The variegated forms of everyday arguments that are not justified in formal propositional terms often are articulated in the horizontal narrative logic.

In general terms, the paradigmatic logic reflects the formal structure of traditional scientific models. The paradigmatic mode is primarily concerned with the construction of equivalence classes and principles of class inclusion and induction. It converts all concepts into the format of attribute categories, in order to subsume them in a hierarchical relationship to a superordinate class. Paradigmatic relationships are founded on principles of similarity between the exemplar and the generic class. Similarity underlies the ascription of class membership and the assignment of properties to the concepts. Class membership may be a function of various criteria, such as shared attributes or functions; the common dimensions mark the various objects as equivalent and determine their class inclusion. This paradigmatic structure thus affords considerable flexibility, since any one object could be conjoined with many other, different ones, depending on the basis for classification. The primary characteristic of the various class members is the common relationship to the category, organized around prototypical examples or defining attributes. Any member may also have distinctive relations with other members; these relations, however are unprincipled, contingent, and highly variable (see Mandler, 1984).

The class inclusion systems are generated by the selective focus on a few criterial features shared by the concepts. Specifically, the paradigmatic mode considers only the formal structure of knowledge, taking little account of the individuating pragmatic dimensions of judgment: motives and goals; and the context of judgment. The paradigmatic logic trades richness for abstract rigor and for generality across domains. Its temporal relations can readily generate equivalent or alternate accounts and associations to related concepts, as is evident in analogy and metaphor. The truth value of its formal propositions is established through external validation—matching concepts to facts.

Paradigmatic thinking thus is indifferent to the relationships *among* the members of a class. Narrative thinking, in contrast, focuses on the principled relations among individual members. It articulates dynamic, sequential links between concepts and a set of combinatorial rules apt for the description of uniqueness, novelty, or change over time. Narrative structuring is rooted in the pragmatic arguments of action, and considers patterns of goal orientation and agency embedded in context, and expressed in a characteristic form of narrative causality.

Narrative logic operates at an intermediate level of abstraction, and focuses on both similarities and differences between phenomena. Narrative seeks to account for the distinctive complexities of the individual phenomenon, and has a retrospective-explanatory emphasis. In addition to patterns of similarity, narrative causality entails a variety of other dynamic associative principles. Narrative logic foregoes rigor to go beyond the information given, and to strive for comprehensiveness and richness. The truth value of its propositions is established, in part, through internal validation: plausibility and coherence.

The sequential links of conjunction or combination are principled or dynamic, rather than merely empirical links. Thus narrative should be distinguished from paradigmatic structures in which elements are joined, *within* the category, by routine temporal connections or other prearranged sequential patterns derived from common practice rather than principle. Thus, scripts (e.g., Schank & Abelson, 1977) are schematic constructs which articulate a stereotyped, temporal sequence of events, in which the horizontal connections between the scenes reflect the conventions of the social episodes. The ''restaurant'' script, for instance, codifies habitual patterns and predetermined relations, from placing the order to paying the check. There are no dynamic links between independent units. The script as a whole serves as a superordinate category, and the primary connection is the vertical link between new exemplars and the generic class ("This is a restaurant?!!").

GOAL ORIENTATION

Human behavior, unlike the motion of physical particles, is shaped by people's understanding of what they are doing and animated by a network of intentions and goals. The purposive orientation of social behavior has long been underscored in the social sciences (e.g., Burke, 1969; Garfinkel, 1967; Nozick, 1981; Weber, 1968). In psychology, the cognitive perspective also emphasizes the active and constructive nature of cognition. The earlier associationist models had depicted essentially passive people prompted by reinforcement contingencies and experimental stimuli. In these models, cognition entailed reactive and retrospective processes, in response to triggering conditions. The cognitive approach, by contrast, treats thinking and behavior as deliberative and prospective, reflecting people's preferences and purposes. Cognition, like behavior, is future oriented, linked to goals and to the uses the individual had in mind, or to anticipated consequences. Miller, Galanter, and Pribram's (1960) seminal cybernetic model for the cognitive regulation of action emphasized the centrality of goals, embodied in the basic feedback unit of behavior—the TOTE (or, Test-Operate-Test-Exit units). Action is guided by "images" of goals, and regulated as a function of tests to determine progress towards achieving them.

For a variety of reasons, however, goals have had a checkered and opportunistic history in psychology, and have remained ill-defined and overcharacterized. While research has repeatedly demonstrated the effects of goals, these goals are typically imposed by the experimenter, and the individual merely responds to an additional constraint in a classic learning task. Inference is studied in terms of its adequation to a host of contingent objectives. These objectives often reflect the experimenters' interests, such as when people are asked to adopt an "impression formation" or a "recall" goal, in studies of the impact of such sets on stages of information processing. In this approach, there is an unprincipled and unlimited repertoire of pragmatic, cognitive, and expressive goals, resulting in an all-encompassing framework of "motivated strategies." Thus, with the recent resurgence of interest in the study of the self, numerous self-related goals have been proposed. They range from objective self-awareness or self-evaluation, to self-serving or self-enhancement processes, to self-handicapping strategies (e.g., Showers & Cantor, 1985; Suls, 1982). In consequence, research has not extensively explored more fundamental goal orientations and the inherently purposive structure of thinking.

Contingent Goals: Narrative Inference and the Base Rate Fallacy

The paradigmatic and narrative modes are associated with fundamental orientations that affect inference in general. The deployment of the two sets of strategies as a function of judgmental objectives was explored in a series of studies on the base rate fallacy in probability estimates (Zukier & Pepitone, 1984). The base rate fallacy is a robust finding that has been described in numerous studies of intuitive prediction. The phenomenon involves the relative underutilization, in probabilistic judgments, of information about the frequency distribution of a phenomenon in the population, and about the prior odds of its occurrence. Instead, people rely unduly on concrete information about particular individuals. In the classic study (Kahneman & Tversky, 1973), people read thumbnail descriptions of several professionals, sampled at random from 100 such profiles of lawyers and engineers. Some people were told that the group included 70 lawyers and 30 engineers; others were given the reverse proportion. Upon reading each profile, people were asked to indicate whether the individual is a lawyer or an engineer. The profiles were designed to sound either like an engineer (or lawyer), or to be totally uninformative about group membership. Typically, people in the two base rate conditions made similar guesses for each description, regardless of whether there were 30 or 70 engineers (lawyers) in the group. In fact, when the sketches were not at all helpful for the judgment, people guessed that both outcomes were equiprobable.

There have been a number of explanations for the underutilization of base rate information. In the present framework, base rate information is paradigmatic information about the frequency of category membership (e.g., in the legal profession) in a given population. The individual profiles, in contrast, clearly are narrative descriptions. The task thus pits paradigmatic against narrative information, with the expectation that people will combine the two kinds of information in accord with paradigmatic rules. The underutilization of the distributional information then is commonly viewed as reflecting limited understanding of the proper meaning and use of abstract ''statistical'' information. However, if there are two fundamental modes of judgment, rather than a unitary set of strategies, the neglect of base rate information may result from the deliberate deployment of the narrative orientation. In narrative judgments, base rate information would properly carry less weight than it should in classic paradigmatic judgments. Consideration of people's judgmental orientation at the time of the task would, in this view, affect the patterns of the base rate fallacy.

The effects of goal orientation were examined in one study (Zukier & Pepitone, 1984) by asking subjects working on the classic base rate problem (Kahneman & Tversky, 1973) to adopt the role of a scientist or of a clinical counselor, and by specifying a sponsorship for the study designed to evoke a paradigmatic or a narrative orientation.

In both conditions, the other instructions and the task were similar to those of Kahneman and Tversky (1973). Subjects were given two personality sketches, supposedly sampled at random from a group of 30 engineers and 70 lawyers. One sketch was designed to evoke the stereotype of an engineer (e.g., "he shows no interest in political and social issues, and spends most of his free time on his many hobbies which include home carpentry, sailing and mathematical puzzles"). The other description was designed to convey no information relevant in any way to the individual's profession (e.g., "he is married with no children . . . ; he is well respected by his colleagues . . .").

The simple manipulation of the sponsorship of the study and of role assignment had a strong effect on subjects' probabilistic judgments. The narrative condition replicated the results of previous studies, and the base rate fallacy. The paradigmatic condition, in contrast, yielded patterns of prediction that accorded with normative expectations. In the narrative orientation, the stereotypical engineer profile was judged to belong to an engineer with an average .76 probability. The neutral profile produced a mean estimate of .42 and a median of .5, thus approximating equiprobability. In the paradigmatic orientation, the probability estimates were lower for both profiles, presumably reflecting the greater weight given to the base rate. Predictions that the stereotypical engineer profile belonged to an engineer were still high (.64), a function of the perceived diagnosticity of that description. The critical neutral profile yielded a mean probability estimate of .31, which was not significantly different from the specified base rate. The patterns of findings suggest that subjects are able to incorporate prior probabilities in their judgments, depending on the specific orientation they have to the task. Subjects in the narrative orientation consider the specific descriptions, and the stories they might tell (or not tell, in the neutral description) about the individuals. In contrast, subjects in the paradigmatic orientation attach little weight to these individual narratives, and base their predictions for the "neutral" profile on the relation of the case to the population from which it is drawn. The base rate fallacy may be so prevalent in previous studies which did not control for judgmental orientation, because the narrative materials (the profiles) may have evoked a narrative mode, or because this mode may dominate spontaneously in many conditions.

The Narrative Orientation as Cognitive Style

The manipulation of goal orientation illustrated the temporary effects of the two orientations, when they are activated in an experimental context. If these orientations are basic features of people's purposive information processing, they may structure judgment in more stable and general ways, in natural contexts. There may be individual differences, related to cognitive style or education, in affinity for each of the modes, and in their relative dominance in particular situations. Enduring individual differences in judgmental orientation may be related, for instance, to medical training. Medical education emphasizes the use of frequency distributions to determine the relative likelihood of various etiologies associated with presenting symptoms, a ruling in and ruling out of possibilities given the patient's symptoms, history, and age. Diagnostic training may thus sensitize people to a paradigmatic orientation, which would remain available in other unrelated domains.

To explore this possibility, Zukier and Pepitone (1984) gave the classic base rate problem to a group of first-year medical students and to a group of surgery residents. Each subject received the standard set of instructions, specifying a group composition of 30 engineers and 70 lawyers, read the neutral and the stereotypical engineer profiles, and estimated the likelihood that each of the sketches actually was that of an engineer. Background information also was obtained, to examine alternative factors which might contribute to any observed group differences. For instance, (self-) selection might occur over the course of studies, such that only students with particular characteristics, associated with a paradigmatic orientation, might reach residency. The registration data for the previous 5 years at the medical school revealed a drop-out rate of 4%, suggesting that the two groups were largely similar. Alternatively, residents might, for instance, evaluate the diagnosticity of the descriptions differently than medical students. Judgments from another group of medical students and residents at the medical school, indicated, however, that there were no such differences.

Given similar background of the two groups, would a medical education lead people to preferentially adopt a paradigmatic orientation in unrelated domains? The data revealed a strong effect of educational level ($p < .0001$) and the expected effect for description ($p < .001$). In all conditions, residents incorporated base rate information in their estimates significantly more than first-year students. In the neutral condition, when the profile had no diagnostic value for the prediction of group membership, 90% of the residents estimated the likelihood at .3, the specified base rate, for an overall mean of .31. In contrast, 45% of the medical students estimated the same probability at .5, for an overall mean of .47.

In the stereotypical condition, the residents' mean estimate was .51, compared to .69 for first-year medical students. The distribution of the residents' responses was bi-modal: the majority guessed a probability of .3, while the remainder assigned probabilities higher than .7. Most residents who gave high estimates indicated in side comments that they did so in spite of an overall probability of .3, because they considered the stereotypical description diagnostic enough.

The results suggest that neither medical students nor residents properly combined prior probabilities and specific information, albeit in different ways. The residents' responses are the mirror image of the medical students' answers. While medical students neglected prior probabilities, the residents in effect over-utilized prior probabilities, and many seemingly discarded entirely specific case information, even when it was considered pertinent to the outcome, in the stereotypical condition. The residents showed a reversal of the base rate fallacy, as extensive as the medical students' traditional tendency to underutilize base rate information. The contrasting judgmental strategies may well reflect the prevalence of the paradigmatic and narrative orientation, respectively.

NARRATIVE CAUSALITY

Paradigmatic causality typically derives from class-inclusion hierarchies. Specific concepts are related to categories, as a function of shared similarity of form or function; or they are located at a class intersection and characterized through the overlap of several independent categories. The cause represents the critical features of the process that produces the outcome, such that a "correspondent inference" is possible from an observed behavior to the underlying set of causal features or relationships. Paradigmatic causality entails intrinsic relations between the outcome and the cause, reflected in structural or functional affinity. The regularities allow prediction of future outcomes under particular conditions. Just as an apple's fall results from gravitational forces to which the apple is subject, so aggressive or submissive behavior are related, in this framework, to correspondent personality characteristics. Particulars are only included if they are shared by the other members of the class. Paradigmatic causes thus often are situated at a higher level of abstraction or of generality than the outcome.

In contrast, narrative causality need not involve class assignment; it introduces external, contextual elements into the causal sequence, which are not necessarily grounded in relations of similarity. Narrative causality may involve the purposiveness of the actors, new occurrences or settings, and other intervening links and triggering conditions. The directionality of the sequence may result from the interaction between the causal antecedent and other elements, at a similar level of abstraction as the outcome. Narrative causality draws on the pragmatic arguments of actions.

The contrast between paradigmatic and narrative structures of causality may also be reflected in the degree of intuitive utilization of base rate information. In the classic problem formulation, base rate information is presented is a purely paradigmatic format and is only useful for determining the prior probabilities of category membership. Formally equivalent problems which evoke a more narrative causality thus might produce different responses. Narrative prior probabilities would suggest discernible pragmatic links to the outcome, through one of several action components.

In a third study (Zukier & Pepitone, 1984), subjects estimated the likelihood of outcomes (professional membership; burglary; divorce) for three different problems in a within-subjects design. The control problem was the standard "engineers–lawyers" problem, and subjects estimated the likelihood that the individuals in the stereotypical and in the neutral profiles actually were, each, one of the 30 engineers.

The burglary problem specified the base rate: "The crime statistics of a certain New York City block shows that 68% of the apartments have been broken into at least once during the last 10 years, and 32% were not." The divorce problem presented a similar statistic: "A recent survey in the New York area has shown that within 3 years of getting married, 27% of the couples are divorced and 73% are still married." For each problem, subjects read one description of individuals unlikely to become burglary victims and likely to get divorced, respectively; and one description which contained no information diagnostic for the predicted outcome.

The "engineer–lawyer" problem replicated previous findings: with a base rate of .3, the mean estimated likelihood that the individual was an engineer was .79 for the stereotypical description, and .50 for the neutral description. However, the same subjects' estimates for the neutral descriptions of the two other problems closely approximated the specified base rate. In the burglary problem, the mean probability for the uninformative description was .26, for a base rate of .32. In the divorce problem, the mean probability of divorce assigned to the neutral profile was .30, for a base rate of .27. None of these estimates was significantly different from the specified base rates. When the statistical information implicitly introduces narrative elements of action (e.g., stories about unsafe neighborhoods or about the vulnerability of marriages) people fully incorporated the information in their judgments.

AGENCY

Arguments of action also emphasize the role of human agency in the understanding of people. The sense of self is encapsulated in the narratives people evolve about their own efficacy, and mastery over events. Indeed, in many domains, people have well-formed expectations about their capabilities. The base rate fallacy, for example, has been commonly attributed to inherent limitations of individual processing capabilities, such as an insensitivity to certain types of statistical information. If subjects share such expectations of ability and agency, these may, in turn, affect performance.

Few cognitive abilities are considered less amenable to change than those skills which are differently distributed among the sexes. One sex difference that has been repeatedly documented is the superiority of males in spatial ability, which culminates at adolescence (Deaux, 1985; Linn & Petersen, 1985; Maccoby & Jacklin, 1974). Within the narrative framework, Felzen and Zukier (1988) explored the possibility of attenuating such sex differences through cognitive changes in self-narratives, which would affect perceptions of agency and competence. The criterial task was the Embedded Figures Test (Witkin, Ottman,

Raskin, & Karp, 1971), on which sex differences at adolescence, favoring males, have been repeatedly found. Indeed, a pretest of the Embedded Figures Test on another group of similar subjects indicated that the response time of girls was on the average 15 seconds longer than the response time of boys.

The Embedded Figures Test (E.F.T.) is a measure of perceptual ability in spatial disembedding, which requires people to isolate a simple geometric figure from a complex and at times confusing background. A group of 15-year-old, 10th grade students at a large high school participated in the study. All students received 8 of the standard 12 items on the E.F.T., and provided several concomitant measures after completion of the task: their attribution for success or failure, their enjoyment of the task, and courses they had taken in school that had a relation to spatial skills.

In the control condition, subjects simply were given the E.F.T. and the other measures. In a competence condition, subjects also received positive performance feedback after the third item was completed, and then at regular intervals. The experimenter explained that the ''puzzles'' had been used at a similar school in the past, and consulted a ''record book'' with lists of scores. He then indicated that the students so far were performing better than 50%, and then 67% of the children at the other school. The feedback also was provided in graphic form: A diagram with a picture of 10 children in a row was presented, and a colored transparent paper was moved along the diagram to illustrate the subject's relative level of performance.

In another condition, the sense of agency and control was manipulated through an ''illusion of choice.'' Subjects were given the choice between the E.F.T. and a coding task, which was a subtest of the W.I.S.C. For the alternative coding task, the experimenter emphasized repeatedly the need to work very fast and accurately, and the demanding nature of the task, to lead people to ''choose'' the E.F.T. and thereby prevent self-selection. In addition, all subjects were asked to indicate their preferred disposition of the room and their seating arrangement. A final condition combined the competence and choice interventions.

The principal measure was subjects' response time in finding the simple form within the larger complex figure, for the eight experimental items. There was a significant interaction effect for sex and treatment. In the control condition, males performed substantially faster than females (males = 52.5 seconds; females = 67.6 seconds). Competence feedback, alone or in conjunction with choice, generally enhanced performance, though primarily so for the girls. As a result of the girls' faster performance, sex differences were eliminated in those conditions. Choice enhanced the girls' performance even more, while it had a deleterious effect on the performance of the boys (girls = 51.6 seconds; boys = 66.7 seconds); the choice manipulation thus produced a reversal in the directionality of the sex differences, reminiscent of the reversal in the base rate fallacy obtained with surgery residents. The concomitant measures reflected similar trends. In the control condition, boys enjoyed the task more than girls. Those differences also were eliminated in the two conditions where competence feedback was provided, due primarily to the enhanced enjoyment of the girls. Choice also enhanced positive affect for the girls, but depressed enjoyment for boys. In contrast to previous studies, there were no significant differences in attribution for success and failures. Boys and girls tended to avoid "ability" attributions, and explained failure by task difficulty ("the puzzle was hard"), and success by effort ("tried hard"). The course background questionnaire revealed a significant correlation for girls between the number of courses using spatial skills and performance on the E.F.T., but no correlation for boys. Boys also took significantly more courses requiring spatial skills than girls.

The effects of the competence and choice manipulations appear related to the narratives people entertain about themselves. Girls traditionally not only perform less well on spatial ability tasks, but seemingly also have corresponding lower expectations. Feedback in the course of the task may serve to dispel such notions, and produce enhanced performance. Choice likely also enhanced subjects' sense of personal involvement and agency for the task. Boys, with higher initial expectations than girls, were confronted with the unexpected slowness on a relatively difficult task, and the disconfirmed expectations further depressed performance and affect. These effects were eliminated as soon as competence feedback was provided. Girls also would derive a greater sense of agency and efficacy from the choice manipulation, but would have fewer expectancies to be disconfirmed. Hence they could enjoy the task without the anxiety about performing "at level."

Together, the various findings illustrate elements of a pragmatically oriented, narrative logic, which affects inference and performance. They also show the need to complement a differential aptitudes perspective, which examines the distribution of particular abilities in different populations, with a social-cognitive perspective, which examines underlying processes and strategies as a function of the context. The course background data in the spatial-ability study suggest that precisely because many skills are, at least in part, malleable, differential practice and different self-narratives people evolve about their competencies may widen, rather than narrow the gap between the sexes, or between groups. More generally, it appears that assumptions of direct and simple, rather than multiple causalities, and of unitary cognitive competencies, will tend to obscure rather than expose the full repertoire of people's abilities.

REFERENCES

Abelson, R. P., & Levi, A. (1985). Decision making and decision theory. In G. Lindzey & E. Aronson (Eds.), *Handbook of social psychology*. New York: Random House.
Aristotle (1973). In R. McKeon (Ed.), *Introduction to Aristotle*. Illinois: University of Chicago Press.
Asch, S. E. (1987). *Social psychology*. New York: Oxford University Press.

Barthes, R. (1977). Introduction to the structural analysis of narratives. In R. Barthes, Image, music text. New York: Hill and Wang.

Bruner, J. S., Goodnow, J. J., & Austin, G. A. (1956). A study of thinking. New York: Wiley.

Burke, K. (1969). A grammar of motives. Berkeley: University of California Press.

Chomsky, N. (1972). Language and mind. New York: Harcourt, Brace, Jovanovich.

Deaux, K. (1985). Sex and gender. Annual Review of Psychology, 36, 49–81.

Derrida, J. (1967/1973). Speech and phenomena, and other essays on Husserl's theory of signs. Trans. D. B. Allison. Evanston, IL: Northwestern University Press.

Einhorn, H. J., & Hogarth, R. M. (1981). Behavioral decision theory: Processes of judgment and choice. Annual Review of Psychology, 32, 53–88.

Felzen, S. L., & Zukier, H. (1988). Bridging the gender gap. Unpublished manuscript. New School for Social Research.

Garfinkel, H. (1967). Studies in ethnomethodology. Englewood Cliffs, NJ: Prentice-Hall.

Greimas, A. J. (1966). Semantique structurale. Paris.

Heider, F. (1944). Social perception and phenomenal causality. Psychological Review, 51, 358–374.

Heider, F. (1958). The psychology of interpersonal relations. New York: Wiley.

Heider, F., & Simmel, M. (1944). An experimental study of apparent behavior. American Journal of Psychology, 57, 243–259.

Kahneman, D., & Tversky, A. (1973). On the psychology of prediction. Psychological Review, 80, 237–251.

Levi-Strauss, C. (1958/1963). Structural anthropology. Trans. C. Jacobson & B. G. Schoepf. New York: Basic Books.

Levinas, E. (1930/1973). The theory of intuition in Husserl's phenomenology. Trans. A. Orianne. Evanston, IL: Northwestern University Press.

Lewin, K. (1951). Field theory in social psychology. New York: Harper.

Linn, M. C., & Peterson, A. C. (1985). Emergence and characteristics of sex differences in spatial ability: A meta-analysis. Child Development, 56, 1479–1498.

Maccoby, E. E., & Jacklin, C. N. (1974). The psychology of sex differences. California: Stanford University Press.

Mandler, J. M. (1984). Stories, scripts and scenes: Aspects of schema theory. Hillsdale, NJ: Lawrence Erlbaum Associates.

Michotte, A. E. (1946/1963). The perception of causality. Trans. T. R. Miles & E. Miles. New York: Basic Books.

Miller, G. A., Galanter, E., & Pribram, K. H. (1960). Plans and the structure of behavior. New York: Holt.

Nozick, R. (1981). Philosophical explanations. Cambridge, MA: Harvard University Press.

Propp, V. (1928/1968). The morphology of the folktale. Trans. L. Scott. Austin: The University of Texas Press.

Ricoeur, P. (1984–1986). Time and narrative (2 vols). Trans. K. McLaughlin & D. Pellauer. Illinois: University of Chicago Press.

Shank, R. C., & Abelson, R. P. (1977). Scripts, plans, goals and understanding. Hillsdale, NJ: Lawrence Erlbaum Associates.

Showers, C., & Cantor, N. (1985). Social cognition: A look at motivated strategies. In M. R. Rosenzweig & L. W. Porter (Eds.) Annual Review of Psychology (Vol. 36, pp. 275–307).

Suls, J. (Ed.). (1982). Social psychological perspectives on the self. Hillsdale, NJ: Lawrence Erlbaum Associates.

Todorov, T. (1977). The poetics of prose. Ithaca, NY: Cornell University Press.

Tversky, A., & Kahneman, D. (1983). Extensional versus intuitive reasoning: The conjunction fallacy in probability judgment. Psychological Review, 90, 293–315.

Weber, M. (1968). Economy and society. New York: Bedminster Press.

White, H. (1981). The value of narrativity in the representation of reality. In W. J. T. Mitchell (Ed.), *On narrative*. Illinois: University of Chicago Press.

Witkin, H. A., Ottman, P. K., Raskin, E., & Karp, A. (1971). *A manual for the Embedded Figures Test*. Palo Alto, CA: Consulting Psychologist Press.

Zukier, H. (1986). The paradigmatic and narrative modes in goal-guided inference. In R. M. Sorrentino & E. T. Higgins (Eds.), *Handbook of motivation and cognition: Foundations of social behavior*. New York: Guillford.

Zukier, H., & Pepitone, A. (1984). Social roles and strategies in prediction. Some determinants of the use of base-rate information. *Journal of Personality and Social Psychology, 47,* 349–360.

IV PERCEPTION

13 Developments in the Gestalt Theory of Lightness Perception

Alan L. Gilchrist
Rutgers University

ABSTRACT

The status of the gestalt theory of lightness perception, particularly as expressed by Koffka, is reviewed with three general conclusions. (1) Key aspects have become established, such as the dependence of lightness on at least two luminances and the crucial role of edges or gradients. (2) The thorny problem of perceptual structure continues to be shunned. It is shown that a very popular embodiment of the edge approach, the so-called contrast theory, is not in fact consistent with gestalt theory. This is seen most clearly in the failure of contrast theories to distinguish illumination edges from reflectance edges. This weakness, tantamount to a failure to engage the gestalt issue of perceptual structure, is shown to afflict both the older adaptation-level theory of Helson as well as the more current models based on Land's retinex approach. (3) Recent developments have moved us closer to a quantification of the prägnanz principle. Attention is drawn to the work of gestalt theorists Bergstrom, Gerbino, and Gilchrist and the potential in the concepts of common and relative components and of the retinal image as layered for launching a successful assault on the crucial puzzle of structure.

What is the current status of the gestalt theory of lightness and color perception? Is it dead? No. But gestalt theory, particularly the work of Koffka, has certainly been neglected by the mainstream. This is ironic since Koffka's (1935) theory can account for a wider range of lightness phenomena than contemporary theories, and with greater economy. Moreover, recent findings, especially those concerning stabilized retinal images, clearly reinforce Koffka's early emphasis on the importance of gradients of light.

Has gestalt theory been assimilated by the field, as in the oft-cited justification for its apparent neglect? There is some truth here, but perhaps the situation is more perverse. The fundamental idea that lightness is based on two luminances, not one, has indeed become accepted fact. Yet this fact is not typically understood in a gestalt way and in many instances, it actually serves to obscure the need for a more thoroughly gestalt analysis by appearing, at least on the surface, to account for the myriad of relational findings in the field.

Most importantly, perhaps, it can be reported that the gestalt approach is being actively and successfully developed in certain quarters. These developments are exciting in part because they have moved us closer to the possibility of a quantitative definition of pragnanz, one that can be applied before the perceptual fact, rather than after.

Before proceeding, we must pause to define a few terms. First, the terms *edge* and *gradient* will be used interchangeably here, and both will embrace gradual changes in light as well as sharp, and temporal changes as well as spatial. As for the gestalt theory of lightness perception, since it was Koffka who wrote in most detail on this topic, we begin with his account.

For Koffka (1935), the fundamental fact is that "perceived qualities depend upon stimulus gradients." By making this claim Koffka is rejecting the constancy hypothesis, according to which sensation at a certain point in the visual field depends on the stimulation at that same point. Even Mach bands are described and used to illustrate that "the local effect is not the result of local stimulation, but depends on the stimulus distribution over a large area" (p. 170).

Koffka insists, however, that not all gradients in the visual field are equally effective in determining lightness, or whiteness as he calls it. The effectiveness of a gradient between two light intensities depends on the degree of appurtenance between them, the degree to which they belong together. The Benary effect (1924), as shown in Fig. 13.1a, is a perfect example. The basic structure is a thick black cross on a white background. Two gray triangles are placed in the display. One appears to lie on the cross and it appears lighter than the other, which appears to lie on the white background, much like the effect in simultaneous lightness contrast. But in this case the physical surrounds of the two triangles are identical. Each borders white on the hypotenuse, and black on the other two sides. It is only perceptually that one triangle seems to "belong" to the cross and one seems to "belong" to the white background. For quantitative results see Gilchrist (1988). Perhaps even more remarkable is the variation created by White (1979) shown in Fig. 13.1b. Here the lighter-appearing gray strips actually border on much more white than do the darker-appearing gray strips. Other examples of this kind are to be found in Kanizsa (1979).

As interesting as these examples are, Koffka described a much stronger and more important example of the relative effectiveness of gradients. He pointed out that retinal gradients are caused by either reflectance gradients in the external environment, or by illumination gradients. It must then be the reflectance gra-

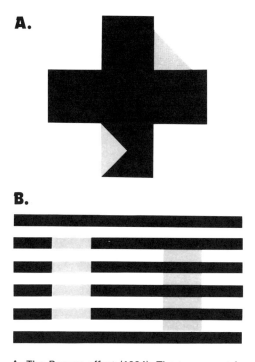

FIG. 13.1.   A. The Benary effect (1924). The two gray triangles have equal surround physically, but the one that appears to "belong" to the cross appears lighter. B. White's effect. The gray bars bordered on their long sides by white appear lighter, not darker, because they appear to "belong" to a black region seen behind the white stripes.

dients that are effective in determining surface lightness, not the illumination gradients. Otherwise lightness perception would be quite nonveridical.

Koffka was fully aware of the multiple dimensions of lightness perception. Every surface is seen as having, not only a surface color, but also a particular brightness of illumination. Koffka (1935) made the connection between these two perceptual dimensions and two fundamental types of gradients. While acknowledging that he could not entirely solve this aspect of the organization question, he nevertheless sharply defined it as the crucial question, as is apparent in the following passage:

> . . . given two adjoining retinal areas of different stimulation, under what conditions will the corresponding parts of the behavioral (perceptual) field appear of different whiteness but equal brightness (or "illumination"), when of different brightness but equal whiteness? A complete answer to this question would probably supply the key to the complete theory of colour perception in the broadest sense. (p. 248)

Here is where the crucial concept of visual organization, or perceptual structure, is brought into the theory. Perhaps the greatest strength of gestalt theory in general is the recognition and explicit treatment of this problem that is so easily overlooked. The visual world we see is composed of objects: chairs, trees—that are not given as such in the optic array. The optic array is a continuous pattern of light, varying in intensity and wavelength. Even the discontinuities do not correlate simply with the boundaries of objects. There are discontinuities in the image that do not represent the boundary of an object, for example a shadow falling across the middle of an object. And there are object boundaries not represented by a discontinuity in the optic array, as for instance when part of one object is hidden behind another. Nor is the problem reduced by the projection of this continuous pattern of light onto the retinal surface composed of discrete receptor units, the rods and cones. The stimulation on a pair of adjacent receptor units may or may not belong to the same object. Thus the very existence in our experience of segregated wholes, not to mention the hierarchical organization of these wholes, represents an impressive achievement by an active visual system.

At a general level, of course, Koffka saw the solution to the problem of organization in the concept of pragnanz. Although intuitively appealing, this concept has eluded rigorous definition. Perhaps the most concrete of Koffka's discussions of pragnanz are those describing processes of minimization and maximization. Nevertheless this apparent ad-hoc quality has often been the justification for rejecting the gestalt approach. The irony is that pragnanz has not been rejected in favor of a stronger approach to the problem of perceptual organization. Rather, the attempt has generally been to avoid this problem altogether, as we shall see. First, however, let us consider those aspects of Koffka's theory that have been widely accepted.

LIGHTNESS BASED ON TWO LUMINANCES

As Wallach (1948, 1976) made clear in his elegant work on ratios, light alone is unable to create the visual impression of an achromatic surface. This requires a gradient between two or more luminances. We know that a ganzfeld fails not only to evoke the appearance of a particular shade of gray, but fails as well to appear as a surface at all. Surface quality only appears when two different luminances are placed side by side. Wallach illustrated this with an elegant series of experiments using the now-familiar pattern of a disk surrounded by an annulus. When the disk has a higher luminance than the annulus, it appears white. When the annulus is brighter, the disk appears gray, the specific shade being a direct function of the disk/annulus luminance ratio.

The concept of lightness as the product of two or more luminances is now universally accepted, but it appears in more than one form. Jameson and Hurvich (1961), for example, hold lightness to be the net effect of two opposing forces, an excitation process associated with the luminance of the target and an inhibition process associated with the luminance of the surround. Citing support from Stevens (1961) and Hess and Pretori (1894), they have claimed that the ratio principle as such only applies to a limited portion of the illumination scale. Wallach, they suggested, had failed to note this because the eight-fold range of illumination represented in his studies was not as large as the eleven-fold range they used. We replicated the Jameson and Hurvich study with a million-fold range of illumination and got systematic ratio results across the entire range (see Fig. 2 of Jacobsen & Gilchrist, 1988a). Our results are consistent with those of a series of other studies (Arend & Goldstein, 1986; Flock & Noguchi, 1970; Haimson, 1974; Noguchi & Masuda, 1971). We found that there are conditions where the ratio principle does not strictly apply, but these conditions are defined by qualitative boundaries, such as whether the target is an increment or a decrement, not by arbitrary quantitative limits.

GRADIENTS AS PRIMARY

Wallach's (1948) ratio concept seems fully congruent with Koffka's gradient concept. Yet there are two interpretations of the ratio/gradient approach that need to be examined. The difference between these two interpretations may seem subtle but, as will be shown, it is far-reaching. The issue is whether luminances are prior to gradients or whether gradients themselves are primary. The usual interpretation is that the ratio or gradient is derived from a comparison of the absolute luminances of two or more adjacent retinal points. I have referred to this interpretation as the photometer metaphor (Gilchrist, Delman, & Jacobsen, 1983). The alternative is more radical. Gradients may be encoded directly, with no intervening encoding of luminances. By this account perception of absolute luminances—that is brightness perception, is derived by combining or integrating gradients, in effect turning the process on its head.

One test of these two hypotheses is provided by the ganzfeld, in which there is a luminance value but no gradient. It is well established that there is no surface lightness perception here, but what about brightness? Can the absolute intensity of a ganzfeld be sensed? Barlow and Verillo (1976) claim to have found an affirmative answer to this question. Using the method of magnitude estimation they obtained brightness estimates for a series of brief flashes in a ganzfeld. Finding that the brightness estimates of each subject increased monotonically with light intensity, they concluded that the visual system is capable of performing as a photometer. The obvious alternative is that these brightness estimates were based, not on absolute luminance per se, but rather on the sensing of temporal luminance changes from trial to trial. Koffka (1935), observing that "Perfect homogeneity would be both temporal and spatial" (p. 120), speculated that we would in fact cease to *see* under these conditions.

We are currently conducting work to resolve this question. An observer is placed in a ganzfeld, the luminance of which is either increased or decreased very gradually—at a below threshold rate—over a large range. After some time, and a substantial change in luminance, the observer is asked to report whether the field is brighter or darker than at the outset. If the ganzfeld fades to so-called "eigengrau," it may be that no subsequent discrimination of brightness levels is possible, even between very bright and very dark fields.

Likewise, Koffka predicted that a chromatic ganzfeld would appear colored only at the outset, and then gradually come to appear neutral. This prediction has since been tested and verified. In a classic study, Hochberg, Triebel, and Seaman (1951) found that the color of a chromatic ganzfeld fades to neutral. The fact that this effect takes at least three minutes to occur could be taken as evidence that the continuing absolute chromatic levels support the chromatic percept long after the effect of the onset has passed. But this of course raises the question of why the ganzfeld ever fades to neutral as long as the absolute chromatic information is present. It is plausible to assume that, in the absence of further change, the effect of the onset is simply extrapolated forward in a temporal filling-in analogous to the familiar spatial filling-in between edges (Krauskopf, 1963).

What constitutes the next logical step in complexity after the ganzfeld? Again it depends on which are primary, luminances or gradients. The general assumption has been that the disk/annulus configuration is the next step since it represents two luminances, not one. The zero luminance of the dark surround doesn't count. Yet if gradients, rather than luminances, are fundamental, an important step has been left out. The ganzfeld contains no gradients while the disk/annulus contains two. Systematic studies are needed of a visual field containing only one edge or gradient. This could take the form of a bipartite ganzfeld or else a disk in a ganzfeld.

My students and I have begun to study this latter configuration: a single disk of light surrounded by a ganzfeld of nonzero luminance. One question we have sought to answer concerns an apparent asymmetry in Wallach's paradigm. There the higher intensity always appears white, while it is the lightness of the darker region that varies with the ratio. Why doesn't the lower intensity always appear black? Or why don't both regions move (in opposite directions) away from middle gray as the ratio increases? Given the relativity of black and white, one might expect such symmetry. We have wondered whether this could be related to the presence of the dark surround of the disk/annulus display. The disk/ganzfeld paradigm eliminates this darkness. Nevertheless our tentative results indicate that the special role of white holds in the disk/ganzfeld paradigm as well, even when the luminance difference is very small. Perhaps a symmetry can be restored by thinking of white not as at one end, but as in the middle, with the gray surface shades below it and with luminous surfaces above it.

The only published report on such a single-gradient visual field is the so-called spot-in-a-void (Land & McCann, 1971) using a single homogeneous target presented within a totally dark surround. In this case the observer clearly has the experience of brightness and color, which is surely based on the nature of the change in light at the boundary of the spot. Here one does not experience perceptual scission of the image into reflectance and illumination. The target invariably appears as a luminous source of light.

Only in the disk/annulus paradigm do we find perceptual structure beginning to emerge. At certain extreme luminance ratios the higher luminance will appear self-luminous, as in the spot-in-a-void. However, over the entire range of less extreme ratios, the two regions appear as achromatic surfaces under a particular brightness of illumination.

THE EDGE AS CRUCIAL

Had Koffka lived he would have appreciated the discovery of stabilized retinal images (Yarbus, 1967). Apparently it is necessary that the retina move across the optic array in order for the image to be experienced. When such relative displacement is eliminated, either by immobilizing the eye, or by causing the image to move in synchrony with the eye, the image disappears within about 3 seconds, producing an experience equivalent to the eigengrau that develops in the ganzfeld.

It would appear that the receptor cells are stimulated by a change of light, not by light per se. A stabilized image that has disappeared can be made visible again by flickering it. Interpreted in the most straightforward way, these facts support the position that gradients are primary, not luminances. Encoding of luminances would only seem to be facilitated by keeping the image stationary on the retina, not hindered. In fact, unless the priority of gradients is accepted it could be said that the disappearance of stabilized images actually contradicts Koffka since gradients of luminance are present on the retina and yet no surface colors are seen. But the obvious conclusion is quite simple. Not only are gradients the basis of lightness perception, as Koffka maintained, they are also the very form in which the image is encoded.

Perhaps the traditional view that luminances are primary cannot yet be decisively ruled out. It can be preserved in two ways. One is the possibility, lacking in elegance, that changing illumination of receptor cells is simply a necessary condition for encoding luminance values. The other is by challenging the facts of stabilized retinal images.

There has indeed been some controversy as to whether a completely stabilized image disappears totally. Earlier work reporting reappearance of stabilized images can now be attributed to incomplete stabilization of the image (Arend & Timberlake, 1986; Barlow, 1963). Certainly the blood vessels in front of the retina never appear under normal conditions. They are completely stabilized, of course, by virtue of being attached to the eye. However, it is still argued by some

(Kelly, 1983) that high contrast and high spatial frequency images do reappear even under complete stabilization. No means currently exist for testing these claims. Consequently the radical possibility that all stabilized images are invisible, with its corresponding implication that absolute luminance information is unavailable, cannot at present be ruled out.

Koffka would presumably find this quite intriguing, even more so an experiment by Krauskopf (1963). Krauskopf presented observers with a disk of one color surrounded by an annulus of another color. The boundary between the disk and the annulus was retinally stabilized while the outer boundary of the annulus was not. The disk disappeared, as expected, but it filled in with the color of the surrounding annulus. The observer saw simply a larger homogeneous disk in the color of the annulus.

The obvious implication is that the homogeneous regions of the image contribute nothing to color perception. These regions are already stabilized, so to speak, the ganzfeld being an extended example. The color system extracts its information from the edges, systematically filling in the homogeneous areas with values based on the edge relationships.

Further insight comes from a color mixing experiment by Walraven (1976). If a projected red disk is exactly superimposed on a projected green disk of the same size, the resulting color will appear yellow when the intensities of red and green are approximately equal. But what happens if both of these disks are superimposed on a larger red disk? Walraven found that the red light of the larger disk, although physically adding to the light of the small red disk, does not contribute to the perceived color of the small disk as long as the small red and green disks continue to have equal edge ratios. Therefore the small disk continues to appear yellow. As Walraven (1976) puts it: "the part of the light that the test stimulus has in common with the surround does not contribute to its perceived hue." Whittle and Challands (1969) have made analogous findings for achromatic light.

These results of Krauskopf, Walraven, and Whittle and Challands fit well with the Wallach disk/annulus results, suggesting that the reason one disk appears equal in lightness to another of different absolute luminance but the same relative luminance is because the retinal cells moving across the two disk borders undergo the same stimulation, in terms of proportionate change in luminance.

CONTRAST THEORIES

Probably the most popular form of the two-luminance approach to lightness perception over the past 3 decades has been the so-called contrast theory. This kind of theory, going back to Hering (1874) and typically linked to the physiological mechanism of lateral inhibition, is based on the notion that the excitation associated with a particular region of the retinal image is inhibited, or distorted in some way, by light from a surrounding or neighboring region, if one is speaking of regions of the image. When speaking in terms of edges or gradients, the concept is one of exaggeration or enhancement of the physical luminance difference.

Contrast theories are often regarded as consistent with a gestalt or relational approach, but they are not. Four points can be made in this regard.

1. First, in contrast theories the correlate of perceived lightness is an *amount, not a relationship*. To be sure, that amount can be influenced by other amounts, such as background luminance, but it still comes down to an amount. As Koffka (1935) wrote, ". . . contrast . . . implies an explanation not in terms of gradient, but in terms of absolute amounts of light" (p. 245).

2. Also there is the idea of *distortion*. The amount in the target region is changed or distorted by the background luminance. In a true relational theory a target luminance may indeed form a relationship with the background luminance, but at the same time, for other perceptual purposes, it may form one or more separate relationships with other parts of the perceptual field. Consider a familiar example. You are in a movie theater and the credits are rolling across the screen, white letters on a black background. Without thinking, the screen appears black. And yet it can easily be seen as white, in relation to other objects in the dim illumination of the theater. Relative to the letters on the screen, however, it appears black. Changes in excitation levels of cells completely fails to address this phenomenon. I may be short relative to Wilt Chamberlain, yet tall next to a midget. But that doesn't mean that when Wilt Chamberlain stands next to me my body actually shrinks. That's the logic of a contrast theory. Contrast theories speak of information loss while relational theories speak of recoding of the input.

3. Contrast theories seem satisfying because they appear to account, at least qualitatively, for the many relational facts of lightness, such as the role of context. But they account for those facts only minimally (often only in direction) and what is meant by the context is very primitive.

4. But the heart of the problem lies in a distinction, embodied in the earlier quote from Koffka, that has until recently been largely ignored. Edges in the retinal image come in two fundamental types: reflectance edges and illumination edges (Gilchrist, 1979, 1980; Gilchrist et al., 1983). The former are produced by changes in the pigment or color of a surface while the latter are produced by changes (either attached, as in the case of a corner, or cast) in the intensity of the illumination. It has not been widely recognized that, when applied to illumination edges, contrast mechanisms fail completely to serve constancy. in fact the constancy problem is exacerbated.

For a concrete example, imagine the paradigmatic display used by Katz (1911) to illustrate lightness constancy. Two achromatic color wheels are set up side by side against a common wall (see Fig. 13.2). A screen is set up between the two wheels so that one disk stands in the higher illumination of a nearby

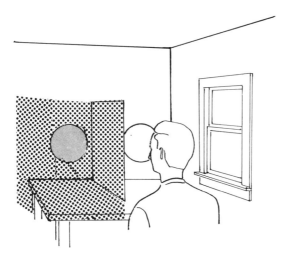

FIG. 13.2. The Katz paradigm. Achromatic color wheels are set up side by side under differing levels of illumination and the observer is asked to adjust the perceived lightness of one wheel to match that of the other.

window while the other disk is in shadow. Some shade of gray is set on one disk and an observer is asked to adjust the other disk so as to give it the same shade of gray. When this is done the disks are found to agree rather closely in reflectance, but not in luminance, the disk in bright illumination having a much brighter luminance.

In general, explanations of this phenomenon focus on the relationship between each disk and its immediate background. According to a widely cited theory (Cornsweet, 1970), although the disk in bright illumination has a much higher luminance that, all things being equal, would produce higher retinal excitation, it also receives much greater inhibition (than the shadowed disk) owing to its very bright surround. The net result, it is held, is that the higher excitation and the higher inhibition associated with the brighter disk cancel out each other leaving the neural rate-of-firing approximately equal for the two disks. The unequal luminances of the two disks have been transformed into equal neural signals through lateral inhibition.

The problem is that the mechanism has been selectively applied. In reality the disks are not the only parts of the display that show constancy. Both the shadowed and illuminated halves of the background wall also appear approximately equal in lightness. Not only is lateral inhibition powerless to rectify their unequal luminances, but in fact when lateral inhibition is blindly applied (as it must be) to the border between the two halves (assume the screen is parallel to the line of sight) the effect on neural signals would be a further exaggeration of the difference, not the reduction of difference required by constancy.

The heart of the problem here is that illumination edges have been ignored. By and large, current lightness theories have been tested only on displays composed exclusively of (or appearing as) reflectance edges. It has for this reason been overlooked that contrast mechanisms work toward constancy only when applied to reflectance edges. When applied to illumination edges they make matters worse, not better, as the earlier example and other studies (Gilchrist, 1977, 1979, 1988) have demonstrated. And when observers are presented with retinal images composed of nothing but illumination edges (Gilchrist & Jacobsen, 1984) using all-black or all-white rooms, predictions from contrast theories bear almost no relationship to obtained results.

Thus it could be said that the contrast solution to the constancy problem works only under conditions where the problem practically does not exist, that is, in a world with no illumination changes.

But the real world and its retinal projection are simply loaded with illumination edges. Any blind mechanism such as lateral inhibition must be applied willy-nilly to all edges in the image. It is surely an advance to recognize the important role of edges, but without an explicit recognition of reflectance and illumination edges and how they are distinguished by the visual system, no solution to the constancy problem is possible. Koffka certainly gave this question central importance.

In a sense, Koffka's question can be read as a restatement of Hering's paradox. Hering asked how reflectance and illumination can be extracted from the simple variable of luminance. Koffka recasts the paradox in a more soluble way—with the added insight that the luminance gradient rather than the luminance point is the appropriate unit of analysis. It is also the appropriate statement of the constancy problem, which has usually been stated in an incomplete, one-sided way. The typical formulation asks how perceived lightness can remain constant when illumination (and therefore luminance) changes. This form of the question has led to "solutions," such as the contrast one we have discussed, that only *appear* to work. For instance, if the constancy of two gray surfaces standing in different illuminations is explained by processes that result in the same rate of neural activity corresponding to the two surfaces, there is nothing left over with which to explain the different brightnesses of the two surfaces. A complete solution must explain how changes in lightness are distinguished from changes in illumination.

The same situation applies to size constancy. Neural mechanisms can be hypothesized, for instance, that could transform an expanding retinal image into one of constant size. But such a mechanism would cause a balloon being pumped up to appear to be getting nearer while remaining constant in size. The complete problem of size constancy is how an expanding object can be distinguished from an approaching object.

Although contrast theories have been singled out for criticism here, it should be noted that virtually all current lightness theories share this crucial failure to deal with illumination gradients.

STRUCTURE

Asking how reflectance edges are distinguished from illumination edges plunges us at once into the central gestalt theme of perceptual structure—the organization of the visual field. Theories have gone to great lengths to avoid confronting this question but these efforts all share a failure to account for visual inputs beyond a set of constrained laboratory-type displays. The fact that we are so far away from the ability to program a computer to identify black and white surfaces in real-world video images makes this point painfully clear.

The problem of perceptual structure is by no means simple, but it simply cannot be avoided. If the gestalt approach has not yet completely answered the question it has at least asked the correct question. And Koffka's theory in particular points the direction to a successful theory of lightness perception. The fact that lightness theories continue to stumble on the question of perceptual structure can be illustrated with two examples, Helson's adaptation-level theory, representing an earlier period of time, and the more recent models of the Land (1977) approach.

Helson's (1943, 1964) approach has strengths that must be acknowledged. One is his observation that various visual mechanisms, such as pupillary change, lateral inhibition, and bleaching of pigment, very likely cooperate in the service of some principle of visual function, and that it is the principle that is important, not the various mechanisms. It must also be noted that Helson's theory is explicitly a gradient theory (as opposed, for example, to a contrast theory). In Helson's case the gradient is not between two adjacent retinal luminances but rather between the luminance of a target region and the average luminance of the entire retinal image. This average luminance which is weighted for proximity to the target he calls the adaptation level (AL).

Let's consider the conditions under which such a formula would identify white and black surfaces correctly. If the entire visual field consists of coplanar surfaces under a single level of illumination and the gray shades are rather randomly distributed, the formula will work just fine. When the distribution of gray shades is strongly biased one way or the other sizable errors will result. Riccio (1986) has found that such errors do occur (up to a point) in human perception under such conditions, although in the all-black or all-white rooms (Gilchrist & Jacobsen, 1984) the Helson model completely fails to predict performance. Here, although there is only a single surface reflectance throughout the entire room, there are many luminances due to the attached and cast illumination edges that result from the spatial complexity. Helson's model must predict that a large variety of gray shades would be perceived but in fact observers see the various surfaces as approximately the same shade of gray.

More important is the distribution of illumination. Spatial variations of illumination make a serious problem for the model. Weighting the AL for proximity to the target helps somewhat but only to the extent that the target is roughly in the center of its given illumination field. Real-world images are not nearly so orderly. And various laboratory displays could be cited for which the model would make sizeable errors (Gilchrist, 1977, 1988; Gilchrist et al., 1983).

To get to the heart of the issue, the model would make correct lightness identification, and indeed predict real human performance, only if the luminance averaging were done entirely within a region of homogeneous illumination. But to identify a region of homogeneous illumination the visual system would need to be able to identify the boundaries of that level of illumination, and that in turn requires the ability to distinguish illumination edges from reflectance edges. So Helson's theory cannot escape Koffka's question. More generally, Helson's theory fails by not confronting the problem of perceptual structure of the field. Averaging luminances is a structure-blind process, as is weighting for proximity.

Recently a new generation of lightness and color constancy theories have arisen (Horn, 1974; Maloney & Wandell, 1986; Marr, 1982). They have been heavily influenced by the Land (1977; Land & McCann, 1971) retinex model and they are closely associated with work on machine vision. They do represent certain advances over the older ratio and contrast models which take the center/surround pattern as paradigmatic. For one thing, the new paradigmatic display, the mondrian, is a bit more complex than a simple center/surround display. Although the mondrian, with its sharp-edged coplanar surfaces and limited luminance range, hardly captures the complexity of everyday life scenes, it is a step in the right direction. As for perceptual structure, at least the reflectance edge/illumination edge distinction is overtly recognized. However, it is hastily dismissed in a quite inadequate manner. According to this emerging cliche, it is suggested that illumination edges tend to be gradual and reflectance edges tend to be sharp. Since the visual system is known to be less sensitive to gradual edges than to sharp ones, it is argued that the illumination edges drop out of the picture by falling below threshold for detection.

There are a number of serious flaws in this story. First, many illumination edges are very sharp. Attached illumination edges are as sharp as the corners that produce them. Even cast illumination edges can be quite sharp, all the more so as the distance of the observer increases. Second, we do in fact perceive levels of illumination, both local and global, even when they are quite blurred. Relative edge sharpness probably does play a role in sorting out the two main types of edges, but it cannot be used in so facile a way to bypass the question of perceptual structure.

In a well-known demonstration, Land and McCann (1971) showed that lightness constancy is quite good when an achromatic mondrian is illuminated from below so as to cast a very gradual illumination gradient over the entire mondrian. They posited a series of luminance comparisons of closely spaced pairs of points which, together with a minimum threshold luminance ratio, would be blind to the illumination gradient, picking up and integrating only the sharp reflectance borders. However, it can be inferred from an analogous experiment by Gilchrist,

Delman, and Jacobsen (1983), that Land and McCann would have obtained almost the same results had their illumination gradient been as sharp as the reflectance borders. Work by Arend (1988) confirms this. The problem of perceptual structure, represented here by the problem of classifying edge types, will have to be confronted sooner or later.

RECENT DEVELOPMENTS

If the problem of perceptual structure is so rarely confronted head on, the reason must surely be that it is such an overwhelming problem. And yet alternative routes of escape have been regularly cut off by the failure of so many efforts to tame the problem either by breaking the image into elements of some kind or by breaking the temporal process into stages. My own contribution to this exercise, a claim that depth processing precedes lightness processing (Gilchrist, 1977), was retracted in a subsequent publication (Gilchrist, 1980). Nonetheless an encouraging constellation of ideas has recently been emerging from the work of third and fourth generation gestaltists, ideas that begin to make pragnanz operational.

COMMON AND RELATIVE COMPONENTS

Bergstrom (1977, 1987; Bergstrom, Gustafsson, & Putaansuu, 1984) has extended the vector analysis approach of his mentor, Gunnar Johansson, to lightness and color perception, as surely would have pleased Johansson's own mentor, David Katz. Bergstrom marshals a wide range of results to show that the visual system analyzes reflected light into common and relative components.

The concept of a relative component is hardly novel, particularly in light of the evidence we have reviewed already. But what about the common component? In fact it too is implicit in the basic edge approach. To say that the perceived color of a homogeneous region is signaled by the change of light at its edge is to say that all points in the homogeneous region have something in common. (It is, of course, quite efficient that such a multitude of points can be represented by a single value—the edge ratio.) The edge defines the way in which all the points inside it differ from all points outside it. In this sense common and relative components are two sides of the same coin.

This approach can be seen in its barest outline in the familiar disk/annulus paradigm. Walraven found, as we noted, that the color of a central disk is determined (under his relatively reduced conditions, of course) only by the difference in light between the disk and the annulus, a difference represented by the boundary between the disk and the annulus. The light that is common to the disk and the annulus, represented by the outer boundary of the annulus, does not contribute to the perceived color of the disk. This common component, however, is not discarded. It plays a different role, as we shall see.

Notice that Krauskopf's results support the notion that the outer boundary of the annulus signals a common component. When the relative component is taken away, by stabilizing the boundary of the disk, the color of the annulus is then revealed as a common layer covering the region of both the disk and the annulus.

Imagine a Wallach experiment with two disk/annulus patterns, side by side. The pattern on the left has the following luminances: annulus 4, disk 1; on the right side: annulus 40, disk 10. In fact, the observer will perceive each pattern as a middle gray disk surrounded by a white annulus, but with ten times more illumination on the right hand pattern. Here the lightness values are signaled by the disk/annulus ratios in each display, but the illumination relationship is signaled by the outer boundary of each annulus. Again the illumination component that is common within a given pattern becomes a relative component when the comparison is between the two patterns. There is a hierarchy of commonness.

THE RETINAL IMAGE AS LAYERED

Musing on his findings, Walraven (1976) makes the intriguing observation that "what the experimenter may consider to be a test field surrounded by an annulus, is treated by the visual system as an increment on a background." The difference is illustrated in Fig. 13.3. The concept of common and relative components is congruent with an analysis of the retinal image into overlapping layers rather than adjacent elements of a mosaic. As Asch (1968) has reminded us, "gestalt psychology is not opposed to analysis. The position it has taken is that analysis is fruitful provided it deals with the units and natural parts actually found in experience." It is natural to think of the retinal image as a pattern of illumina-

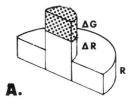

A.

FIG. 13.3. A disk/annulus display can be treated as a disk surrounded by an annulus (A), or as an increment added to (or a decrement subtracted from) a background (B). The visual system seems to work according to the latter. From Walraven (1976).

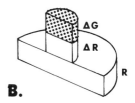

B.

tion superimposed on a pattern of surface colors. In fact, when measurements of perceived illumination are taken (in relatively complex images) along with measurements of perceived surface lightness, the two patterns of measurements, when combined, yield a good approximation of the raw image itself (Gilchrist, 1979; Gilchrist et al., 1983; Gilchrist & Jacobsen, 1984). This can be seen as an example of what Rock, Auster, Schiffman, & Wheeler (1980) would call apportionment. We find a reference to this result in Koffka's (1935) observation that "a combination of whiteness and (perceived illumination), possibly their product, is an invariant for a given local stimulation under a definite set of total conditions" (p. 244).

One of the curiosities in the history of lightness perception work is the strange neglect of the perception of illumination. Our obvious and regular experience notwithstanding, illumination perception is typically ignored by theories of lightness only when it is not denied. This prevalent view is made even more curious by the absence of empirical data supporting it. The explanation, however, may lie in the tacit influence of the photometer metaphor, the deeply rooted and widespread assumption that visual processing begins with a point by point record of luminance (and chromaticity) values in the retinal image. The variety of lightness theories are primarily distinguished by the ways in which they would process these point-wise values. These values are allowed to influence one another in various ways, but in the end one is left with only a single value at each point in the image. This value is most naturally assigned to the surface color, with nothing left over to account for the perceived illumination level at that same point.

Here is where the edge approach proves its worth. Because the perceived value of a given point in the image is associated, not with that point itself, but rather with the contour that surrounds it, a single point can have two or more perceived values, just as a point falling within two overlapping Venn circles. In this context one can appreciate the irony that lightness models based on Land's approach perpetuate the neglect of illumination perception when the edge approach that they have embraced has such potential in this respect.

The question of how the retinal image is split into two overlapping illumination and reflectance images is, of course, merely a variation of Koffka's question of how illumination edges are distinguished from reflectance edges. But perhaps it is a more useful variation. For example, the analysis of the image into common and relative components seems particularly helpful here. Imagine a shadow cast across a multicolored surface. All the colored regions within the shadow have something in common—namely a reduced luminance. Of course this common factor only has meaning relative to surfaces outside the shadow, and this is signaled by the constant luminance ratio along the entire length of the shadow's boundary, regardless of what surface color it lies across. At the same time, a red surface that falls partly inside and partly outside the shadow has its own common component. The red surface inside the shadow is redder than other surfaces inside the shadow just as much as the red surface outside the shadow is redder than other surfaces outside the shadow.

The region of intersection between the boundary of the shadow and the boundary of the red surface has been shown (Gilchrist, 1987) to provide the visual system with crucial information. In this case the luminances in the four quadrants of the intersection exhibit a property that can be termed ratio-invariance; the luminance ratio of each edge is unchanged by the crossing. This property signifies that the two intersecting edges belong to separate, overlapping images. In other cases, where two illumination edges intersect, for instance, there is no ratio-invariance. Here another pattern, difference-invariance, signifies that the intersecting edges are part of the same illumination image (though cast by different sources of light).

The concept of overlapping layers has been most explicitly recognized, not surprisingly, in the case of perceptual transparency (Fuchs, 1923; Koffka, 1935; Metelli, 1974). Kanisza's protege Gerbino (1988), working in this tradition, has found a way of quantifying simplicity through an application of coding theory (Leeuwenberg, 1971). Given that a surface can be considered to have three properties: reflectance, transmittance, and degree of illumination, the classic transparency pattern shown in Fig. 13.4a can be partitioned in innumerable ways. However the significant ones are illustrated by parts b, c, d, and e of Fig. 13.4.

In the first partitioning (Fig. 13.4b), each region of the pattern (A, P, Q, and B) is seen as having its own surface color and its own illumination. Although one

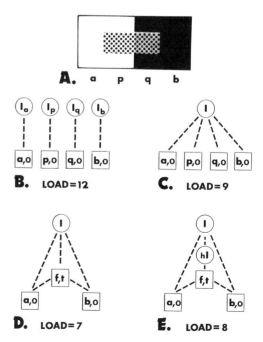

FIG. 13.4. The transparency pattern shown in A can be perceptually organized in at least four ways. The information load of each organization can be computed by counting the total of three types of parameters, referring to (1) surface lightness (a, p, g, b, f), (2) degree of transparency (o, t), and (3) intensity of illumination (l, hl). According to Gerbino's extension of coding theory, the visual system prefers the organization with the lowest load.

never perceives according to this partitioning, it is a theoretical possibility, a complex organization with an information load of 12 (four regions times three parameters).

The second partitioning (Fig. 13.4c) consists of four differently colored surfaces under a common illumination, for an information load of nine. The third partitioning (Fig. 13.4d) is possible only within a certain range of luminance values. Here one transparent surface (two parameters) is seen on top of two adjacent background surfaces (two parameters each) with a common illumination (one parameter) on both layers, for a total of seven parameters.

Equal illumination on the layer and the background would be a limiting case. The final partitioning shown (Fig. 13.4e) is the more general case. There are separate levels of illumination on the transparent layer and the background surfaces. This organization has a slightly higher information load (eight) here but might well have the lowest load when embedded in a richer context.

The important point is that partitionings 3 and 4 both involve the unification of two regions into a single layer, and the partitioning of the corresponding luminances into layer and background. This organization into common and relative components is consistent with the minimum principle.

The riddle of lightness perception will be solved either by cracking the problem of perceptual structure or by skirting it. Neither logic nor the empirical record offer much hope for the latter approach. The developments described here are not dramatic breakthroughs. Yet they represent advances toward a definition of pragnanz that may one day prove equal to the devilish problem of structure. The burgeoning field of machine vision is bringing new urgency to questions of surface color perception. With it comes both swifter rejection of inadequate models as well as a no-nonsense demand for operational definition. Only time can reveal the correct approach, but recent findings have shown that the gestalt theory of lightness perception is anything but outdated.

REFERENCES

Arend, L. E. (1988). Eye movements and spatial vision. Unpublished manuscript.
Arend, L. E., & Goldstein, R. (1987). Simultaneous constancy, lightness and brightness. *Journal of the Optical Society of America, 4,* 2281–2285.
Arend, L. E., & Timberlake, G. T. (1986). What is psychophysically perfect image stabilization? Do perfectly stabilized images always disappear? *Journal of the Optical Society of America, A, 3,* 235–241.
Asch, S. E. (1968). Gestalt theory. *International Encyclopedia of the Social Sciences,* 158–175.
Barlow, H. B. (1963). Slippage of contact lenses and other artefacts in relation to fading and regeneration of supposedly stable retinal images. *Quarterly Journal of Experimental Psychology, 15,* 36–51.
Barlow, R. B., & Verillo, R. T. (1976). Brightness sensation in a ganzfeld. *Vision Research, 16,* 1291–1297.
Benary, W. (1924). Boebachtung zu einem Experiment uber Helligkeitskontrast. *Psychologische*

Forschung, 5, 131–142. Reprinted in W. Ellis (Ed.), *A source book of gestalt psychology,* Selection 8, The Humanities Press, 1950.

Bergstrom, S. S. (1977). Common and relative components of reflected light as information about the illumination, color, and three-dimensional form of objects. *Scandanavian Journal of Psychology, 18,* 180–186.

Bergstrom, S. S. (1987). Colour constancy: Support to a vector model for the perception of illumination, colour, and depth. *DAPS: Report No. 26,* Department of Applied Psychology, University of Umea, Umea, Sweden.

Bergstrom, S. S., Gustafsson, K., & Putaansuu, J. (1984). Information about three-dimensional shape and direction of illumination in a square-wave grating. *Perception, 13,* 129–140.

Cornsweet, T. N. (1970). *Visual perception.* New York: Academic Press.

Flock, H. R., & Noguchi, K. (1970). An experimental test of Jameson & Hurvich's theory of brightness contrast. *Perception & Psychophysics, 8*(3), 129–136.

Fuchs, W. (1923). Experimentelle Untersuchungen uber das simultane Hintereinandersehen auf der selben Sehrichtung. *Zeitschri. F. Psychologie, 91,* 145–235.

Gerbino, W. (1988). Models of achromatic transparency: A theoretical analysis. *Gestalt Theory, 10*(1), 5–20.

Gilchrist, A. (1977). Perceived lightness depends on perceived spatial arrangement. *Science, 195,* 185–187.

Gilchrist, A. (1979). The perception of surface whites and blacks. *Scientific American, 24,* 88–97.

Gilchrist, A. (1980). When does perceived lightness depend on perceived spatial arrangement? *Perception & Psychophysics, 28*(6), 527–538.

Gilchrist, A. L. (1987, November). *Edge intersections contain lightness information.* Paper read at annual meeting of the Psychonomic Society, Seattle, Washington.

Gilchrist, A. L. (1988). Lightness contrast and failures of constancy: A common explanation. *Perception & Psychophysics, 43,* 415–424.

Gilchrist, A. L., Delman, S., & Jacobsen, A. (1983). The classification & integration of edges as critical to the perception of reflectance and illumination. *Perception & Psychophysics, Vol. 33, No. 5,* 425–436.

Gilchrist, A., & Jacobsen, A. (1984). Perception of lightness and illumination in a world of one reflectance. *Perception, Vol. 9, No. 6,* 936–944.

Haimson, B. R. (1974). The response criterion, the stimulus configuration, and the relationship between brightness contrast and brightness constancy. *Perception & Psychophysics, 16*(2), 347–354.

Helson, H. (1943). Some factors and implications of color constancy. *Journal of the Optical Society of America, 33,* 555–567.

Helson, H. (1964). *Adaptation-level theory.* New York: Harper & Row.

Hering, E. (1874/1964). *Outlines of a theory of the light sense.* (Translated from the German by L. M. Hurvich & D. Jameson.) Cambridge, MA: Harvard University Press.

Hess, C., & Pretori, H. (1894/1970). Quantitative investigation of the lawfulness of simultaneous brightness contrast. *Perceptual and Motor Skills, 31,* 947–969. (Translated by H. R. Flock & J. H. Tenney).

Hochberg, J. E., Triebel, W., & Seaman, G. (1951). Color adaptation under conditions of homogeneous visual stimulation (Ganzfeld). *Journal of Experimental Psychology, 41,* 153–159.

Horn, B. K. P. (1974). Determining lightness from an image. *Computer Graphics and Image Processing, 3,* 277–299.

Jacobsen, A., & Gilchrist, A. L. (1988a). The ratio principle holds over a million-to-one range of illumination. *Perception & Psychophysics, 43,* 1–6.

Jacobsen, A., & Gilchrist, A. L. (1988b). Hess and Pretori revisited: Resolution of some old contradictions. *Perception & Psychophysics, 43,* 7–14.

Jameson, D., & Hurvich, L. M. (1961). The complexities of perceived brightness. *Science, 133,* 174–179.

Kanizsa, G. (1979). *Organization in vision: Essays on gestalt perception.* New York: Praeger.

Katz, D. (1911). *The world of color.* Translated from the 2nd German edition by R. B. MacLeod & C. W. Fox. London: Kegan Paul, Trench, Trubner.

Kelly, D. H. (1983). Spatiotemporal variation of chromatic and achromatic contrast thresholds. *Journal of the Optical Society of America, 72,* 1238–1243.

Koffka, K. (1935). *Principles of gestalt psychology.* New York: Harcourt, Brace, & World.

Krauskopf, J. (1963). Effect of retinal image stabilization on the appearance of heterochromatic targets. *Journal of the Optical Society of America, 53,* 741–744.

Land, E. H. (1977). The retinex theory of color vision. *Scientific American, 237*(6), 108–128.

Land, E. H., & McCann, J. J. (1971). Lightness and retinex theory. *Journal of the Optical Society of America, Vol. 61, No. 1,* 1–11.

Leeuwenberg, E. L. J. (1971). A perceptual coding language for visual and auditory patterns. *American Journal of Psychology, 84,* 307–349.

Maloney, L. T., & Wandell, B. A. (1986). Color constancy. A method for recovering surface spectral reflectance. *Journal of the Optical Society of America, Vol. 3*(1), 29–33.

Marr, D. (1982). *Vision.* San Francisco: W. H. Freeman.

Metelli, F. (1974). The perception of transparency. *Scientific American, 230,* 90–96.

Noguchi, K., & Masuda, N. (1971). Brightness changes in a complex field with changing illumination: A re-examination of Jameson and Hurvich's study of brightness constancy. *Japanese Psychological Research, 13*(2), 60–69.

Riccio, G. E. (1986). *An ecological investigation of surface color perception.* Unpublished doctoral dissertation, Cornell University.

Rock, I., Auster, M., Schiffman, M., & Wheeler, D. (1980). Induced movement based on subtraction of motion from the inducing object, *Journal of Experimental Psychology: Human Perception and Performance, 6*(3), 391–403.

Stevens, S. S. (1961). To honor Fechner and repeal his law. *Science, 133,* 80–87.

Wallach, H. (1948). Brightness constancy and the nature of achromatic colors. *Journal of Experimental Psychology, 38,* 310–324.

Wallach, H. (1976). *On perception.* New York: Quadrangle.

Walraven, J. (1976). Discounting the background; The missing link in the explanation of chromatic induction. *Vision Research, 16,* 289–296.

White, M. (1979). A new effect of pattern on perceived lightness. *Perception, 8,* 413–416.

Whittle, P., & Challands, P. D. C. (1969). The effect of background luminance on the brightness of flashes. *Vision Research, 9,* 1095–1110.

Yarbus, A. L. (1967). *Eye movements and vision.* New York: Plenum Press.

14 Metamorphosis from Rod and Frame to Visual-Vestibular Interaction

Sheldon M. Ebenholtz
Schnurmacher Institute for Vision Research and Department of Vision Sciences, SUNY/College of Optometry

ABSTRACT

Evidence is described showing the rod and frame effect (RFE) to be sensitive to characteristics of the retinal image such as size and/or eccentricity, and spatial frequency. On the other hand, certain dimensions of phenomenological experience, such as apparent size, apparent depth, and form-quality appear not to influence the RFE. Accordingly, an account of the RFE was proposed in terms of visual-vestibular-proprioceptive interactions. The role of orientation detectors in the RFE and in the inhibition of orientation channels by peripheral visual stimuli also was developed.

BACKGROUND

In 1948 Solomon Asch and Herman Witkin published a series of four now-classical papers on spatial orientation. The studies were inspired largely by the concept of frame of reference and the tenet of relational determination so central to Gestalt Psychology as developed by Max Wertheimer (1912) and Kurt Koffka (1935). Like other great scholars before them, Asch and Witkin sharpened and transformed a critical concept so that it could be treated empirically in the confines of a laboratory. Max Wertheimer (1912) had taken a step in this direction with his observations on spatial orientation through a tilted mirror but only small numbers of subjects were used and hence the analytical power afforded by hypothesis testing and statistical decision-making was lacking.

In the first of the four studies replicating and extending Wertheimer's original observations, Asch and Witkin (1948a) had subjects view a laboratory scene through a mirror tilted at a 15° pitch angle around a horizontal axis. Subjects were required to adjust the image of a 2½ ft. long rod, seen in the mirror, to an angle that appeared parallel with their own apparent longitudinal body axis. In the second study (Asch & Witkin, 1948b) the exemplar of the frame of reference concept was somewhat more controlled over that of the initial study by the use of a miniature room, 4 ft. wide, 4 ft. deep, and 6 ft. high, open at one end with no ceiling and fixed at a counterclockwise roll angle of 22° from the subject's point of view. The view of the wall in the observer's frontal plane contained a picture, a chair and table, and the response measurement apparatus, a rotatable rod 1″ wide by 39″ long. In this and the two subsequent studies, only roll-plane, i.e., left-right, tilts were investigated and instead of a body-centered reference, the rod, used as the principal dependent variable, was to be adjusted in the roll plane to match the direction of the gravitationally defined vertical or horizontal directions. For example, the rod was to be set ". . . parallel to the wall of the [unseen] room in which the S [subject] was standing . . ." (Asch & Witkin, 1948b, p. 456). The same gravitational reference was utilized in the third study (Witkin & Asch, 1948a), which exclusively manipulated head and body tilt without visual reference in a dark room. The rod was made visible by coating it with luminous paint and exposing it to a light source prior to the experiment. The fourth study (Witkin & Asch, 1948b) instantiated the concept of frame-of-reference in the form of a luminous rod and frame. The latter was square, each side of which was 1 in. wide, 40 in. long, and was capable of ready variation in its tilt in the roll plane. The rod, 1 in. wide, 39 in. long, rotated about an axis at the frame center. The strong tendency for rod settings to appear upright when in fact they were rotated in the direction of frame tilt represented what has come to be termed the "rod-and-frame effect," while the use of a tilted frame as the laboratory surrogate for spatial frame of reference has attained near universal acceptance.

OTHER SALIENT EFFECTS

In addition to its influence on the apparent position of the rod, the frame has a powerful influence on the apparent position of the observer's body[1] and head (Ebenholtz & Benzschawel, 1977; Sigman, Goodenough, & Flannagan, 1978, 1979; Witkin & Asch, 1948b) and also is productive of some degree of disorientation and vertigo (Witkin & Asch, 1948b). Furthermore, rotation of the frame is capable of producing vection in the observer, i.e., the sense of body rotation accompanied by the perception of a stable nonmoving frame (Babler & Ebenholtz, 1989; Witkin & Asch, 1948b).

Not all frames are equally effective. There is ample data now, 40 years after the

---

[1]Similar observations were made by Witkin, 1949, in the case of a subject placed within a tilted 3-dimensional room.

original ground-breaking studies, to clarify further the nature of the frame of reference for orientation. It is of theoretical importance that the rod and frame effect (RFE) is dependent on retinal image size, larger sizes producing larger effects, but not on apparent or phenomenal size (Ebenholtz, 1977a; Ebenholtz & Callan, 1980) and is equally effective whether the rod and frame share the same depth plane or are in differing non-parallel planes[2] (Ebenholtz & Glaser, (1982) as shown in Fig. 14.1. In these respects at least, the frame does not meet the criteria for a framework for spatial orientation as proposed by Koffka (1935, ch. 4–7) since the several different field organizations, implied by the differing apparent sizes and the various depth relations between line and frame, yield only a singular effect. Furthermore, not only do *apparent* depth and size relations fail to influence the RFE, but equivalent form-organizations appear to produce drastic changes in the size of the effect. For example, the seven patterns represented in Fig. 14.2, seen as luminous against a dark background, all represent a tilted square or square-like form sometimes also described as a "diamond" or "box" (Streibel, Barnes, Julness, & Ebenholtz, 1980). Despite the varying proximal input, however, processes of perceptual organization (Koffka, 1935) produce a certain equivalence of global form-quality in experience. One would therefore be led to expect a corresponding equivalence in their respective capacities as frames of reference. Yet they do not produce equivalent effects (Ebenholtz, 1985a; Streibel et al., 1980). Every form with a curved element within it exhibited a marked decrement in effectiveness. Corner (2b) and sides only (2g) displays tended to be equally effective (Ebenholtz, 1985a) and more effective than the curved element displays, while the full frame generally, was maximally so.

In addition to small retinal image size other inhibiting factors include the extent of blur associated with the frame (Ebenholtz, 1985b), and a circumscrib-ing circular contour enclosing the frame (Ebenholtz & Utrie, 1983). High blur significantly degrades the RFE, thus indicating that retinal patterns with ex-clusively low spatial frequency content, i.e., below about .25 cpd, are not supportive of the RFE. Large inhibitory effects also occur when a tilted luminous frame is itself surrounded by a circular luminous contour. Reductions in RFE to about 25% of the initial effect have occurred (Ebenholtz, 1985c; Ebenholtz & Utrie, 1982, 1983).

Tentative Model and Potential Explanations

The RFE represents a large and nearly ubiquitous influence of vision on spatial orientation. The RFE therefore is intimately tied to problems of spatial orienta-tion in general.

---

[2]Small frames, having a frame edge less than about 8 deg of arc per side, and a frame tilt of 15 deg do exhibit a reduction in effect with a depth interval between rod and frame (Ebenholtz & Glaser, 1982; Gogel & Newton, 1975). Small-frame patterns, however, produce only small illusions of less than one or two degrees and differ from the RFE in other respects as well.

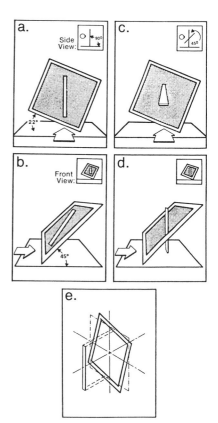

FIG. 14.1. All frames have a 22-deg CW rotation. Line and frame are both in the observer's frontal plane in 1a, while both are inclined top away by 45 deg in 1b. The frame is in the frontal plane, but line is inclined 45 deg top away in 1c, while the relations between line and frame are reversed in 1d. Parallel depth planes between line and frame are shown in 1e. From Ebenholtz and Glazer (1982).

Figure 14.3 represents the flow of information in a hypothetical system in which gravitational reference for the head (i.e., plumb line) and egocentric reference (Rock, 1954), e.g., the capability to detect a line-target as parallel with a longitudinal chin-forehead axis, are maintained as controlled quantities. A theory of orientation perception requires both quantities since the system must encode the location of the retinal image of the target relative to the head along with the location of the head relative to the gravitational direction, in order to derive the gravitational orientation of a target. Accordingly, for the purpose of modelling the egocentric reference, a retinal reference for head-vertical is posited. This permits the formulation of a head-centered egocentric coordinate system that remains relatively stable regardless of head and body tilt even in the absence of any substantial gravitational signal in outer space (Graybiel & Miller, 1971). A visual bias is represented as summing with and hence affecting the retinal reference signal, since a tilted luminous frame has been shown to alter the egocentric orientation of a line in supine observers, in the direction of frame rotation (Goodenough et al., 1982; Rock, 1966). The ocular torsion angle also is represented and subtracted at this point since some degree of compensation for

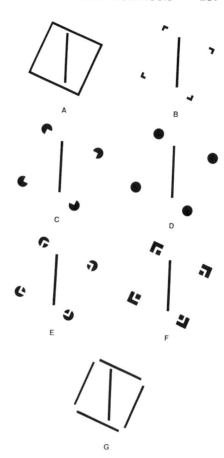

FIG. 14.2. Luminous displays representing full frame (a), corners only (b), subjective surface (c), disks in a square pattern (d), subjective frame on disks (e), subjective frame on squares (f), and sides only (g). After Streibel et al. (1980).

ocular torsion has been demonstrated (Nakayama & Balliet, 1977). The head-centered coordinate system that emerges at the right is based on a neural signal that marks a particular retinal meridian as consistent with a particular direction with respect to the head. Thus, e.g., in the absence of visual or other bias, stimulation of the vertical retinal meridian represents an apparent direction parallel with the median plane of the head.

The system controlling head-centered egocentric orientation is represented as a feed-forward system. Thus the meridian representing egocentric vertical, for example, is only as veridical as the combination of visual bias, neural reference, and ocular torsion angle will permit. A feedback loop, on the other hand, would allow correction to the meridian signaling egocentric vertical in the face of some external perturbation. Since the latter seems quite unlikely, only a feed-forward signal is represented in Fig. 14.3.

It is not known with certainty whether the gravitational and egocentric systems are in fact interrelated as this and other treatments presume (Mittelstaedt,

238

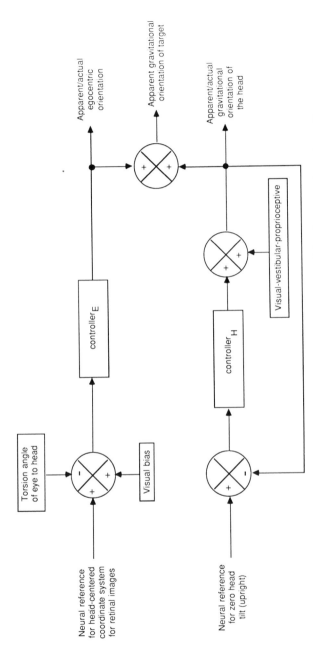

FIG. 14.3. One of several possible control system models of egocentric and gravitational orientation. Note that the head centered coordinate system for egocentric orientation is a feed-forward type, with no provision for error correction, whereas error correction for head orientation occurs via a negative feedback loop. The relevant motor systems for head and body righting reflexes are not represented in the diagram. Controllers determine the amplitude of the output relative to input signal (gain) as well as the rate parameters or system time constants.

1983), nor is it known which of these is ascendant and which is derivative of the other. Thus several possibilities remain to be explored empirically.

Inputs from visual, vestibular, and proprioceptive sources (e.g., Cohen, 1981; Lechner-Steinleitner, 1978) are shown entering at the lower right and contributing negative feedback to the neural reference for head (and body) orientation. The output on the right, represented as the apparent/actual gravitational orientation of the head, depending on whether or not it is veridical, is then added with the egocentric signal. This has the purpose of undoing or compensating for the effects that changes in gravitational orientation of the head, produced by e.g., body tilt, might otherwise have on the orientation of the head-centered egocentric coordinate system, and hence on the stability and veridicality of apparent vertical. For example, a constancy for the gravitational vertical (Ebenholtz, 1977b) results when the particular retinal meridian that signals a target at the gravitational vertical is rotated away from the egocentric reference, opposite the direction of the body tilt by a magnitude that is some function of body tilt. For another example, consider the head to be tilted 10 deg cw with a target stimulating the vertical retinal meridian. In this case the apparent gravitational orientation of the target would be signalled as 10 deg cw, whereas without the addition of the signal from the head-tilt loop only a nonveridical 0 deg (vertical) would be indicated.

Since evidence exists for a confluence of visual and vestibular signals at the level of the vestibular nuclei (Daunton & Thomsen, 1979; Waespe & Henn, 1977) it seems likely that visual inputs such as the image of a tilted frame mediate their influence on apparent target orientation via activity in the vestibular nuclei. Furthermore, from the point of view of brain centers upstream from the nuclei, such as the vestibular cerebellum, allowing for differences in signal strength or gain, there may indeed be a functional equivalence between visual and vestibular sources of afference. Thus a frame tilted in one direction may actually be the neural equivalent of a body tilt in the opposite direction, viz., both types of input cause a compensatory rotation of the retinal direction representing the gravitational reference for target orientation. A similar equivalence may also hold for proprioception and the afference arising from direct gravito-inertial stimulation, but direct evidence on this possibility is not presently available.

Given the great importance of certain characteristics of the retinal image of the frame and the findings that visual inputs are capable of modulating nervous activity in the vestibular nuclei, it seems likely that the RFE is mediated by such basic stimulus attributes as spatial frequency and orientation. The hypothesis offered here is that the frame-pattern enters the system via receptive fields in the periphery of the retina that are selective with respect to contour orientation. It may be assumed that, for reasons not yet understood, linear contours 90° apart, like those found at the corners of a frame, do not inhibit processing in each others orientation channels, but both bias the gravitational coordinate system in the same direction. If orientation channels were stimulated in a symmetrical fashion around the gravitational reference axis, then no bias would be present and no RFE should occur (e.g., Goodenough, Cox, Sigman, & Strawderman, 1985). Likewise, if all orientation channels were stimulated simultaneously, again no bias would enter the system to rotate the gravitational coordinate system. These considerations, plus the fact that the most peripheral of several competing patterns dominates the effect (DiLorenzo & Rock, 1982; Ebenholtz & Utrie, 1983), form the logical and empirical basis for an explanation of the inhibitory effect of a surrounding circular pattern on the RFE as well as for an account of the RFE itself.

Although the thin edges of the circular pattern surrounding the frame probably are processed by relatively large peripheral receptive fields (Ransom-Hogg & Spillmann, 1980), nevertheless the truly circular retinal contour will approximate a linear contour when only the section falling on a receptive field is considered. For example, a circle whose circumference lies 50° eccentrically, radius of 50°, will have a circumference of $2 \pi r$ or 314° of arc, and a receptive field with, e.g., a 10° diameter, will analyze only 3.2% of its total circumference. If it is true that these small sections of arc are treated as though they were linear, then they probably will stimulate orientation-selective cells in striate cortex (DeValois, Yund, & Hepler, 1982) and elsewhere. In fact, since an entire circle is represented on the retina, every type of orientation-selective cell will be stimulated over the entire orientation bandwidth. Thus all orientation channels will be activated. If the biasing effect of a tilted frame occurs according to the relative activity in all orientation channels in comparison with those channels signaling only the tilted frame edges, then the ratio of such activity will vary depending upon the presence or absence of a surrounding circle. Considering the activity in channels conveying the tilted-frame orientation as signal (S) and the entire remaining activity as noise (N) then the ratio with circle present is $S/N + B$ while in the absence of circle the ratio is S/B where B represents base level nervous activity. Since the ratio will be higher in the absence of the surrounding circle, a greater RFE is to be expected in that case.

One may deduce the inhibiting effect of the circular surround from yet a slightly different approach based on the premise that orientation channels stimulated by peripheral patterns have a controlling influence on spatial orientation relative to less peripheral patterns, i.e., an orientational anisotropy. For example, of two concentric frames, the tilt of the outer frame controls the RFE (DiLorenzo & Rock, 1982), while the inhibitory effect of a circular contour depends on its *relative* eccentricity with respect to a tilted frame. Thus a circular contour *within* a frame is virtually without effect whereas the inhibition is maximal when the contour surrounds the frame (Ebenholtz & Utrie, 1983). From these considerations together with the premise that the image of a large circular pattern is analyzed by orientation detectors as though the pattern was truly linear, no RFE should occur since all orientation channels would be more or less equally stimulated by the circle while the less eccentric frame would stimulate few controlling orientation channels.

It needs to be added perhaps that underlying the approach is the assumption that orientation detection in the retinal periphery subserves the task of only limited form perception, but functions primarily to control the spatial orientation of the observer and of visual targets (Ebenholtz, 1985c; Leibowitz & Post, 1982). Thus seeing the surrounding pattern as a circle or as any other form probably is irrelevant to its effectiveness in modulating the RFE.

ACKNOWLEDGMENT

Much of the research on the Rod and Frame Effect authored by S. M. E. was supported by Research Grant BNS 8201441 from the National Science Foundation.

REFERENCES

Asch, S.E., & Witkin, H. A. (1948a). Studies in space orientation: I. Perception of the upright with displaced visual fields. *Journal of Experimental Psychology, 38,* 325–337.

Asch, S. E., & Witkin, H. A. (1948b). Studies in space orientation: II. Perception of the upright with displaced visual fields and with body tilted. *Journal of Experimental Psychology, 38,* 455–477.

Babler, T. G., & Ebenholtz, S. M. (1989). Effects of peripheral circular contours on dynamic spatial orientation. *Perception & Psychophysics, 45,* 307–314.

Cohen, M. M. (1981). Visual-proprioceptive interactions. In R. D. Walk & H. L. Pick, Jr. (Eds.), *Intersensory perception and sensory integration.* New York: Plenum.

Daunton, N., & Thomsen, D. (1979). Visual modulation of otolith-dependent units in cat vestibular nuclei. *Experimental Brain Research, 37,* 173–176.

DeValois, R. L., Yund, E. W., & Hepler, N. (1982). The orientation and direction selectivity of cells in Macaque visual cortex. *Vision Research, 22,* 531–544.

DiLorenzo, J. R., & Rock, I. (1982). The rod-and-frame effect as a function of the righting of the frame. *Journal of Experimental Psychology: Human Perception and Performance, 8,* 536–546.

Ebenholtz, S. M. (1977a). Determinants of the rod and frame effect: The role of retinal size. *Perception & Psychophysics, 22,* 531–538.

Ebenholtz, S. M. (1977b). The constancies in object orientation: An algorithm processing approach. In W. Epstein (Ed.), *Stability and constancy in visual perception: Mechanisms and processes.* New York: Wiley.

Ebenholtz, S. M. (1985a). Absence of relational determination in the rod-and-frame effect. *Perception & Psychophysics, 37,* 303–306.

Ebenholtz, S. M. (1985b). Blur-modulated orientation perception in the rod-and-frame task. *Perception & Psychophysics, 37,* 109–113.

Ebenholtz, S. M. (1985c). Depth separation fails to modulate the orientation-inhibition effect. *Perception & Psychophysics, 37,* 533–535.

Ebenholtz, S. M., & Benzschawel, T. L. (1977). The rod and frame effect and induced head tilt as a function of observation distance. *Perception & Psychophysics, 22,* 491–496.

Ebenholtz, S. M., & Callan, J. W. (1980). Modulation of the rod and frame effect: Retinal angle vs. apparent size. *Psychological Research, 42*, 327–334.

Ebenholtz, S. M., & Glaser, G. W. (1982). Absence of depth processing in the large-frame rod-and-frame effect. *Perception & Psychophysics, 32*, 134–140.

Ebenholtz, S. M., & Utrie, J. W., Jr. (1982). Inhibition of the rod-and-frame effect by circular contours. *Perception & Psychophysics, 32*, 199–200.

Ebenholtz, S. M., & Utrie, J. W., Jr. (1983). Peripheral circular contours inhibit the visual orientation control system. *Aviation, Space, and Environmental Medicine, 54*, 343–346.

Gogel, W. C., & Newton, R. E. (1975). Depth adjacency and the rod-and-frame illusion. *Perception & Psychophysics, 18*, 163–171.

Goodenough, D. R., Cox, P. W., Sigman, E., & Strawderman, W. E. (1985). A cognitive-style conception of the field-dependence dimension. *Cahiers de Psychologie Cognitive, 5*, 687–705.

Goodenough, D. R., Nowak, A., Oltman, P. K., Cox, P. W., & Sigman, E. (1982). A visually induced illusion of body tilt in a horizontal plane. *Perception & Psychophysics, 31*, 268–272.

Graybiel, A. M., & Miller, E. F. (1971). Human otolith function—Experiment M009. *Gemini Program Biomedical Science Experiments Summary.* NASA TM x-58074, pp. 155–170.

Koffka, K. (1935). *Gestalt psychology.* New York: Harcourt Brace.

Lechner-Steinleitner, S. (1978). Interaction of labryinthine and somatoreceptor inputs as determinants of the subjective vertical. *Psychological Research, 40*, 65–76.

Leibowitz, H. W., & Post, R. B. (1982). The two modes of processing concept and some implications. In J. J. Beck (Ed.), *Organization and representation in perception.* Hillsdale, NJ: Lawrence Erlbaum Associates.

Mittelstaedt, H. (1983). A new solution to the problem of the subjective vertical. *Naturwiss enschaften, 70*, 272–281.

Nakayama, K., & Balliet, R. (1977). Listings law, eye position sense, and perception of the vertical. *Vision Research, 17*, 453–457.

Ransom-Hogg, A., & Spillman, L. (1980). Perceptive field size in fovea and periphery of the light- and dark-adapted retina. *Vision Research, 20*, 221–228.

Rock, I. (1954). The perception of the egocentric orientation of a line. *Journal of Experimental Psychology, 48*, 367–374.

Rock, I. (1966). *The nature of perceptual adaptation* (pp. 71–72). New York: Basic Books.

Sigman, E., Goodenough, D. R., & Flannagan, M. (1978). Subjective estimates of body tilt and the rod-and-frame test. *Perceptual and Motor Skills, 47*, 1051–1056.

Sigman, E., Goodenough, D. R., & Flannagan, M. (1979). Instructions, illusory self-tilt, and the rod-and-frame test. *Quarterly Journal of Experimental Psychology, 31*, 155–165.

Streibel, M. J., Barnes, R. D., Julness, G. D., & Ebenholtz, S. M. (1980). Determinants of the rod and frame effect: Role of organization and subjective contour. *Perception & Psychophysics, 27*, 136–140.

Waespe, W., & Henn, V. (1977). Neuronal activity in the vestibular nuclei of the alert monkey during vestibular and optokinetic stimulation. *Experimental Brain Research, 27*, 523–538.

Wertheimer, M. (1912). Experimentelle Studies uber das seben von Bewegung. *Zeitschrift fur Psychologische und Physiologische Sinnesorgane, 61*, 161–265.

Witkin, H. A. (1949). Perception of body position and of the position of the visual field. *Psychological Monographs: General and Applied, 63*, 1–46.

Witkin, H. A., & Asch, S. E. (1948a). Studies in space orientation. III. Perception of the upright in the absence of a visual field. *Journal of Experimental Psychology, 38*, 603–614.

Witkin, H. A., & Asch, S. E. (1948b). Studies in space orientation. IV. Further experiments on perception of the upright and displaced visual fields. *Journal of Experimental Psychology, 38*, 762–782.

15

The Frame of Reference

Irvin Rock
University of California, Berkeley

ABSTRACT

,One of the fundamental concepts in the Gestalt revolution, and one that deeply influenced and interested Solomon Asch, was the notion of the frame of reference or framework. Although this concept played a central role in Gestalt thinking, it is not as well known as other Gestalt contributions, such as those concerning organization, holism, and prägnanz. Moreover, with respect to the topics to which the Gestaltists most directly related it, namely, the perception of motion and of the upright of space, little use has been made of the concept by subsequent investigators and, if anything, attempts have been made to explain its phenomena in terms of entirely different mechanisms. The occasion of this volume honoring Asch thus provides an opportunity to remind the scientific community of this important concept, to clarify its meaning and to re-examine its application to several topics in perception.

THE GESTALT CONCEPT OF FRAMEWORK

What did the Gestaltists mean by "framework" and, apart from that historical question, what would be the clearest way to define it? The Gestalt meaning is best understood in terms of their critique of elementaristic theories. For example, Hering (1861) sought to explain the perception of the orientation of a line in terms of the sum of the elementary sensations of the directions of its separate points within a retinal coordinate system centered on the fovea. The vertical image of a line would then give rise to the perception of a vertical line because each retinal locus stimulated would have a constant X coordinate and a varying Y coordinate. Now consider how that same vertical image appears through a tube

243

pointed at a tilted mirror, as suggested by Wertheimer (1912). (See also, Koffka (1935), p. 215.) After a few moments, in which the mirror world looks tilted, a "righting" occurs so that it looks upright. Now a vertical contour in the scene that gives rise to an oblique image on the retina appears to be vertical and, conversely, any tilted contour in the scene that happens to produce a vertical image on the retina appears to be tilted.[1]

Therefore, one cannot explain perception as the sum of elementary sensations but rather one must consider the relationships of components to one another. The vertical image produced by a contour in the mirrored scene appears tilted, not vertical, because it is tilted with respect to all those other contours in the scene that collectively serve to define the main axes of environmental space. There are *two* distinct claims here. One concerns relational determination and the other a causal asymmetry with respect to relational determination. In certain cases, such as in perceived orientation, a unit is perceived that serves as the reference or center of coordinates *with respect to which* certain properties of other units are perceived. This is the framework. However, the converse is not true, the perception of the framework is not governed by how it relates to other units unless they in turn happen to serve as frames of reference.

There is another implication of the framework concept that is, to my way of thinking, extremely important. The perception of one's own self, i.e., the phenomenal body, is also governed by its relationship to the framework. If one is upright with respect to gravity but is inside a tilted room (Witkin, 1949), one will perceive oneself as tilted. This follows from the theses of relational determination and reference to framework. The representation of the body, however (about which, more later) is such that it is not parallel to that of the room. But the room as framework is taken to be upright. Therefore one's body must be tilted. Precisely the same conclusion can be drawn from an experiment in which a stationary observer is surrounded by a moving environment, whether it is an experimentally created structure or room (Dichgans & Brandt, 1974; Duncker, 1929; Lishman & Lee, 1973), a nearby train, or the current in a surrounding body of water. If the moving environment becomes the framework, then it is perceived as unmoving. But the relative motion between framework and self is, of course, detected. Therefore that relative motion is ascribed to the motion of the self.

The self qua body is thus an object in the field and how it is perceived is a function of how it relates to other objects in the field and, in particular, to whatever is taken to be the framework. This is of course a very different theoretical perspective than one in which everything external is held to be perceived in terms of purely egocentric mechanisms. Thus, for example, the orientation of a contour is perceived in terms of how its retinal orientation must be assessed

---

[1]This is an example of the incorrectness of what the Gestaltists referred to as the constancy hypothesis (not to be confused with constancy *phenomena*). The same proximal stimulus does not always give rise to the same sensation or perception.

given information about the direction of gravity. While such a process indeed accounts for a good deal about the perception of object orientation, if that were the whole story, a tilted room surrounding an observer would have to look tilted. That it looks upright instead and the observer sees him or herself as tilted adds a whole new dimension to the problem of perception.

The definition of framework implicit in Gestalt theorizing as summarized earlier seems clear and correct to me. To repeat, a framework is a unit or organization of units that collectively serves to define a coordinate system with respect to which certain properties of all objects, including the phenomenal self, are gauged.

The framework concept can, therefore, be thought of as a principle of organization although somewhat different than other such Gestalt principles that bear on what is grouped with what in the field or on configurational effects of organization. Framework as an organizing principle concerns what *relates* to what and on how object properties are governed by such relationships. However, insofar as whether or not an object is or is not perceived to be encompassed by a framework, Gestalt principles that affect belongingness will presumably come into play.

THE PERCEPTION OF THE UPRIGHT

Given the fact that we ourselves are often tilted, the orientation of contours that are vertical in the environment will not always give rise to images that are vertical with respect to the retina. Yet such contours in the environment continue to appear vertical regardless of our bodily orientation. We refer to this fact as orientation constancy. Because such constancy occurs (within certain limits of accuracy) even in viewing a single visible rod in an otherwise dark room, it must be the case that the perceptual system makes use of information about the direction of gravity in solving the problem of what orientation along the retina signifies the vertical of space.

So far then there is no need to invoke the concept of framework. However, the fact is that ordinarily in daily life we do not see single isolated objects but an entire array of objects in a scene whether outdoors or indoors, and given the presence of structures such as the ground, trees, walls, floors, and the like, it is entirely possible that these structures serve to define a framework. If that is so, we cannot say that gravity has been isolated as the sole determinant of the perception of the upright. The utilization of a tilted mirrored scene or tilted room, therefore, can be thought of as an experimental method of separating gravity and framework from one another as determinants. In these examples, however, the observer is inside the tilted scene and, since this can be considered to a special case, it would be better to postpone discussion of it.

What we need, then, is an experiment in which an object is seen within a tilted framework but not a framework within which the observer is located. That is precisely the condition of the now classical experiments by Asch and Witkin (1948a, 1948b) and Witkin and Asch (1948). They used either a small tilted room or a tilted luminous rectangle. An important feature of the experimental method was the inclusion of a rod within the framework, the orientation of which could be varied and measured. The subject was asked to indicate when the rod appeared to be vertical (or horizontal). If gravity alone determined perception of the upright, the subject should select a gravitationally vertical rod. If the framework alone governed perception of the upright, the subject should select an orientation of the rod parallel to the longer axes of the framework. In fact the average setting of the rod selected was a compromise between the two predictions. This phenomenon has come to be known as the rod-and-frame effect.

One might think that this evidence of the potency of the framework as a determinant of the perception of the upright is clear enough, given the conflict condition in which gravity—already known to be such a determinant—must be expected to play a role. But in the years following the publication of these experiments, the role of the framework has been increasingly deemphasized, if not entirely denied. In its place a number of other determinants have been suggested, i.e., determinants that would account for the role of a surrounding framework without regarding it as a framework effect per se as suggested by the Gestaltists and by Asch and Witkin.

For example, some have suggested that the framework effect is simply another example of contrast, in this case of angle, in which a difference in orientation of contour is exaggerated (Gogel & Newton, 1975; Goodenough, Oltman, Sigman, Rosso, & Mertz, 1979; Wenderoth, 1974). The angular relation between the rod and the sides of the frame most nearly parallel to it is said to be overestimated, thereby resulting in the rod's phenomenal deflection away from the frame. This same kind of hypothesis has been used as explanation of certain geometrical illusions in which it is said that acute angles are overestimated and it is thought to be based on lateral inhibition (Békésy, 1967; Blakemore, Carpenter, & Georgeson, 1970; Carpenter & Blakemore, 1973). However, such a contrast effect would be expected to be quite small in angular degrees, and indeed under the conditions used by these investigators the magnitude of the effect obtained is as little as 1 degree to a maximum of 3 degrees; whereas the rod-and-frame effect of Asch and Witkin is, on the average, roughly 6 degrees. Moreover, there is no theoretical reason why the rectangular framework need be large to test this hypothesis and indeed, in the relevant experiments, they have been small: 10 degrees or under (in contrast to the angular subtense of the frame used by Witkin and Asch which I compute to be around 36 degrees). Yet we now know that there is a linear relationship between the magnitude of the rod-and-frame effect and the angular size of the frame measured in visual angle (Ebenholtz, 1977; Ebenholtz & Callan, 1980; Ebenholtz, this volume). In one study, using a frame that subtended an angle of 6.5 degrees, the illusory tilt of a vertical line within it was of the order of 1 degree, a far cry from the kind of effect obtained by Asch and Witkin (Wenderoth, 1974).

Others have suggested that the Asch and Witkin effect is the result of induced ocular eye torsion (Goodenough et al., 1979; Hughes, 1973). This would occur were the eyes to respond to a tilted frame by rotating in the direction of that frame's tilt. If this eye rotation were not registered centrally—i.e., if the brain did not "know" about it—then the rod would be set in accordance with the vertical retinal meridian of the eye, which would be slightly in the direction of the frame's tilt. But this effect has been found to of the order 0.5 degrees and thus can hardly account for the rod-and-frame effect.

Still others have suggested an induced head-tilt-hypothesis according to which the tilted frame induces a perception that the head is tilted in the opposite direction (Ebenholtz & Benzschawel, 1977; Sigman, Goodenough, & Flannagan, 1978, 1979). Were that to happen, then a rod stimulating the retina vertically would no longer look vertical. In fact, the framework may indeed affect how the observer experiences his or her own orientation and not merely that of the head, even if the observer is not *in* a tilted framework, so that such a fact is something predictable from the standpoint of the framework hypothesis rather than an alternative explanation for this hypothesis, and I therefore return to this matter later.

Finally, it has been suggested that the effect of the framework, particularly of one large in angular subtense, is a direct neurophysiological outcome of stimulation of the peripheral retina (Ebenholtz, 1977; Ebenholtz, this volume; Ebenholtz & Callan, 1980) in determining spatial attributes of perception such as orientation or self-motion. This suggestion is in keeping with recent evidence that there are two modes of perception, one concerning attributes such as form, based on foveal and near-foveal stimulation, and one based on spatial attributes, such as of orientation and motion, based on peripheral retinal stimulation (Held, 1968, 1970; Held, Dichgans, & Bauer, 1975; Ingle, 1967; Leibowitz & Post, 1982; Schneider, 1967; Trevarthen, 1968).

All of these suggested explanations either make no reference to the concept of frame or reference as explanation or explicitly seek to replace it entirely.[2] Given the prevailing silence or skepticism concerning the framework explanation of the perception of the upright, Joseph Di Lorenzo and I set out to rescue it (DiLorenzo & Rock, 1982). We reasoned that what was needed was evidence that when an appreciable rod-and-frame effect occurred, such as the one originally demonstrated by Asch and Witkin, it was based on an acceptance of the framework as either upright or as less tilted than it in fact was. For if the tilted frame's

---

[2]I cannot help noting that there has always been a preference for peripheralistic explanations in terms of sensory mechanisms over more central ones in the history of the field of perception, and these would seem to be good examples of it. As we shall see, a similar fate has befallen the concept of framework in it application to the phenomenon of induced motion.

orientation is veridically perceived, then the prediction based on Werthmeimer's notion of righting hardly seems appropriate. However, alternatively, one might still maintain that the frame can be expected to serve as frame of reference for the rod contained within it regardless of how the orientation of the frame is perceived. Such an expectation would be in keeping with the concept of *separation of systems* developed by Duncker (1929) in connection with the phenomenon of induced motion. The inducing structure or frame that moves can be perceived veridically to move and still induce motion in a stationary spot within it, or so it was claimed. What matters is the relation of contour or spot to the surrounding framework and not to a framework once removed, as it were, surrounding the immediate framework. In other words, the inner object is insulated from direct influence by that outermost framework by virtue of the presence of the innermost framework.

So while one might still predict a rod-and-frame effect regardless of how the frame is perceived, it seemed to us that there were both logical and empirical reasons for not doing so. *Logically,* if the frame's tilted orientation is perceived veridically, then the perception of a vertical rod within it as substantially tilted, in the opposite direction, is a violation of transitivity. That is, if the frame, tilted by θ degrees clockwise, is perceived veridically and the rod is vertical and perceived to be θ degrees counterclockwise from the frame (given by the stimulus relationship on the retina), then it follows that the rod is vertical. *Empirically,* for a separation of systems effect to occur, it ought not to matter (as far as I can see) what the angular size of the frame is. With a small tilted frame, however, as we have seen, the effect is miniscule, being of the order of only 1 degree (Wenderoth, 1974). Moreover, Gogel and Newton (1975) who also used a frame the visual angle of which was small, roughly 10 degrees, included a measure not included by Asch and Witkin, or any previous investigators for that matter, of the perceived tilt of the frame itself. Not surprisingly, they found the frame's orientation was perceived veridically.

Given these facts and arguments, it seemed to us that in the Asch and Witkin experiments, what was probably going on was a tendency of the frame to right itself, i.e., the perceived tilt of the frame was *underestimated*. The large angular size of the tilted room or rectangle would be expected to make that possible because, the larger its size, the more likely it would serve as a world surrogate: a framework that defined the main axes of space. In our experiments, therefore, we made use of a large square frame that subtended a visual angle of 54 degrees. The subject had two tasks: first, to indicate the apparent tilt of a frame tilted by 20 degrees, without the rod present and, second, to set the rod to the apparent vertical when it was seen within that 20 degree-tilted frame. (See DiLorenzo & Rock, 1982 for details of procedure and apparatus.) What we found was an appreciable underestimation of the frame's actual tilt, the mean being 7.6 degrees. The rod-and-frame effect was 9.8 degrees. Moreover the two measures were highly correlated as they also were in the experiments described later.

When the same experiment was conducted with the subject's head tilted by 45 degrees—a condition that has repeatedly been shown to increase the rod-and-frame effect, presumably by decreasing the effectiveness of gravity information—the mean underestimation of the frame's tilt was now 14.1 degrees and the rod-and-frame effect was 13.5 degrees.

In another experiment two concentric rectangular frames were used with the angular orientation of each different from the other. In one condition, the outer rectangle was upright and the inner one tilted. According to a separation of systems theory, the presence of the outermost frame should not eliminate the rod-and-frame effect but, according to the theory of righting as advocated by Weitheimer, Koffka, Asch and Witkin, it should. The tilted inner rectangle can hardly be perceived as upright or as less tilted given the upright rectangle surrounding it. The result was that neither righting nor a rod-and-frame effect occurred in this condition. It is interesting to note that in an analogous condition for studying induced motion, no effect occurs when a moving frame surrounding a stationary spot is itself surrounded by a stationary frame (Brosgole, 1968; Farber, 1979).

But the opposite condition, of an upright inner frame *surrounded by a tilted one,* is another story. For here it is plausible to suppose that the outermost frame might serve as a reference to define the axes of space, in which the phenomenal tilt of the inner upright rectangle as well as of a rod within it would be expected to be affected accordingly. That is precisely what happened. The outer rectangle's orientation was underestimated by 8.3 degrees and the rod-and-frame effect was 5.8 degrees. The inner rectangle appeared upright only when it was tilted by 8.7 degrees. One might interpret these results to mean that the inner rectangle undergoes an appreciable rod-and-frame effect whereas the innermost object, the rod, undergoes a lesser one, by virtue of *it* being immediately surrounded by an upright rectangle. There is thus some tendency toward separation of systems in that the inner rectangle has a slight insulating effect on the perceived orientation of the rod within it. Once again, when the experiment was repeated with the observer tilted 45 degrees, the effect increased considerably, with the outermost tilted rectangle now appearing close to upright on the average. And once again analogous effects have been found for induced motion. An outer moving frame does induce motion on a spot within an inner stationary frame and on that inner frame itself (Brosgole, 1968; Farber, 1979).

We take all these findings to provide firm support for the proposition that when a structure is such that it can serve as a framework, because it is large enough in relation to the observer or surrounds the observer, it will tend to define or at least to influence the definition of the main axes of space and thus to be perceived as either upright or as far less tilted that it actually is. Given that, other objects, including the self, will be perceived accordingly.

So far we have primarily been considering conditions in which the observer is not inside the structure. Here gravity information ought to be expected to indicate the true vertical. Thus the results of Asch and Witkin and our experiments just described can be regarded as a measure of the potency of a framework to dominate perception in spite of the potential conflict between it and gravity information. What happens when an (upright) observer is inside a tilted framework, however, is that he or she now perceives him/herself as tilted, usually by as much as the angular discrepancy between the framework and body (Witkin, 1949). No doubt there is a tendency for this misperception of self orientation even in the more typical condition of the rod-and-frame experiment where the observer is *not* inside the structure, as witnessed by the finding referred to earlier of Ebenholtz and Benzschawel (1977) and Sigman et al. (1978) concerning the perception of head orientation. No doubt such misperception of self orientation occurred in my experiment with Di Lorenzo but we did not measure self perception. But with the subject *inside* the tilted framework the perception of body orientation is more or less completely governed by the visual state of affairs. What we have here, I believe, is an example of visual capture (Hay, Pick, & Ikeda, 1965; Rock & Harris, 1967; Rock & Victor, 1964; Tastevin, 1937). Given the conflict between vision and proprioception (and subsuming vestibular cues under the latter category), vision is dominant. What this means is that gravity information is rendered more or less ineffectual and the observer both looks and feels to be tilted. If the observer is now tilted so as to be in the same orientation as the tilted structure, he or she will now look and feel to be upright.

If one now tests for the perceived orientation of an object within the structure, such as a rod, it will come as no surprise to learn that that object will only look upright when it is aligned with the tilted framework. That is, the rod-and-frame effect is no longer only partial, a compromise outcome, but complete. After all, with proprioceptive information not merely neutralized but captured by vision, there is no longer any conflict of cues.

THE PERCEPTION OF MOTION

Just as in the case of perceived orientation, we cannot immediately conclude that perceived motion is relationally determined simply because in daily life a moving object is always seen within a structured stationary field. For after all, we have information about the moving object's changing location with respect to ourselves as origin of directions and would perceive the object as moving even if only *it* were visible. That is what makes the induced-motion paradigm so crucial. It is not merely the fact that an illusion occurs, but the fact that here there is no egocentrically based reason to see the stationary spot as moving and, in fact, every reason to see it as stationary. So, induced motion attests to relational determination and, by virtue of the asymmetry (a moving spot will not induce motion in a stationary rectangle that surrounds it), attests also to the role of a framework. We also know that if that framework is large enough or surrounds the observer, induced self motion occurs.[3] So again we see that the phenomenal self can be thought of as an object in the field, the perception of which is governed by how it is seen with respect to the surrounding framework. When such induced self motion occurs, the surrounding moving framework is perceived to be stationary.

Once again, however, with the exception of those working in or influenced by the Gestalt tradition, (e.g., Wallach (1959), Brosgole, (1968), Johansson, (1950), Rock, (1975), investigators of induced motion, in the years since Duncker (1929) published his seminal paper on this topic, have not sought to support the concept of framework as an explanation, but to substitute other explanatory mechanisms. For example, it has been suggested that there may be neural feature detectors that respond to the motion of one contour relative to others (Bridgeman, 1972). The discharging of such a cell would presumably explain both real and induced motion perception without the need to refer to the framework concept. Although this does not deal with asymmetry to which we have referred, it could conceivably explain phenomenal motion in the so-called two-point induced-motion paradigm (Mack, Fendrich, & Fisher, 1975). Other research has questioned the framework concept by demonstrating that induced motion occurs even with a diminutive rectangle and even when it is adjacent to rather that surrounding the stationary spot (Day, Millar, & Dickinson, 1979).

A very serious difficulty with the framework interpretation of induced motion, as advocated by the Gestalt Psychologists, concerns the perception of the frame during its actual motion. If it is taken to be the reference with respect to which the spot's change of relative position is referred, then ought it not to appear stationary? This would be analogous to the righting of the frame in the perception of object orientation. The fact is that at below-threshold speeds of the frame, its motion is, by definition, not detected, and "pure" induced motion of the spot occurs. But it is also true that induced motion occurs at supra-threshold speed. Presumably then, again by definition, the frames motion *is* perceived, and yet the spot appears to move.

As already noted, Duncker dealt with this problem using his concept of separation of systems. The frame does serve as reference for the spot within it, but frameworks external to it—such as the room or the egocentric system of directions of the observer—serve to affect *its* perceived motion. There are, however, difficulties with this view analogous to those already discussed in connection with perception of the upright. First, there are certain factual discrepancies: As mentioned earlier, if one surrounds the moving frame by a stationary one, induced motion of the spot is abolished (Brosgole, 1968; Farber, 1979); if the frame moves too rapidly, induced motion is abolished (Duncker, 1929).

---

[3]When the surrounding structure moves forward, backward or sideways, the illusion has been referred to as linearvection whereas when it moves around the observer the illusion is called circularvection.

Neither of these factors ought to eliminate induced motion according to the separation-of-systems account.

There are also certain logical difficulties. Once again, to perceive *both* the moving frame and the stationary spot moving is to deny transitivity in perception. Such a phenomenal outcome has been referred to as the perception of excess motion because, for a given magnitude of relative displacement in the proximal stimulus, measured in degrees, twice as much motion is seen, since both the spot and frame are each seen to move the distance of that relative displacement. A related question concerns the phenomenological character of induced motion. Is it egocentric or object relative? By that I mean, do we have the impression that the induced spot is moving relative to ourselves or only relative to the frame? Either way there are difficulties. If the motion is perceived only relative to the frame, then that would occur if induced motion did not occur and only the frame was seen to move. We would be aware that the spot had changed its location vis-à-vis the frame. So how would we distinguish perception of spot motion from perception of frame motion? If, however, induced motion is phenomenologically egocentric, then the frame ought to appear stationary. Because the frame appears stationary, displacement of spot with respect to it would imply displacement of spot relative to ourselves. My own view, based on such reasoning and casual observations of induced motion, is that induced motion is egocentric in character. That is why one often has the impression that one is tracking the spot back and forth as it appears to move.[4] If that is true, then one might ask whether or not the frame really does appear to move at those moments when induced motion of the spot is occurring, despite the fact that its motion is, by definition, above-threshold. We need to know how the frame appears when induced motion of the spot occurs. The reader will once again note the similarity of these issues regarding motion to those regarding the upright. There we had asked how the tilted frame appeared when a rod-and-frame effect occurred and there was little if any data available to answer that question.

My associates and I, therefore, set out to investigate this question (Rock, Auster, Schiffman, & Wheeler, 1980). The experiments consisted of obtaining quantitative judgment of the perceived motion of a stationary spot as well as of the surrounding moving rectangle on each trial. Varying speeds of the rectangle were used because it was expected that, at very rapid speeds, its motion would be perceived more or less veridically and thus that induced motion would not occur. But at slower speeds, although above threshold, it was predicted that either the

---

[4]In several brilliant experiments, Arien Mack and her associates (Mack et al., 1985) have sought to test the hypothesis that induced motion is egocentric and found it wanting. The basic idea was to require the subject to saccade to the direction perceived to be straight ahead the moment an induced motion sequence ends. If the eyes are indeed felt to be pointing in a direction off to the side, because the induced motion would have carried the spot to that egocentric location, then the eyes should now move in the opposite direction, beyond the straight ahead. There is only a slight tendency in this direction. Despite this, I consider the matter as not yet fully resolved.

rectangle would appear to be stationary, in which case induced motion would be complete, or it would appear to be moving slower than (or less than) its actual motion, in which case some partial degree of induced motion was expected to occur. The guiding hypothesis, then, was that the actual displacement of rectangle with respect to spot would result in an equivalent amount of perceived motion, whether entirely attributed to the rectangle's motion (no induced effect), partially attributed to some motion of rectangle *and* of spot (a partial induced effect) or totally attributed to the motion of the spot (complete induced motion). We referred to this as the *apportionment hypothesis:* if and only if the frame's motion is under-perceived is it the case that it is subtracted from the frame's notion and attributed phenomenally to the spot.[5]

That is precisely what we found. The most dramatic aspect of the result was that about 40 per cent of the time the frame was perceived to be stationary, despite the fact that even at its slowest speeds it moved at a rate known to be above the subject-relative threshold for the detection of motion. One can only surmise that with the presence of the spot and the relative displacement that occurs and the tendency to "take" the frame as defining the zero point or stationarity, its actual motion vis-à-vis the observer is no longer detected. As might be expected, the frame was seen as stationary more often when its motion was objectively the slowest. On the other 60% of the trials, phenomenal motion was divided between spot and frame, so that induced motion was only partial. Overall, the results provided no evidence for the separation of systems or, otherwise expressed, for the occurrence of excess motion.

We interpret these findings as vindicating the Gestalt thesis concerning framework, and they precisely parallel the findings on the perception of the upright. There too we can formulate the hypothesis in terms of apportionment: Greater righting of the tilted frame, so that its tilt is either entirely or partially under-perceived, produces greater illusory tilt of the rod. Together, the two perceptions always account for the angular discrepancy between frame and rod. However, the results of both investigation challenge Duncker's thesis about separation of system, to which we return later.

How does induced *self* motion fit into the scheme of things? If an observer is surrounded by an appropriately moving structure, then induced self motion occurs. Now consider a spot in front of the observer that remains stationary. One

---

[5]There is an effect that, superficially considered, seems to be one of induced motion but which does not follow this rule. A stationary spot seen within a rectangular frame or window will appear to move in a direction opposite to that of a pattern of contours moving across the window. A good term for this effect is *simultaneous motion contrast* (Over & Lovegrove, 1973; Loomis & Nakayama, 1973; Mack, 1986; Anstis, 1976; Day & Dickinson, 1977). The presence of the window frame effectively eliminates any impression that the spot is changing its location, as is characteristic of induced motion. Instead the effect is paradoxical, in which the spot does yield a sensation of motion, but not one in which it appears to change its location with respect to anything else. It is probable that such motion contrast is a low level sensory effect.

can think of the induced-object paradigm, when the self is *not* induced to move, as a conflict situation, in which certain egocentric information indicates the object's stationarity—namely the absence of retinal-image motion or eye motion. At slow frame speeds, the framework effect is powerful enough to overcome that egocentric information, but at rapid frame speeds it overpowers the framework effect. However, when induced motion of the observer occurs as well, the conflict is eliminated. That is because self and external object, the spot, are yoked together as it were. The spot remains in the same egocentric location, e.g., straight ahead, since neither moves. When both are induced to move in the direction opposite to that of the moving structure, no conflict arises because the phenomenally moving spot always *should* remain straight ahead of the phenomenally moving observer. Hence, we should predict that induced object motion will *always* accompany induced self motion, regardless of the speed of the moving structure. To the best of my knowledge, this is indeed the case. So here we see the causal efficacy of the framework in all its splendor, precisely as is the case when an observer is inside a tilted structure. *Objects in the field, including the self, are perceived on the basis of how they relate to the framework.*

SEPARATION OF SYSTEMS RECONSIDERED

It would seen that our work has shown that Duncker's separation of systems concept is either incorrect or unnecessary. Still, there is the nagging doubt that such a description seems to be absolutely correct for certain phenomena. Consider such well know effects in daily life as a person on a moving train waving goodbye to people on the platform. One perceives the hand as moving up and down, vertically. Yet its motion in space, and thus the motion of its image on the retina as well (assuming the eye doesn't track the train's motion), is sinusoidal, since the train's motion carries the hand forward. One might say, therefore, that the motion of the hand is perceived entirely in terms of its displacement relative to the hand-waving person or train and not at all in terms of its motion relative to any frame of reference external to these. Is this not separation of systems? Duncker describes another example of this kind, namely that of the perceived motion of a distinct point on the periphery of a rolling wheel. The point appears to revolve around the hub rather than to move along the cycloidal path it in fact does traverse in space, unless *only* that point is visible. Johansson (1950) has created a number of other demonstrations of this kind.

I suggest that while a separation of systems effect does indeed occur in these cases, its theoretical meaning is importantly different than what Duncker had in mind. The important difference is that these cases reveal a *hierarchical organiza-*

tion.[6] The element under consideration (hand, point on wheel, etc.) is indeed perceived primarily in terms of its changing relation to its immediate frame of reference rather than to any external frame (including the observer's egocentric coordinates) *but*—and this is crucial—that element is also perceive as *partaking of* the motion of its frame. For example, the hand, as part of the person and train configuration, partakes of the horizontal motion of the train. In Johansson's terms, there is a common motion component in addition to the relative motion component of the object in relation to its reference frame.

In Duncker's example of ordinary induced object motion, however, hierarchical organization is not implied. The spot is not alleged to be partaking of the frame's motion.[7] The reader may feel that the distinction drawn here is overly subtle and of no particular consequence. Yet it seems to me that the distinction is important with respect to the issue of whether or not perception conforms to principles of logic or, as some have put it, whether or not a ratiomorphic approach to perception is justified. Separation of systems as Duncker and later Wallach (1959) defined it entails excess motion and violates transitivity as I have already pointed out. Separation of systems understood as hierarchical organization does not.

The same is true for orientation perception. Consider again the rod-and-frame effect. If a tilted frame induced a strong impression of tilt in a vertical rod, in the direction opposite to that of the frame, at the same time as the frame's tilt were to be perceived veridically, this would clearly illustrate separation of systems á la Duncker in the sense that there would be ''excess tilt'' perceived. Suppose the frame is tilted 30 degrees clockwise and the rod appears to be tilted 30 degrees counter clockwise. If the frame's orientation were perceived veridically, then one might say that 60 degrees of tilt is seen, whereas there is only 30 degrees of tilt in the proximal stimulus. Transitivity is violated, as explained on p. 248. Now, from all that we know, it does *not* seem to be the case that a substantial rod-and-frame effect ever occurs when the frame's tilt is perceived veridically. Therefore, separation of systems as defined by Duncker does not seem to occur

---

[6]''Hierarchical organization'' as defined here in relation to the perception of the upright and of motion is essentially the same concept that Palmer (1977) referred to as ''hierarchical structure'' in the perception of form.

[7]Logically it is possible for such an effect to occur. The spot would appear to move in one direction with respect to the frame and, simultaneously, to partake of the frame's motion in the other direction. The two motions being equal and opposite would cancel each other out so that the spot would remain egocentrically straight ahead. Were this to occur it would indeed be an example of hierarchical organization. However it doesn't occur in the usual induced-motion display. In a unpublished experiment, however, Joseph Di Vita and I were able to obtain such an effect by making use of a three-dimensional realistic model of an open box in the bottom surface of which was a small sphere. The sphere was held rigidly in place by a hidden mechanism as the box moved back and forth. The sphere appeared to move along the bottom surface but also to partake of the box's motion. We believe that the emphasized belongingness made this hierarchical effect possible.

in the case of perception of the upright. There is no perception of excess tilt. Still, one might describe the state of affairs in the above example in terms of hierarchical organization. That is, the rod will certainly look tilted within the frame, i.e., with respect to the frame, and the frame will look tilted in the scene or with respect to ourselves and yet, because the rod partakes of the frame's tilt, we will be aware that it is upright in the scene and with respect to ourselves.

Returning to motion perception, it is interesting to note that where induced motion of objects is a fragile effect, easily disrupted by factors such as speed of the frame, the presence of other stationary objects or stray light and characterized by individual differences, what I am here calling hierarchical effects are robust and can occur under full daylight conditions. One such effect, first studied by Wallach, Bacon, and Schulman (1978) consists of a vertically moving spot seen within a horizontally moving rectangle. The spot appears to be moving obliquely (with a horizontal component opposite to that of the rectangle) and the effect reliably occurs under a wide range of conditions. Let us call it the oblique effect. Now, under one interpretation, the effect is a vectorial combination of the real vertical motion and the induced horizontal motion of the spot. If so we must have separation of systems because the frame's horizontal motion, which is well above threshold, is perceived veridically. Yet we know that rapid speed of the frame and/or the presence of a stationary frame surrounding the moving one will destroy induced motion and thus should destroy the oblique effect. But they do not! However, suppose the oblique effect is one of hierarchical organization. While the oblique motion of the spot is salient, the spot is also seen as *belonging* to the rectangle and thus of partaking of its horizontal motion. Therefore there is no excess motion and no violation of transitivity. The spot has two motions in a horizontal direction that precisely oppose one another. With respect to the rectangle, it moves, let us say, to the left; as part of the rectangle configuration, it moves with it to the right. What remains is its vertical motion with respect to the observer. Belongingness is thus an important factor in hierarchical organization, and this together with the spot's leftward movement relative to the frame, produces the perception of oblique motion.

There are certain additional facts concerning induced motion of the *self* that bear on separation of systems. Suppose the observer is entirely surrounded by two structures rather than one, either of which can remain stationary or be set in motion. Such an experiment was performed many years ago by A. Weisz (1955) under the supervision of Hans Wallach, but never published. The observer was surrounded by two cylindrical drums of differing radii that rotated about the Y axis centered on the observer's position. The outer drum could be seen through alternate spaces between vertical stripes in the inner drum. The experiment asked the question of what the effect would be of holding one drum stationary and rotating the other. Which, if either, would be more effective in generating induced self motion? One might think that the inner one would, according to separation of systems, since it ought to serve as the immediate reference system for the observer. In fact, however, the opposite was the case. With the outer drum stationary and the inner one rotating, no induced motion of the self occurred. With the outer drum moving and the inner one stationary, however, such induced motion did occur. The inner stationary drum also appeared to rotate along with the observer. A similar effect was later obtained by Brandt, Wist, and Dichgans (1975).

From the standpoint of the original notion of framework as described by Wertheimer and Koffka, however, this result makes perfect sense. The outermost, visible, surrounding structure ought to define the stationary framework with respect to which all objects in the field, including the self, would be referred. That structure would then be expected to be perceived as stationary, as was indeed the case in the Weisz experiment, just as it is in more typical experiments on induced self motion using a single surrounding structure. Given that, the inner stationary drum, stationary with respect to the observer, would be expected to appear to be rotating along with observer and such was indeed the case. With outer drum stationary, however, and serving as the framework, the inner moving drum would have to be seen as rotating. Given that, it could hardly be expected to induce rotary motion on the observer. Thus there is no separation of systems occurring here.

INDUCED SELF MOTION IN DAILY LIFE

Whenever we move about we change our location with respect to the framework of the environment. Since that change is brought about by our locomotion it might seem inappropriate to explain the perception of such change in terms of induced motion of the self. Still, it is a fact that the visual state of affairs under such typical conditions is precisely the same as it would be were the environment moving and we stationary. Therefore, it has been suggested that the displacement of the entire scene with respect to the observer during observer motion, is indeed information to the effect that the observer is in motion. Gibson (1966) has referred to such information as visual kinesthesis. Presumably the observer would then misperceive him or herself to be in motion whenever the entire visible scene is set in motion and the observer is stationary. That is precisely the case in conditions of induced self motion.[8]

Suppose, however, that the observer is in a state of passive motion, as in

---

[8]However the prediction is not quite that simple. First, there is a latency period during experiments on induced motion of the self. This undoubtedly concerns the fact that were the *observer* to have initiated the motion there would be signals from the inner ear signalling acceleration. Thus the *absence* of such signals is at first information opposing self-motion perception. Second, other methods of causing the location of the scene to move such as viewing a stabilized image during saccadic eye motion do not result in induced self motion. The transition is probably too abrupt.

being transported in a vehicle. Aside from the knowledge about how the motion is accomplished, there would seem to be no difference whatsoever in the stimulus conditions that prevail in such a case and in one in which the environment is moved and the observer-and-vehicle is stationary.[9] Therefore it seems correct to infer that during such passive transportation the perception of oneself and vehicle can be understood as instances of induced self motion. Assuming smooth motion of the vehicle such that there is no accelerative information from the inner ear, why else should the observer perceive him or herself and vehicle as moving rather than the world around them? (See Rock [1968] for an experimental demonstration of this phenomenon.)

Therefore we can conclude that in virtually all cases of motion in vehicles in daily life, at least during linear motion of constant speed, our veridical perception of ourselves as moving through a stationary environment is based on the principles that yield induced self motion, namely the tendency to interpret the surrounding framework as stationary and thus to interpret change of location of self to framework as based on motion of the self.

Consider also the case where a current of air or water passively displaces an organism with respect to the visible environment. That can happen to a person in a boat but it can also happen to an animal such as a fish. If the fish experiences itself as being transported downstream when it has not intended to swim in that direction, then it may attempt to counter that unwanted motion by swimming upstream. It is known that such rheotaxis occurs if and only if the stationary sides or bottom of the waterway is visible. Otherwise, the fish cannot distinguish between being carried along by a current from remaining stationary in still water. So the fish swims in order to remain in place with respect to the visible environment. But this is precisely what occurs in the laboratory condition when a fish in a stationary tank is surrounded by a rotating striped drum. The circular swimming of the fish is an example of what is referred to as the optomotor response.

The optomotor response is similar to the optokinetic response in humans, in which the eyes track the drum as far as they can before snapping back to a straight-ahead direction, and has therefore generally been explained as a reflex-like behavior the "purpose" of which is to maintain stabilization of the retinal image (Duke-Elder, 1958; Walls, 1942). However, I am suggesting an alternative explanation here. The swimming is based on the tendency to undo the unwanted induced self motion that occurs by virtue of the motion of the surround, which, in the life of the fish, is often created by its passive transportation by a current. Evidence in support of this interpretation derives from experiments with tropical fish which made use of two independent striped drums surrounding the water tank (Rock & Smith, 1986). As in the experiment of Weisz (1955) with human subjects, the outer drum was visible through the inner one. When the

---

[9]As investigators of perception are aware, *knowledge* about prevailing conditions rarely affects perception.

outer drum was stationary and the inner one rotated, the optomotor response did not occur. It did occur, however, when the reverse was the case, i.e., when the inner drum was stationary and outer one rotated. However, as compared to a control condition using only one rotating drum, the presence of a inner stationary one in the double-drum condition did somewhat inhibit the optomotor swimming response. In another experiment, using only a single drum, it was shown that a series of black circles roughly 2 cm. in diameter placed on the inside of the drum, instead of using the more typical black stripes, failed to produce the optomotor swimming response. We took this to be further evidence against the retinal-image-stability hypothesis. The circles should have been adequate to elicit swimming, if such were the explanation, but not to elicit induced self motion. They were too small to serve as a surrounding frame of reference.

It should be noted that the concept of visual kinesthesis alone cannot explain the optomotor response. That is because such visual feedback attesting to the organism's own locomotion occurs whether the locomotion is actively initiated or passively imposed. But when it is actively initiated—as when the fish intends to swim downstream—it is not immediately counteracted by swimming upstream. Only when the self motion is unintended does the organism seek to undo it.

There is one important point about the perception of the self on the basis of the perception of the framework that to my knowledge has not been brought out by the Gestaltists or others since. Earlier I referred to the body as an object in the visual field. For some animals, including humans, parts of the body are often visible. In man, everything but the head is often seen and even part of the head (the nose) is visible. But for other animals, such as a fish, its own body is not visible. Moreover, even in man, parts of the body are not always visible. I would venture to say that sight of the body is *not crucial* at all for the self to be thought of an object in the field and for perception of the self to be governed by how the body relates to the rest of the field, or to the framework. Rather, the body is an implicit object in the field.

While the direction, orientation, distance, and motion of things can be seen in relation to other objects, they are also seen in relation to the self as an origin. Thus we speak of egocentric localization (or radial direction), meaning the angular direction of an object outward from the mid-eye cyclopean position as origin; we speak of egocentric orientation, meaning how an extended contour such as a line or rod is oriented in a fronto-parallel plane with respect to our head or body axis; we speak of egocentric or subject-relative (rather than object-relative) motion, meaning the motion of a thing with respect to ourselves. In all these cases the self is the origin and thus is implicit in the perception. Therefore, when the structure such as the cylindrical drum rotates around the observer, it is at first perceived as rotating with respect to the self as implicit origin of directions. If shortly later the rotating drum is reinterpreted as the stationary framework, still its changing egocentric direction continues to be detected. Therefore, if the drum is now seen as stationary, that changing relation must now be attributed to motion of the observer's own body. The situation is similar with respect to an observer in a tilted room. It may be that as the observer steps into the room it is perceived as tilted. If the observer remains upright, the room certainly is perceived as tilted egocentrically because its vertical and horizontal axes are tilted with respect to the retinal axes. Only contours aligned with those retinal axes will appear to be egocentrically vertical or horizontal. When righting occurs, so that the tilted room appears to be upright, the observer must reinterpret the lack of egocentric alignment as resulting from a tilted body, i.e., a body tilted with respect to the room.

One source of confusion here is between the observer thought of as organism and the observer thought of as phenomenal object in the field. The point I am making is that the organization of sensory information in the brain of the organism is such that the perceptual field consists of framework and objects within it and one such phenomenal object—albeit a very special one located at the center of the field—is the self. How the self-as-object is perceived depends on its relation to the framework and that relation can be given whether the self-as-object is visible or not.[10]

FRAMEWORK AND PHENOMENAL SHAPE

It has been known ever since Ernst Mach (1914/1959) noted the difference in appearance between a square and a diamond that the orientation of an object affects its phenomenal shape. However orientation can be defined in terms of differing reference systems, namely, an egocentric one based on retinal coordinates, an environmental one based on the direction of gravity, or one based on a visual frame of reference which may or may not be aligned with the other reference systems.

We now know that change of orientation with respect to each of these reference systems alone can affect phenomenal shape (Rock, 1973). For example, if the observer looks at a figure that is in a horizontal plane, e.g., either on the floor or ceiling, by bending over or lying supine, and only that figure is visible, its appearance is strictly a function of its egocentric orientation. A square rotated around its center by 45 degrees will look like a diamond. Or if an upright

---

[10]This analysis is relevant to the question that has been raised by some thinkers of why the phenomenal world is localized as outside rather than as inside the head, given the fact that the brain events that give rise to the phenomenal world take place inside the head. As pointed out by Wolfgang Köhler (1938) this question reveals a confusion between organism and phenomenal self. The world of perceived objects is located by us as outside the phenomenal self just as one object is located as outside and apart from another object. The ontological status of the self is, in this regard, like that of other objects, namely, an object in the phenomenal field. Presumably the same is true at the level of brain process, namely, that there is some structure in the brain that represents the self just as there are structures that represent objects. They are all "outside" of one another.

observer views a glowing square in the fronto-parallel plane in an otherwise dark room, it will look like a diamond when it is tilted by 45 degrees around the Z axis. Here only change with respect to gravity occurs. Finally, if an upright observer views a square in a fronto-parallel plane such as on the wall of a *tilted room,* it will look like either a square or a diamond depending upon how it is oriented with respect to the vertical and horizontal axes of the room rather than how it is oriented with respect to gravity. In one experiment, subjects' recognition of previously seen novel shapes declined appreciably when the figures were presented within a scene that was tilted by means of a Dove prism (Rock, 1956).

The last example, of the effect of a tilted room, would seem to be another case of a framework effect analogous to the others considered in this essay. The parallel can be extended because the strong effect on phenomenal shape seems to depend upon how the visual framework is perceived, i.e., on whether or not righting occurs. In one experiment, figures were seen within a *large* tilted rectangle which itself was seen within an upright room. Essentially no effect of this tilted frame on recognition occurred (where recognition was used as an index of phenomenal shape). Thus one might think that separation of systems does not occur for shape any more than it does for perception of the upright (see pp. 255–256). On the other hand, there is some evidence of hierarchical organization, as in the perception of the square and diamond embedded in the tilted rectangle in Fig. 15.1 in the well known Kopfermann (1930) effect. The diamond in the tilted rectangle does tend to look like a square and, to a lesser extent, the square in the tilted rectangle does tend to look like a diamond. But the orientations of these figures with respect to the page and to the observer is given veridically by virtue of the veridical perception of the surrounding rectangle. Thus it may be that the orientation of these figures relative to the page is given by transitivity operations

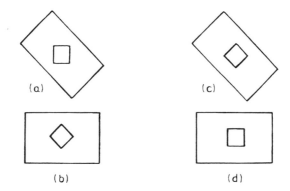

FIG. 15.1.   The Kopfermann effect. The inner squares in (a) and (d) look different as do the inner diamonds in (b) and (c) because of their differing relation to the surrounding rectangular frame of reference.

and that is what interferes somewhat with the framing effect on phenomenal shape. Nonetheless, there clearly is some effect.

This brings up the more recent, ingenious series of experiments by Stephen Palmer and his coworkers in which the effect of reference frames on the perceived shape of figures has been demonstrated by using the sensitive measure of reaction time (RT). See Palmer (1980, 1985, 1988, 1989); Palmer and Bucher (1981, 1982). In many of his experiments the test figure was an equilateral triangle which had previously been shown to be ambiguous with respect to which way the triangle appears to point (Attneave, 1968). However, Palmer went on to show that certain configurations of several triangles established a bias to perceive all these triangles as pointing in a particular direction, either aligned with the long axis of the configuration, or orthogonal to the bases of the triangles (see Fig. 15.2). I leave out the details of the procedure and method.[11] Thus the overall pattern of triangles seems to serve as a frame of reference. Similarly squares, rectangles, textural stripes, or even single straight lines can bias the perception of the triangles' orientation. Palmer has obtained similar effects of reference frames on the perception of figures such as squares and diamonds, plusses (+), and X's, and the like.

More recently Palmer (1989) has addressed the question of separation of systems using the ambiguous triangles. In one study he varied the size of the rectangular frame surrounding a triangle and found that the smaller the rectangle, the greater its effect on the phenomenal pointing of the triangle. The optimum effect occurred when the rectangle was about the same size as the triangle. In another study Palmer made use of two rectangular frames, each in a differing orientation, one immediately surrounding the triangle and the other surrounding that inner rectangle. Here he found that the inner rectangle exerted a much greater effect than the outer one.

At first glance these findings appear to be at variance with effects obtained in the rod and frame paradigm discussed earlier, in which it was shown that the larger the frame the greater the likelihood of obtaining an appreciable effect on the perceived orientation of the rod. Other experiments with dual frames also showed that it was the outer, not the inner frame that affected perception of the innermost rod (DiLorenzo & Rock, 1982).

Yet I believe these seeming contradictions can be adequately reconciled. When an effect depends on altering the directions seen as vertical and horizontal in the environment, i.e., in establishing a new set of directional coordinates, the

---

[11]Palmer's method, which he calls the "interference paradigm" was to require subjects to report whether a triangle pointed in one of the three possible direction, e.g., horizontally, rather than in either of the other two directions and the time it takes them to do so is measured. If the triangle is presented inside a frame whose orientation biases perception of pointing in a direction consistent with the required response, then RT will be faster than if the triangle is presented inside a frame whose orientation biases a direction inconsistent with the required response. The difference between these two RT's is then a measure of the magnitude of the perceptual bias by the kind of reference frame under study.

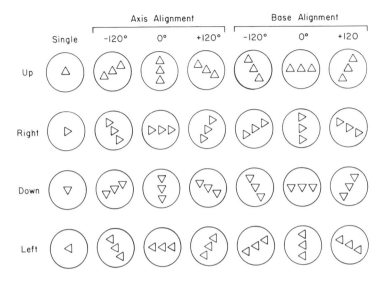

FIG. 15.2.   Triangles pointing up, down, right, or left were shown singly or in configurations aligned along their axes or bases. The configural line was oriented so that it was either consistent or inconsistent with
the required directional response.

larger frames increase the likelihood that it can serve as surrogate for environmental coordinates. Similarly only the outermost frame is likely to be able to
play this surrogate role, as found in the results of the experiments by Di Lorenzo
and myself described earlier. Similar logic applies to induced motion of the self
as shown in the experiments by Smith and myself, by Weisz (1955) and of
Brandt, Wist, and Dichgans (1975).

Now if the directions taken as the vertical and horizontal of the environment
can be altered by a tilted frame, then we should expect that the phenomenal shape
of figures seen within such a tilted frame will be affected. That explains the
outcome of the experiment in which subjects viewed figures in a prismatically
tilted scene. Why did we not obtain a similar effect when the figures were viewed
within a large tilted rectangle? For two reasons. First the rectangle was clearly
seen as tilted within an upright room, so that there was no change in environmental coordinates. Second, because we now know from Palmer's work that a
hierarchical effect of a circumscribed frame of reference requires a relatively
small frame.

A similar analysis applies to Palmer's experiment with two differently oriented rectangular frames. Here neither frame can be expected to serve as world
surrogate of coordinate directions. The outer one is still relatively small and in
any event is seen within an upright room. So only hierarchical effects are to be
expected, and from that perspective, by definition of what is meant by hier-

archical effect, it would be the inner frame that would be expected to have an effect on the appearance of the enclosed triangle. Since it is undoubtedly crucial that the triangle be organized as belonging to the inner frame, a smaller frame would be more effective in that regard.

But why, one might ask, is there any effect at all of a circumscribed frame on the appearance of a figure seem within it? The general answer to this question is the importance of stimulus relationships in perception, both within and between organized units and the tendency of the perceptual system to organize units of the field hierarchically. What exists or occurs in the real world is often most veridically described if hierarchical relationships are taken into account. It is a better description of the motion of an animal's limb if it is described with respect to its torso than if it is described with respect to some external coordinate system.

More specifically, if a figure or object is seen within an organized structure that has a definite intrinsic axis or coordinate axes, such as a rectangle, then these directions serve as reference frames of directions for objects seen within it. Thus, while such a frame of reference is not a world surrogate, in that we do not take its directions as equal to the coordinates of the environment, it does operate in an analogous fashion. That is, such a frame seems to define what is at the top, bottom and sides of an object within it.[12] At the same time we remain aware that the frame—and thus its contained objects as well—is tilted with respect to the vertical and horizontal of this environment. By virtue of this hierarchical organization there thus remains a certain ambiguity as to which directions are the top, bottom and sides of a figure. The tilted square within the tilted rectangle frame in the Kopfermann effect is a square with respect to the rectangle, but by virtue of partaking of the rectangle's tilt, is a diamond with respect to the environment or with respect to the observer's egocentric coordinates.

According to this reasoning there ought to be a rod-and-frame effect even when the rod is surrounded by a circumscribed small reference frame that itself can appear tilted. There ought to be a hierarchical effect. Yet, as was mentioned earlier, only a miniscule illusory tilt effect occurs when a small frame, whose tilt is veridically perceived, surrounds a vertical line. The problem here may be that the instructions clearly call for a judgment of how the line is oriented in the world, with respect to gravity. Whether by a transitivity operation (in which the rod's orientation in the world is inferred by combining its given orientation with respect to its frame and the frame's given orientation in the world) or by some other operation, the observer can perceive more or less veridically how the rod is oriented in the world. Another factor here may be that we are particularly sensitive to the rod's vertical orientation so that the use of this unique or prägnant

---

[12]Strictly speaking, a rectangular frame can only define what is vertical and horizontal but not the polarity of top and bottom or left and right along these axes. The unambiguous attribution of top-bottom must result either from gravity information or the observer's egocentric coordinates but attribution of left and right can only be based upon the egocentric coordinates.

orientation works against finding a hierarchical effect. Therefore, I would suggest that if a rod in some oblique orientation is seen within a tilted, relatively small rectangle and if the task is to compare its orientation to that of another rod (which itself might be seen within a rectangular frame either upright or tilted at some other angle), then a strong effect of the tilted frame on the appearance of the rod's orientation would indeed occur. It would be a hierarchical rod-and-frame effect.[13]

REFERENCES

Anstis, S. (1986). Motion perception in the frontal plane: Sensory aspects. In K. R. Boff, L. Kaufman, & J. P. Thomas (Eds.), *Handbook of perception and human performance* (Vol. 1.). New York: Wiley.

Asch, S. E., & Witkin, H. A. (1948a). Studies in space orientation: I. Perception of the upright with displaced visual fields. *Journal of Experimental Psychology, 38,* 325–327.

Asch, S. E., & Witkin, H. A. (1948b). Studies in space orientation: II. Perception of the upright with displaced visual fields and with body tilted. *Journal of Experimental Psychology, 38,* 455–477.

Attneave, F. (1968). Triangles as ambiguous figures. *American Journal of Psychology, 81,* 447–453.

Békésy, G. von (1967). *Sensory inhibition.* Princeton, NJ: Princeton University Press.

Blakemore, C., Carpenter, R. H. S., & Georgeson, M. A. (1970). Lateral inhibition between orientation detectors in the human visual system. *Nature, 228,* 37–39.

---

[13]There are several other perceptual phenomena that are based on the effect of a frame of reference that space limitations prevent me from discussing in this chapter. For the sake of inclusiveness I mention them here but the reader is referred to the references cited for a more thorough discussion of these phenomena: *The velocity transposition effect* (Brown, 1931; Wallach, 1939; Rock, Hill, & Fineman, 1968; Rock, 1975; Di Vita, 1983; Epstein, 1978; Epstein & Cody, 1980). This effect refers to the fact that the perceived velocity of moving objects is governed by the rate at which they traverse a reference frame. The principle has been invoked to explain the constancy of perceived velocity at varying distances of a moving object (Wallach, 1939). *The size proportionality effect* (Rock & Ebenholtz, 1959; Künnapas, 1955; Gogel & Sturm, 1972; Wenderoth, 1976; Epstein & Cody, 1980). This effect refers to the fact that perceived size is governed by the size of an object in relation to a frame of reference in the same plane, i.e., by the proportion of a frame of reference subtended by the object. Since such proportionality remains invariant over distances, it can also be considered to be an explanation of size constancy. *The Roelofs effect* (Roelofs, 1935; Dietzl, 1924; Rock, 1975; Kleinhans, 1970; Harris, 1974; Rock, Goldberg, & Mack, 1966). This effect refers to the fact that the perceived direction of an object is affected by the presence of a frame of reference placed asymmetrically or eccentrically with respect to the observer. Similarly, perceived egocentric direction is affected by the slant of a reference frame. In the first case, the error is in the direction of the center of the reference frame and, in the second case, it is toward that direction in which the line of sight is orthogonal to the plane of the reference frame.

Regarding all three of these phenomena, further research, following the initial discoveries, has questioned both the magnitude of the effect and the theoretical explanation offered. In any event, in my opinion, these effects are not as good examples of the frame of reference concept as defined and discussed in this chapter as are those of the perception of motion, the upright, and orientation of form.

Brandt, T., Wist, E., & Dichgans, J. (1975). Foreground and background in dynamic spatial orientation. *Perception & Psychophysics, 17,* 497–503.

Bridgemen, B. (1972). Visual receptive fields sensitive to absolute and relative motion during tracking. *Science, 178,* 1106–1108.

Brosgole, L. (1968). An analysis of induced motion. *Acta Psychologica, 28,* 1–44.

Brown, J. F. (1931). The visual perception of velocity. *Psychologische Forschung, 14,* 199–232. (Reprinted in I. M. Spigel (Ed.), *Visually perceived movement.* New York: Harper & Row).

Carpenter, R. H. S., & Blakemore, C. (1973). Interactions between orientations in human vision. *Experimental Brain Research, 18,* 287–303.

Day, R. H., & Dickinson, R. G. (1977). Absence of color selectivity in Duncker type induced visual movement. *Perception & Psychophysics, 22,* 313–320.

Day, R. H., Millar, J., & Dickinson, R. G. (1979). Induced movement as nonveridical resolution of displacement ambiguity: Effect of closure and number of field elements. *Perception & Psychophysics, 25,* 23–28.

Dichgans, J., & Brandt, T. (1974). The psychophysics of visually induced perception of self-motion and tilt. In F. O. Schmidt & F. G. Worden (Eds.), *The neursciences* (Vol. 3, pp. 123–129). Cambridge, MA: MIT Press.

Dietzl, H. (1924). Untersuchungun über die optische Localisation der Mediane. *Zeitschrift für Biol., 80,* 289–316.

DiVita, J. (1983). *Temporal determinants of perceived velocity.* Unpublished doctoral dissertation, Rutgers University.

DiLorenzo, J., & Rock, I. (1982). The rod and frame effect as a function of righting of the frame. *Journal of Experimental Psychology: Human Perception and Performance, 8,* 536–546.

Duke-Elder, S. (1958). *The eye in evolution.* St. Louis, MO: Mosby.

Duncker, K. (1929). Uber induzierte Bewegung. *psychologische Forschung, 12,* 180–259.

Ebenholtz, S. M. (1977). Determinants of the rod and frame effect: The role of retinal size. *Perception & Psychophysics, 22,* 531–538.

Ebenholtz, S. M., & Benzschawel, T. L. (1977). The rod and frame effect and induced head tilt as a function of observation distance. *Perception & Psychophysics, 22,* 491–496.

Ebenholtz, S. M., & Callan, J. W. (1980). Modulation of the rod and frame effect: Retinal angle vs. apparent size. *Psychological Research, 42,* 327–334.

Epstein, W. (1978). Two factors in the perception of velocity at a distance. *Perception & Psychophysics, 24,* 105–114.

Epstein, W., & Cody, W. J. (1980). Perception of relative velocity: A revision of the hypothesis of relational determination. *Perception, 9,* 47–60.

Farber, J. M. (1979, April). *Peripheral dominance in dual-surround induced motion.* Paper presented at the meeting of the Eastern Psychological Association, Philadelphia.

Gibson, J. J. (1966). *The senses considered as perceptual systems.* Boston: Houghton-Mifflin.

Gogel, W. C., & Newton, R. E. (1975). Depth adjacency and the rod and frame illusion. *Perception & Psychology, 18,* 163–171.

Gogel, W. C., & Sturm, R. D. (1972). A test of the relational hypothesis of perceived size. *American Journal of Psychology, 85,* 201–216.

Goodenough, D. R., Oltman, P. K., Sigman, E., Rosso, J., & Mertz, H. (1979). Orientation contrast effects in the rod and frame test. *Perception & Psychophysics, 25,* 419–424.

Harris, C. S. (1974). Beware of the straight-ahead shift—a nonperceptual change in experiments on adaptation to displaced vision. *Perception, 3,* 461–476.

Hay, J. C., Pick, H. L., & Ikeda, K. (1965). Visual capture produced by prism spectacles. *Psychonomic Science, 2,* 215–216.

Held, R. (1968). Dissociation of visual functions by deprivation and rearrangement. *Psychologische Forschung, 31,* 338–348.

Held, R. (1970). Two modes of processing spatially distributed visual stimulation. In F. O. Schmidt (Ed.), *The neurosciences: Second study program.* New York: Rockefeller University Press.

Held, R., Dichgans, J., & Bauer, J. (1975). Characteristics of moving visual scene influencing spatial orientation. *Vision Research, 15,* 357–365.

Hering, E. (1861). *Beitrage zur Physiologie.* Heft 1. W. Englemann.

Hughes, P. C. (1973). The influence of the visual field upon the visual vertical in relation to ocular torsion of the eye. Doctoral dissertation, University of Oklahoma. *Dissertation Abstracts International, 33,* 468B. (University Microfilms No. 73–91, 58B).

Ingle, D. (1967). Two visual mechanisms underlying the behavior of fish. *Psychologische Forschung, 31,* 44–51.

Johansson, G. (1950). *Configuration in event perception.* Uppsala, Sweden: Almkvist and Wiksell.

Kleinhans, J. (1970). *Perception of spatial orientation in sloped, slanted, and tilted visual fields.* Unpublished doctoral dissertation, Rutgers University.

Koffka, K. (1935). *Principles of gestalt psychology* (p. 25). New York: Harcourt, Brace.

Köhler, W. (1938). *The place of value in a world of facts* (pp. 126–141). New York: Liveright.

Kopfermann, H. (1930). Psychologische Untersuchungen uber die wirkung zweidimensionale Darstellungen Korperlicher Gebilde. *Psychologische Forschung, 13,* 293–364.

Künnapas, T. M. (1955). Influence of frame size on apparent length of a line. *Journal of Experimental Psychology, 50,* 168–170.

Leibowitz, H. W., & Post, R. B. (1982). The two modes of processing concept and some implications. In J. J. Beck (Ed.), *Organization and representation in perception.* Hillsdale, NJ: Lawrence Erlbaum Associates.

Lishman, J. R., & Lee, D. N. (1973). The autonomy of visual kinesthesis. *Perception, 2,* 287–294.

Loomis, J., & Nakayama, K. (1973). A velocity analogue to brightness contrast. *Vision Research, 18,* 425–428.

Mach, E. (1914/1959). *The analysis of sensations.* (Translated from the German edition, 1897). New York: Dover.

Mack, A. (1986). Perceptual aspects of motion in the frontal plane. In K. R. Boff, L. Kaufman & J. P. Thomas (Eds.), *Handbook of perception and human performance* (Vol. 1). New York: Wiley.

Mack, A., Fandrich, R., & Fisher, C. B. (1975). A re-examination of two-point induced movement. *Perception & Psychophysics, 17,* 273–276.

Mack, A., Heuer, F., Fendrich, R., & Chambers, D. (1985). Induced motion and oculomotor visual capture, *Journal of Experimental Psychology: Human Perception and Performance, 11,* 329–345.

Over, R., & Longrove, W. (1973). Color selectivity in simultaneous motion contract. *Perception & Psychophysics, 14,* 445–448.

Palmer, S. E. (1977). Hierarchical structure in perceptual representation. *Cognitive Psychology, 9,* 441–474.

Palmer, S. E. (1980). What makes triangles point: local and global effects in configurations of ambiguous triangles. *Cognitive Psychology, 12,* 285–305.

Palmer, S. E. (1985). The role of symmetry in shape perception. *Acta Psychologica, 59,* 67–90.

Palmer, S. E. (1988). Reference frames in the perception of shape and orientation. In B. Shepp & S. Ballesteros (Eds.), *Object perception: Structure and process.* Hillsdale, NJ: Lawrence Erlbaum Associates.

Palmer, S. E. (1989). *Effects of multiple frames on perceived pointing of ambiguous triangles.* In preparation.

Palmer, S. E., & Bucher, N. M. (1981). Configural effects in perceived pointing of ambiguous triangles. *Journal of Experimental Psychology: Human Perception and Performance, 7,* 88–114.

Palmer, S. E., & Bucher, N. M. (1982). Textural effects in perceived pointing of ambiguous triangles. *Journal of Experimental Psychology: Human Perception and Performance, 8,* 693–708.

Rock, I. (1956). The orientation of forms on the retina and in the environment. *American Journal of Psychology, 69,* 513–528.

Rock, I. (1968). The basis of position constancy during passive movement of the observer. *American Journal of Psychology, 81*, 262–265.

Rock, I. (1973). *Orientation and form.* New York: Academic Press.

Rock, I. (1975). *An introduction to perception.* New York: Macmillan.

Rock, I., Auster, M., Schiffman, M., & Wheeler, D. (1980). Induced movement based on subtraction of motion from the inducing object. *Journal of Experimental Psychology: Human Perception and Performance, 6*, 391–403.

Rock, I., & Di Vita, J. (1973). Unpublished experiment performed at Rutgers University.

Rock, I., & Ebenholtz, S. (1959). The relational determination of perceived size. *Psychological Review, 66*, 387–401.

Rock, I., Goldberg, J., & Mack, A. (1966). Immediate correction and adaptation based on viewing a prismatically displaced scene. *Perception & Psychophysics, 1*, 351–354.

Rock, I., & Harris, C. S. (1967). Vision and touch. *Scientific American, 216*, 96–104.

Rock, I., Hill, L., & Fineman, M. (1968). Speed constancy as a function of size constancy. *Perception & Psychophysics, 4*, 37–40.

Rock, I., & Smith, D. (1986). The optomotor response and induced motion of the self. *Perception, 15*, 497–502.

Rock, I., & Victor, J. (1964). Vision and touch: An experimentally created conflict between the senses. *Science, 143*, 594–596.

Roelofs, C. O. (1935). Optische Localisation. *Archiv für Augenhellkunde, 109*, 395–415.

Schneider, G. E. (1967). Contrasting visuomotor functions of tectum and cortex in the golden hamster. *Psychologische Forschung, 31*, 52–62.

Sigman, E., Goodenough, D. R., & Flannagan, M. (1978). Subjective estimates of body tilt and the rod-and-frame test. *Perceptual and Motor Skills, 47*, 1051–1056.

Sigman, E., Goodenough, D. R., & Flannagan, M. (1979). Instructions, illusory self-tilt, and the rod-and-frame test. *Quarterly Journal of Experimental Psychology, 31*, 155–165.

Tastevin, J. (1937). En partant de l'experience d'Aristote. *L'Encephale, 1*, 57–84.

Trevarthen, C. (1968). Two mechanisms of vision in primates. *Psychologische Forschung, 31*, 229–337.

Wallach, H. (1939). On constancy of visual speed. *Psychological Review, 116*, 541–552.

Wallach, H. (1959). The perception of motion. *Scientific American, 201*, 56–60.

Wallach, H., Bacon, J., & Schulman, P. (1978). Adaptation in motion perception: Alteration of induced motion. *Perception and Psychophysics, 24*, 509–514.

Walls, G. L. (1942). *The vertebrate eye and its adaptive radiation.* New York: Hafner Press.

Weisz, A. (1955). Visual determinants in perceiving movement of self. Unpublished doctoral dissertation, New School for Social Research, New York.

Wenderoth, P. M. (1974). The distinction between the rod-and-frame illusion and the rod-and-frame test. *Perception, 3*, 205–212.

Wenderoth, P. M. (1976). The contribution of relational factors to line-length matches. *Perception, 5*, 265–278.

Wertheimer, M. (1912). Experimentelle studien uber das Sehen von Bewegung. *Zeitschift fur Psychologie, 61*, 161–265.

Witkin, H. A. (1949). Perception of body position and of the position of the visual field. *Psychological Monographs, 63* (7, Whole No. 302).

Witkin, H. A., & Asch, S. E. (1948). Studies in space orientation: IV. Further experiments on perception of the upright with displaced visual fields. *Journal of Experimental Psychology, 38*, 762–782.

V

GESTALT PSYCHOLOGY

16 The Vanishing World and Köhler's Inkwell

Rudolf Arnheim
Professor Emeritus of the Psychology of Art, Harvard University

ABSTRACT

A current philosophical trend tries to discredit the objective reality of the experienced world and to describe the human self as a detached universe left to its own wishes and phantasies. In this vein, a recent attempt to reduce organic functioning to the principle of self-regulation has suggested an affinity to gestalt theory. Such an analogy, however, risks to misinterpret the basic epistemological attitude of the theory's founders.

An urgent first task of human beings, soon after they are born, is that of sorting out the self from things that are not the self. Foremost under the control of the self are the body's limbs and the eyes. Partially controllable are the mother and the teddy bear. Other things again are entirely beyond the control of the self, as for instance the clouds. This first advance toward the facts of reality takes place in an entirely unitary world of things among things.

As cognition becomes more wary, it begins to separate mere appearances from objective existences. Some visual percepts turn out to be misleading, but they are considered exceptions in an otherwise reliable world. Such a worldview suffices for daily living, and it also suffices for psychologists who are untouched by the refinements of epistemology. They study, for example, optical illusions or dreams as curious deviations from a reality that otherwise is directly given.

Cognition becomes specifically human and psychologists become truly psychologists when they take to wondering how the world manages to persist once we close our eyes. Since the experienced world reaches beyond what is supplied by direct perception, it must be imported from somewhere beyond perception, from a realm entirely unreachable by the direct access of our senses. When this duality is accepted, it leads to a philosophical division between people who trust the reliability of given experience and those who do not. Natural science is dependent on the given world as the source of clues from which to make inferences about the nature of what exists transphenomenally. To this end, science examines the totality of the given perceptual world as to its consistency. In the context of the whole, the chaff of the misleadingly accidental is winnowed out.

With ever refined instrumentation, it became convincingly probable that whatever facts are suggested by circumstantial evidence can eventually be found in direct experience, whether it be a missing planet or a needed gene—with one spectacular exception, namely the recent realization that in the realm of quantum physics the very fact of information gathering prevents the simultaneous measurement of the position and momentum of particles such as electrons. The resonance created by this discovery in our entire culture, far beyond the realm of physical science, is a telling example of the phenomenon to which my chapter is devoted. When the physicists turned to calling the laws of nature "statistical," they meant as a rule that "a particular physical system is incompletely known." Werner Heisenberg (1955), making this statement, added: "When it comes to macroscopic processes, this statistical element of atomic physics is generally irrelevant because in the large the statistical laws lead to so strong a probability that in practice the event can be called deterministic" (pp. 24–30). Given the state of mind of the culture, however, the uncertainty principle was taken by many to proclaim that causality had gone out of the window, even though everywhere in the physical world events are measured and predicted to a fraction of a second or millimeter and any violation of causality would be even more profoundly disturbing today than it would have been in the days of Laplace.

We are driven to suspect that such readiness to dismiss the principle of causality in its most general sense derives not so much from what is demanded by the findings of science but rather from an urge to deny objective reality, an urge that has darkened our philosophy like a cloud of poison gas. If I am not mistaken, this pathology of our spirit has acquired its destructive power from the fusion of two influential trains of thought. One is the insistence of the British empiricists on accepting the reality of nothing but the most immediate and tangible evidence of our senses, whereby—if I may stay with the example of causality for another moment—David Hume (1739) was led to say about necessity that it is "nothing but an internal impression of the mind or a determination to carry our thoughts from one object to another." And further: "The efficacy and energy of causes is neither placed in the causes themselves, nor in the Deity, nor in the concurrence of these two principles, but belongs entirely to the soul, which considers the union of two or more objects in all past instances."

The other ingredient of the toxic philosophical concoction derives from the Continent and from an entirely different frame of mind. It claims the privilege of powerful individuals, and more broadly of human beings in general, to mold the world according to their own wishes and needs. The most eloquent promoter of this claim is, of course, Nietzsche (1887), who in *Der Wille zur Macht* has a section on the will to power as cognition [Erkenntnis]. There, inveighing against "causalism," he asserts that "truth," which he puts in quotes, is not "something that exists and is to be found and discovered but something to be created, something that provides a name for a process or rather for a will to overpower, which is actually endless."

Evidently, this blend of a cognitive insistence on perception as the sole generator of connection and interaction and the moral license to wilful interpretation has had an irresistible influence on the mood of our times. In consequence, we are caught in a climate in which philosophers, psychologists, anthropologists, and aestheticians vie with one another in asserting that there is no objective world, no binding truth, no factual value, no inherent meaning. It is a frightening example of what Wolfgang Köhler has called "the obsessions of normal people" (Henle, 1971). Solomon Asch (1952) in a chapter of his *Social Psychology* on "the fact of culture and the problem of relativism" has pointed out that the determinants derived from social and individual conventions and preferences do not exclude the ability of human beings to consider objectively given conditions according to their intrinsic demands. In the present essay I propose to discuss the resonance of the negativistic worldview in certain recent reinterpretations of the relation between sentient organisms and their surroundings and the consequences of such views for principles of gestalt theory.

An attempt by two Chilean biologists, Humberto R. Maturana and Francisco J. Varela, to define the nature of living systems clearly exhibits the effect of this alienation on the interpretation of a strictly scientific matter and the resulting response evoked well beyond the confines of a professional specialty. Maturana and Varela define the organism as a self-regulating system, an approach that would offer little novelty, were it not for their insistence that the self-regulation of the isolated system in and by itself is its only relevant trait. Other essentials of organic nature, such as reproduction and evolution, are described as secondary operations of the self-regulatory process. This process, together with the other mechanisms it generates, is given the name *autopoiesis,* meaning roughly self-creation or self-production. What matters for my purpose is that everything beyond the process of self-regulation, the organism's relation to its environment as well as the effects of its past and the goals to be attained in the future are strictly bracketed out. They are evident to an observer who can look beyond the spatial and temporal boundaries of the system, but they appear within the system as mere stimuli, generated externally or internally, in the play of forces constituting the homeostatic process. They are mere "perturbations," as Maturana and Varela (1980) call them with a characteristically negative term. The organic system, devoted exclusively to the maintenance of its equilibrium, is totally closed. "What occurs in a living system is analogous to what occurs in an instrumental flight where the pilot does not have access to the outside world and must function only as a controller of the values shown in his flight instruments. . . . When the pilot steps out of the plane he is bewildered by the congratulations of his friends on account of the perfect flight and landing he performed in absolute darkness'' (p. 51).

This description of self-regulation in the darkness of an isolated system is obviously correct. It is also valuable by stressing the fundamental importance of the homeostatic process. It is, however, acceptable only if one is willing to think of perceptual or hormonal stimuli as mere perturbations, that is, as mere challenges, acting without any rationale of their own but simply to be met by countermoves reestablishing balance.

Needless to say, Maturana and Varela deny neither the existence of the niche constituting the organism's ambience nor its metabolism or temporal context in ontogeny or evolution. But not only do they restrict these external factors to the cognitive domain of the observer; the observer, too, is described as an autopoietic system, which receives its knowledge about the outer world only through translations into the stimuli accessible to him as ''boundary conditions'' of his own internal system. Such a confined worldview is not entirely remote from what we know psychologically about some human behavior; for example, people may respond to the urges of the sexual instinct without any explicit conception of reproduction as the biological purpose it serves in its broader context. But we recognize such a limited outlook as a deplorable insensitivity to the privileges of human cognition, to the ability, that is, to look beyond the local information of our immediate stimuli. Such, however, is the perspective suggested by Maturana and Varela (1980). The relationship between what is externally given and what is internally received is weighted entirely in favor of the latter. They observe that ''there is no possible distinction between internally and externally generated states of nervous activity'' (p. 23), no way for the nervous system to distinguish between perception and hallucination (p. XVI). Autopoietic systems ''do not have inputs or outputs. They can be perturbated [sic] by independent events and undergo internal structural changes which compensate these perturbations'' (p. 81).

From such more technically physiological statements the reader is led without warning to affirmations like the following: ''Language does not transmit information, and its functional role is the creation of a cooperative domain of interactions between speakers through the development of a common frame of reference, although each speaker acts exclusively within his cognitive domain where all ultimate truth is contingent to [sic] personal experience'' (p. 57). There is no communication. The man in the flight cabin is deprived not only of his view of the world but also of his copilot. We are told that this is so because ''language is connotative and not denotative, and its function is to orient the orientee within his cognitive domain without regard for the cognitive domain of the orienter'' (p. 32). Consequently there is no object of knowledge (p. 53), and ''no absolute system of values is possible and all truth and falsehood in the cultural domain are necessarily relative'' (p. 57). (Maturana & Varela, 1980)

All this philosophical and psychological superstructure is derived by Maturana and Varela from the concept of self-regulation as a basic trait of organic functioning—a foundation coinciding, of course, with that of gestalt theory. "Dynamic self-distribution," wrote Köhler (1947), "is the kind of function which gestalt psychology believes to be essential in neurological and psychological theory" (p. 132). Although no acknowledgement of this debt is found in Maturana's and Varela's text, the kinship has not been lost on the members of the *Gesellschaft für Gestalttheorie,* who have been carrying on the tradition in Germany. In fact, the 1985 convention of the Society was devoted to exploring contact points and similarities between gestalt theory and the "theory of self-organization in complex systems." In a characteristic contribution to this discussion, however, Stadler and Kruse (1986) warned that they intended to concentrate on a "specifying application" of this basic principle to the cognitive systems stated first by Maturana and Varela and further developed by others; and they proceeded, in the spirit of "an ironical self-criticism," to insist on the "wide-ranging overlap" between gestalt theory and the "radical constructivism" propounded by Heinz von Foerster and his circle.[1]

Radical constructivism, we are told by Stadler and Kruse, states that human perceiving, thinking, and behaving dwell in a realm of semantic seclusion and that, in consequence, the world of material objects is located beyond human experience (p. 76). This formulation involves a curious ontological contamination of the transphenomenal (physical) world with what one might call the world of phenomenal invariants. It is a distinction with which Stadler and Kruse are not unfamiliar, but which they choose to ignore. Color vision, for example, does indeed derive ultimately from an electromagnetic spectrum to which human experience has no direct access. But our basis for distinguishing the so-called optical illusions from what the world is "really" like is by no means beyond the reach of our perception. Rather we compare such deviations with the phenomenal invariants, that is, with the totality of perceptual experience by which we establish the objective reality of our world through a continuous process of integration, comparison, and correction.

Nothing would be more alien to the spirit of gestalt psychology than an attempt to use perceptual deviations for the purpose of describing human experience as sequestered from the outer world in which life takes place. Gestalt psychology has been distinguished from the beginning by a deep respect for the objective conditions to which the human mind must respond if it is to act appropriately. As early as 1924, Köhler stated that the way in which the field of vision segregates gestalten of particular properties from the ground is "*sachlich bestimmt,*" meaning that it corresponds to the objective nature of the given

---

[1]Radical constructivism, strongly influenced by the theory of autopoiesis, proposes "an epistemology that argues that what we can know is a function of the observer rather than what is observed" (Segal, 1986, p. 8) and proclaims a kind of collective solipsism.

things (Köhler, 1924). By referring to the objects on his desk, the inkwell, the book, the pencil, he took pains to insist that the shapes given in perception inform us reliably. Although the transcendental physical world is indeed inaccessible to us in any direct fashion, the stable, invariant presence of the inkwell in our experience permits legitimate inferences to a transcendental world whose existence must be assumed to account with corresponding properties of form and structure for the solidity of the things we see.

Most characteristic of the misreading to which Stadler and Kruse, under the influence of "radical constructivism," subject the gestalt approach is their reference to Asch's experiments on group forces in the modification and distortion of judgments (Asch, 1952; chapter 16). Under the heading *Incompatibility of social and individual reality* they cite Asch's findings together with the "asocial reality" of schizophrenics, hallucinations, and dreams to illustrate the difference between what is considered real and what is variously experienced. Actually, of course, Asch's experiments were conceived in response to the view, popular among psychologists even then, that cognition is helplessly at the mercy of social and other subjective forces preventing people from doing justice to the facts before their eyes. He showed that while some individuals yield to such pressure, others resist it courageously.

In a broader sense, Asch's work goes with the many ways in which gestalt psychologists have undertaken to show that human behavior, and cognition in particular, is brought about by the interaction between externally generated stimuli and the complex forces that activate the responses of the nervous system and the mind. The former provide the information about the environment needed to make behavior biologically and psychologically appropriate, the latter organize the input according to the principles that control the perceptual and motivational processes. It was this internal organization that was shown to operate as a field process, in which "all local changes must be such that, when considered in their totality, they bring the system nearer to the balance of forces" (Köhler, 1947, p. 132). To explore these principles, gestalt psychologists studied phenomena such as optical illusions, figural aftereffects, and groupings, which differed from the raw data provided by the sense organs. And far from using these symptoms of gestalt organization for the purpose of demonstrating that the mind conjures up a world unrelated to whatever may exist outside, they had to be concerned with the problem of how the mind manages to do justice to the facts of external reality, even though the brain processes the imported materials according to autochthonous principles of its own. In the field of vision, for example, the resulting perceptual organization

fits in general the subdivision of our environment into singular objects, for the reason that the single object, by way of its natural origin or because of the shape and color given it by its human maker, tends to meet the conditions that bring about an optical stimulus configuration suitable for the formation of a visual unit (Köhler, 1924, p. 186).

Gestalt theory does not deny that the organism can be considered a self-contained unit operating within its own boundaries. It acknowledges the existence of subwholes as components of a broader gestalt. But subwholes are bound to the organization of the whole of which they are a part, and therefore the gestalt theorist cannot afford to forgo the privilege of looking beyond the outer shell of the organism. Only when the context is extended into the surroundings of space and time, do the stimulus signals within the organism cease to be meaningless disturbances of the equilibrium.

Two further observations conclude this chapter. First, the ontogenetic development from the single cell to the complete organism and from the self-centered infant into a social being suggests a view of complex wholes as being brought about by an agglomeration of individual units. This tendency will be all the stronger in an approach such as that of autopoiesis, where the individual is conceived of as a detached gyroscope, self-sufficient and complete in its own organization. In opposition to such a view, much modern biology, anthropology, and other social science considers dynamic and social structure as being governed by the principles of the overarching whole. Perhaps this gestalt approach may be said to have proceeded in too unilateral a fashion by laying principal stress on the direction from the top down to the parts, although it did not overlook the interaction by which each part on the basis of its own organization contributes structural features to the overall play of forces. The very nature of a part viewed as a structure rather than an arbitrarily bounded quantity of material presupposes an internal organization that creates constraints toward its surroundings while interacting with them at the same time. Any description uniquely favoring the role of either the part or the whole will fail to do justice to the richness of field processes.

A second observation concerns the static character attributed to organic systems when they are treated exclusively as self-regulatory mechanisms. "A living system is not a goal-directed system," write Maturana and Varela (1980), "it is, like the nervous system, a stable state-determined and strictly deterministic system closed on itself and modulated by interactions not specified through its conduct" (p. 50). Living systems, they say, are purposeless. By relegating the goal-directed aspect of organic life to the domain of the observer, they table it in effect. This revives a problem for which there are well-known precedents. Sigmund Freud (1941), in the definitive statement on his theories, said of the instinctual drives, that although they are the ultimate cause of all activity, they are conservative by nature. "Any state attained by a creature generates a tendency to reestablish this state as soon as it has been left behind" (p. 71). And we remember that Walter B. Cannon (1963), after giving his magisterial description of how the homeostatic balance of the body keeps the internal environment constant and thereby frees us "from the limitations imposed by both internal and external agencies or conditions that could be disturbing," raised the question: Freedom for what? (p. 302). His answer referred to the higher nervous system as being made free to "have all our intelligent relations to the world about us." In this way, Cannon gave the goal-directedness of the organism its due, but he did so by separating the static physiological infrastructure as a mere foundation from the dynamics of creativity, aspiration, and the yearning for love. This left psychologists with the task of how to integrate the forces maintaining the self with those carrying the self toward its targets.

I have tried to show how a current philosophical trend to discredit the objective reality of the world we live in and to describe the human self as a detached universe left to its own wishes and phantasies has slanted some recent interpretations in biology and psychology and has attempted to enlist gestalt theory as an ally. There is no telling whether the ominous visions of a vanishing world are the forewarnings of a dying civilization or whether a coming generation will recover from the attack. In the meantime, gestalt theory remains available in support of the many who do not doubt that they are in direct communication with the world in which they live and the fellow human beings with whom they share it. Not many inkwells are left in our studies nowadays, but the objects on Wolfgang Köhler's writing desk maintain their reassuring presence while the debate continues.

REFERENCES

Asch, S. E. (1952). *Social psychology.* Englewood Cliffs, NJ: Prentice-Hall.
Cannon, W. B. (1963). *The wisdom of the body.* New York: Norton.
Freud, S. (1941). *Abriss der Psychoanalyse. Schriften aus dem Nachlass 1892–1938.* London: Imago.
Heisenberg, W. (1955). *Das Naturbild der heutigen Physik.* Hamburg: Rowohlt.
Henle, M. (Ed.). (1971). *The selected papers of Wolfgang Köhler* (pp. 398–412). New York: Liveright.
Hume, D. (1739). *A treatise of human nature. Part III: Of the idea of necessary connection.*
Köhler, W. (1924). Gestaltprobleme und Anfänge einer Gestalttheorie. (Reprinted in *Gestalt Theory,* August, 1983, Vol. *5,* 178–205).
Köhler, W. (1947). *Gestalt psychology.* New York: Liveright.
Maturana, H. R., & Varela, F. J. (1980). *Autopoiesis and cognition.* Dordrecht: Reidel.
Nietzsche, F. W. (1887). *Der Wille zur Macht,* Book III, paragraph 552.
Segel, L. (1986). *The dream of reality. Heinz von Foerster's constructivism.* New York: Norton.
Stadler, M., & Kruse, P. (1986, June). Gestalttheorie und Theorie der Selbstorganisation. *Gestalt Theory,* Vol. *8,* 75–98.

17

Some Neo-Gestalt Psychologies and Their Relation to Gestalt Psychology

Mary Henle
New School for Social Research

ABSTRACT

Renewed interest in problems first investigated by Gestalt psychologists has brought forth a variety of so-called "Neo-Gestalt" theories. Although they differ among themselves, they have in common an interest in such phenomena as perceptual grouping and Prägnanz; and most of them take an information processing approach to their material. This chapter examines the underlying assumptions of several of these new psychologies and compares them to those of Gestalt theory.

The present decade has seen revived interest in problems raised by Gestalt psychologists some three-quarters of a century ago. In 1981 Michael Kubovy and James R. Pomerantz prefaced their edited volume with the remark: "This is the first volume devoted to perceptual organization since Köhler's last book, *The Task of Gestalt Psychology,* was published in 1969" (1981, p. x). Soon after the publication of Kubovy and Pomerantz's collection, Jacob Beck edited a volume on *Organization and Representation in Perception* (1982). These books may be taken as representative of a now substantial literature on perceptual organization. In the collections mentioned, several authors explicitly label themselves Gestalt psychologists with specific qualifications. In these cases and others, I will raise the question: What is their relation to Gestalt psychology? I will consider a variety of issues that arise in connection with these new efforts to deal with problems of organization. My treatment will be selective confining itself, for example, to visual perception and resisting the temptation to go beyond—or even to cover completely—the two collections in question, since too many issues arise for adequate treatment in a single chapter.

It may be remarked at the outset that most of the authors here discussed have in common an interest in certain problems investigated by Gestalt psychologists, especially grouping and Prägnanz, and that most take an information processing approach to these problems.

ANALYTIC GESTALT PSYCHOLOGY

W. R. Garner (1981), after criticisms of Gestalt psychology, states:

> I have long been interested in Gestalt phenomena and believe that they are very important in perception. But along with this interest is a desire to maintain what I consider to be a fruitful scientific approach to the problem; thus I suppose I am an analytic Gestalt psychologist. (p. 130)

Garner uses the term *analysis* in at least two senses, which are not always sufficiently distinguished. The naive observer, he says, may perceive forms as unitary wholes in a completely unanalyzed way; the scientist, on the other hand, must use the sophisticated techniques at his disposal to understand the perception. But these are two quite different tasks, the one perceptual, the other scientific. The scientist perceives a whole in the same manner as the layman before he begins his specific tasks of developing constructs and investigating the conditions and functional consequences of the phenomenon. Since Garner is an "analytic Gestalt psychologist" as an investigator rather than as a perceiver, I will first discuss this meaning.

Garner (1981) approves the early Gestalt tradition culminating in Korte's laws (1915), which concern relations of distance, intensity, and time of presented forms for optimal phi movement. "Thus the beginning of Gestalt psychology was based on a thoroughly analytic approach to stimulus properties" (p. 129). Later, he believes, "Gestalt psychologists undertook simply to catalog phenomena that were more or less holistic but ceased utterly to be analytic about their phenomena" (p. 129).

This criticism of Gestalt psychology is made in the complete absence of any reference to its experimental literature, except for the mention of Korte as reported by Boring in 1942. Since Max Wertheimer's paper on perceived motion (1912) antedates Korte's, it presumably comes within the "analytic" period of Gestalt psychology and need not be discussed here. Suffice it to say that in all respects this investigation is the very model of Garner's analytic method. Its aim is to test then existing theories of perceived movement and to work in the direction of a more adequate one.

Garner's criticism is directed, however, to a later period in the development of Gestalt psychology. Rather than trying to describe a large number of the experimental investigations which would satisfy his demand for analytic methods, I will concentrate on one particularly impressive study of a later date which can certainly not be dismissed as "[shrugging] our shoulders and [saying] that there is little further we can do about it as perceptual scientists" (Garner, 1981, p. 131).

Köhler and Wallach's monograph on figural aftereffects was published in 1944. In dozens of experiments, one factor after another in the production of such effects was investigated. For example, shape of inspection and test figures, their size, use of solid vs. outline figures, use of three-dimensional inspection figures, distance relations between inspection and test figures, duration of inspection, spatial orientation of inspection figures, to name only a few. Results were obtained not only by inspection; necessarily crude first measurements of size changes in test figures were made by a method of constant stimuli, as well as measurements of displacement of test figures. Binocular transfer of figural aftereffects was demonstrated and, indeed, proved useful as an experimental procedure. Later, figural aftereffects in kinesthesis (Köhler & Dinnerstein, 1947) and in the third dimension (Köhler & Emery, 1947) were demonstrated. Like Wertheimer's, Köhler's major interest in all this work was in developing a theory of the phenomena under investigation and, by way of figural aftereffects, a theory of visual processes. This theory was later investigated more directly (cf. for example, Köhler, Held, & O'Connell, 1952).

In this volume it is particularly appropriate to mention Asch's work on forming impressions of personality (e.g., Asch, 1946), his work on independence and conformity (e.g., Asch, 1951, 1956), and that on the nature of associations (e.g., Asch, Ceraso, & Heimer, 1960) as investigations which Garner would surely call analytic (although they are not mainly perceptual). Much more experimental work of the Gestalt psychologists could be cited in this connection. It is only by ignoring their specific experimental research that Garner can say that Gestalt psychologists simply catalog interesting phenomena, shrug their shoulders, and find nothing further to say about them.

The foregoing examples should suffice to show that Gestalt psychologists, like all other experimental psychologists, do indeed specify what Garner calls "stimulus properties," as well as employ different tasks, with their differing demands (Garner's converging operations), in investigating a problem.

Now I leave the question of scientific analysis and come to that of perceptual analysis. As mentioned earlier, Garner seems to say that the scientist, but not the layman, perceives in an analytic way. He quotes Boring (1942) as saying that a visual form is a unitary whole. This statement, with which he takes issue, seems to be equated (not by Boring) with the assertion that perceptions "are processed in an unanalyzed way" (Garner, 1981, p. 119). Garner accepts Boring's statement for *some* perceptions only. Here we find a confounding of the perception with the way, in Garner's terms, it is processed.

With regard to perception, "holistic" or unanalyzed perceptions are not characteristic of our experience. Ordinarily we, layman and scientist alike, perceive articulated wholes, which means that they have parts, boundaries, inner structure, that they constitute parts of groups and are differentiated into figure and ground. Only in exceptional cases (e.g., the Ganzfeld) is the visual scene undifferentiated or holistic.

The conceptual question of how these differentiated wholes are to be analyzed must be distinguished from the question of their appearance. For most cases, Garner (1981) looks to attributes, that is, to features or dimensions: "Any stimulus can be described in terms of its components, and if in fact we describe all the components of a stimulus, then in some sense we have described or defined a whole" (p. 124). Again, (Garner, 1981): "When we want to understand a phenomenon, we must somehow analyze it, take it apart, see what its components are, and otherwise subdue the holistic percept into analyzed components" (p. 119). To these attributes, he maintains, configurational properties, such as symmetry, repetition, intersection (good continuation?) may somehow be added (p. 126), or such properties may somehow emerge from the attributes (p. 124).

This approach to the analysis of perceptual wholes clearly distinguishes Garner from the Gestalt psychologists who start with wholes, which may be analyzed, not into predetermined attributes, but into their natural parts and other substructures.

In sum, since Garner has chosen analysis as his arena, this is the aspect of his psychology discussed here. It can be seen that he totally neglects the experimental analyses of the Gestalt psychologists. In addition, his conception of perceptual analysis is altogether different from, indeed opposite to, that of Gestalt psychology: he wants to "subdue the holistic percept into analyzed components" rather than respecting the natural parts of an articulated whole.

INFORMATION PROCESSING

It has been pointed out that a number of the authors of the two volumes under consideration approach problems of perceptual organization by way of the concepts of information processing. That this approach has no relation to Gestalt psychology can easily be seen. I can do no better than quote Ulric Neisser (1976), who refers to the "mechanistic information processing models, which treat the mind as a fixed-capacity device for converting discrete and meaningless inputs into conscious percepts" (p. 10). Criticism of mechanism, or of machine theory, along with an alternative to it, has been one of the main thrusts of Gestalt theory. While recognizing the existence, even the necessity of constraints, the components of machines, in the organism, Gestalt psychologists insist on the dynamic factors that organisms and their nervous systems share with all of nature. These invariant dynamics keep machines as well as organisms functioning. Yet they have been neglected by most theories, including the ones now under review.

A mechanistic model, which relies on constraints in the nervous system to produce orderly perceptual fields, necessarily precludes free interaction among the relevant processes. Connections and even networks of fibers are no substitute for interactions of processes. Such a system, entailing as it does "discrete inputs," is therefore atomistic, though the elements of contemporary theorizing are likely to be features, dimensions, and attributes rather than the sensations of earlier times. In its elementarism, too, information processing contradicts the basic propositions of Gestalt psychology.

The question that concerns us here is whether a system that contradicts the essential assumptions of Gestalt psychology can do justice to Gestalt problems. More important, can it carry forward the work begun by Gestalt psychologists? The work of James R. Pomerantz will be considered in relation to these questions, which have relevance to other authors too; although he does not call himself a neo-Gestaltist, his work is consistent with this tradition, which attempts to apply the concepts of information processing to Gestalt problems.

Pomerantz is concerned with finding performance measures of grouping and other phenomena which he believes Gestalt psychologists have investigated by phenomenological methods only (not an accurate assessment, as we have seen). Surely there can be no objection to the use of performance measures if they are appropriate to the problem. The phenomenological method, or as Attneave (cited in Pomerantz, 1981) calls it, the "look-at-the-figure-and-see-for-yourself" method, Pomerantz (p. 143) finds "wholly subjective," though the meaning of subjective in this context is never explained; and he believes that it cannot go beyond establishing the existence of a phenomenon to an analysis of it.

The Gestalt psychologists are not properly to be criticized on this ground; they regard phenomenology as a preliminary step that must be taken before experimental investigation can be made meaningful, a procedure to insure that the analysis will be relevant. As has already been pointed out, acquaintance with the research literature would not permit Pomerantz to imply that Gestalt psychology stops with demonstration. And in the same connection, it is interesting to find this author (Pomerantz, 1981) citing as evidence an experiment which he has never performed "because the effect it demonstrates is so obvious that it needs no experiment" (p. 148). Why is he permitted, in some cases, to stop with demonstration, while the Gestalt psychologists are criticized for the same procedure? Again, why in many cases does Pomerantz take pains to compare results obtained by his performance measures with phenomenological observations if the latter are considered to be of so little scientific value?[1]

---

[1]Similarly, Garner (1981) plans "to write a book on all that we know from the experiments we know better than to do. We usually know so much about the perceptual process that we only run our experiments to clarify what we don't know. But what we don't know is then often the small or subtle part of the broader question" (p. 136) *How* does Garner know that part of perception in which he knows better than to do experiments?

It must be added that, if performance measures and phenomenological observations were scrutinized, they would be found not to differ epistemologically and thus to constitute no basis for questioning those results of Gestalt psychologists (and information processors) obtained by phenomenological methods. Who, for example, is to read the reaction time measures? In this sense they are no more objective than phenomenological observations: both depend on the experience of the investigator.

Pomerantz (1981) inclines to the belief in a two-stage theory of perceptual processing, the preliminary parsing being carried out by a gatekeeper below the level of attention and of consciousness.[2] Then selective attention takes over, grouping being the consequence of a failure of selective attention: "We may define a perceptual group as a set of parts that are processed as an all-or-none unit even when we try to attend selectively to a single part" (p. 149).

It is unclear to me why Pomerantz is willing to consign the main work of perceptual grouping to a murky, preattentive level, at the same time (without analysis) rejecting a theory such as Köhler's much more specific one of the cortical processes corresponding to perception. This theory is simply dismissed as nativistic and automatic (see Pomerantz, 1981, pp. 150, 163, 164), which it is not. Nor do I understand why grouping is made a *failure* of selective attention rather than a *positive achievement* of the perceptual system.

How does grouping occur? For Pomerantz the main question is whether it is a matter of bottom-up (data driven, beginning with the "raw stimulus") or top-down (conceptually driven) processing.[3] Proximity, similarity, and common fate, he believes, can be taken care of by bottom-up processing; good figure, good continuation, and Prägnanz seem to depend on top-down processing, starting with a hypothesis and applying it to the data.

But Gestalt psychology, Pomerantz (1981) believes, is neither top-down nor bottom-up; rather it involves "wholistic processing," patterns being "organized preattentively into unitary configurations" (p. 163). He believes that he has evidence that "wholes are not perceived by independent processing of parts" (p. 165). Wholes possess emergent features which are detected directly. Emergent features seem to be what Gestalt psychologists call whole properties or Ehrenfels qualities; the latter expressions seem to me more appropriate since they do not raise the problem of the process of emergence, or emergence from what, thus necessitating a two-level theory in advance.

Direct perception of wholes and whole properties thus seems to be consigned

---

[2] It must be added that Pomerantz sees some difficulties with the gatekeeper analogy. Nor does he regard it as completely adequate, since perception also has "strategic" (i.e., hypothesis testing) properties.

[3] As Michael Wertheimer (1985) has pointed out in a comparison between Gestalt psychology and contemporary cognitive psychology, "the similarity between 'from above down' [an expression of the Gestalt psychologists] and 'top-down processing' . . . is purely verbal" (p. 26).

by Pomerantz to the unknown level of preattention. Nothing is said about it except that emergent properties are "not derived from the output of line detectors," but are a "pure or unmediated perceptual experience" (p. 171). If these features are directly perceived, why not others? And how these formulations fit Pomerantz's original question remains to be shown: "How should a perceptual system begin the task of synthesizing global representations from local information?" (p. 142).

Still, consistency is not the main issue here. Is Pomerantz moving toward a more adequate approach to his material? or is he merely consigning the interesting questions to an unknown realm where they need not disturb us?

NEO-GESTALT PSYCHOLOGIES

Calling his theory Neo-Gestalt psychology, Frank Restle (1982) admits that "any theory given the name 'Neo-something' is not well defined" (p. 39). He relates to Coding Theory theoretical ideas that he feels "owe heavy debts to Gestalt theory" (p. 39). His aim is "to integrate parts of Gestalt theory with information processing theories through the use of coding theory" (p. 31). Since Restle believes that information processing models of perception "do not seem to be apposite to Gestalt Theory" (p. 47), it is hard to see what is gained by such an integration.

In applying coding theory to the description of a figure, Restle (1982) enumerates parts of the figure—lines, angles, and other features that, he believes, permit "reconstruction of all the essential characteristics of the display" (p. 31). The next step is to simplify the code by the use of the rules developed by Emanuel Leeuwenberg (1982). "Simplifying a code reduces its information load" (p. 32) or the number of data points needed. The code is likened to a "computer program to reconstruct the essential properties of the display" (p. 32). It is hypothesized that that interpretation of the visual display will be selected which yields the simplest code.

Restle sees at least two relations of coding theory to Gestalt psychology. He is interested, not in what is seen at first glance, but after careful inspection since, presumably, it takes some time to find the simplest code among its competitors. Thus a sort of phenomenological method is used, and Restle (1982) believes that "for this reason, Coding Theory may serve to analyze experiments and observations that belong to the Gestalt tradition" (p. 33). It should be pointed out, however, that Gestalt psychology has no monopoly on phenomenological observation; nor, as has been seen, is this the only method employed by Gestalt psychologists. And Gestalt psychologists do not limit themselves to perceptions requiring careful inspection.

In another respect, Restle (1982) relates his approach to Gestalt psychology. He believes that "the Gestalt laws, in the main, can be shown to be consequences of Coding Theory'' (p. 34). He thus attempts to restate Wertheimer's "laws" in terms of coding theory. Although he has trouble with proximity, Restle indicates how coding theory would deal with similarity, good continuation, and common fate, seeing these principles ''as applications of certain effective ways of making a code more economical'' (p. 35). It should be noted that similarity is reduced to identity, a different matter. Nor can similarity be treated in terms of lines and angles, the important simple elements of coding theory, as Goldmeier (1936/1972) has shown much earlier.

Restle's chief interest in Gestalt psychology seems to be in a principle of simplicity. He deals with Wertheimer's principle of Prägnanz as consisting of simplicity, regularity (itself reduced to repetition), symmetry, and minimum energy (pp. 37–38), each of which is described in terms of coding theory which, Restle believes, unifies Wertheimer's various principles of organization.

Restle (1982) acknowledges that coding theory is concerned with the end result of a perceptual process, not the process itself (p. 36). This constitutes an important difference from Gestalt theory. He states:

"Coding theory begins with a primitive code that consists entirely of a close analysis of local details of the display" (pp. 49–50). Again, "the 'earliest stage' of coding of a line drawing or figure is the extraction of line and angles" (p. 47). Thus, "a square may be coded as continued repetition of an angle α and a length L" (p. 48). The procedure, in short, is to start from the parts in order to arrive at a whole.[4]

The procedure of Gestalt psychology is exactly the opposite. As Wertheimer (1924/1944) expressed it:

The basic thesis of gestalt theory might be formulated thus: there are contexts in which what is happening in the whole cannot be deduced from the characteristics of the separate pieces, but conversely; what happens to a part of the whole is, in clear-cut cases, determined by the laws of the inner structure of its whole. (p. 84)

Whatever Neo-Gestalt ideas owe to Gestalt theory, it is not this basic thesis. Add to this discrepancy the contrast between coding theory's concern with end results only and that of Gestalt psychology with the processes of perception— and there seems to be no basis for considering the one psychology a revision of the other. What they have in common is the interest of coding theorists in certain phenomena to which Gestalt psychologists have called attention; but these are the property of psychology, not of any particular approach. Coding theory and Gestalt theory seem to me to be opposite approaches to these phenomena.

---

[4]Cf. also Leeuwenberg (1982): "We will assume that the information content of a pattern is expressible in terms of the independent pieces of data necessary to reproduce the pattern" (p. 58).

Another Neo-Gestalt theory of perception is put forth by D. N. Perkins (1982). Since given proximal stimuli might be projections of any number of objects in space, Perkins argues that the observer "adds something"—most likely geometrical assumptions—to produce the percept.

> The perceiver often resolves the projective ambiguity of stimuli by "reading in" certain geometric regularities such as rectangularity or symmetry and deriving a three-dimensional interpretation, one both exhibiting these regularities and consistent with the stimulus. Thus, the perceiver uses regularity assumptions plus a geometric capacity to achieve a spatial encoding of an essentially indeterminate stimulus. (p. 73)

There have been numerous theories in the history of psychology in which some external process is thought to have been imposed on, or added to, retinal stimulation (or, in some cases, sensory data) to yield a percept. Of these the most famous is Helmholtz's; he held that from physiological stimulation (or sensory data) inferences are drawn as to the external object which gave rise to the stimulation. Since no evidence of such inferences can be found in consciousness, the inferences, which derive from previous experience, were said to be unconscious. Similar theories have become popular in the field of perception today; and there have been a number of variants of Helmholtz's theory.

It can be seen that Perkins's (1982) theory is of the same type: retinal stimulation whose ambiguity is resolved by the imposition on it of geometric assumptions. He states that "no subject ever reported any conscious geometric strategy for performing the task" (p. 80). Thus his geometric assumptions must be as unconscious as Helmholtz's inferences.

Although Perkins (1982) calls his theory a "neo-Gestalt theory of perception" (p. 92), it is interesting that this kind of theory has many times been criticized by Gestalt psychologists. Transposing the criticisms to the present theory, the Gestalt psychologist would ask: How does the perceiver know which geometrical assumptions to apply in a particular case? Must one not perceive a rectangle before one can apply to it the assumption of rectangularity rather than, say, that of circularity? The proximal stimulation itself does not possess this organization. This is a question that Perkins himself sees (p. 90) and, of course, does not answer. Again, how is geometrical knowledge possible at all—knowledge of rectangularity, symmetry, parallelism, etc.—in advance of actual perception of rectangles and the others? In both respects, organized perceptions are presupposed, not explained; the problem of organization is not addressed.

Perkins (1982) relates the Gestalt principle of Prägnanz to a minimum energy principle or a "relaxation of a system into a minimum energy state" (p. 87). He regards his principle as dealing with the behavior of quasi-mechanical systems (p. 88). This view of it is reinforced by the alternative theories which he does not reject. (He prefers his own on the basis of parsimony only.) Although he criticizes the atomism of Attneave's dipole model (cf. below), he finds it very similar in spirit to his own; "the difference in the end might well reduce to nothing more than contrasting levels of description" (p. 89). Another acceptable alternative would be an information processing account, "a cybernetic procedure involving some sort of feedback and control mechanism" (p. 91).

Perkins's minimum energy principle (and the other theories he finds acceptable) differ from the principle of Prägnanz in Gestalt psychology in important respects. Again it is the difference between machine theory and a dynamic theory. Why, according to Gestalt psychologists, do systems achieve increasing regularity, symmetry, and simplicity in the distribution of their material and forces as they approach equilibrium? Referring to Mach, Köhler (1969) points out:

> When such regular distributions are being established, more and more components of the acting forces are likely to balance each other, which means that under these circumstances the equilibrium or a steady state is quickly or gradually approached. . . . It is therefore not surprising that during this operation the distributions within the system become more regular, symmetrical and simple. (p. 59)

Given this state of affairs, it takes only the hypothesis of psychophysical isomorphism to show the relevance to perceptual processes.

The process of achieving Prägnanz here envisaged is thus seen to be entirely different from Perkins's own minimum energy principle or any of the other mechanistic theories he finds acceptable.

A SOAP BUBBLE SYSTEM

Fred Attneave (1982), in what he calls "the best Gestalt tradition" (p. 20), develops a "soap bubble system" of perceptual organization. Such systems "progress to equilibrium states by way of events in interconnected and recursive causal sequences so numerous that their effects must be considered in the aggregate rather than individually" (p. 12). All variables in Attneave's system must be interdependent; their effects "integrated in a common medium . . . a neuronal manifold" (p. 13). This manifold contains a very large number of *dipoles,* that is, "points in space considered two at a time" (p. 16), each dipole requiring one unique neuron (p. 22). Among activated dipoles there is mutual inhibition and facilitation; the latter occurs within certain "kinship sets" whose relevance to Gestalt organizational principles of similarity, good continuation, and proximity is pointed out, although Attneave reminds his readers that this discussion is restricted to dipoles, i.e., to points in space considered two at a time (p. 16). The latter qualification, as Attneave seems to recognize, raises questions about such relevance.

Attneave (1982) freely admits that his dipole may be a neurological fiction (p. 21). In any case, the analogy with the soap bubble breaks down: Soap bubbles attain their spherical shape by the attraction of the soap particles and the pressure against them of the air inside the bubble. They do not do so by the activation of points in space considered two at a time. In Attneave's theory, the interactions within the system appear to occur piecemeal; they are not the result of forces within the system as a whole.[5] This is a drastic difference from Gestalt psychology.

Whatever might underlie an economy principle, and thus the principle of Prägnanz, is seen by Attneave (1982) to be a product of evolution leading to adaptive behavior. "We may suppose," he adds, "that the specific bases for mutual facilitation between dipoles reflect ecological contingencies, as a result either of evolutionary pressures or of associative learning in the individual" (p. 21).

If it was not previously clear, this statement leaves no doubt that the principle of Prägnanz, or any economy principle, is here made to depend on constraints, either inherited, thus a product of evolution, or acquired.[6] In Gestalt psychology, any such principle would describe the working of dynamic forces within the system.

Again, when Attneave (1982) is considering the plausibility of his theory, he asks: Are there enough neurons in the visual cortex?—that is, constraints within the nervous system. His own formulation is more specific and more revealing; he asks "whether a system like this is within realistic bounds in the quantity of neural machinery that it would require" (p. 22). It is clear that he is thinking in terms of neural machinery—that is, mechanisms or constraints, not in terms of dynamic processes within the limits permitted by existing constraints, which is characteristic of the thinking of Gestalt psychologists.

Attneave (1982) regards the exercise he has undertaken in this chapter as an exploration of theoretical possibilities, making no claims for its truth (p. 27). Nor am I concerned primarily with its truth, rather with the relation it claims to Gestalt psychology. For the reasons given—the viewing of interaction piecemeal and the emphasis on neural machinery, not dynamics—I would suggest that Attneave is mistaken if he considers "this exercise to start from the general point of view of the classical Gestalt psychologists" (p. 13).

A FINAL WORD

Kubovy and Pomerantz (1981) found interest among their colleagues in Gestalt psychology, mentioning it, however, "with faint embarrassment, brought on by concern that one's audience might think one enjoyed it for the wrong reasons" (p.

---

[5]"I would remind the reader that we are restricting ourselves (so far, at least) to relations that may exist between dipoles; that is, points in space considered two at a time" (Attneave, 1982, p. 16).

Perkins's criticism of Attneave's atomism has already been noted.

[6]In this discussion I will omit the empiristic possibility, which presents the same problem as the evolutionary one.

IX). I doubt whether they would be embarrassed if they were talking about the same psychology that Wertheimer, Köhler, and Koffka discussed. I do not know whether the misunderstandings arise from lack of knowledge of the literature (including the research literature), from the inhospitality of the current intellectual climate to Gestalt ideas, or from both. This is not the place, however, to discuss current misunderstandings of Gestalt psychology, some of which can be gleaned from the above discussion. I would only point out that if the Neo-Gestaltists want to build on Gestalt psychology, they would do well first to get it right. Then they would know what has to be done.

All investigators have the privilege, indeed the obligation, to carry their thinking in any direction that seems fruitful to them. What they label their approach is also their own concern. But to call such different theories as information processing and Gestalt theory by the same name seems to me confusing. Theoretical psychology is difficult enough without adding semantic confusion.

Needless to say, we should welcome the new interest in Gestalt problems and should welcome new work in the spirit of Gestalt theory, work that advances the task of Gestalt psychology and corrects the theory where appropriate.

ACKNOWLEDGMENT

I am grateful to Professor Solomon Diamond for correcting an error in an earlier draft of this paper.

REFERENCES

Asch, S. E. (1946). Forming impressions of personality. *Journal of Abnormal and Social Psychology, 41,* 258–290.

Asch, S. E. (1951). Effects of group pressure upon the modification and distortion of judgments. In H. Guetzkow (Ed.), *Groups, leadership and men* (pp. 177–190). Pittsburgh, PA: Carnegie-Mellon Press.

Asch, S. E. (1956). Studies of independence and conformity: I. A minority of one against a unanimous majority. *Psychological Monographs, 70*(9). (Whole No. 416).

Asch, S. E., Ceraso, J., & Heimer, W. (1960). Perceptual conditions of association. *Psychological Monographs, 74*(3). (Whole No. 490).

Attneave, F. (1982). Prägnanz and soap bubble systems: A theoretical exploration. In J. Beck (Ed.), *Organization and representation in perception* (pp. 11–29). Hillsdale, NJ: Lawrence Erlbaum Associates.

Beck, J. (Ed.). (1982). *Organization and representation in perception.* Hillsdale, NJ: Lawrence Erlbaum Associates.

Garner, W. R. (1981). The analysis of unanalyzed perceptions. In M. Kubovy & J. R. Pomerantz (Eds.), *Perceptual organization* (pp. 119–139). Hillsdale, NJ: Lawrence Erlbaum Associates.

Goldmeier, E. (1972). Similarity in visually perceived forms. *Psychological Issues, 8,* No. 1, Monograph 29. (First published in 1936, translated and enlarged by E. Goldmeier.)

Köhler, W. (1969). *The task of Gestalt psychology.* Princeton, NJ: Princeton University Press.

Köhler, W., & Dinnerstein, D. (1947). Figural after-effects in kinesthesis. In *Miscellanea psychologica Albert Michotte* (pp. 196–220). Louvain: Éditions de l'Institut Supérieur de Philosophie.

Köhler, W., & Emery, D. A. (1947). Figural after-effects in the third dimension of visual space. *American Journal of Psychology, 60*, 159–201.

Köhler, W., Held, R., & O'Connell, D. N. (1952). An investigation of cortical currents. *Proceedings of the American Philosophical Society, 96*, 290–330.

Köhler, W., & Wallach, H. (1944). Figural after-effects: an investigation of visual processes. *Proceedings of the American Philosophical Society, 88*, 269–357.

Kubovy, M., & Pomerantz, J. R. (Eds.). (1981). *Perceptual organization.* Hillsdale, NJ: Lawrence Erlbaum Associates.

Leeuwenberg, E. (1982). Metrical aspects of patterns and structural information theory. In J. Beck (Ed.), *Organization and representation in perception* (pp. 57–71). Hillsdale, NJ: Lawrence Erlbaum Associates.

Neisser, U. (1976). *Cognition and reality.* San Francisco: W. H. Freeman.

Perkins, D. N. (1982). The perceiver as organizer and geometer. In J. Beck (Ed.), *Organization and representation in perception* (pp. 73–93). Hillsdale, NJ: Lawrence Erlbaum Associates.

Pomerantz, J. R. (1981). Perceptual organization in information processing. In M. Kubovy & J. R. Pomerantz (Eds.), *Perceptual organization* (pp. 141–180). Hillsdale, NJ: Lawrence Erlbaum Associates.

Restle, F. (1982). Coding theory as an integration of Gestalt psychology and information processing theory. In J. Beck (Ed.), *Organization and representation in perception* (pp. 31–56). Hillsdale, NJ: Lawrence Erlbaum Associates.

Wertheimer, M. (1912). Experimentelle Studien über das Sehen von Bewegung. *Zeitschrift für Psychologie, 61*, 161–265.

Wertheimer, M. (1944). Gestalt theory. *Social Research, 11*, 78–99. (Translation of lecture at the Kant Society, Berlin, 1924.)

Wertheimer, M. (1985). A Gestalt perspective on computer simulations of cognitive processes. *Computers in Human Behavior, 1*, 19–33.

The Publications
of Solomon E. Asch

1932

An experimental study of variability in learning. *Arch. Psychol.*, *143*, pp. 1–55.

1934

With O. Klineberg & H. Block. An experimental study of constitutional types. *Genetic Psychology Monographs*, *16*, 141–221.

1936

A study of change in mental organization. *Arch. Psychol.*, *195*, 30–79.

1938

With H. Block & M. Hertzman. Studies in the principles of judgments and attitudes: I. Two basic principles of judgment. *J. Psychol.*, *5*, 219–251.

1940

Studies in the principles of judgments and attitudes: Determination of judgments by group and by ego standards. *J. Soc. Psychol.*, *12*, 433–465.

1946

Forming impressions of personality. *J. abn. soc. Psychol.*, *41*, 258–290.
Max Wertheimer's contribution to modern psychology. *Social Research*, *13*, 81–102.

1948

The doctrine of suggestion, prestige and imitation in social psychology. *Psychol. Rev.*, *55*, 250–276.

With H. A. Witkin. Studies in space orientation: I. Perception of the upright with displaced visual fields. *J. exp. Psychol., 38,* 325–337.

With H. A. Witkin. Studies in space orientation: II. Perception of the upright with displaced visual fields and with body tilted. *J. exp. Psychol., 38,* 455–477.

With H. A. Witkin. Studies in space orientation: III. Perception of the upright in the absence of a visual field. *J. exp. Psychol., 38,* 603–614.

With H. A. Witkin. Studies in space orientation: IV. Further experiments on perception of the upright with displaced visual fields. *J. exp. Psychol., 38,* 762–782.

1951

Effects of group pressure upon the modification and distortion of judgments. In H. Guetzkow (Ed.), *Groups, leadership, and men* (pp. 117–190). Pittsburgh, PA: Carnegie Press.

1952

Social Psychology. Englewood Cliffs, NJ: Prentice-Hall, p. 646.

1955

Opinions and social pressure. *Sci. Amer., 193,* 31–35.

On the use of metaphor in the description of persons. In H. Werner (Ed.), *On expressive language.* (pp. 29–38). Worcester: Clark University Press.

1956

Studies of independence and conformity: I. A minority of one against a unanimous majority. *Psychol. Monogr., 70,* 1–70.

1958

With W. C. H. Prentice. Paired association with related and unrelated pairs of nonsense figures. *Amer. J. Psychol., 71,* 247–254.

The metaphor: A psychological inquiry. In R. Tagiuri & L. Petrullo (Eds.), *Person perception and interpersonal behavior* (pp. 86–94). Stanford University Press.

1959

The practical use of theory. *Social Research, 26,* 127–166.

A perspective on social psychology. In S. Koch (Ed.), *Psychology: A study of a science* (Vol. III, pp. 363–383). New York: McGraw-Hill.

1960

With H. Nerlove. The development of double function terms in children: An exploratory study. In S. Wapner & B. Kaplan (Eds.), *Perspectives in psychological theory* (pp. 47–60). New York: International University Press.

With J. Ceraso & W. Heimer. Perceptual conditions of association. *Psychol. Monogr., 74,* no. 3, pp. 1–48.

With J. Hay & R. Mendoza. Perceptual organization in serial rote-learning. *Amer. J. Psychol., 73,* 177–198.

1961

Issues in the study of social influences on judgment. In I. A. Berg & B. M. Bass (Eds.), *Conformity and deviation*. New York: Harper.

1962

With S. M. Ebenholtz. The principle of associative symmetry. *Proc. Amer. philos. Soc., 106,* 135–163.
A problem in the theory of associations. *Psychologische Beitrage, 6,* 553–563.
With S. M. Ebenholtz. The process of free recall: Evidence for non-associative factors in acquisition and retention. *J. Psychol., 54,* 3–31.

1963

With M. Lindner. A note on "Strength of association," *J. Psychol., 55,* 199–209.

1964

The process of free recall. In C. Scheerer (Ed.), *Cognition: Theory, research, promise* (pp. 79–88). New York: Harper & Row.

1968

The doctrinal tyranny of associationism. In T. R. Dixon & D. L. Horton (Eds.), *Verbal behavior and general behavior theory* (pp. 214–228). Englewood Cliffs, NJ: Prentice-Hall.
Gestalt theory. In *International Encyclopedia of the Social Sciences,* pp. 158–175.
Wolfgang Kohler (1887–1967). *Amer. J. Psychol., 81,* 110–119.

1969

A reformulation of the problem of associations. *Amer. Psychol., 24,* 92–102.

1970

Perceiving and thinking (Review of *Visual Thinking* by R. Arnheim). *Science, 169,* 361–362.

1974

Preface to David Rapaport: *The history of the concept of the association of ideas* (pp. VII–XIII). New York: International University Press.

1984

With Henri Zukier. Thinking about persons. *Journal of personality social Psychology, 46,* 1230–1240.

1987

Social psychology. (Reissue of 1952 book in paperback, with new preface.) Oxford: Oxford University Press.

Author Index

Ford, M. E., 155, *157*
Fraser, B., 28, *37*
Frazer, J. G., 101, 102, 104, *109*
Freud, S., 139, *141, 277, 278*
Friedrich, P., 30, *38*
Fuchs, W., 229, *231*
Fuller, S., 40, *51*

G

Galanter, E., 200, *208*
Garfinkel, H., 200, *208*
Garner, W. R., 280, 281, 282, 283, *290*
Georgeson, M. A., 246, *265*
Gerbino, W., 229, *231*
Giacomini-Biraud, V., 154, *157*
Gibson, J. J., 48, *52,* 257, *266*
Giere, R. N., 49, *52*
Gilchrist, A., 217, 221, 223, 224, 225, 226, 228, 229, *231*
Gilman, A., 28, 30, *37*
Glaser, B., 128, *141*
Glaser, G. W., 235, 236, *242*
Glass, A. L., 176, 182, *193*
Goffman, E., 24, *38,* 128, *141*
Gogel, W. C., 235, *242,* 246, 248, *266*
Goldberg, L. R., 61, 73, *75*
Goldmeier, E., 286, *290*
Goldstein, RR., 217, *230*
Goodenough, D. R., 234, 236, 240, *242,* 246, 247, 250, *266, 268*
Goodnow, J. J., 195, *196*
Goody, E. N., 24, *38*
Gordon, D., 27, *38*
Gottschaldt, K., 176, 177, *193*
Graybiel, A. M., 236, *242*
Green, F. L., 155, *157*
Greene, D., 81, *96*
Greimas, A. J., 198, *208*
Grice, H. P., 24, *38*
Griffin, D. W., 81, 84, 87, 89, *95,* 96
Gruber, H., 4, 5, 6, 8, *19,* 154, 155, *157*
Grunfeld, D. I., 102, 105, *109*

H

Habermas, J., 48, *52*
Haimson, B. R., 217, *231*
Hardison, O. B., Jr., 128, 139, *141*

Harris, C. S., 250, *268*
Hartshorne, H., 78, *95*
Hastorf, A., 91, *95*
Havemeyer, L., 128, *141*
Hay, J. C., 14, *19,* 250, *266*
Heider, F., 72, *75, 86, 95,* 196, 197, *208*
Heimer, W., 14, *19,* 114, 117, *125,* 160, *165,* 177, *193,* 281, *290*
Heisenberg, W., 272, *278*
Held, R., 247, *266, 267,* 281, *291*
Helson, E., 224, *231*
Heng, J. H., 30, *37*
Henle, M., 273, *278*
Henn, V., 239, *242*
Hepler, N., 240, *241*
Hering, E., 220, *231,* 243, *267*
Herrnstein, R. J., 14, *19*
Herskovits, M. J., 40, *52*
Hertzman, M., 11, *19,* 41, *51*
Höffding, H., 176, *193*
Hoffman, S., 77, 81, *96*
Hogarth, R. M., 195, *208*
Holland, P. C., 168, *173*
Hollis, M., 40, *52*
Holmes, D. S., 81, *95*
Horn, B. K. P., 225, *231*
House, P., 81, *96*
Hughes, P. C., 247, *267*
Hull, C. L., 16, *19*
Hull, D. L., 40, *52*
Hume, D., 138, *141,* 272, *278*
Hurvich, L. M., 216, *231*

I

Ikeda, K., 250, *266*
Ingle, D., 247, *267*
Inhelder, B., 146, *157*

J

Jacklin, C. N., 205, *208*
Jacobs, R. C., 43, 44, *52*
Jacobsen, A., 217, 221, 223, 224, 225, 226, 228, *231*
Jameson, D., 216, *231*
Jarvie, I. C., 40, *52*
Johansson, G., 251, 254, *267*
Jones, E. E., 78, 85, *95,* 139, *141*
Julness, G. D., 235, 237, *242*

Subject Index